The publisher gratefully acknowledges the generous contribution
to this book provided by the General Endowment Fund
of the University of California Press Foundation.

Friends of God

FRONTISPIECE. This plan of the Prophet's mosque in Medina, al-Haram an-Nabawī, shows (with green domes) the burial places of Muhammad and Fātima (top left); Muhammad's wife Zaynab (in courtyard); in the cemetery at bottom: Muhammad's uncle ʿAbbās, grandson Hasan, Muhammad Bāqir, and Jaʿfar as-Sādiq (second, fifth, and sixth Shīʿī imams, all on the right); legal scholar Mālik ibn Anas and third caliph ʿUthmān (to the left); further left outside the cemetery, Muhammad's legendary uncle Hamza. Arabia or India, eighteenth–early nineteenth century; The Nasser D. Khalili Collection of Islamic Art, MSS 745.2.

Friends of God

Islamic Images of Piety, Commitment, and Servanthood

JOHN RENARD

University of California Press

BERKELEY   LOS ANGELES   LONDON

University of California Press, one of the most distinguished university presses in the United States, enriches lives around the world by advancing scholarship in the humanities, social sciences, and natural sciences. Its activities are supported by the UC Press Foundation and by philanthropic contributions from individuals and institutions. For more information, visit www.ucpress.edu.

University of California Press
Berkeley and Los Angeles, California

University of California Press, Ltd.
London, England

Library of Congress Cataloging-in-Publication Data

Renard, John, 1944–
    Friends of God : Islamic images of piety, commitment, and servanthood /
John Renard.
        p.   cm.
    Includes bibliographical references and index.
    ISBN: 978-0-520-24291-3 (cloth : alk. paper)
    ISBN: 978-0-520-25198-4 (pbk. : alk. paper)
    1. Islamic hagiography—History and criticism.   2. Legends, Islamic—History
and criticism.   I. Title.
  BP189.43.R46   2008
  297.6'1—dc22   2007028542

Manufactured in the United States of America

17   16   15   14   13   12   11   10   09   08
10   9   8   7   6   5   4   3   2   1

This book is printed on New Leaf EcoBook 50, a 100% recycled fiber of
which 50% is de-inked post-consumer waste, processed chlorine-free.
EcoBook 50 is acid-free and meets the minimum requirements of
ANSI/ASTM D5634-01 (Permanence of Paper).

With gratitude to my parents, Virginia M. Renard (1915–2006) and George J. Renard (1911–), for sharing their desire for God's Friendship

Contents

Illustrations

Preface

Islamic hagiography is a rich, expansive repository of religion, history, and culture. As with so many areas of the still-young field of Islamic studies, countless written sources have yet to be rediscovered and edited, and translation remains in most instances a still-more-remote prospect. A cursory search for "Muslim Saints" in the Library of Congress online catalog turns up over two hundred titles of fairly recent vintage, the vast majority of which are (evidently) by Muslims writing in non-European languages. Though the topic is by no means a museum piece, material is still largely inaccessible to the wider reading public. With few exceptions, European and American scholars interested in the hagiographical sources have used the documentation to reconstruct historical and cultural contexts, institutional developments, and the careers of major individual figures.

The majority of scholarly analysis, originating particularly in the disciplines of history, anthropology, and political science, has focused on the history of Sufism. But the story these sources tell is a much bigger one, and a study of Friends of God must look to a broader canvas than that of Sufism. The immense patrimony of Islamic hagiographical sources has yet to generate adequate interest in the windfall of insights into the religious and ethical life of Muslims that await discovery in these sources. Interrogating the sources about "what really happened" is, of course, an essential ingredient in understanding them. However, we must also let the sources speak for themselves, even—perhaps especially—when they seem to venture into the realm of the preternatural. To do so by no means calls for a naïve, uncritical reading of this often multilayered material. It simply acknowledges that though many written sources offer potentially important historically verifiable data, much hagiographical material offers a great deal more. Even when an author appears to have slipped off the straight path of "fact" onto the mucky byways and quick sands of credulity, we can learn something from such sources. Here the challenge is to find a solid methodological basis for evaluating the less verifiable claims of many hagiographical sources. In this book, I suggest such a broad method.

Storytelling remains the most effective way to tell a story. This statement is no mere tautology. The larger story is how and why accounts of colorful religious figures have captured the attention of countless millions of Muslims for nearly fourteen hundred years. To explore these questions, we need to situate written hagiographical sources in the broader context of the humanities and appreciate their distinctive and even unique features. To tell the larger story, we must fashion a set of tools for appreciating how the numerous smaller stories communicate the ineffable. Great poetry has some potential to inform readers about the life and times of the poet, but scholars generally acknowledge that this potential is very limited. Readers of a great poem do not ordinarily feel constrained to ask whether the poem's subject "really happened." A successful poem reveals far more about the inner life of the poet—and that of his or her reader. As in poetry, imagination in the hagiographies I look at here is an essential key to letting the smaller tales unfold the larger narrative.

This book tells stories about a host of characters whom many Muslims have regarded as astonishing despite their ordinariness. In the chapters that follow, I hope to offer a way of understanding how those characters have functioned in the lives of Muslims of diverse cultural, social, economic, and political contexts. Questions of historicity, though generally shifted to the background, have their place here, particularly in looking at institutional developments. But above all, readers need to become travelers in the realms of the religious imagination as well as in those of space and time. This book offers a broad introduction to the global phenomenon of Islamic personalities who function as embodiments or personifications of sanctity. With such a broad thematic overview, one cannot also provide in a single volume the kind of in-depth historical and literary analysis necessary to appreciate the many faces of individual Friends in the varied accounts of them and to understand the ways in which diverse historical contexts have shaped these multifaceted portrayals. A companion anthology now in preparation, will provide further literary and historical context and supply additional depth and breadth through multiple examples of hagiographical texts in over a dozen languages.

An important organizational-methodological premise here is that Islamic hagiography is not limited to accounts of the post-prophetic figures called "Friends of God" in the narrower, more technical sense of the term. Stories of the prophets, from Adam to Muhammad, as well as accounts of exemplary individuals of the earliest generations of Muslims and the Shiʿi imams of the subsequent two and a half centuries or so, are all considered here as part of a continuum of tradition and lore that has perdured down to our day.

This volume is both premature and long overdue. It is premature in the sense that much detailed work remains to be done in the study of individual texts and regional traditions of hagiography. Scholarly analysis of the vast caches of material, in well over a dozen major languages from across the globe, is still in its infancy. And the next level of needed scholarship, diachronic studies of primary sources' interpretations of individual Friends across time and over cultural and linguistic boundaries, has similarly just begun. This book is also long overdue, for several reasons. Given the historical and cultural pervasiveness of the lives and stories of Friends of God, a need exists for a useful and evocative thematic overview that approaches the story of Islam as a global tradition. In addition, the increasing tendency of extremist interpretations of Islam to denounce Friends of God and all they stand for, as part and parcel of the wholesale rejection of history and culture, increases the importance of presenting an alternate narrative—a narrative cultivated and preserved by countless Muslims for many centuries.

THE STRUCTURE OF THE BOOK

A brief introductory overview of Islamic hagiography in all its color and variety begins the story. Three perspectives then give structure to the unfolding narrative. Part 1, gathers accounts of key moments and aspects of the literary life experiences of Friends of God from birth to death. Major thematic elements begin to emerge with a look at nativity and infancy narratives, often sprinkled with the miraculous (chapter 1). Stories of many of the Friends begin a bit later than infancy, often starting with a moment of "conversion" (chapter 2) that establishes a new tone in the Friend's relationship to God from then on (chapter 3). A common theme in many life stories is that of the miracle or saintly marvel, and one can again discern a wide range of specific themes and subtypes among stories of such extraordinary events (chapter 4). Intimations of mortality provide an unmistakable counterbalance to the spectacular, as manifest in accounts of ordinary human foibles and frailties. Friends also die, and remembrances of their earthly departures are essential to their stories (chapter 5).

Situating individual prophets and Friends' life cycles in broader contexts is the overriding concern of part 2. These contexts include the larger collectivity of saintly lives and the history of the many local, regional, and even global communities that have called these Friends their own. In the stories in this section, Friends of God relate to their respective societies and local communities in a variety of ways. They function as moral and spiritual exemplars and engage in the world as advocates for their people, warriors, and missionaries. Some Friends choose to stay on the margins of society, and others, particularly women, are relegated to the fringes through no choice of their own (chapter 6). Many Friends of God have ties to a variety of institutions, whether as founders or as eponymous ancestors. Some have contributed to the development of organizations of spiritual seekers, generally known as Sufis. Most are identified to some degree with important burial places (chapter 7). In addition, hagiographical accounts link Friends of God to many important holy sites, creating interlocking networks of sacred geographies. The presence of exemplars of devotion and holiness has been an important ingredient in many Muslims' sense of the larger world and their place in it (chapter 8). So much information about Friends of God is historical and often quite ancient. But hundreds of millions of Muslims across the globe today still calibrate their moral and spiritual compasses by the lives and deeds of the great ones (chapter 9).

Finally, part 3 addresses the challenge of interpreting the larger implications of this treasure house of tales. Chapter 10 provides an outline of major hagiographic literary forms and functions, dipping into the sources for clues to how their authors intended them to be used and understood. Large theoretical issues about the theological, cosmological, and psychological dimensions of the accounts are the focus of chapter 11.

A NOTE ON USING THE BOOK

Pedagogically speaking, I have designed the four sections of the book to build gradually in complexity and technical precision. The introduction describes a broad historical development, highlighting several types of literary material, but does so in fairly general terms. The five chapters of part 1 rely almost entirely on anecdotes, arranged thematically, so that the reader can gradually make acquaintance with major figures and become familiar with episodes from the lives of diverse personalities. Part 2's four chapters blend increasingly noticeable, but still generally unthreatening, elements of historical data and theoretical concepts into the narratives. Finally, part 3 shifts from narrative elements to focus almost entirely on background issues.

I situated these two chapters at the end of the book rather than at the beginning because many readers might be daunted by an immediate immersion in theory and technical terminology. Readers already broadly familiar with the

Islamic religious tradition, including teachers who want to incorporate this volume into formal courses in Islamic studies, might want to begin with chapters 10 and 11, thereby establishing a theoretical and methodological framework for reading the stories in parts 1 and 2. Alternatively, teachers might opt to tap into segments of the last two chapters selectively, in the course of reading parts 1 and 2 (referring, for example, to chapter 11's section on miracles and marvels when students read chapter 4).

My choice of a generally thematic structure neither means to suggest, nor reflects the conclusion, that Islamic hagiography is essentially a patchwork of formulaic accounts. Some patterns do emerge from a broad study of the material, and my decision to focus on many of those common themes and "types" of story or character is largely pedagogical in intent. This volume's primary goal is to allow readers to make an introductory acquaintance with a vast subject. In no way do I mean to sidestep the methodological complexity and sophistication a deeper study of the subject requires, and which mark the works of so many scholars on which I have relied.

The remarkable hagiographical works I discuss in this book are far more than the sum of the engaging tales gathered here; their structures and plans are far more substantial than would be possible in mere collections of interchangeable narrative units and plots; and their subjects are ultimately far more subtle and rounded than one can tell from the sometimes hit-and-miss effect of a thematic approach. I hope that these stories and themes will kindle in readers a desire to fill in the countless gaps by further pursuing this most rewarding tributary to the greater Islamic tradition.

RESOURCES AND TECHNICALITIES

Research for this volume has relied on a relatively limited store of primary sources, both in their languages of origin and in translation, as well as a much larger trove of secondary research. My non-English access to the former is confined to works in Arabic and Persian, and in the latter instance, to publications in French, German, Spanish, and Italian. (Though I give most titles both in their original languages and in English, my presentation of a title in English is strictly for the reader's information and does not necessarily mean that the work is available in translation.) Throughout the book, I have drawn especially on sources that tend to recount the stories of the Friends in generally fulsome narratives and less so on those that compile hadithlike briefer anecdotes and sayings. I confess a personal bias toward ʿAttār's Persian *Tadhkirat al-awliyāʾ*, truly a masterpiece of narrative art and a vastly influential work in its own right. Paul Losensky has done a most welcome translation of much of this text for the Paulist Press Classics of Western Spirituality series, but when the present volume went to press, that work had not yet appeared. Much as I would have liked to acknowledge in greater detail the countless intertextual connections among the great hagiographies, I have limited such cross-references because of constraints of time and space. Serious attention here to that dimension of the larger hagiographical story would have required a multivolume product.

In the hopes of making this volume useful to scholars interested in pursuing the subject further, I have included a considerable amount of bibliographical material. To maximize utility of this material and make the most efficient use of space, I have provided bibliographical information in endnotes rather than in a formal bibliography, presorting relevant entries as cleanly as possible according to historical, thematic, and geographical context.

Technical terms often require some clarification or special consideration in translation. I have leaned toward calling the book's many paradigmatic figures "Friends of God" but have also retained the most commonly used "non-Islamic" renderings of *walī* and *walāya*—namely, "saint" and "sainthood"—as well as cognates such as "saintly" and "saintliness," and analogous terms such as "sage" or "righteous or authentic one" (some of which appear as synonyms or subcategories of the Islamic notion of Friend of God). My first bias rests on the conviction that because the paradigmatic figures in this book exhibit a number of characteristics in Islamic sources not found in the sources of Christianity or other traditions, one needs a way to acknowledge their uniqueness. At the same time, the desirability of avoiding cumbersome circumlocutions calls for some flexibility in the use of terms.

Transliteration always poses certain technical problems, but in a book whose subject covers as many linguistic and cultural contexts as this one does, the challenges are huge. My overarching concern has been to achieve a consistency in transliteration that would facilitate reading and cross-referencing. To that end, I have privileged a modified standard system of transliterating Arabic and have tried to use that system consistently where the language of origin (especially of personal or place names) was Arabic or Persian. I have also used this system for technical terms of Arabic or Persian origin that are in other linguistic contexts (e.g., if a Malay source mentioned an "evidentiary miracle," I used *muꜤjiza* rather than *mujiza*). I have simplified the system by placing long marks over vowels as well as using the Ꜥ for the ayn and ꜣ for the hamza, but I have not included the sub- and supralinear dots with consonants. My rationale is that whereas the nonspecialist reader will find clues to correct pronunciation in the macrons, only specialists would appreciate the sub-/supralinear apparatus that betokens more difficult variations in pronunciation. With those specialists in mind, however, I have retained a full system of transliteration in the index. Terms that are now in wide usage, such as *shaykh, hadith,* and *imam* are spelled according to the conventions of *Merriam-Webster's Collegiate Dictionary,* Eleventh Edition.

I have included death dates for individuals, when they were readily available, in both the Hijrī lunar and Gregorian solar date systems, in the index. I did so to make chronological data readily available without interrupting the flow of reading. Dual dates also appear throughout the text: a date expressed in the Islamic lunar calendar is given first (Hijrī, i.e., after the Hijra of 622), followed by a slash and the date in the Gregorian calendar— for example, 1/622. Finally, I use the term Islamicate to refer to societies, cultures, and artifacts deeply influenced by the religious tradition of Islam but not "Islamic" in the strictly religious sense.

ACKNOWLEDGMENTS

I wish to thank fellow specialists in Islamic religious studies Ahmet Karamustafa of Washington University in St. Louis and Frederick Denny of the University of Colorado for their generosity in reading and commenting on drafts of the book. I am indebted to a host of other colleagues in Islamic religious studies of the American Academy of Religion Islamic Studies Section for dozens of helpful comments, suggestions, and bits of advice about resources and topics related to hagiography. To the scores of other scholars whose relevant works I cite or list in the notes, I express my gratitude for their studies in various regions, individual figures and organizations, and individual hagiographical texts, without which a book of this kind would be impossible.

In addition, my thanks go especially to Catherine Scine of Saint Louis University for her consistent and patient assistance in researching and editing the large volume of material that forms the basis of this book. I thank also Christine Baudin, Lisa Marie Duffield, Danny Dunivan, and Tomas O'Sullivan, members of a seminar on medieval hagiographies at Saint Louis University in the fall of 2005, who along with Catherine Scine provided much helpful criticism of the evolving drafts of the volume; and Ben O'Connor and Robert Porwoll of Saint Louis University for their assistance during the final phase of manuscript preparation and indexing. Special thanks to Reed Malcolm and Kalicia Pivirotto (Religious Studies) and Rachel Berchten (editorial), all at the University of California Press, and to Adrienne

Harris for their outstanding attentiveness and assistance in the completion of this and two earlier publications.

For help in securing permissions for illustrations, I thank especially Elaine Wright and Sinead Ward of the Chester Beatty Library in Dublin and Nahla Nassar of the Nasser D. Khalili Collection of Islamic Art. I am grateful to Saint Louis University for a Provost Faculty Research Leave during which to advance writing on the initial drafts, SLU Mellon Grant funding to support art-program research, Summer Research Award funds for art-program expenses, and a sabbatical leave during which to complete the volume.

And, as always, my deepest gratitude and appreciation go to my spouse, Mary Pat, for her constant support, wisdom, and good humor as this project unfolded.

Introduction

An Overview of Islamic Hagiography

Every major faith tradition has devised important ways of acknowledging and communicating the paradigmatic status and magnetism of its central personalities. Whether religious adherents describe these personalities as founders, companions of founders (who are custodians of the tradition), prophets, saints, martyrs, sages, seers, or teachers, they locate in each of these figures a particular revelation, wisdom, insight, authority, organizational genius, or model of perfect commitment.

One of the richest repositories of lore about such irresistible exemplary characters resides in the tales told by the approximately 1.3 billion people who identify themselves as Muslims. Like other treasuries of stories about amazing people, this repository belongs, in a way, to all of us. However, scholars, non-Muslim and Muslim alike, have barely begun to mine this extraordinary mother lode of marvelous tales. Important exceptions exist: Many stories circulate about Muhammad, the prophets who preceded him, and the most important members of the first and second generations of Muslims, the Prophet's Companions and Followers. Moreover, hundreds of millions of Egyptians, Iraqis, Moroccans, Turks, Nigerians, Pakistanis, and Indonesians are familiar with tales of later Muslim exemplars of regional and local importance. And one can point to a small handful of post-Prophetic models of holiness, such as the sixth-/twelfth-century ʿAbd al-Qādir al-Jilānī, who have enjoyed virtually global celebrity. Scores of other exemplary men and women, lauded in their times and places as embodiments of authentic Islamic faith and values, await rediscovery by a wider public.

Both in the past and in more recent times, religious authorities in some predominantly Muslim societies have deemphasized (or even denied) the possibility that "holiness" can inhere in an exemplary way in ordinary human beings. They have decried as blasphemous, and denounced as mere "folk piety," the age-old narratives, beliefs, and practices through which many communities of Muslims celebrate certain individuals as "Friends of God." During certain periods of history, they have mounted vigorous campaigns to purge such aberrations from the general populace, in the interest of restoring the tradition that they deem to be pristine Islam. Pure Islam, they believe, existed only at the time of Muhammad, and with each succeeding generation, this once-pure form has become more elusive and diluted.

HAGIOGRAPHY IN THE PROPHETIC AGE

Despite resistance to recognizing holiness in ordinary human beings, even the most stringent critics of "popular" or "folk" Islam throughout history have recognized that telling the life stories of some exemplary figures is essential to passing along the faith. Such exceptional human beings include the prophets, beginning with Adam; proceeding with such major figures as Abraham, Moses, and Jesus;, and culminating in Muhammad—a list that already numbers over two dozen people. In addition, even the guardians of "pure" Islam did not hesitate to list several score men and women who lived with and around Muhammad and enjoyed spiritual and religious favor. At the least, they acknowledged the importance of these people's eye- and ear-witness relationships with the last Prophet. But the list did not stop with these Companions of Muhammad. The Followers, descendants of the Companions, continue to enjoy elevated status as custodians of the community's most precious memories. They are still human, to be sure, but they are hardly run-of-the-mill figures.

The faithful have enshrined stories of these prophetic and postprophetic figures since the earliest generations. Many tales of the prophets, including those about Muhammad, sparkle with intimations of the extraordinary, from signs and wonders surrounding their births and infancies to spectacular divine interventions to protect the people to whom God sent his emissaries. Though the Qur'ān is by no means a hagiographical work, some of its narrative elements share important features with hagiographical accounts. In fact, Muhammad's critics charged that his Qur'ānic utterances were little more than warmed-over "fables of the ancients."[1] The Qur'ān clearly indicates that its prophetic narratives have an essentially ethical purpose: to teach lessons and motivate listeners to mend their ways. As we shall see, authors of many hagiographical works share this motive. Although the Qur'ānic narratives perhaps focus more explicitly on this purpose than do hagiographic narratives generally, one can argue persuasively that the scriptural materials provide important continuity with post-Qur'ānic hagiographic literature.

Stories of causes for amazement did not vanish after Muhammad's death. An important literary subgenre celebrates the unique gifts of Muhammad's Companions and Followers. It focused on the "excellences" or "special virtues" (fadā'il) of these remarkable figures, giving prominence to the Prophet's wives. Significant chapters in the most authoritative collections of hadith literature, of primary importance in preserving the words and deeds of Muhammad, extol similar strengths in his successors. The qualities of these figures go far beyond the mundane and well into the realm of at least preternatural characteristics.

Companions such as Abū Bakr and ʿUmar, for example, partook of marvelous events in Muhammad's presence and enjoyed gifts of remarkable dreams, striking clairvoyance, and the ability to know of events occurring at a great distance. Two excellent examples of miracle stories from the hadith come from Abū Hurayra, a highly revered transmitter of traditions. The reports cite Muhammad's accounts of extraordinary experiences of talking animals. In one, an individual uses his ox to tote baggage. Deeply offended, the ox complains that it was created to plow the earth and draw water and was meant for more than carrying heavy loads. In the other story, a shepherd chases after a wolf that has snatched a goat, only to have the wolf remind the shepherd that a day may come when only the wolf is keeping an eye on the flocks.[2] The hadith collections also mention a number of early Muslims who later gained recognition for their piety, which grew out of their unique relationships with Muhammad (Uways, Abū 'd-Dardā', and Salmān the Persian).[3]

In addition to the various preternatural elements I have mentioned, a noteworthy hagiographical feature in the stories of the earliest Muslims is the quality of their relationships with Muhammad. The figures came first not only chronologically but also in the intensity of their personal attachment and loyalty to the Prophet and in his affection for them. Stories about the warmth and intimacy of their bonds to Muhammad offered an important model for subsequent hagiographers who sought to describe later examples of piety and devotion.

POST-PROPHETIC DEVELOPMENTS

Within less than a century after the death of Muhammad, more integrated historical and literary approaches to the "life stories" (siyar, pl. of sīra) of the Prophet and early exemplary Muslims began to emerge. Ibn Ishāq's second-/eighth-century Life of Muhammad, amplified substantially several generations later by Ibn Hishām, was to become a foundational work in the history of Islamic hagiographical literature. After tracing Muhammad's genealogy back to Adam, the work situates the Prophet on the Arabian Peninsula in the late sixth/early seventh century. Countless reports of Muhammad's words and actions, along with other stories about him and poetic reflections on the meaning of his life, appear in this substantial volume.[4] Muhammad's exploits, and those of his chief Companions (Abū Bakr, ʿUmar, ʿUthmān, and ʿAlī, known as the Rightly Guided Caliphs) were also the subject of two new literary genres: *maghāzī*, "raiding stories," and *futūh*, "conquest narratives." Al-Wāqidī was the best-known author of the former, and although neither genre precisely qualifies as hagiography, both include elements that connect them to the larger traditions from which hagiographical works draw their material.[5]

By the mid-second/-eighth century, another important genre, the biographical dictionary, had come into being within the larger movement of hadith scholarship. The earliest generations of Muslims had not systematically committed to writing the sayings attributed to Muhammad or the anecdotes about him. They had entrusted these treasures to the memory of Muslims who had become the custodians of tradition by an organic process of oral transmission. But as the Muslim community expanded into new social and cultural contexts, a growing need to turn to the Prophet's authority in the regulation of community affairs required a systematic and reliable effort to preserve prophetic tradition. Scholars fanned out across the Muslim communities of the Middle East and North Africa, gathering and writing down countless hadiths as well as the names of the hundreds of individuals acknowledged as transmitters of the material. Whenever a reporter cited a hadith, he or she prefaced the "quote" with a retrospective chain (*isnād*) of transmitters: people who had heard it from someone, who heard it from someone else, and so on, all the way back to either the Prophet or to an authoritative early Muslim (typically a Companion or Follower).

Because the text, or body (*matn*), of a hadith was only as trustworthy as the least reliable link in the chain of transmitters, scholars needed to devise a means of evaluating the veracity of individuals named in the chains. Thus was the biographical anthology invented as a principal tool in the "science of men" (*ʿilm ar-rijāl*), providing scholars a ready reference by which to rank hadiths on a scale of trustworthiness. Ibn Saʿd's *Great Book of Classifications* (*Kitāb at-tabaqāt al-kabīr*), for example, begins with a life of Muhammad, proceeds through often rather detailed sketches of the Companions, and includes generally less fulsome entries on later individuals. Though this genre does not qualify as hagiography, it eventually became the model for an explicitly hagiographical genre dedicated to stories of Friends of God.

Another important related genre that began to emerge in the third/ninth century is that of the "universal history." Works of this type situate the stories of the prophets in global history. Their purpose is quite different from those of the other genres I have discussed. Sometimes commissioned by the princely class, the histories sought to bolster the reputations of their patrons as cosmopolitan rulers. They include stories and characters from a wide range of religious traditions (Buddha, Jesus ʿ[Īsā], and Zoroaster, for example)—not always presenting these figures in an entirely favorable light, to be sure, but nevertheless acknowledging them as part of the known world. Their intended public was generally smaller than were the audiences that enjoyed *qisas* ("tales") and *hikāya* ("narrative") forms (about which more shortly) but was perhaps broader than those addressed by the biographical dictionaries. Among the earliest examples are the Arabic histories of Yaʿqūbī, Tabarī, and Masʿūdī. Their accounts of the great religious figures, especially of the prophets from Adam to Jesus, have much in common with those of, for example, the *Tales of the Prophets* (to be discussed shortly). Persian and Turkish authors likewise composed in this genre. Rashīd ad-Dīn's early eighth-/fourteenth-century *Universal History* (*Jāmiʿ at-tawārīkh*), Hāfiz-i Abrū's early ninth-/fifteenth-century *Compendium of History* (*Majmaʿ at-tawārīkh*), and Sayyid Luqmān's late tenth-/sixteenth century Turkish *Cream of Histories* (*Zubdat at-tawārīkh*) all include important episodes from the lives of prophets and saints. In these universal histories, the emphasis shifts from edification to education and entertainment for the already well educated. The tenth-/sixteenth-century Ottoman Turkish work *Rosary of Historical Reports* (*Subhat al-akhbār*), for example, does in abbreviated fashion what the universal histories do at length: it traces the lineages of the sultans all the way back to the beginning of creation via the prophets. A "theology of history" is at work here, similar to the one that carefully traces Muhammad's lineage back to Adam in the first great biography of the Prophet. In this case, the historian also positions the sultans over a line of mostly Persian heroes and mostly Arab rulers. The genre's potential for expressing at least an implied theory of political legitimacy, and its positioning of members of a royal line, such as the Ottoman sultans, as successors to the prophets, makes a powerful claim to religious as well as temporal authority.

TALES OF THE PROPHETS AND THE HAGIOGRAPHICAL ANTHOLOGY

One major genre, whose development occurred chiefly from the fifth/eleventh century on, focused on the prophetic material that was but one ingredient of the "universal histories." A number of works entitled *Tales of the Prophets (Qisas al-anbiyā²)* focused on a more or less common set of two dozen or so major sacred figures from Adam to Jesus and unfurled a sweeping historical panorama of divine providence and revelation. Thaʿlabī, Tarafī of Cordova, and Kisāʾī wrote in Arabic, and they were eventually joined by a number of Persian and Turkish contributors to the genre. These works, which frequently found use as aids for preachers and professional story-tellers, provided a host of interesting and entertaining details about how God worked through his principal messengers to humankind.[6]

Other works that qualify as "biographical anthology," though they have a more distinctly hagiographical flavor, are the collected lives of important Sufis, which came into vogue in the early fifth/eleventh century and remained popular. The earliest of these works preserved the "classification" format of the hadith scholars' key reference tool, the biographical diction-ary of transmitters, but transformed the notion of "classes" or "categories" *(tabaqāt)* into that of "generations." Sulamī's Arabic *Generations of the Sufis (Tabaqāt as-Sufiya)* and Ansārī's Persian reworking of it established the pop-ularity of the genre, emphasizing the importance of spiritual genealogy and lineage in establishing spiritual credibility and authority. Later developments of the hagiographical anthology form shifted the emphasis somewhat to underscore their subjects' conversions, miraculous deeds, and sayings. Examples of this genre include Abū Nuʿaym al-Isfahānī's Arabic *Ornament of the Friends of God (Hilyat al-awliyāʾ)* and Farīd ad-Dīn ʿAttār's Persian *Remembrances of God's Friends (Tadhkirat al-awliyāʾ).* Such works have provided an enormous amount of narrative material for subsequent chap-ters of this book.[7] An important variation on the biographical anthology includes major works whose authors limit their material to sketches of revered individuals they knew personally, or of members of a particular Sufi organization.

Treatments of the lives of individual holy figures gradually became more common throughout the Middle East, the Maghrib (North Africa and Spain), and South and Southeast Asia. Taking their cue, at least indirectly, from Ibn Hishām's life of Muhammad, works of this sort naturally afforded greater scope for details of all kinds, both marvelous and mundane. Among the earliest Arabic and Persian examples were biographies of the mystics and Sufi founders Ibn Khafīf, Abū Ishāq al-Kāzarūnī, and Abū Saʿīd ibn Abī 'l-Khayr. In Southeast Asia, the *hikāyat* (narrative) became a popular vehicle for recounting the stories of individual prophets as well as later Friends of God. A narrative form akin to the genres of autobiography and diary also provided a great deal of information with hagiographical elements. Finally, another important source on individual figures, one that emphasizes the sayings of the principal subject rather than his or her deeds, is the *malfūzāt*, "utterances" or "discourses." Chapter 10 discusses these and similar works in greater detail.

This brief initial overview of the history of Islamic hagiography can only hint at the immense wealth of this vast tradition and the host of characters it enshrines. For now, however, the important point is that from the earliest years of Islamic history, Muslims have cherished the uniqueness and importance of certain divinely favored individuals. This elevated status did not end with the last Prophet but was shared, albeit in a somewhat diminished form, by persons of subsequent generations. Though Muslim sources began to distinguish rather early on between prophets and Friends of God, the tradition has in fact made room for a broad spectrum of exemplars of holiness and piety. I begin this book with the dual conviction that a credible overview of Islamic hagiography must take into consideration this sense of historical and spiritual continuity and that one can account for this element without diminishing the distinctive role of prophets in Islamic belief. Many classic Islamic works give ample foundation and precedent for this conviction.

HAGIOGRAPHY AND ITS SUBJECTS

A recent study of the life of a major fourteenth-/twentieth-century Muslim figure describes hagiography as "an active process of identity formation in conceptual space somewhere between memory and history. That is, hagiography retains origins as diffuse as memory, yet it is as purposeful and politically driven as history."[8] For present purposes, I suggest a working distinction among the following types of sources: works whose primary purpose is to retell the stories of paradigmatic religious figures; works that include elements of such stories as part of a larger historical or cultural framework; and works that include theoretical or systematic analyses of key elements of the lives of prophets and Friends of God. No matter how one defines hagiography, however, one has to appreciate the range of characters that make up its subject matter.

Among the many terms for exemplars of devotion and conduct, and for embodiments of the loftiest relationships to God, arguably the most important is *walī*. I have generally translated it as "Friend (of God)," though "protégé" would also be apt. The term appears in the Qurʾān in various contexts but has been most widely understood in postscriptural Islamic religious literature as suggesting protection, patronage, and even intimacy. Scholars have spent considerable time discussing the meanings and interrelationships of two cognate substantive nouns, *walāya* and *wilāya*. Vincent Cornell suggests a useful distinction, defining the former term as "the nature/essence of a person's sainthood" and the latter as "the actions of the saint as experienced by others"—that is, "the outward visage" of Friendship with God. Cornell associates the "inner" *walāya* especially with the epistemological concerns of more speculative Sufism and the "outer" *wilāya* with manifestations of spiritual power.[9]

Another important term or title in Middle Eastern lore is *Qiddīs*, "holy one." Arabic-speaking Christians use this term to refer to their "saints," individuals elevated by an often-complex process of examination and authentication. Interestingly, Middle Eastern Christians have named many of their parishes and local church communities after figures whom European or "Latin" Christian churches rarely identify as "saints." They principally name them after figures more typically identified as prophets or patriarchs, such as Abraham. "Saint Abraham" may strike the Western ear oddly, but it sounds fine to the Christians of Iraq and Iran. Other commonly used and rather generic terms in the classic sources are *sālih* (righteous) and *sādiq* (truthful).

Stories of the Friends of God have been preserved in a wide variety of literary forms. But one can discern equal, if not greater, diversity in the types of holy persons depicted in this vast and still largely untapped historical record. These sources depict a variety of social contexts and spiritual odysseys, and they often tailor their presentations of Friends' lives and personalities to their intended audiences. Some depict Friends in urban contexts, whereas others place their protagonists in more rural settings.[10] Some saintly figures enjoy a fairly direct and apparently effortless journey toward union with God. They find themselves "being drawn" (*jadhb*) to God, and sources refer to them as *majdhūb*. Others, the "wayfarer" (*sālik*), clearly need to struggle and exercise constant vigilance as they seek God. Finally, some accounts so emphasize elements of the fantastic, marvelous, and seemingly superhuman that they inspire no more than distant admiration for the Friends they depict. Friends in other stories are more accessible to the ordinary person. Because their deeds are more down to earth, more obviously within reach of the average believer, well-intentioned folk can imagine imitating these Friends.[11] Finally, a dichotomy exists between the socially respectable holy person, and the "fool for God." Whereas Friends in the former category are typically connected with organizations with some standing and authority in their communities, those in the latter category are frequently loners who choose to live on the margins of society and are sometimes referred to as *muwallahs* (those who are ecstatically crazed) or *malāmatīs* (those who are willing to incur blame and derision). One might consider *malāmatīs* to be a subset, or perhaps an extreme example, of renunciants (*zāhid*), who are best known for their asceticism (*zuhd*).

Perhaps the largest category of terms for describing Friends of God refers to the individual's relationship with God, either conveying a direct relationship or placing the Friend within a cosmic hierarchical structure. Those who are believed to be closest to God are often described as "fully realized" (*muhaqqiq*), or as "intimate or experiential knowers" (*ʿārif*), whereas major figures in the cosmological structure might be the "pole or axis" (*qutb*), "pegs" (*awtād*), and "substitutes" (*abdāl*). Because Friends stand between humankind and God, they often function as mediators or intercessors. Wielding the gift of marvels, Friends perform countless deeds that benefit and astonish their constituencies, including healing and managing otherwise untamed elements of nature. In many historical and geographical contexts, arguably the Friend's knowledge-intensive role as "power broker" is the factor that comes to the fore most often.[12]

Many hagiographical works emerge explicitly from Sufi organizations and thus describe their subjects largely in terms that derive from the historic structures, and related ranks and offices, of those groups. The most important Friends of God are often individuals credited with founding Sufi orders, and their immediate successors are then ranked next in the organizational hierarchy. Hagiographies of some orders present the groups as microcosms of the larger community of Muslims, with its spiritual descent from Muhammad and his Companions. Orders also appear as miniature versions of the cosmos itself. They may have structural features such as the "axis of the age" at the pinnacle, followed by "substitutes" and other subordinate figures whose task is to hold the universe together spiritually.[13]

I could delve much more deeply into background details at this juncture. But without the personalities of the prophets and Friends, to present more theory now would be like offering so many fleshless bones. The stories are the real treasure. They are waiting to be told, so let us allow them to speak for themselves.

PART I

Stages in the Lives of God's Friends

. . . . .

God's Friends, and the stories of their lives and times, come in a variety of shapes and sizes. As personalities, these characters span a broad spectrum, from shy and reclusive to extroverted and colorful; from vigorously youthful to mellow in their seniority; from confident, perhaps even brash, to consumed with self-criticism. Narrative sources on these paragons of piety and commitment are equally diverse in tone and content. Moreover, these tales offer a fascinating repertoire of story types, literary forms whose signature motifs and structures have made their way across the globe and now preserve a host of distinctive cultural interpretations of the Friends.

In five chapters, part 1 outlines dominant themes in the lives of some of God's Friends in all their richness and diversity. Nativity and infancy narratives, among the most distinctive story types, offer a glimpse of the origins of prophets and saints, charging elements of ordinary humanity with wonder and divine power (chapter 1). Chapter 2 then traces exemplary footsteps along the road of conversion and ongoing spiritual struggle. On that path, prophets and Friends enjoy unique guidance from their divine patron in the form of dreams and visions, voices and visitors (chapter 3). Even more arresting are the countless manifestations of power that God works through his earthly representatives, as told in chapter 4's tales of miracle and marvel. Spectacular prerogatives notwithstanding, prophets and Friends are human, and chapter 5 brings their life stories full circle with reminders of frailty and mortality.

1. Beginnings Both Humble and Spectacular

Among the various subgenres within the expansive category of Islamic hagiography, those that recount the births, infancies, and childhood years of God's Friends are among the most intriguing for both religious and literary reasons. From a religious perspective, whatever the specific faith tradition, these accounts underscore the mystery and marvelous nature of divine involvement in human affairs. As literary forms, the stories have remarkable similarities in content and narrative art. Not all biohagiographical sketches start with stories of beginnings. Those that do share some themes, symbols, and character types.[1] This chapter considers several nativity and infancy narratives, as well as some tales that follow youthful Friends as they emerge from childhood.

Except in stories of the early lives of the Friends themselves, children do not often appear as subjects of hagiographical narratives. Some famous Sufis report that talking with children is one of several actions (along with hobnobbing with one's enemies and befriending women) sure to erode one's spiritual life.[2] Other hints of a somewhat negative attitude toward children occur in various Islamicate literary strands, a topic that is a major study in its own right. Here I look at the more positive descriptions of how God uses aspects of the beginnings of the lives of his Friends as vehicles for communicating the message of divine providence and power.[3]

FIGURE 1. *(opposite)*   After the infant Moses slaps Pharaoh, the ruler threatens to kill the child. Pharaoh's daughter intervenes, insisting that the baby was unaware. As proof, she places a pearl and a live ember before Moses. When the infant begins to reach for the pearl, Gabriel guides his hand to the ember, which he then raises to his lips. Juwayrī, *Qisas al-anbiyaʾ*, Columbia University Rare Book and Manuscript Library, X 829.8 Q1/Q (1574–75), 75a.

13

NATIVITY NARRATIVES

Nativity narratives appear in both major types of hagiographic accounts, those of prophets and those of Friends of God. "Birth" stories of both groups arguably represent a single literary form. However, because these two groups of personalities embody theologically distinct presuppositions, certain subtle thematic variations set them apart. I therefore begin here with prominent examples of the Islamic tradition's enshrinement of the origins of God's premier spokespersons, the prophets, and suggest some principal thematic differences from similar accounts of God's Friends. Although no clear formal distinction exists between nativity and infancy accounts, I treat them separately here purely for organizational purposes. Thus, in this chapter, the category of "nativity" story embraces occurrences before the holy person's conception, during gestation, and at birth.

From the Tales of the Prophets

Most of the major prophets are the subjects of Qurʾānic texts, although these scriptural accounts are typically brief and fragmentary, and appear sporadically in various contexts. Many of these briefer allusions function as moral examples, reminding listeners and readers of the consequences of rejecting God's messengers and the revelations they bring. In many instances, the works of Qurʾānic exegetes fill in details and expand context, and in the unique instance of Joseph (Yūsuf), the prophet's story unfolds in a single literary unit (sura 12). But the genre we call "tales of the prophets" provides extended coherent narratives that go well beyond the scriptural accounts. Tales of the prophets are in the category of hagiographical anthologies or "collected lives." Among the most famous and influential works in the genre are the Arabic works of Thaʿlabī and Kisāʾī. My goal here is to illustrate elements of genre and theme rather than to rehearse the traditional Islamic structure of revelation history. I therefore discuss the stories of the prophets by theme rather than in the order in which they typically occur in the major sources.

The story of the Arabian prophet Hūd features an important theme: the revelatory dream anticipating the blessed birth. In a dream, Khulūd, of the tribe of ʿĀd, sees a chain—a common metaphor for progeny or lineage—emerging from his loins that is as bright as the sun. A voice informs him that when he witnesses the chain in a dream again, he is to marry the young woman chosen for him. He is later instructed to marry a cousin, and when Hūd is conceived, all creation exults and the tribe's orchards overflow with fruit. The baby is born on a Friday. Another significant (and often-used) metaphor in such dreams is that of the tree emanating brilliant light from its many limbs, as in the dream of Rebecca that she would bear Isaac's sons Jacob and Esau.[4]

Kanūh (called ʿUbayd in Thaʿlabī and other sources), the father of another distinctively Arabian prophet, Sālih, experiences similar revelatory signs. When the seed that would grow into the new prophet becomes mobile within the father-to-be, a blazing light emits from his body, and he hears a voice that identifies the light as that of Sālih. Significantly, Kanūh has heretofore served the idols of the tribe of Thamūd—a parallel to Abraham's father's making his living by carving idols. Kanūh, in his fright, has recourse to the chief idol, but just before it comes crashing down, the image concedes that the light is indeed that of a great prophet. Here, as in other tales, an evil king responds to the perceived threat to his rule by trying to assassinate the principal characters; but in this instance, the target is the father, Kanūh. God intervenes and spirits the man away to a remote valley, where he sleeps for a century. Back home a hundred years on, Kanūh's wife continues to grieve his presumed death, when a marvelous bird suddenly appears in her courtyard. It identifies itself as the raven that showed Cain how to bury his brother Abel. It then offers to lead the woman to her husband. The couple reunites and conceives Sālih; but God takes Kanūh to himself, and the bird leads his pregnant wife back home. There, on Friday, the tenth of Muharram (the first lunar month), she delivers the child, who immediately begins to praise God.[5] This detail of timing is also a common feature in nativity narratives in tales of the prophets, and the annual date continues to be important both to Sunnī and (especially) to Shīʿī Muslims.

Abraham's (Ibrāhīm's) story is among the most extensive in the genre. The tale begins well in advance of his birth, with anticipatory dreams in this instance coming to two wicked rulers in succession. Canaan dreams of his own destruction, and his astrologers inform him that a shepherdess has conceived a child that will threaten Canaan's rule. The infant, Nimrod, survives various attempts to exterminate him and grows up to overthrow Canaan and establish his own evil regime. These activities set the stage for a second round of revelatory events, which inform the tyrant that a child will soon be born who will overthrow him. This time, the newcomer is a prophet rather than a rival king. A pair of white birds, one of the East and one of the West, enter the scene to foreshadow a series of dreams and apparitions. As in other dream stories, Nimrod's dream features brilliant lights emanating from the father-to-be. As in other stories, too, the evil ruler learns that his destruction will come from within his own house. This time the nemesis will be Abraham, whose father, called Āzar in most Islamic sources, has long been a trusted servant of Nimrod.[6] Nimrod immediately initiates a murderous seven-year hunt for all male children, only to find that Abraham has not yet been conceived. Āzar's wife is old and barren but reports to him that she has mysteriously begun to menstruate again. When the two conceive Abraham, a new star ascends in the heavens and sends the idols in the Ka'ba crashing down from their pedestals. As we shall see, rising stars and falling idols go with the territory.

Again Nimrod launches a slaughter of innocents, and another dream informs him that his nemesis is yet to be delivered. His agents go to Āzar's house, but God conceals the pregnancy from the visitors. And when the time for childbirth arrives, according to Kisā'ī's account, an angel leads the child's mother to the cave where the prophets Idrīs and Noah were born, and she delivers on Friday, the tenth of Muharram. She hides the baby in the cave, where wild animals protect him, and she visits him every three days. In an interesting variation, Tha'labī includes an account in which Abraham's mother bears him in a wadi, a seasonal riverbed that was then dry, and hides him in some rushes. Thereafter, his father takes the baby to a riverside and excavates a tunnel in which to hide him. Turning over a new generation, Abraham's own wife, Sarah, eventually conceives their son Isaac on the night on which God had destroyed Lot and his family. When the child is born, his forehead radiates light, and he immediately prostrates himself before God.[7]

The birth of Moses (Mūsā) is likewise foreshadowed by ominous dreams, in which Pharaoh gets a glimpse of his own ignominious end, through the auspices of a child born within his own household. Like Nimrod, the Egyptian ruler sets out to slaughter all male children. Amram ('Imrām), Moses's father, has been accustomed to sleeping at the foot of Pharaoh's bed, but God now carries Amram's wife to the royal bedchamber on the wings of a bird so that the couple can conceive the prophet. When a new star arises, Pharaoh's astrologers deliver the bad news to his majesty, who again seeks the lives of all male children. But Moses's mother hides the baby in the stove. Unaware of this fact, her daughter lights the oven; and when guards come shortly thereafter in search of the baby, they look everywhere but the stove. There God has kept the baby safe, and when his mother returns and flies into a panic at her daughter's actions, the infant reassures her from within the stove that all is well. Tha'labī also includes a version of the oven incident but prefaces it with an account of the effect of the child's birth on the Egyptian midwife whom Pharaoh has sent to kill the baby. When the infant emerges, a light from between his eyes shines on the midwife, causing her to love him totally. In this version, Moses's mother is the one who casts the baby into the oven, to discover after the guards have left that the oven has cooled miraculously.[8]

Stories of a host of lesser figures, also of biblical fame, provide intriguing twists on the main thematic elements of the genre. Most prominent in Noah's (Nūh's) story, for example, is the idea that age is a barrier to the birth of the special child. Here, however, the initial problem is not age beyond fertility but a woman who is not yet marriageable, however old she may sound. According to Kisā'ī, Noah's father meets a woman to whom he is attracted, but when he inquires about her age, she initially claims that she is one hundred eighty years old—twenty years short of marital maturity. When he continues to express interest, she reveals that she is actually two hundred twenty years old, and they marry and have a son. As in the story of Abraham (among others), Noah's mother fears the evil king of the age and gives birth sequestered in a cave. But after the child's birth, she wants a way to emerge safely from hiding, so her infant speaks up (like the baby Jesus and others) and assures her that she need not worry because God will take care of him. She then leaves the baby in the cave (as Abraham's mother left hers) and returns to her family. After forty days, a cohort of angels retrieves the baby and brings him to his mother.[9] Other stories that feature an unlikely pregnancy are those in the "historical books" about Islamic prophetic figures or "former prophets" of the Bible. As in the biblical story of Samuel, Tha'labī's version highlights the pregnancy of the aged and barren wife of Samuel's father. Like Hanna of the biblical First Book of Samuel, the woman prays and the next day begins to menstruate again. Hearing of her pregnancy, the people conclude that the baby will be a prophet, for women otherwise incapable of bearing children give birth only to prophets; one need only witness the mothers of Isaac and John the Baptist.[10]

Tales of the prophets include stories of the conception and birth of Mary, mother of Jesus, with Tha'labī providing greater detail than Kisā'ī does. When the story starts, Mary's mother has been childless, and her husband has a dream that he is to have intercourse with her. She has prayed for a son and promised to dedicate him to the temple if her prayer is answered. Her husband takes her to task, however, for dedicating a child whom he knows will be (or thinks might be) a girl. While Mary's mother is still pregnant, her husband dies and she bears a girl, who later comes to be one of the four premier female models in Islamic tradition: Mary, Āsiya, Khadīja, and Fātima. Mary's mother takes her immediately to the temple for dedication, inciting a competitive stir among the priests, for they all want to claim the child. The priests cast lots, tossing their quills onto the water. That of Zakarīya, father of John, stands upright in the water, and Mary becomes his charge. Like other wonder children, Mary begins to grow much more rapidly than her peers.[11]

Nativity accounts of Jesus (ʿĪsā) and his cousin John the Baptizer, known in Arabic as Yahyā, are intimately linked. John is wondrously conceived by an elderly, infertile woman. Thaʿlabī notes that Zakarīya had faith that his wife might yet have a son and prayed accordingly. When his mother is carrying him, John bows to the still-unborn Jesus, and immediately at birth, John gains note as a precocious infant.[12]

Mary is likewise impregnated under improbable circumstances. Gabriel meets her on the "longest and hottest day of the year" as she seeks water in a cave. The angel breathes into an outer garment that Mary has laid aside, and when she again dons the robe, she conceives. In Thaʿlabī's account, Joseph and Mary have an extended discussion of how this conception could have occurred. In Kisāʾī's version, when Joseph interrogates Mary about her pregnancy, Jesus rebukes Mary's husband-to-be from the womb. Mary explains to Joseph that Jesus, like Adam, is to be born without ordinary parentage. When Mary later encounters the expectant mother of John, the two prophets exchange gestures of greeting with an intrauterine bow. Variant traditions put the length of Mary's pregnancy from the usual nine months to as little as one hour, the abbreviated terms underscoring the miraculous nature of the prophet's genesis.

At the onset of labor, Mary takes hold of an unproductive date palm beneath which lie a livestock manger and a stream. According to Qurʾān 19:24–26, and Muhammad's biographer Ibn Ishāq, Jesus speaks to her immediately upon birth (some variant traditions say that Gabriel speaks instead), telling her not to grieve, for God has placed a river under her.[13] He instructs her to shake the palm tree so that ripe fruit will rain down upon her.[14] Shortly after delivery, Jesus speaks to Joseph, announcing that he has come as a messenger from the darkness of the womb into the light. Idols across the world reportedly toppled at the time of the birth of Jesus as well as upon the birth of several other prophets, including Muhammad. Jesus caught the devil by surprise, for before Mary's secret pregnancy, Iblīs had had foreknowledge of every human conceived.[15] This theme of frustrating the devil's agenda and restoring joy and vitality to the earth is important, occurring in many stories. When Solomon (Sulaymān) was born, for example, all the world's devils became comatose, and Satan sank into the ocean for seventy days. For the first time since Nimrod threw Abraham into his bonfire, the earth laughed again.[16]

Ibn Ishāq's *Life of Muhammad* tells several intriguing stories about the conception of Muhammad. In each instance, the author is careful to note that he cannot vouch for the veracity of these "allegations" or "folktales." Muhammad's grandfather, ʿAbd al-Muttalib, prays to God and tells the

Almighty that if He will grant him ten sons, he will sacrifice one in gratitude. God fulfills the prayer for ten boys. ʿAbd al-Muttalib takes them all to
the Kaʿba to cast lots, and as they do so, he prays that ʿAbd Allāh, his youngest,
might be spared. ʿAbd Allāh loses the lot. When his father takes him to the
place where the ruling Quraysh tribe performs its sacrifices, the tribe members protest, saying that they will go to any length to redeem the young
man from his father's vow. The Quraysh insist that ʿAbd al-Muttalib take
the youth to see a sorceress to get her verdict. She instructs him to return
to Mecca and cast lots again, and every time the lots fall against his son, to
add ten more camels to the blood money. The lots fall against ʿAbd Allāh
over and over, until the blood money reaches one hundred camels. The
Quraysh declare the deity will now be satisfied, but ʿAbd al-Muttalib insists
that he must cast lots three more times. Each draw is in favor of his son, so
he slaughters all the camels, and his son lives to become the father of
Muhammad.

In another account, as the Prophet's grandfather takes his son ʿAbd Allāh
for betrothal to the woman destined to become Muhammad's mother,
another woman offers herself to the son. ʿAbd Allāh declines. After he has
consummated his marriage to Āmina, he encounters the woman again. Now,
however, she is no longer interested in him, and he asks her why she has
changed her mind. She explains that her Christian brother, Waraqa ibn
Nawfal, has informed her that his scriptures foretold the birth of a prophet
among their folk. When ʿAbd Allāh had passed by before, she goes on, he
had borne a light between his eyes, but that light was no longer there. She
recognized instinctively that the Prophet had already been conceived, and
her sole interest in ʿAbd Allāh vanished.

Muhammad was born after a very brief and painless labor, and he immediately lifted his head heavenward. Other signs heralded Muhammad's antic-
ipated arrival as well. A new star rose, and his pregnant mother saw a light
emanating from her so bright that she could see castles as far as Syria. A voice
explained that she would bear a leader of the people, instructing her to com-
mend him to the protection of God and name him Muhammad. An important feature of his life story (and that of several other prophets) is that his
father dies before he is born, emphasizing the centrality of divine protection
for the child.[17]

Some stories report that Muhammad's cousin and, later, son-in-law, ʿAlī,
also had a wondrous gestation and delivery. In such stories, his pregnant
mother is unable to pray before idols with ʿAlī in her womb. In a twist reminiscent of the relationship between Jesus and John, ʿAlī speaks to his older
cousin Muhammad from the womb. ʿAlī's mother experiences a protracted

and difficult labor until she enters the sacred precincts of the Kaʿba. There she bears the perfect child, beaming and oriented to the heavens.[18] And here begins the remarkable story of the Shīʿī imams.

How the Imams Came into the World

Among the accounts of the Shīʿī imams, Husayn's gestation and nativity have attracted more attention than most others. Traditional sources report that Gabriel three times announced to Muhammad the imminent birth of a grandson who would suffer martyrdom for his community. Twice Muhammad sends the angel away, insisting that the world has no need of such a child. On his third visit, Gabriel adds that the child's offspring will guard the imamate and divine authority. Muhammad immediately gives his approval to the arrangement. His daughter, Fātima, likewise balks initially at the announcement, until Muhammad explains that Husayn will stand at the head of the imams. According to at least one traditional source, the child is conceived the day his older brother, Hasan, is born, clearly suggesting a miraculous conception. Before his daughter conceives, Muhammad tells her he perceives a revelatory light from her countenance. According to one tradition, Husayn's gestation, like that of Jesus, lasted a mere six months, but the timing is less spectacular in other versions of the story.

During the pregnancy, Fātima is never hungry or thirsty and experiences peculiar signs. Like Mary in the Qurʾān, she goes into seclusion. At six months, she hears the fetus exalting God and finds that she sheds light wherever she goes. Early in the seventh month, three angels in succession visit her at night, causing her great consternation. When she visits her father and his wife Umm Salama the next day, a white dove enters her robe. The Prophet then identifies the angels as ʿIzrāʾīl (angel of death and guardian of the womb), Michael (guardian of the wombs of the women in the Prophet's family), and Gabriel (who will attend the child). Some popular hagiographies even suggest that Muhammad himself delivers his grandson, further emphasizing the baby's intimate relationship to the Prophet. In a feature reminiscent of the New Testament's acknowledgment of Mary's future loss of her son, Shīʿī traditions report that angels consoled Muhammad (not the boy's mother) in advance for Husayn's eventual martyrdom on the tenth of Muharram 61/680.[19]

Conceptions and Births of the Friends of God

Friends of God, like their senior predecessors the prophets, often enter the world under most unusual circumstances. Though the settings are sometimes quite spectacular, accounts of the Friends typically lack the larger historic and cosmic dimensions that so often characterize the genesis of the prophets.

For example, a Friend's impending arrival rarely touches off astronomical pyrotechnics or bestirs potentates to scramble for their thrones and clutch at their crowns. Arresting effects in general tend to be more localized and may even be indiscernible except to those close to the special child. Stories of conception and gestation deal less with how the divine overcomes impossible obstacles (such as barrenness) than with remarkable ways in which the child communicates his divine message precociously. As often as not, the unusual concomitants seek to underscore the humility and piety, rather than the power and prerogatives, of the Friend. Conception and gestation stories are arguably less crucial to the tales of Friends than to those of prophets. A brief look at examples of the subgenre reveals some of its principal themes.

Accounts of the pregnancies of mothers of God's Friends often highlight the need for ritually pure (*halāl*) food. The story typically follows a formula. Every time the mother-to-be ingests something forbidden or even legally discouraged, the fetus in her womb becomes so agitated that the mother eventually realizes the problem and modifies her behavior. In some cases, the mother needs only one instance of intrauterine commotion to take the cue. ʿAttār says that Sufyān ath-Thawrī has been scrupulous from birth, but his abstemiousness seems to have earlier origins. The fetus reacts to his mother's eating a pickle and gets her attention by squirming. When Bāyazīd al-Bistāmī is in the womb, he becomes upset whenever his mother takes a bite of a food that is of questionable ritual purity. ʿAttār is careful to note that Bāyazīd himself later confirmed this story.[20]

At the birth of Rābiʿa, her family is so poor her parents have no oil for her navel and no swaddling clothes, and her father goes to bed deeply distressed. The Prophet appears to the father in a dream and assures him that the child will have the authority to intercede for seventy thousand Muslims. Muhammad tells the baby's father to go to the emir of Basra and ask him for four hundred gold coins to make up for the fact that the governor has neglected his usual Friday wish for four hundred blessings on the man. Delighted that the Prophet has mentioned him by name, the governor not only gives the man four hundred gold pieces but gives an additional ten thousand in alms.[21] Maʿrūf Karkhī's conception also occurs in a peculiarly marvelous way, in a story designed to aggrandize a Friend of God named Dawūd at-Tāʾī. Dawūd once gave a hungry Christian passerby a piece of his bread, for he always tried to be generous. That night the man's wife conceived Maʿrūf.[22]

Aflākī's monumental hagiography of Rūmī's family and followers includes a remarkable set of reports about the conception and birth of Rūmī's grandson Chalabī Amīr ʿĀrif. The day after Rūmī's son Sultān Walad had intercourse with his wife, Fātima Khātūn, Sultān Walad encountered his father. Rūmī asked Sultān Walad whether he had been searching for ʿĀrif in hope after he and his wife had lost twelve or thirteen children in their infancy. Thus does Aflākī set the scene for a marvelous offspring to arrive against great odds and amid intense longing. It was on that occasion that Sultān Walad and his wife had indeed conceived the child they would name Chalabī Amīr ʿĀrif. Apparently experiencing some sort of depression after so many losses, however, Fātima Khātūn tried unsuccessfully to end this new pregnancy. But she was at length persuaded that she would bear a healthy child. She began to take care of herself, and at last "ʿĀrif transferred his foot from the world of eternity to the plain of existence."[23]

A variety of stories focus on the gestational life of later medieval great South Asian Friends as well. When Bībī Zulaykhā was pregnant with Nizām ad-Dīn Awliyāʾ, a voice in a dream told her that she must choose between her unborn child and her husband. She preferred the clearly special child and widowhood, and her husband died when the Friend was an infant.[24] Before Shāh Mīnā was "born a saint," his uncle foretold that the "candle of our household" would soon come forth to give luster to the family name. People could hear the sound of the fetus engaged in *dhikr* and Qurʾān recitation in his pregnant mother's womb.[25] A later medieval Indian hagiography records extraordinary occurrences during the gestation and infancy of ʿAbd ar-Rahīm, the successor of a major Friend named Bābā Musāfir. In one story, ʿAbd ar-Rahīm's mother, having borne five daughters, prays for a son. A mendicant visits her one day and after she makes a donation, he promises that she will have an important male child. After she becomes pregnant, the mother reports having a dream in which she embraces the sun. She recalls that during gestation, she experienced no need of food, drink, or sleep, and wanted only to pray continually.[26]

INFANCY NARRATIVES: PRODIGIES AND SIGNS

Tales of striking circumstances in the conceptions and gestations of God's most extraordinary servants are only the beginning of their stories. Traditional sources also feature accounts of the conditions and manner in which prophets and Friends engaged the outer world. They detail not only the feats of these servants of God as infants and toddlers but also the responses of their families and larger constituencies. I begin with stories of prophets and continue with God's tiniest Friends.

Baby Prophets

Stories of the early childhood years of prophets use various devices to describe the young heroes' introduction to their world. In one of the more unusual accounts, Hūd's mother reminisces with her son that shortly after he was born, she placed him on a black rock that immediately turned white. She soon encountered an enormous "man," who raised the child up to a group of white-faced persons in the heavens, and these figures in turn gave Hūd back to his mother with a green pearl on his arm and light on his head.[27] These events are among the more novel manifestations of a prophetic infant's inherent uniqueness and portentousness, including the striking image of the offering of the child to the heavenly court as a sign of his divinely sanctioned authority. Solomon's debut was much less spectacular but nonetheless remarkable. Baby Solomon fasted until he was three years old, at which time his father, David, initiated the boy in the study of Jewish scriptures. When the king read to the child, Solomon memorized the words immediately, and by the time the boy turned four, he had mastered the whole Torah. At that age, he began to perform a hundred cycles of ritual prayer daily. One day his mother instructed him to kill an ant crawling on his clothes, but he declined. The prospect of hearing the ant say on Judgment Day that it had died at Solomon's hand terrified the royal child.[28]

Abraham's first encounter with his larger environment is equally dramatic in its way, but it focuses on an extraordinary kind of conversion for one so young. When Abraham was a mere four years of age,[29] God sent Gabriel to instruct the boy to emerge at last from the cave in which he had been born. God then showed him signs in the heavens—star, moon, and sun, all of which set—that revealed to the child the transcendent oneness of the true deity (Qurʾān 6:76–79). Gabriel then took the child to his parents' home, where he confronted his father, who had been a carver of idols, with his true belief. Nimrod had Abraham brought before him and then instructed Abraham's father, Terah, that perhaps the boy could be returned to his senses with time and patience, so long as Terah taught the child to worship only Nimrod.[30]

Islamic sources elaborate on the biblical account of Moses, with which many readers are already familiar. These sources expand the network of persons involved in Moses's prophetic debut. Another telling feature is the irony in the child's thinly veiled hostility toward Pharaoh, which nearly unmasks the infant as the nemesis about whom the ruler has been warned. Not long after the newborn Moses is saved by being hidden in the oven, his mother has a carpenter build a tiny ark in which she plans to set the forty-day-old baby afloat on the Nile. (Moses's father dies at about this time, and early loss of the father has already emerged as an important theme.) According to one of Thaʿlabī's sources, the carpenter tries to tell her secret to Pharaoh, but God renders him mute. On each of two attempts, the carpenter is dismissed as crazy and is driven away, until he vows that if God restores his speech, he will serve as Moses's faithful guard.

Once the baby is entrusted to the river, God causes the wind to blow the ark toward Pharaoh's palace. There the oldest of the king's seven diseased daughters finds the child glowing like the sun. Upon contact with the baby prophet, she is healed, as are all her sisters. When Pharaoh's wife, Āsiya, brings him the child, the king immediately suspects the baby is to be his downfall and resolves to kill him. Āsiya persuades him that he need not hurry because the child is now in his power, and he relents. As in the biblical accounts, Moses is returned to his mother for nursing, but some accounts suggest that he continued to spend considerable time in the palace. On one occasion when Pharaoh dandles the baby on his lap, the child suddenly grabs his beard and slaps the king so hard that his crown falls off. Again Pharaoh swears that he will kill the child, but Āsiya persuades him that the infant is without awareness and therefore blameless. As a test, she places a pearl and a hot coal before the child; when he reaches for the pearl, Gabriel guides his hand toward the coal, and the child raises his hand to his mouth in agony. Again Pharaoh relents (see Fig. 1).[31]

In the story of Jesus, themes of refuge in a cave, rapid growth, and escape from the evil intentions of a threatened monarch combine with overtly heroic deeds of power. This last element is more evident in this story than in many other tales of baby prophets. Tha'labī reports that Joseph took Mary and the child Jesus to a cave, where she recovered from childbirth for forty days. In only one day, Jesus showed a full month's development. Mary's family members are prepared to disown her when she brings the newborn Jesus to them. Spectacularly again, but not out of character for a prophet, the infant speaks in defense of his mother's virtue.[32] Kisā'ī includes a variety of episodes in Mary and Joseph's journey with the child to Egypt to escape the murderous designs of Herod. First, they encounter a lion. Jesus instructs them to put him down in front of the beast. When the baby asks the lion why he is there, the animal responds that he is waiting for an ox to eat. Jesus cautions the lion that perhaps the ox's owners are impoverished and suggests that the lion head to a place where he can find a camel to eat. The lion obeys. The family later comes to a town where a mob is forming around a home, evidently threatening its inhabitants. Jesus tells the people in the crowd that the owner is a believer and then tells them where they can find a stash of treasure that once belonged to a dead man with no descendants. Take that treasure, he orders them, and so they do.[33]

Muhammad's introduction to his social environment is through growing up in a kind of foster family and experiencing purification by mysterious "angelic" figures when he is a child. After his birth, his grandfather, ʿAbd al-Muttalib, goes in search of a wet nurse for him. A woman named Halīma and her husband happen to have traveled to Mecca looking for more children for her to nurse, for they are destitute and have a new baby of their own. There the infant Prophet's family offers him to every interested woman, but none want him when they hear that his father has died, making recompense for their service unlikely. In the end, all the women find a child to nurse except Halīma. She convinces her husband that they should accept the Prophet rather than return home unsuccessful. When she begins to nurse the baby, her breasts overflow with milk, as do the udders of their previously dry she-camel. These marvels prompt her husband to proclaim that his Halīma has been given a wondrous child. Even when others' flocks graze on the same pasture as Halīma's, they remain dry.

These features of Muhammad's story recall important aspects of traditional accounts of Jonah (Yūnus). Jonah is conceived on the eve of the tenth of Muharram, and his father dies just after his birth. Unlike Muhammad, Jonah miraculously supplies his destitute mother with daily sustenance. Unable to nurse the baby, she takes him to shepherds and asks them to let him suckle the sheep.[34] The latter feature of the story is consistent with the Islamic tradition in which God takes every prophet from shepherding when the time comes for his new role, and the theme recurs in the stories of many youthful prophets and Friends of God.

After two years, Halīma brings Muhammad back to Āmina and begs her to let him stay longer with Halīma's family; Muhammad's mother agrees. Soon thereafter, Halīma's own boy comes running to report that two men in white have laid his stepbrother (Muhammad) on the ground, opened his chest, and searched his innards. Terrified that the boy might be possessed by a jinn, Halīma returns him to his birth mother. After Halīma departs, the boy explains to playmates that he is the one whom the prophet Abraham has prayed for and the very message Jesus has brought. He explains that the two men in white extracted a black drop from his heart and cleansed it with snow.[35]

Infant Friends

Stories of nonprophetic children with unusual abilities and preternatural powers appear as early as the hadith literature. Speaking precociously is a common feature in stories of the prophets, but it also occurs in other curious contexts. Both Hujwīrī and Qushayrī include in their handbooks of spirituality the "Hadīth of Jurayj," in which Muhammad describes three infants who have spoken precociously. The first is the prophet Jesus (who spoke from the womb and later as a newborn to defend his mother). The second is an infant who saved the reputation of a monk named Jurayj. In this story, the monk's mother pays her son a visit only to find him too engrossed in prayer to see her. When the same scene plays out the next day, the woman asks God to cause her son to lose his good name because the monk has mistreated her so. A woman of questionable virtue who lives nearby resolves at that moment to seduce the monk. But when she accosts Jurayj in his cell, he ignores her. Departing in anger, the woman spreads rumors about the monk and shortly thereafter sleeps with a shepherd. Nine months later, she bears the shepherd's son and claims that Jurayj is the boy's father. When the king hails the monk to court, Jurayj asks the infant to name his father. The infant discloses that his father is a shepherd and that the wicked woman has defamed Jurayj. In the third story, an otherwise unidentified infant speaks to contradict an adult's pronouncements. A woman sits at her front door and asks God to make her son like an attractive stranger she sees riding past, but the child insists he does not want to be like the stranger. Not long thereafter, a lighthearted (and therefore probably undignified) woman passes, and the mother prays that God will keep the child from becoming like her. Again the infant disagrees, insisting that he wants to be exactly like the woman. When his puzzled mother questions him about his responses, the baby explains that he discerned that the horseman was a tyrant whereas the woman was good-hearted and did not deserve her questionable reputation.[36] In general, however, precocious speech is reserved to prophets. Baby Friends of God have other wondrous ways of communicating.

The theme of early rearing under striking circumstances, though rather common in tales of the prophets, occurs infrequently in stories of Friends. When it does appear, it signals the storyteller's intent to connect the Friend with the prophets. When Hasan al-Basrī was born, he received his name from no less a luminary than the Companion and caliph-to-be ʿUmar ibn al-Khattāb, who declared him "handsome" (*hasan*). Hasan grew up in the home of Muhammad's wife Umm Salama, for whom the child's mother worked. If the baby cried because his mother was otherwise occupied, Umm Salama gave him her breast. She prayed that God would make the child an exemplar for all, thus bestowing countless blessings on the boy. Once when the Prophet visited Umm Salama's house while the baby was there, he prayed for little Hasan and again bestowed blessings. On one occasion, the child drank water from the Prophet's water jug. Noticing some water missing, the Prophet learned that the child had drunk it. Muhammad declared that the boy would receive knowledge from him in proportion to the water he had imbibed.[37]

Like their prophetic counterparts, God's Friends are often dedicated to or presented for the exclusive service of God. According to legendary accounts about Hallāj's beginnings, for example, the mystic's mother promised during her pregnancy to dedicate the child to a life of service to the spiritually poor. Tradition holds that the baby had foreknowledge of this dedication and that his mother made good on her promise when he reached the age of seven.[38]

When a follower asked the adult Bāyazīd how he had arrived at his advanced spiritual condition, he recounted a story about his childhood that brings to mind Hūd's presentation at the heavenly court. One night, he recalled, he walked to the outskirts of his hometown of Bistām. There in the tranquil moonlight, he envisioned a "presence" that rendered the rest of creation meaningless. Transported into an ecstatic state, the awestruck boy humbly expressed to God his surprise that the "court" he had seen was so deserted. A heavenly "voice" responded that the divine court was deserted only because God is choosy about whom to invite. At that point, he reported, he felt the desire to intercede so that all creation might receive an invitation. He stopped short when he realized that only the Prophet Muhammad enjoyed the prerogative of intercession. In honor of that precocious and most appropriate reticence, God told the boy that he would henceforth be called the "Sultan of Mystics."[39]

In an important variant on presentation and initiation themes, the Friend's father brings the child to a prayer gathering, only to have the tyke steal the show. Abū Saʿīd ibn Abī 'l-Khayr was born on a Sunday, the first day of Muharram (an exception to the more common day of Friday and the more usual date of the tenth). His mother asks her husband to take the infant along with him to a regular *samaʿ* meeting of dervishes so that they might look upon the child. The baby's presence prompts the repeated recitation of a quatrain, which the child memorizes. Returning home, the child asks his father about the meaning of the ecstasy-inducing verses. His father rebukes the little boy, saying that such mystical things are not meant for him. Later, when his father is building the family a house in Mayhana, the child asks his father to build a room where none but Abū Saʿīd can go. So his father adds a room on the roof just for the boy, and the child requests that the name of God be inscribed repeatedly on every surface. When his father asks the boy the meaning of this request, his son responds that he wants only to do what his father has done in the rest of the house: to instruct the workers to decorate it with the name and image of the sultan and his kingdom. After the child explains that everyone inscribes on his walls the name of the object of his devotion, the father experiences a conversion and removes all signs of homage to the earthly sultan.[40]

Abū Saʿīd himself reported that when his father took him to the mosque one Friday, a famous mystic and Traditionist asked whose child he might be.

The old scholar—whose function in the story is much like that of Simeon in the New Testament—bent down and rubbed his cheek against the child's.[41] He wept as he explained that he could now die in peace, content that the child assured the future leadership of the spiritual quest. A sign reinforced the old Sufi's conviction shortly thereafter: Abū Saʿīd's father brought the boy into the shaykh's room, and the old man instructed the father to lift the child so that the boy could reach a loaf of bread from a niche in the wall. Breaking the loaf in half, the old man shared it with the child only. He explained to the father that he had put the loaf there thirty years earlier upon receiving a promise that the one whose touch warmed the loaf as though it had just been baked would be a long-awaited spiritual leader, the "seal" of the Friends of God.[42] The old man, Pīr Abū 'l-Qāsim Bishr-i Yāsīn, continued as the boy's shaykh for several more years. Abū Saʿīd's main biographer, Ibn-i Munawwar, records a number of anecdotes about the boy's spiritual formation. Ibn ʿArabī tells an analogous story of the infant daughter of Mawrūrī, one of his shaykhs. The little girl was so in touch with the spiritual condition of her father that during sessions at the shaykh's house, the infant used to slide off her mother's lap and stand in their midst. There she manifested ecstatic experience, and even before she was weaned, God took her from this life.[43]

Mentoring of a younger Friend by an elder saint is an important related theme. When Rūmī's new grandchild, ʿĀrif Chalabī, was born, the grandfather visited the mother and asked to take the baby with him. He breathed into the child the gifts of light (i.e., of knowledge) and the ability to open hearts and then returned the baby to his mother and her attendants. Rūmī declared that he saw the light of seven Friends of God (three of Rūmī's family members and four of his intimate personal friends) in the child. He told the boy's father to give him the honorific title Farīdūn, the name of the great Iranian national epic hero. In another account, a woman brings ʿĀrif's crib to Rūmī in the courtyard of his madrasa. Grandfather instructs the six-month-old child to say "Allāh, Allāh," and, like the precociously articulate Jesus, the child does so. Rūmī dies when Fātima Khātūn is still nursing the new grandson, but the mother is so distraught that she can no longer nurse him. More ominously, the child will not (following the example of Moses) take milk from other nurses either. One night Rūmī appears to Fātima in a dream and consoles her. She awakes and finds herself able to nurse again. But the light of Rūmī shines so effulgently in the boy's eyes that she experiences ecstasy and becomes a disciple of her own child.[44]

In a story about the infancy of an Egyptian Friend of God named Muhammad Wafāʾ, an important mystic and religious leader comes to visit.

Seeing the child, the visiting Ibn ʿAtāʾ Allāh al-Iskandarī kisses him and declares (Simeon-like) that the infant is already endowed with full knowledge of the highest realities. He reports that the baby will compose numerous mystical works before he is ten years old. When Muhammad Wafāʾ himself becomes a father, he passes along to his six-year-old son, ʿAlī, the gift of composing poetry, by investing the boy with his own belt just before he himself dies.[45]

In another tale of infancy, a contemporary of Abū Saʿīd, Abū Ishāq al-Kāzarūnī, manifests signs of extraordinary altruism even as a nursling. He refuses his mother's breast until she allows another child to nurse before him. When he is still very small, his Qurʾān tutor asks whether the boy's family can supply him a bit of wheat, for the land is suffering a shortage. Kāzarūnī's family is too poor to help. On the following day, when the child goes to the barn to scrape up a few grains, he finds it overflowing with wheat.[46]

As an infant, fifteenth-century Chishtī shaykh Shāh Mīnā refuses to nurse both during Ramadan and at other times, the story goes, until his mother purifies herself ritually. When his mother awakes at night, she invariably notices the infant prostrate in prayer beneath his cover. When he is only two or three, the child's grandfather instructs sparrows to flock to Shāh Mīnā. They do so and remain until the infant releases them. At the age of five, the boy is a challenge to his teachers. Already endowed with greater knowledge than the instructor can impart, the boy spends the day in *dhikr*. When he is just ten, the boy reads Suhrawardī's major manual of spirituality, *The Benefits of Intimate Knowledge*, and rises to the rank of Pole of the universe.[47]

In another story, the newborn Indian Friend ʿAbd ar-Rahīm always nurses from his mother's right breast, and as a child, he refuses to wear fancy clothes. At two and a half years, the toddler dresses as an ascetic and recites Qurʾān in secret; and by four, he has read the entire sacred book.[48] Amadou Bamba of Senegal is similarly possessed of astonishing self-control as an infant. He does not cry, insists on remaining only in rooms devoted to prayer, and becomes seriously agitated if anyone in his presence acts in any way contrary to Islamic law.[49] When ʿĀrif Chalabī is eight months old, a tumor in his throat prevents him from taking nourishment for a week, causing his mother great anxiety. The baby's father takes him to the roof of the madrasa and has a vision of his own father, Rūmī, pacing anxiously. Rūmī responds to his son's anguish by assuring him that the boy will not perish. The grandfather takes a pen and inscribes seven lines on the baby's throat, causing the tumor to burst and restoring him to health. ʿĀrif's beauty is such that people consider him a second Joseph, and one glance at his face is all anyone can bear without losing control.[50]

First-person nativity and infancy accounts are, not surprisingly, rare. ʿAbd al-Qādir ibn ʿAbd Allāh al-ʿAydarūs, whose family had migrated from South Arabia to the Indian region of Gujarat, records in an autobiography several unusual occurrences in his earliest life. He notes that two weeks before his birth, his father dreamt of two Friends of God and decided to name the boy after them. One was his namesake, the great ʿAbd al-Qādir al-Jīlānī. ʿAydarūs claims that the ancient Friend had appeared in the dream to ask his father for a favor—clearly including this feature to add stature and religious legitimacy to the author's family. ʿAydarūs then narrates an event passed on to him by "a reliable source." When a prominent politician came to ask baby ʿAbd al-Qādir's father to pray for him, the infant recited Qurʾān 61:113, indicating that the visitor would be granted blessing and rapid success. The infant's father added that the visitor could consider this pronouncement virtually a message from God![51]

In modern times, too, Muslim authors have left such rare autobiographical works. Ibn ʿAjība, a major Moroccan Sufi shaykh, composed the *Fahrasa,* or *Chronicle,* to document his mother's recollections of his childhood. As an infant, he had an innate sense of the prescribed time for ritual prayer and frequently pestered his mother until she decided to perform the proper *salat.* As a child, he never missed the appointed prayer times, performing ritual ablution so enthusiastically that his clothes became soaked. His mother, worried that he might ruin his clothes, insisted that he perform the waterless ablution allowed in Islamic Law when water is unavailable. Eventually his mother allowed him to return to ablution with water.[52]

YOUTHFUL PROPHETS AND FRIENDS

One last category of narratives offers details of the prepubescent and adolescent lives of the great ones, beginning with Abraham. Many stories feature the prophet's inauguration into an active prophetic ministry, including his struggle with the unbelief of the people to whom God has sent him.

Preadolescent Prophets

Divining the revelatory signs in the heavens was not quite enough to free Abraham from associating with idolaters. His father forced him to spend some years peddling his father's carved images alongside his somewhat less reluctant brother Aaron. Abraham spoke against the idol trade with every would-be customer, but at length a turning point occurred. An old woman came to the shop looking for a replacement idol, for hers had been stolen in a package of clothes. Assuring her that no authentic deity could be stolen,

Abraham miraculously produced her clothes, and she became a believer.[53] At the age of seven, Abraham's son Isaac was due to become Abraham's sacrificial victim, but the son was miraculously delivered by further divine intervention (see Fig. 2).[54]

Revelatory dreams attended the nativity and infancy of many prophets, but Joseph became most famous as a dreamer in his own right. Joseph had the first of his many revelatory dreams when he was only four, thus establishing the emblematic feature of his story. The youthful prophet was twelve when he had the most significant dream of his life, in which he saw eleven stars, sun and moon, doing him homage. This dream was the harbinger of things to come in his relationship with his brothers. Joseph's suffering as a result of sibling jealousy is surely the most famous element in his story. He is arguably unique among the prophets in that the "people" who rejected him were his own kin. Like Moses and Abraham , Joseph became an honorary member of the household of the ruler who would become his bitterest enemy—in this instance, one of the pharaohs.[55]

The insights that Joseph gained in dreams, others acquired through either assiduous study or infused knowledge. Some prophets reportedly received significant forms of higher religious insight when they were still very young children. Elijah (Ilyās) plays a relatively minor role in Islamic lore, but Kisā'ī notes that when Elijah was born, he was much like Moses in both physical characteristics and fiery temperament. More important, the child had memorized the entire Torah by age seven without the aid of a teacher.[56] At the tender age of seven, the prophet Jonah began his life of asceticism and scholarship, marking the story of even this relatively minor prophetic figure with widespread themes. Holiness in extraordinary personages is often signaled by this combination of spiritual and intellectual discipline.[57]

Moses's godly struggle with unbelief was embodied from the outset in his stormy relationship with Pharaoh. Even as a lap child, Moses was a handful for his adoptive father. Throughout his childhood, Moses continued to test Pharaoh's patience, each time raising the ante with a more spectacular sign of the true God. At the age of five, the boy interpreted the crowing of a rooster as a recommendation to praise God. Pharaoh said the boy was merely putting words in the rooster's mouth, whereupon the prophet instructed the bird to speak intelligibly. After exacting Moses's promise of protection, the rooster repeated itself in Egyptian; the king slaughtered the bird only to have God raise it back to life. At nine years old, Moses kicked over the king's chair, causing Pharaoh to break his nose. Again Pharaoh was on the point of killing the boy, when Āsiya persuaded him of the value of having a son so strong to fight his foes for him. At twelve, the boy brought

back to life a camel that had been destined for the evening's entrée, and Āsiya again pointed out the wonder of having a son who could do such marvels. A year later, a man spotted Moses performing his ritual ablutions in the river and asked if the youth worshipped other than Pharaoh. When the boy vilified the king, the man vowed to inform on Moses. Moses caused the earth to half-swallow the man until he swore not to tell, but he turned the child in nonetheless. When Pharaoh asked Moses whom he worshipped, the boy said it was the Master who reared him, and Pharaoh was sure that Moses was referring to him. The king then executed the accuser.[58]

Not all prophetic prodigies have such direct confrontation with the nemesis. Solomon was empowered with wonders as a young boy. His gifts included bestowing fertility on a bereft turtledove that sought his assistance—and every dove since then has been this one's descendant. He was particularly talented in communicating to all the animal kingdoms, and his positive relationship with his father stands out as especially formative and symbolic. In one story, a cow makes its way to David's (Solomon's father's) door with a request. There, in the presence of Solomon, she asks the king to save her from certain slaughter, but he declines, saying that she was made to be slaughtered. Solomon intervenes, allowing the cow to guide him to her owner's house, where the boy asks to buy the animal to save it from slaughter. When the owner asks how Solomon knows he had planned to kill her, Solomon replies that the cow has informed him. At that statement, the owner gives him the cow, for a voice had announced the day before that when such a lad appeared, his whole tribe would meet its end.[59]

Jesus's knowledge was infused, but he nevertheless went to school, where his influence on his teachers and peers alike took center stage. According to Kisā'ī, when Jesus was about nine, Mary sent him off to study. He proved quite precocious, for he knew before being instructed what his teacher was about to teach him. One day while among his schoolmates, Jesus fashioned a bird from a lump of clay, and by God's permission, breathed upon it and caused it to take wing. In Tha'labī's account, the tiny prophet is even more remarkable. In this story, when Jesus is a mere nine months old, Mary enrolls him in school. There Jesus reveals to his astonished teacher the mystical

FIGURE 2. *(opposite)* In a dual-image page, Abraham sits in the comfortable garden into which God has converted the flames of Nimrod's fire (with Nimrod in the tower at right and the catapult above). Below, Abraham prepares to sacrifice his child Isaac/Ishmael (Ishāq/Ismāʿīl), and the sacrificial ram appears in the bush at right. Ottoman Turkish; ©The Trustees of the Chester Beatty Library, Dublin, T414:68.

meanings of the Arabic alphabet. Tha῾labī also includes a number of other stories not found in Kisā᾽ī, such as those recounting events in Jesus's twelve years in Egypt. Among the young prophet's powers are clairvoyance—a gift for which he is much reviled as a dangerous magician—healing, the ability to provide food and drink (including the transformation of pots and jars of water into meat and wine), the power to make a single dyer's vat produce multicolored garments, and the ability to restore life to the dead. The boy's knowledge was legendary: lessons that took others a day, a month, or a year to learn, he absorbed in an hour, a day, or a month.[60]

Muhammad's childhood accounts include elements common to many other tales of prophets. Even as a very small child, Muhammad considered himself a shepherd, thereby linking himself with all the previous shepherding prophets. Muhammad's mother died when he was six, leaving the boy in the care of his grandfather; but only two years later, ῾Abd al-Muttalib died too, and Muhammad's uncle Abū Tālib took custody of the orphan. When Abū Tālib heard that an important seer resided in Mecca, he took Muhammad to see him. The seer discerned something special about the child and insisted that his grandfather bring the boy back immediately, but Abū Tālib spirited him away. Some time later, the Prophet's uncle had to mount a caravan to Syria and agreed to let the boy go with him. Arriving at Busrā (whose castles the child's mother, Āmina, had seen by the light of her wondrous pregnancy), the caravan passed by the cell of a monk named Bahīra. He had seen a cloud sheltering the boy as he went along, so the monk spread a feast for the travelers, hoping to get a closer look at the youngster. This hospitality surprised the caravaneers, for Bahīra had never been so kind to them before. When the monk failed to see the boy in the crowd gathered to eat, he asked to see him. The travelers brought the boy, who had been left to guard the baggage, and the monk examined him closely for signs of which his scriptures had spoken. He detected a mark between Muhammad's shoulder blades and questioned the boy. Muhammad responded with the answers that Bahīra knew signaled a special child. He warned Abū Tālib to protect the Prophet from the Jews, who might do him harm.[61] In this story, Bahīra plays a role not unlike that of sage figures in traditions like Christianity and Buddhism, in that he possesses the knowledge requisite to identify a person of great promise. In this instance, the impact of his perspicacity is all the greater because he is a Christian validating the Muslim prophet.

Early Years of the Shī῾ī Imams

Like so many of the prophets, the imams enjoyed the bestowal of a pedigree early in life, along with exemplary knowledge. Muhammad's cousin and son-in-law, ʿAlī, was among the most prominent of the Prophet's Companions. More importantly for the world's Shīʿī communities, ʿAlī was the first imams in the line of familial and spiritual descendants of Muhammad to represent distinctively Shīʿī tradition. In that tradition, ʿAlī was an unsurpassed exemplar of devotion and heroism and a living embodiment of God's power in the post-Prophetic age. He thus possessed extraordinary qualities that made him "equal to two of the prophets, apostles and proofs of God." This statement is remarkable, and many Muslims would reject it outright, for it elevates ʿAlī to the level of the prophets. As a boy, ʿAlī possessed an exceptional wisdom that was related to his call, reportedly at between seven and ten years of age, to the Muslim faith. His spiritual and intellectual precociousness likened him to the young Jesus and John the Baptist, for Muhammad saw fit to entrust him with esoteric knowledge.[62]

ʿAlī's sons by Muhammad's daughter Fātima, Hasan and Husayn, were the second and third imams. According to tradition, Hasan's mother took the seven-day-old child to Muhammad swaddled in a silken wrap that Gabriel had brought down to the Prophet. When Husayn was a year old, a group of twelve angels descended on Muhammad to console him for the inevitable loss of this portentous child, destined to become the protomartyr. The angels assumed mysterious guises, four of them resembling the angelic symbols of the Christian evangelists and the others entirely in animal shapes. When, on one occasion, Fātima later brought her boys to visit Muhammad, the Prophet acknowledged her sons' advanced spiritual states and announced that they carried his authority. Hagiographer Shaykh al-Mufīd observes that Muhammad's entrusting so lofty a commission to the two boys is the equivalent of Jesus's possessing the gift of speech as a newborn (see Fig. 3).

Shaykh al-Mufīd makes similar statements about the youthful wisdom and authority of later imams as well. He recounts, for example, a lengthy episode in which religious authorities examined the nine-year-old fifth imam Abū Jaʿfar al-Jawād (i.e., Muhammad al-Bāqir), concluding that the boy was indeed wise beyond his years. Several accounts of Hasan and Husayn tell of their being lost. An anguished Muhammad discovers them under the care of an animal, who surrenders the boys after speaking to the Prophet. When the tykes wrestled, Muhammad rooted for Hasan, but because Gabriel cheered on Husayn, the result was naturally a draw.[63]

Youthful Friends of God

Numerous stories refer to conditions or qualities that distinguished individual Friends from their peers from childhood on. Stories of God's Friends at this stage of life have more in common thematically with those of prophets

FIGURE 3. Khwāja Yahyā ibn ʿAmmār ash-Shaybānī of Nishapur, in upper right, is saying that he will have a successor even as the Prophet had four caliphs (as he gestures to the left to reveal Muhammad preaching before ʿAlī and his two young sons, Hasan and Husayn). The painter uses an intriguing device to join two moments far separated in time. Jāmī, *Nafahāt al-uns* (Ottoman, 1003/1595), ©The Trustees of the Chester Beatty Library, Dublin, T474:177v.

than do nativity and infancy stories. According to ʿAṭṭār, Sufyān ath-Thawrī was hunchbacked from his early youth. People wondered at this condition and enjoined him to straighten up. He explained that fear of ending his life in unbelief or rejection by God had run up his spine and broken it.[64] Sahl at-Tustarī recalled that when he was only three, he kept night vigils, to his uncle's consternation. At the age of seven, he knew the Qurʾān fully and engaged in continual fasting, eating only bread, until he was twelve. When he turned thirteen, Sahl struggled with a spiritual question, and his family sent him to consult religious scholars in Basra, but these learned men were unable to satisfy his concern. He soon traveled to ʿAbbādān and studied for a time with Abū Habīb Hamza and then returned to Tustar.[65]

Junayd, one of the great second-/ninth-century Friends, experienced the chronic pain of spiritual longing, had wisdom beyond his years, and demonstrated the power of clairvoyance. One story told by ʿAṭṭār (among others) has the boy traveling to Mecca for the hajj with his uncle Sarī as-Saqaṭī. There four hundred religious scholars debated the meaning of gratitude, and when his uncle prompted the boy, he weighed in with his opinion: gratitude means not using God's favor as a pretext for disobedience. As all the shaykhs shouted their approbation, Junayd's uncle said, to the boy's dismay, that Junayd's tongue was God's preeminent gift to him. This uncle was the one who had also declared that Junayd had outstripped him in spiritual rank. In turn, the nephew acknowledged that his uncle enjoyed divine disclosure but lacked heart, and was angelic but lacked the experience of suffering that had made Adam such a kindly man.[66]

Many stories outline the origins of a saintly child's sacred trajectory. The parents of Abū ʿAbd Allāh ibn Jallāʾ, for example, dedicated the boy to God from his youth.[67] One of the more engaging stories of the parents' early purposeful detachment from their child is that of Bāyazīd al-Bisṭāmī. As a very young student in Qurʾān school, Bāyazīd asks his teacher about the meaning of the verse, "Give thanks to me [God] and to your parents" (31:14) in the sura of Luqmān. The boy is troubled by this divine command that he divide his loyalties, so he goes home early to talk to his mother. Experiencing his first ethical-spiritual dilemma, the boy explains to her that he has come home unexpectedly to ask her to resolve it for him. His view is that she must either surrender him totally to God or request that God give him unreservedly to her. Without hesitating, she tells the child that he will henceforth belong entirely to God, for she will make no further claim on her son. The hagiographer, ʿAṭṭār, indicates that the son then departed from his mother for thirty years of ascetical rigor, wandering from town to town.[68]

Sālih al-Kharrāz of Seville, a childhood companion of Ibn ʿArabī, began his life of divine service at seven, avoiding games and companionship with his peers. Even as a young boy, he earned his livelihood as a cobbler and studied assiduously.[69] Ahmad ash-Sharīshī (from Jerez in Andalusia) was likewise dedicated to God as a child. When he was barely ten years old, a state of ecstasy caused him to fall into a fire, but God protected him from harm. Ibn ʿArabī reports that such things happened to him often and that the Friend was never aware of what was occurring in those moments.[70] As a young girl, Rābiʿa became an orphan, and a stranger made her his slave. Abū ʿUthmān al-Hīrī, in contrast, was a child of relative wealth and privilege and had four slaves travel with him to school. Passing the ruins of a caravanserai on one occasion, he spied therein a bedraggled donkey and a crow pecking at the poor beast's wounded back. He removed his fine garment to cover the donkey and wrapped its wounds with his turban, and the animal experienced communion with God.[71]

As a young boy, ʿAbd al-Qādir al-Jīlānī and some playmates were once walking behind a cow as it plowed a field when the cow suddenly spoke up to assure the boy that he was meant for bigger things than sleeping and playing with his mates.[72] This account is an evident variation on the earlier-told story of an ox that insisted it was meant for higher purposes than plowing. Some young Friends enjoyed very extroverted powers. As a boy, the founder-to-be of a major Central Asian Sufi order, Ahmad Yasawī, fed a crowd of thousands from just one bit of bread when a local ruler put him to the test. The youngster later stirred up a tempest and cleared land for his future home and tomb by disposing of an entire mountain.[73]

Stories told by Aflākī and Jāmī, for example, recount emblematic events of Jalāl ad-Dīn Rūmī's childhood. At a very early age, Rūmī was already habituated to fasting for up to seven days at a stretch. Just five years old, he received visits from the recording angels in human guise. One Friday when the boy was six and was sitting on the roof of his home reciting Qurʾān, some other neighborhood children drifted over to join him. One challenged his buddies to bet on who could jump from one roof to another. Jalāl ad-Dīn responded that if the boys really wanted to act in accord with their higher natures, they should rather aspire to fly to the heavens. He then disappeared, to the considerable alarm of his companions. When they yelled for help, Rūmī reappeared, and the other boys humbly acknowledged that they would be his followers. Rūmī then explained to his friends that a group of figures dressed in green had accompanied him through the many levels of the cosmos, offering him a glimpse of the marvels of the universe.[74]

Every morning, Rūmī tearfully recited sura 108, recalling that in that text, God granted the Prophet all good things, telling Muhammad to perform his devotions and that anyone who was inimical to him would have no progeny. The thought of such divine protection was overwhelming to the boy. When God appeared to the boy, he passed out and soon heard a voice inform him that by God's *jalāl* (majesty), he would no longer engage in jihad with himself but would henceforth enjoy immediate vision of God. This experience prompted the boy to dedicate himself wholly to God's service.[75] A story that underscores the importance of special knowledge in the young Rūmī 's life notes that people with spiritual insight often saw Khidr visiting the boy when he was in Damascus.[76]

Another account describes Rūmī's frequent trips to the Tigris to bring water to his father when the family lived in Baghdad. As the boy walked through the city, every locked gate opened miraculously before him. Stories of his youth also say that while he was a student in Aleppo, he often left his room at midnight, raising suspicions that he was up to no good. Other students who were jealous of the attention his teacher gave him as the son of a great scholar (Bahā᾿ ad-Dīn Walad) made sure the city's administrator knew of this odd behavior. The mayor hid by the gate of the school and followed the youth as he headed out through the city, with every door and gate miraculously unlocking and opening before him. Rūmī continued all the way to Hebron, to the tomb of Abraham, where a group of green-clad figures welcomed him. The mayor became totally disoriented, and after his staff found him, he immediately became a follower of the young Rūmī.[77]

A story about Abū Saʿīd ibn Abī 'l-Khayr has a similar ingredient and offers a fine example of the use of formulaic material. Ibn-i Munawwar relates that the boy's father would lock the door and wait till the youngster had fallen asleep before retiring for the night. One night, the father awoke around twelve and was concerned when he noticed that his son was not in bed. Near dawn, the boy returned and fell asleep. But when the father noticed that this behavior continued for several more nights, he decided to follow the lad on his nightly adventure. Shadowing Abū Saʿīd, the father saw him enter a mosque within a *ribāt*, in which there was a pit. As the father watched through a window, the youngster took a piece of wood, tied a rope to it, placed it across the opening of the pit, and lowered himself. He remained suspended by his foot while he recited the whole Qurᵓān. His astonished father continued to observe this disciplined behavior for the next few nights.[78]

At the tender age of five, Rūmī's grandchild, Chalabī ʿĀrif could foresee the deaths of others. He could read minds and unveil secrets of all kinds. He once took a bowl of food from another child and returned the bowl empty. He told the other boy to cover the bowl and go along, but when the other boy looked into the bowl, he saw that it had miraculously refilled with food. The boy returned to become ʿĀrif's servant. When ʿĀrif was six, he studied the Qurʾān. His father often paid him homage, to the surprise of others. Sultān Walad explained that he did so because he experienced the presence of his own father whenever his boy entered the room, so dramatically did the child copy every mannerism of his sanctified grandfather.[79]

Many of the Friends of God had particularly strong bonds with their mothers and struggled with filial piety and responsibility in their youth. Al-Hakīm at-Tirmidhī, for example, planned to leave home in search of knowledge with two fellow students. His mother, however, was frail and alone and besought him to stay and look after her. Tirmidhī gave up the opportunity to travel and regretted that he had missed out on a life of learning. As he sat one day grieving in a graveyard, a shaykh appeared to him and after hearing the cause of the young man's sadness, offered to teach him daily. The youth gladly accepted the offer, and three years later, he recognized the teacher as Khidr. Tirmidhī realized that his devotion to duty had been the key to this extraordinary good fortune. After some time, Khidr offered to bring his student with him on a privileged journey. The two travelers came to a barren desert where a gold throne sat in an oasis. The person seated there arose and yielded his place to Tirmidhī, as forty people gathered. At the group's gesture, food materialized. There ensued a discussion of esoteric topics in a foreign tongue with the one who had been sitting on the throne. The story explains that the place was the desert in which the Israelites had wandered and that the person on the throne was the cosmic axis (*qutb*) surrounded by the forty substitutes (*abdāl*).[80]

Famous Friends of God have only occasionally left us first-person accounts of the spiritual experiences of their younger days, whether in the form of autobiographical narrative or briefer diary entries. Rūzbihān Baqlī recorded the following in a "memoir":

> I reached the age of seven, and in my heart there occurred a love of remembering and obeying him, and I sought my conscience and I learned what it was. Then passionate love occurred in my heart; my heart melted in passionate love. I was mad with love in that time, and my heart was at that time a diver in the ocean of pre-eternal remembrance and in the scent of the perfumes of sanctity. . . . And at that time I was seeing all of existence as though it was beautiful faces, and during this period I grew fond of seclusions, prayers, devotions, and pilgrimage to the great shaykhs.[81]

He reports further that when he was just fifteen, a message from the Unseen Realm informed him, to his shock, that he was a prophet. He protested that he surely could not be so, because no prophet could follow Muhammad and because he himself had too many obvious shortcomings and human foibles. Taking to the desert in fear, he exchanged his life as a shopkeeper for a life of bewilderment and ecstatic experience.[82]

According to the autobiography of the eighteenth-century Moroccan Friend Ahmad ibn ʿAjība, the author attended Qurʾān school from an early age and frequently arose at midnight to hurry to the mosque, so great was the love of solitude that God had bestowed on him. He ignored the reproaches of the mothers of the other children, who told him he should not hold himself aloof from his peers, and memorized the entire Qurʾān at a very young age. Ibn ʿAjība recalls that he soon took up pasturing sheep for two important reasons. Shepherding not only gave him time to read, but, following the saying of Muhammad that "every prophet began as a shepherd," instilled in him a certain political savvy as well as the compassion and goodness required of an authentic spiritual leader. Throughout his youth and adolescence, he reports, God preserved him in chastity, though more than a few women tried to seduce him.[83]

Many Friends are born saintly; some (like Rūzbihān and Ibn ʿAjība) seem to experience a youthful conversion.[84] Others undergo major transformations later in life, and to their stories we now turn.

FIGURE 4. Two disciples consult Naqshbandī shaykh Khwāja ʿUbayd Allāh Ahrār (d. 896/1490) in a cave. Depicted here as an ascetic, the shaykh was noted for his extensive founding of institutions. Jāmī, *Nafahāt al-uns* (Ottoman, 1003/1595), ©The Trustees of the Chester Beatty Library, Dublin, T474:219v.

2. Conversion and Asceticism on the Road to Sanctity

Conversion in one form or another is an essential ingredient in the stories of countless Friends of God. As chapter 1 indicates, stories of prophetic and saintly origins share many thematic and structural features. From here on, God's Friends appear to follow a rather different path from that of the prophets. This departure reflects the fact that prophets, in most accounts, typically do not need to undergo a major change of heart before becoming genuine servants of God. Conversion, which accounts also describe as repentance or a turning back (to God, *tawba*), calls for a deliberate reassessment of one's priorities and values.

Whether a Friend's conversion is dramatic or gradual in biographical tales, the experience is only the larger framework of a life that typically embraces a host of specific practices that symbolize and facilitate the Friend's reorientation. Hagiographical sources characterize the refocused spiritual life generally as the pursuit of piety, devotion, or servanthood (*ᶜibāda*). This pursuit includes adherence to all the religious requirements of the expansive body of traditions known as sharia, Revealed Law. It also presupposes a high degree of commitment, not merely to perform the associated actions and ritual requirements but to absorb and interiorize the deepest significance of the practices of the faith. "Presence of the heart" is the fundamental attitude of the true servant of God, and Friends of God embody that presence most intensely.

According to traditional Islamic hagiographical sources, conversion typically bears fruit in a life of asceticism. For God's closest Friends, servanthood invariably requires a greater emphasis on a wider range of spiritual practices and attitudinal changes than one might expect of more ordinary folk. Sources describe these actions and attitudes in a variety of ways, from renunciation, self-discipline, or asceticism (*zuhd*) to spiritual reticence, scrupulousness and ethical purity (*waraᶜ*), withdrawal from society to a life of seclusion (*ᶜuzla*), and the deliberate embrace of a life of poverty (*faqr*) (see Fig. 4). In keeping with this complex set of choices, many Friends of God are noted for both the intensity of their fasting (*sawm*) and their unstinting generosity, or charitable giving (*sadaqa*), to the less fortunate.[1] In this chapter, I explore important aspects of these symbols of spiritual commitment. These features of the saintly life provide a backdrop for the discussion in chapter 3, which looks at the devices storytellers use to describe how God communicates with His Friends and how they respond.

CONVERSION STORIES

A common convention in Islamic hagiographical material is the conversion account. As in several other major religious traditions, Islamic conversion narratives typically fall into two large categories. Some accounts describe the principal character's spiritual awakening as a gradual unfolding, through evaluation of ordinary experience via ever-deeper introspection. Others show more of a flare for the dramatic, depicting the Friend's transformation as a sudden and unexpected turnabout. English Jesuit poet Gerard Manley Hopkins characterized the classic dichotomy beautifully when he wrote that Paul's conversion occurred "as once at a crash," whereas that of Augustine resulted from a divine "lingering-out sweet skill."[2]

Each type of conversion story encompasses a variety of scenarios that suggest further distinctions, not in the temporal sequence of the change but in the qualitative outcome, the difference between the individual's former and latter states. Some characters emerge, whether slowly or suddenly, from the gloom of erroneous belief into the full light of true faith. Others experience a metamorphosis, either abandoning their outright enmity toward the divine plan to embrace full intimacy with God or turning away from the flamboyant pursuit of wealth and power to commit to unyielding rejection of the world and all its trappings.

Conversion does not figure prominently in the stories of some select Friends of God, including Bāyazīd al-Bisṭāmī, Ḥallāj, Ibn Khafīf, and Sufyān ath-Thawrī, the last of whom, ᶜAṭṭār says, was "born scrupulous."[3] But such ever-saintly characters seem to be in the minority. One could argue that the beginning of a Friend's awakening to a deeper spiritual life is structurally parallel to God's sending his prophets on their initial missions in His name. As chapter 1 suggests, an important theme in the tales of the prophets is the idea that "every prophet began as a shepherd." The implication is that before their ultimate calling, God's ambassadors already shared a common vocation in the care and leadership of creatures unable to fend for themselves.

Evolving Conversion: From Untested Belief to Keen God Awareness

Two general types of sources supply the vast majority of conversion stories. First-person accounts, cast in the form of autobiographical recollections, provide an important insight into the use of more or less standard, perhaps even formulaic, themes. Among the most celebrated of spiritual autobiographies that center on a transforming summons to the inward quest is Abū Hāmid al-Ghāzālī's *Deliverance from Error* (*Al-munqidh min ad-dalāl*), often likened in a very general way to Augustine's *Confessions*. Ghazālī's narrative is an engaging, if stylized, account of an extended odyssey precipitated by a psychospiritual "crisis" during his tenure as professor at the Nizāmīya madrasa (college of theological and legal studies) in Baghdad. He had enjoyed the patronage of the Saljūqid vizier (minister to the sultan) Nizām al-Mulk and for a time reveled in the prestige and influence of his academic position. He began to experience great difficulty in communicating and eventually had to admit to himself that he no longer entirely believed what he was teaching. Renouncing his position, Ghazālī embarked on an extended quest for spiritual certitude. He sought out in succession specialists in a wide range of sciences and at length concluded that only the Sufis could credibly claim access to genuine knowledge. Ghazālī's "conversion" was thus a transformation from concern for the outward aspects of Revealed Law to fuller engagement in the life of the spirit. He had been a Muslim all along and, to appearances at least, was a devout and observant one. His story is one of the best examples of conversion through intensification of one's personal commitment.[4]

In a more recent account that resonates strongly with that of Ghazālī, the eighteenth-century Moroccan Sufi Ibn ʿAjība describes how he, too, underwent a change of mind and heart. Not until the age of forty-six did he join the Darqāwīya Sufi order. Before that time, Ibn ʿAjība had given most of his life to the academic profession. He recalls that his encounter with the great shaykhs of the order was the event that led him to forsake his academic focus on the traditional, exoteric religious disciplines (especially scriptural exegesis, hadith scholarship, and jurisprudence) in order to pursue the life of renunciation, poverty, and devotion in the order. Significantly, however, Ibn ʿAjība describes his "conversion" as a gradual process that began with several years of steeping himself in the writings of classic Sufi spiritual masters, including Ghazālī himself.[5]

Two other telling, if lesser-known, conversion-centered first-person narratives are those attributed to Al-Hakīm at-Tirmidhī, author of a seminal early theoretical work on sainthood, and ʿAlāʾ ad-Dawla as-Simnānī, a major

Persian Sufi theorist. Unlike many other autobiographical reminiscences, Tirmidhī's account spends little time on his educational credentials, moving with dispatch to a description of several life-altering experiences. His life thus "begins" at the age of twenty-seven with a desire to embark on a pilgrimage. In Mecca, he prays for and receives a change of heart, marked by a new assessment of worldly values. He emphasizes the need for self-discipline and his search for a personal guide, and he then describes a series of revelatory dreams (including some experienced by his wife).[6]

ʿAlāʾ ad-Dawla as-Simnānī penned more than one autobiographical account, including an early eighth-/fourteenth-century text entitled *The Bond for the People of Reclusion and Unveiling*, in which he spotlights his experience of conversion.[7] He recalls that as a young man, he thought only of himself and of his selfish ambitions. Beginning when he was fifteen, Simnānī served the sultan and curried the royal favor for ten years, while neglecting his religious duties. However, during a conflict between his patron and the sultan's uncle, Simnānī experienced a dramatic openness to things of the next world and a desire to withdraw from society to dedicate himself to a life of piety. Unable to extricate himself from the royal court, he remained there for about two years, but he began to suffer an illness that gave him a reason to request leave to return home to Simnān in north-central Iran just east of present-day Tehran. En route, Simnānī was mysteriously and suddenly healed. Viewing this healing as confirmation of his quest, he set about steeping himself in the spiritual masterpiece of Abū Ṭālib al-Makkī, *The Sustenance of Hearts (Qūt al-qulūb)*. Simnānī's struggle to pursue the correct course was not over, however. He recounts in some detail how Satan contrived to sidetrack him by presenting multiple temptations to turn away from his desire for a life of self-discipline.[8]

Far more numerous than such "autobiographies"—and more important for present purposes—are the third-person hagiographical narratives that prominently feature spiritual turning points in the lives of their subjects. Conversion accounts play a crucial role in the life stories of dozens of major figures and in a wide variety of hagiographical genres, particularly in anthologies of holy lives. Toward the beginning of many of their major biographical sketches, ʿAṭṭār and Hujwīrī, among others, insert a statement such as the following: "This was the beginning of [this individual's] conversion." ʿAṭṭār, for example, follows such statements with stories of fairly dramatic transformation, spurred by an experience of the futility of wealth, power, beauty, and fame. He often recounts almost verbatim bits of stories that Hujwīrī tells in his generally much shorter sketches.

ʿAṭṭār's story of Hasan al-Basrī relates that the great ascetic began his adult life as a successful jewel merchant. He once visited the Byzantine emperor's court, and the vizier invited him to travel with him into the desert. There Hasan saw a lavish tent, to which came in succession a large army, four hundred scholars, elders, and four hundred beautiful servant maids. The vizier explained that each year since the emperor's handsome young son had died of an illness, these throngs of Byzantine subjects had come to pay respects to the dead prince. After all these categories of royal subjects had entered and departed, the emperor and his chief minister would go into the tent and explain to the deceased boy, in turn, how it grieved them that neither their might, nor learning, nor wisdom, nor wealth and beauty, nor authority had been sufficient to prolong his promising life. The striking scene persuaded Hasan of the need to be ever mindful of his mortality, and he was transformed from a prosperous businessman into a veritable archetype of the world-renouncing ascetic.[9] Hasan was known for the abundance of tears he shed out of compunction for his sins. On one occasion, he wept so copiously when he prayed in his rooftop retreat that the liquid ran off through the downspouts upon a passerby, who inquired whether the water was clean. Hasan replied that it was not, for these were a sinner's tears; he advised the passerby to wash them off forthwith.[10]

Dramatic Conversions: From Sinner to Saint, King to Beggar

As the story of Hasan suggests, one cannot necessarily draw a neat line between gradual and sudden conversions. Two of the paragons of flamboyant transformation in Islamic hagiography are Fudayl ibn ʿIyād and Ibrāhīm ibn Adham. Fudayl lived much of his adult life as a brigand, sending his minions out to steal from travelers along the roads of northeastern Persia, while he remained in his tent wearing sackcloth and fingering his rosary beads. This story clearly spotlights the theme of hypocrisy. One member of a nearby caravan, alerted by rumors of highway robbers in the area, decides to entrust his money to a stranger in a tent out in the desert. After the crew of robbers hit the caravan, the savvy traveler returns to the tent in hopes of reclaiming his wealth, only to spot the bandits sharing their spoils outside the tent. The caravaneer begins to head back in despair, but Fudayl spots him and calls him over. When the man tells him that he has returned for his stash, Fudayl tells him that the money is right where he left it. Fudayl's henchmen scold him for returning the money after they had scored such a paltry haul from the travelers. In reply, he announces that just as the merchant trusted him, so he now trusts God. One account notes that he returned all that he had stolen to the owners.[11]

ʿAttār tells a follow-up conversion story about Fudayl that has a hint of polemical intent. Fudayl falls in love and begins to send the woman of his dreams all of his ill-gotten loot. But one night he hears a voice from a passing caravan reciting a verse from the Qurʾān that challenges him to consider whether the time might have come for him to improve his relationship with God. Seeking solitude amid ruins, he happens upon a place in which some travelers have sought refuge as well. Unaware of Fudayl's identity, they tell him that they had hoped to be on their way but were afraid that Fudayl might lie in wait for them along the road. Fudayl assures them that the bandit has changed his ways and is as eager to avoid the travelers as they are to steer clear of him.

Setting out to make restitution, Fudayl comes across a Jew and asks how he can atone for his former misdeeds. Intent on humiliating Fudayl, the Jew tells him he must go to a certain sand dune and clear it away to level ground. After Fudayl has labored for several days, a mighty breeze comes up and finishes his work for him. When the Jew sees the results, he tells Fudayl that he cannot forgive him until the bandit returns his gold. Fudayl must go the Jew's bed, retrieve a bag of gold and hand it to the Jew. Fudayl does so, and the Jew insists that the befuddled Fudayl make him a Muslim. The Torah says that authentic conversion turns dust to gold in the hands of the repentant person, and the Jew confesses that he had left only dirt under his pillow. Thus does the power of the legendary robber's conversion transform another person's life.[12]

In stories reminiscent of the Buddha's renunciation, Ibrāhīm ibn Adham first appears in hagiography as king of Balkh (now in northwestern Afghanistan). Surrounded by unimaginable wealth, Ibrāhīm falls asleep one night on his throne. Suddenly from up on the roof comes a ruckus, and the king asks who is there. A voice replies that the interloper is someone looking for a camel. When Ibrāhīm expresses his surprise at the foolishness of searching for a camel on the rooftop of a palace, the voice replies that the quest is no more bizarre than looking for God while wrapped in finery and seated on a throne of gold. Thus begins in Ibrāhīm a process of introspection that continues through several more remarkable episodes.

Once during a royal assembly, when all the courtiers are duly arranged, a stranger bursts in and declares to the king that he means to spend the night at his "inn." When Ibrāhīm corrects the man, reminding him that the court is no inn but a palace, the interloper begins a series of questions to determine who owned the palace before Ibrāhīm. "My father," the king replies. "And before that?" the man asks. At length, he gets the king to admit that all previous tenants have died—just as lodgers come and go in an inn. The man departs as suddenly as he arrived, and Ibrāhīm pursues him, hoping to speak further with him. He presses the stranger about his identity, and the visitor admits that he is Khidr, the mysterious prophet-guide who appears so often as the spirit who initiates famous individuals into the Sufi Path.

When Ibrāhīm asks Khiḍr's leave to make a quick trip home before going on, the guide refuses to wait and disappears.

As Ibrāhīm's agitation intensifies, he orders his mount saddled and heads to the desert to hunt. In a daze, he loses track of his retinue and finds himself alone, hearing voices trying to wake him up. Suddenly a gazelle confronts the hunter and speaks, challenging him to consider whether he might have a higher purpose than hunting a defenseless creature for sport. Even the pommel of his saddle and the button on his collar harangue him in that vein, until Ibrāhīm is suddenly swept into an experience of ecstasy. Coming across a shepherd, the king changes places with him, thereby linking Ibrāhīm with the great tradition for both prophets and Friends of God: lives of spiritual leadership begin with shepherding. He embarks on a long journey of spiritual discovery, his own pilgrimage to Mecca.[13]

These two colorful characters have plenty of company among the better-known Friends of God. In the story of another famous ascetic, Bishr al-Ḥāfī ("the barefoot"), the protagonist begins his life in anything but an ascetical mode. As he walks about in a drunken stupor one day, he spots a piece of paper on the ground. Reading its message, "In the name of God, the Gracious and Merciful," Bishr does the paper homage, anointing it with a perfume he has purchased for that purpose. Elsewhere that night, a stranger dreams that he must go tell Bishr that just as he anointed, glorified, and purified God's name, so God will anoint, glorify, and purify him. But because the dreamer is aware of Bishr's questionable reputation, he ignores the dream; not until it returns a second and third time does he set off on his mission. Bishr's acquaintances tell the messenger that Bishr is drunk in a local saloon. The dreamer sends word to Bishr, who asks who has sent the message. The messenger replies that the message is from the Lord, at which Bishr weeps for fear that God is angry with him. When the messenger assures him that God is not angry, Bishr informs his drinking companions that he is leaving them for good. He ambles out of the bar and sets off barefoot—hence, the nickname al-Ḥāfī—on his lifelong journey of repentance and self-discipline.[14]

Surely one of the more striking and eccentric of the earlier Friends of God is Dhū 'n-Nūn of Egypt. One day he visits a legendary ascetic and finds him suspended from a tree, chastising his body and threatening to leave it there to die if it does not help him learn obedience. To the ascetic's surprise, Dhū 'n-Nūn is moved to tears at the sight. The ascetic explains the rationale for his self-discipline. He tells Dhū 'n-Nūn that he will find someone even more austere up the path of a nearby mountain. Dhū 'n-Nūn ascends the hill and discovers a man in the doorway of a hut. The man has cut off one foot, and he explains to his visitor that after thirty years of self-denial, he had seen a beautiful woman walk by and succumbed to the temptation to step out for a better look. Ashamed of his betrayal, he had removed his foot. He then tells Dhū 'n-Nūn that if he wants to see a real ascetic, he should climb to the summit of the mountain.

Unable to advance higher, Dhū 'n-Nūn inquires about the man and learns that the ascetic refuses to take any nourishment not divinely provided for him and that God has sent bees to supply him with honey. Dhū 'n-Nūn reflects on the absolute trust of these renunciants, and as he descends, he notices a blind bird. Wondering where such a creature finds sustenance, he sees the bird fly down and strike the earth with its beak. Two bowls suddenly materialize, one gold and one silver, containing sesame seed and rosewater, and the bird partakes freely. Filled with confidence in God, the traveler finds a building in ruins down the road. Inside is a bucket of gold covered by a plank with God's name on it. Dhū 'n-Nūn's companions head for the gold, but he wants only the plank. Later, in a dream, a voice tells him that in honor of his choice he will have access to knowledge.[15]

CONVERSION AND THE GREATER STRUGGLE

Whatever the type and function of conversion in a Friend's story, nearly all of the paragons of piety and virtue model in some way an ideal for devout Muslims. An underlying theme in conversion stories is the concept of the "greater struggle" (al-jihād al-akbar) against one's baser tendencies, a struggle that requires constant vigilance. Chapter 6 discusses hagiographical traditions that cast Friends of God as warriors in the "lesser struggle" (al-jihād al-asghar). In common parlance, the term jihād (struggle, exertion, effort) most often refers to the latter sense of combat against an outward enemy. Muslim hagiographers, however, place far greater emphasis on the way God's Friends model the intractable battle against the inward foe than on their prowess with sword and shield. According to a hadith, Muhammad told warriors coming home from a military campaign that though they had returned safely from the lesser jihad, they still faced the greater struggle against the "enemy between their two sides." That inner nemesis is the ego-soul, the nafs. Constantly at war with the spirit (rūh), the ego marshals all its wiles and stratagems to hijack the heart (qalb) for its own selfish purposes. The heart is the contested inner land over which the armies of good and evil wage incessant combat for the highest of all stakes, the individual's relationship with God. Read in this context, nearly every story in which Friends of God confront the obstacles of ignorance, selfishness, pettiness, hypocrisy, and deceit is a reminder of the greater struggle.[16]

Our exploration begins with accounts of Friends whose inner lives do not appear especially remarkable and moves into stories of more sustained and deliberate spiritual rigor. Among the various permutations of the ascetical ideal, some of the more prominent themes include watchfulness over one's hypocrisy, avoidance of positions of power and influence, rejection of pretense to fame, scrupulous honesty, complete reliance on divine providence, and renunciation of even the desire for renunciation itself: conversion can become a source of inappropriate attachment. Virtually all stories of asceticism in its diverse forms play out in a Friend's conversion.

Many Friends of God reportedly pursued lives of rather ordinary, and at least superficially acceptable, Muslim piety. ʿAttār's version of Mālik ibn Dīnār's conversion tells of Mālik's ambition to become an official of the great mosque of Damascus. To improve his chances of selection, the wealthy, good-looking man makes sure that visitors to the mosque see him praying there at all hours. He knows his behavior is hypocritical and often reminds himself of that fact, but the message makes no significant impression on him. Then one night when he is enjoying a musical performance with some friends, he hears a voice from the lute asking what prevents him from repenting sincerely. Returning to the mosque, he prays for the first time with a heart cleansed of hypocrisy. When a group of worshippers arrive the following day, they notice signs of deterioration in the building and decide that they can find no more suitable trustee than Mālik. But when they ask him to undertake the responsibility, he confesses to God his past hypocritical behavior and departs for a life of spiritual discipline.[17]

Habīb al-ʿAjamī (the "non-Arabic speaker/foreigner") started out as a moneylender and was guilty of exacting usury. On his daily collection rounds, he commonly charged a fee if the debtor could not make payment due. One day a wife who had no money to pay offered him some meat. When Habīb returned to his house, his wife informed him that they had no fuel or bread. The next time he returned home from his rounds, a passing beggar hailed him, and Habīb rebuffed him callously. At this moment, his wife reported that the food she was preparing had turned to blood and declared that they were being punished for his treatment of the beggar. Habīb was stricken with remorse, and he resolved never again to exact usury. On Friday, he headed for Hasan al-Basrī's prayer session and fainted when he heard the sermon. He then proclaimed an amnesty for all his debtors and returned their money. Some years after Habīb resolved to spend more time studying with Hasan, his wife became very ill, and still Habīb returned home each night penniless. After ten days, God sent a succession of visitors to his home who brought abundant supplies. Stunned at the blessings, Habīb dedicated himself totally to the Generous One.[18]

One day Dāwūd at-Tā'ī heard a person who was grieving a loved one's death recite a verse about the frailty of human life. He was overcome with sadness and resolved to retire from social interaction altogether. But his teacher, the great jurist Abū Ḥanīfa, persuaded him that he would do better to attend class in patient silence. After a year, Dāwūd concluded that his quiet attentiveness was preferable to thirty years of effort.[19] Dāwūd's later companion, Maʿrūf al-Karkhī experienced a different form of conversion. The son of Christian parents, Maʿrūf converted to Islam, and his parents followed suit.[20] Maʿrūf's disciple Sarī as-Saqatī grew up as a Muslim and made his living as a grocer. He maintained the highest standards of honesty. One day when his shop was the only one to survive a fire in the Baghdad bazaar, Sarī decided to give his possessions to the poor and to begin a life of extreme austerity.[21]

An associate of Ibrāhīm ibn Adham named Shaqīq of Balkh recounted a conversion nearly as dramatic as Ibrāhīm's. One year a famine in Balkh was so dire that people turned to cannibalism to survive. Like most of his fellow citizens, Shaqīq was horrified, but he encountered a young man in the market who laughed heartily in the face of this horror. Shaqīq asked the laughing youth how he could behave so cavalierly under the circumstances. The boy replied that he had no worries, because his master owned a whole village and would provide for him. Shaqīq reasoned that if a human master with only one village could be so provident, he should turn himself over unreservedly to a master who owns the universe. From then on, he considered the young man his most important teacher.[22]

Some Friends of God experience a conversion simply because they have the desire to do so. In one such conversion tale, Abū 'l-Husayn an-Nūrī spends forty years in seclusion, austerity, and renunciation, only to realize that his effort has been rife with hypocrisy and that his ego-soul remains in control of his choices. He resolves to take another tack, first discerning what his ego-soul urges him to do and then doing the opposite. When Nūrī confronts his ego directly, it identifies itself as a "gem from the mine of disillusionment" and instructs him to inform his disciples accordingly. The shaykh then goes to the river and declares that he will wait for a fish to jump onto his hook as a sign that his struggle has ended. When he catches a fish, he assumes that he has seen the light and seeks out his friend Junayd to tell him about the marvel. Junayd remains convinced that Nūrī's baser self is still calling the tune. He reminds Nūrī that though he could have claimed a marvel if he had caught a snake instead of a fish, he still has too much ego invested in his claim to be credible. Even the greatest Friends of God must strive for continual conversion, particularly for detachment from marvels.[23]

Abū Saʿīd ibn Abī 'l-Khayr's conversion story turns on his meeting with Shaykh Luqmān of Sarakhs during his studies in Sarakhs (in the north-eastern Persian province of Khurasan). Abū Saʿīd calls Luqmān "one of the wise madmen," a man who has lost his reason as a result of a divine unveiling. He represents the ultimate spiritual freedom. After telling Abū Saʿīd that he has sewn him onto his cloak along with his patch, Luqmān leads the young man to a *khānqāh* (Sufi residence) and places his hands into those of the *pīr* ("elder," spiritual guide) Abū 'l-Fadl. The old master tells his new disciple that the prophets' mission is to proclaim to humankind the name of God and instruct people to pay attention to this reality. At this point, Abū Saʿīd resolves to forsake his former life of study in the religious disciplines and to dedicate himself wholly to devotion and reflections. Remarkably, Abū Saʿīd's principal biography seems to suggest that he later experienced a reversal of this early transformation. In the second book of the biography, he "suddenly" appears to be far more carefree and even showy.[24]

ASCETICISM IN THE LIVES OF PROPHETS AND FRIENDS

A serious commitment to cultivating a God-focused life presupposes, according to many of our sources, rejection of all that might threaten this single-minded commitment. Whether one calls this orientation asceticism, renunciation, hard-core self-discipline, or inner combat, the commitment is not for the lazy or the fainthearted. "Die before you die," Muhammad reportedly said. This pithy yet stringent directive has arguably been the inspiration of many important Muslim ascetic themes. One might expect champion practitioners of *zuhd* to be dour, unregenerate curmudgeons: life is a series of hardships, and the next life will be still more joyless for those who are not willing to forego all delights in this one. But stories about the asceticism of God's Friends are full of surprises. For example, some accounts cite the necessity of renouncing renunciation itself, for satisfaction with one's own self-discipline poses the greatest and most insidious danger of all. This section highlights the prominent features of the committed spiritual life, beginning with stories from the lives of prophets, who set the example for subsequent generations of Muslims. Major themes include self-denial, flight from too-conspicuous engagement with the public, the symbolic dimensions of food and fasting, and the complex relationships between sexuality and asceticism. These stories recall a number of prophetic and saintly personalities we have already met and introduce several new characters who are celebrated for their success in the greater struggle.

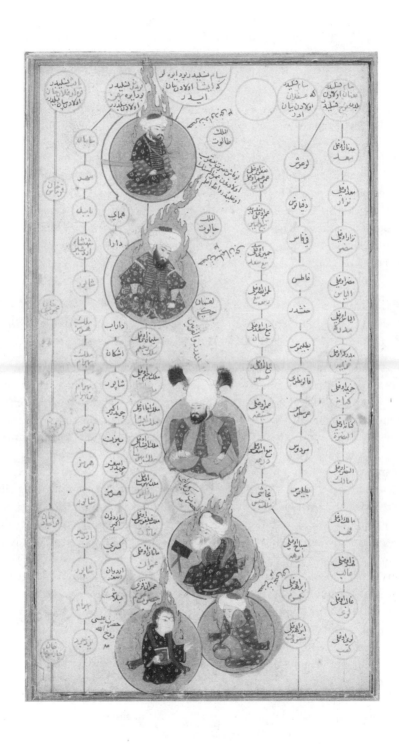

Prophetic Paradigms of Asceticism

In asceticism, as in so many other aspects of the spiritual life, the prophets set the bar—often quite high. Their spiritual discipline, however, is not the result of a "conversion" experience but is the fabric of their beings. According to Thaʿlabī, Abraham was the first to perform a host of actions that Muslims have long considered part of the discipline of good hygiene. He willingly gave all his sustenance to needy guests, prepared to sacrifice his son at God's command, suffered in the midst of Nimrod's bonfire, and surrendered his heart entirely to God.[25]

God permitted Satan to strip Job (Ayyūb) of nearly everything he might have called his own. But after each loss, Job acknowledged God alone as the owner of all good things. Satan was continually frustrated by Job's acceptance of his sufferings and was painfully aware that nothing he could inflict on the prophet gave him access to Job's heart. The harder Iblīs (the most common proper name of Satan, perhaps related to the Greek *diabolos*) tried to separate the faithful servant from God, the closer Job came to his Lord. Not until Job believed he had lost everything—his children and wife as well as all his possessions—did he acknowledge God as most compassionate, at which point his fortunes reversed. Job had never taken food when he knew someone hungered, never used a shirt when he new someone was naked. Junayd observed that God had allowed Job to sink to the status of a beggar so that he would know definitively the divine favor (see Fig. 5).[26]

Even as a child, John the Baptist (Yahyā) lived the life of a serious renunciant, refusing to play with his peers and preaching repentance to adults. In one account, John asks his mother to make him a tunic of hair in imitation of the rabbis and monks he has seen performing their austerities in the temple. The merest mention of hellfire is enough to set his determination to live a more severe life, to such an extent that he gave his parents cause for alarm.[27] His cousin Jesus was also a model ascetic in many ways. He went barefoot, had no fixed abode, and had no assured source of income, sustenance, or clothing.[28]

Not surprisingly, Muhammad's preference for simplicity of life remains the paramount prophetic example of asceticism. Descriptions by Hasan al-Basrī and other celebrated ascetics emphasize the Prophet's abstemiousness

FIGURE 5. *(opposite)* This "genealogy" represents prophets from across the ascetical spectrum, from (top to bottom) royal David and Solomon to world-conquering Alexander the Great, to Zakarīya, his son and celebrated ascetic, John the Baptist (Yahyā), and John's cousin Jesus (ʿĪsā), also noted for his ascetical ways. *Silsila Nāma*, ©The Trustees of the Chester Beatty Library, Dublin, T423.21a.

and renunciation of even the hint of excess. Muhammad ate the bare minimum, dressed in rough garments, rode a donkey, and devoted many hours to night vigil.[29]

Friends' Self-Denial, Hardship, and Flight from the Public

With the prophets setting so lofty an example of the committed spiritual life, Friends of God have faced a daunting challenge. One of Ibn ʿArabī's shaykhs, Abū ʿAbd Allāh ibn Jumhūr, used to keep vigil and recite Qurʾān until he was exhausted. When he lay down to sleep on a pillow, he reminded himself that because his cheek rested softly now, it would rest on a stone in his grave. At the man's burial, Ibn ʿArabī noted that God had left a large rock in the grave. Before lowering the body, someone moved the rock so that the shaykh's cheek would rest upon it, thus fulfilling the shaykh's premonition.[30]

One of Dhū 'n-Nūn's followers engaged in severe austerities, including forty-day fasts and protracted periods of night vigil. Even so, he complained to his shaykh that God had yet to acknowledge his efforts. Dhū 'n-Nūn instructed the man to eat hearty that night and to skip his rigorous disciplines, in the hope that God might respond, if only to chastise the servant. The disciple dined well, but could not bring himself to skip his prayers before sleeping. In a dream that night, the prophet Muhammad relayed a message from God that the servant should have persevered and that his prayers would now be answered. But the message also instructed the disciple to take his shaykh to task as a presumptuous liar for daring to issue such an instruction to a seeker. Dhū 'n-Nūn was delirious with joy at receiving even this scathing response from God. ʿAttār explains that the shaykh had issued the instruction because, like a physician, a teacher must on occasion prescribe poison. Dhū 'n-Nūn knew, however, that the student would not skip his night prayers and would remain spiritually protected. ʿAttār draws a parallel between this type of instruction from a Friend and God's command that Abraham sacrifice his son, knowing that he would not go through with the deed. So too, God expressed the desire, but not an explicit command, that Khidr kill a boy destined to grow up an unbeliever, thus saving the boy from eternal punishment (Qurʾān 18:74). Sometimes the seeker must confront apparently unlawful demands on his or her spiritual quest.[31]

Some Friends manifest their absolute devotion to God by rejecting the "world" and assiduously avoiding the company of other people. Seclusion and deliberate shunning of society become a symbol of the desire to belong to God alone. A favorite metaphor for the painful separation from social interaction is that of "breaking one's lute" to stop revelry. In one story, Bāyazīd al-Bisṭāmī encounters a young man playing the lute in a graveyard at night. The musician approaches Bāyazīd, declares that God is the sole source of strength and power, and wallops Bāyazīd on the head, breaking both lute and head. Bāyazīd manages to make his way back to a shrine and the next day sends an assistant to pay the musician the price of the lute, along with some candy. He sends an apology, whereupon the young musician and some companions come to see him and repent at his feet.[32]

In another story, Maʿrūf al-Karkhī, as he walks through Baghdad with some disciples, comes across a group of youngsters besporting themselves musically. Maʿrūf offers a prayer that God will give the wayward youths enjoyment in the next life as well. Catching sight of the saint, the revelers smash their lutes, empty their flagons and repent before the teacher. Their actions answer his prayer.[33] A similar tale focuses on Shāh Shujāʿ of Kerman's son, who was a fine musician and occasionally walked the neighborhood singing and playing the ʿūd (lute). When his music moves a sleeping woman to come to the window, the woman's husband yells to the boy that he should repent and repudiate music. Suddenly the youth realizes that the man is right. He breaks his ʿūd, secludes himself at home for forty days, and then departs for a life of renunciation. At last, ʿAttar notes, the name "Allāh" that had been written on the boy's chest in fine hair settled into his heart.[34]

Many ascetics have regarded ordinary contact with humankind as a major source of spiritual contamination. Hagiographer Tādilī tells a story about a fourth-/tenth-century Egyptian jurist named Abū 'dh-Dhikr who was strong-armed into a position of chief judge that he did not want. He took to moonlighting, hoping that selling dates after hours would get him fired. Apprised of the judge's activities, the caliph set up a sting and sent his minions incognito to buy dates. The ruler distributed the dates to some sick people because he knew the holy man's blessing would heal them, and eating the dates indeed relieved these people of their fevers. Hailed before the caliphal court, the ascetic was granted one request. Removal from his judicial post was all he wanted, and he got his wish.[35]

Dates often feature in stories about the importance of fasting and the symbolism of food in the larger story of asceticism in the spiritual life. A saying attributed to the ʿIraqi Friend Dāwūd at-Ṭāʾī aptly connects flight and fasting: "Fast from the world and death will break your fast; shun people as you would run from a ravening beast."[36] As we saw in chapter 1, many Friends begin fasting even in the womb.

Fasting and the Symbolism of Food

The symbolic importance of dates is evident in the traditional Muslim practice of enjoying some fresh dates to break times of fasting, as Muhammad did. All Muslims are enjoined to fast between sunup and sundown during the ninth lunar month of Ramadan. Fasting in this instance includes more than renunciation of food. Tradition calls Muslims to refrain from a host of potentially harmful practices, such as complaining or criticizing others. Given the Islamic calendar's dependence on lunar cycles, the month occurs about eleven days earlier in the solar calendar each year, making the practice particularly challenging when Ramadan falls during the long, hot days of summer. As demanding as the annual practice can be, many of God's Friends have sought out still more severe forms of food-related asceticism. In the colorful accounts that follow, the symbolism of food suggests that more is at stake than whether one eats or not.

In one tale, Uways al-Qaranī embarks on a three-day fast, after which he spies a gold coin on the road. He thinks about using it for food but reasons that someone has probably lost it and will return to look for it. As he is about to break his fast with grass, a sheep appears with a loaf of fresh bread in its teeth. Again, Uways's first thought is that the bread belongs to someone else and that he should not eat it. But suddenly the animal speaks up, informing Uways that God has sent her with food for the faster. As he grasps the bread, the sheep vanishes.[37]

In another story, Malik ibn Dīnār has a reputation for avoiding savory foods for years at a time and typically breaks his day's fasting with a loaf of fresh bread. But when he takes ill and has an overwhelming desire for meat, he drops by his local butcher shop and slips out with three animal hooves. The butcher sends an assistant to follow Mālik. The spy reports back that Mālik gave the meat, as well as bread, to some poor folk, telling himself that with any luck he would soon be dead. Contrary to the popular conception that going meatless for forty days weakens the mind, Mālik finds that after twenty years' abstinence, his mind is clearer than ever. In a struggle against his attachment to another delicacy, Mālik refrains from eating dates for forty years, but he is then overcome by a craving. He makes a deal with his ego-soul: if he can fast entirely for seven days, he will earn the right to indulge in dates. He wins the deal and takes some dates to the mosque one day, where a child exclaims that he sees a Jew eating in this place of prayer. The boy's father moves to drive Mālik out but then recognizes him and apologizes: only a Jew would eat during the day, the man explains, and Mālik is the last person the worshippers expected to see eating. Mālik begins to pray, thinking that God has mysteriously spoken through the child. Because God has had him labeled as a Jew even before he could eat the dates, Mālik believes that God will surely allow him to be branded as an unbeliever if he proceeds to eat them. Thus, he swears off the fruit permanently.[38] In both anecdotes, Mālik appears to be flaunting "conventional" religious observance, thus risking public censure, all to deny satisfaction to his inner enemy, the ego.

A story of Rābiᶜa takes place in a similar setting and exemplifies a Friend's willingness to risk offending others to get God's attention. Two hungry shaykhs visit Rābiᶜa, and she brings out two loaves of bread, but when a beggar asks for food, she takes the bread from her guests and gives it to the poor person. As the shaykhs sit in amazement, a neighbor's servant brings in eighteen more loaves. Rābiᶜa insists that this offering must be a mistake and tells the servant to take the bread back. The servant's mistress then adds two more loaves and sends her back to Rābiᶜa. Rābiᶜa's guests eat the bread, and she explains what has happened. Initially embarrassed that she had only two loaves to offer such important people, she had given the bread to the beggar in hopes that God would make good on his promise to recompense all gifts tenfold. When only eighteen loaves materialized, she knew there must be a mistake.[39]

On another occasion, Rābiᶜa uses food in a very different way. The saint prepares to break a fast with a soup that her servant girl is making. When the girl says she needs to go borrow some onions, her mistress tells her that she refuses to seek assistance from anyone but God. Just then, a bird flies by and drops some peeled onions into the soup. Rābiᶜa bemoans the difficulty of avoiding temptations and opts for bread only.[40] She apparently wants desperately to forgo the pleasure of condiments in her soup. She then concludes that the bird was sent to remind her that even soup without onions is too elegant to break the fast, and she repents by settling for plain bread.

Another anecdote exemplifies the danger of inattentiveness to the ritual appropriateness of certain foods. Ibrāhīm ibn Adham asks to meet a young man noted for his self-denial. After being with the youth for three days, Ibrāhīm becomes envious of his abilities, even suspecting that the young man is influenced by a demon. How else could his companion go without sleep? Indeed, on closer investigation, the young man appears to be eating unlawful foods. Ibrāhīm invites the youth to visit him for a while, during which time he feeds the guest the food Ibrāhīm himself typically eats. The guest quickly loses his spiritual strength and angrily asks what Ibrāhīm has done to him. Ibrāhīm explains to the young man that the demon has gained access to him through food.[41]

Ibrāhīm was therefore especially vigilant in renouncing the gift of sustenance. During Ramadan, he plucked grain and sold it so that he could give alms to the poor. He refused to sleep and kept extended night vigil, explaining that constant weeping for his sins kept him awake. On another occasion, Ibrāhīm went seven days and nights without receiving anything to eat. As his strength ebbed, he prayed for sustenance. Out of nowhere came a youth, who asked if the shaykh was hungry and took Ibrāhīm to his own home to feed him. At Ibrāhīm's probing, the youth identified himself as the shaykh's former servant who felt a debt to Ibrāhīm. Ibrāhīm refused to take back anything he had left to the young man and departed hungry.[42]

Friends of God sometimes bargain with the ego-nemesis, thinking that they can outwit the *nafs* in the end. In one story, Dhū 'n-Nūn makes a deal with his ego-soul: if he responds to his ego's incessant pleading for vinegar beef stew on a feast day, his ego must help him recite the whole Qurʾān during two cycles of ritual prayer prostration. After prayers the next morning, Dhū 'n-Nūn begins to eat some stew and then removes it from his mouth. To his puzzled companions the shaykh explains that by taking the mouthful of stew, he denied his ego-soul the ability to claim victory. Shortly thereafter, a visitor appears with a large portion of savory stew and explains that he had prepared the dish for his family's feast day, but the Prophet had come to him in a dream and told him that if he wants to encounter the Prophet at the resurrection, he must take the stew to Dhū 'n-Nūn. He is to tell the shaykh that the Prophet bids him indulge just this once. The shaykh obediently eats the stew.[43]

Ibn Khafīf ("son of the light one") was one of the most vigorous fasters among the Friends of God, engaging in no fewer than four forty-day fasts every year. He did so even during the year of his death and reportedly died while fasting. When he broke his fast each night, he ate only seven hard raisins. On one occasion, he inadvertently consumed eight raisins that his well-intentioned servant gave him. But when Ibn Khafīf realized that his prayers that night did not bring the accustomed consolation, he questioned the servant, who confessed that he had added a raisin. Ibn Khafīf fired the servant, for if the man had truly been a friend, he would have reduced the number to six.[44]

In the midst of his periods of often-dire austerity, Ibn Khafīf did not lose sight of the need to acknowledge the rights and dignity of each person he encountered. Even as a young man, Ibn Khafīf was so noted for his renunciation of food that a dervish once visited him to observe how fasting affected him. The dervish invited him to his house and served rancid meat. His intent was good, and he did not intend to poison his guest. He tried to encourage Ibn Khafīf to eat it but was embarrassed when he realized the extent of the shaykh's revulsion at the prospect. Ibn Khafīf departed on a trip with a group that became lost and had not brought food for such an eventuality. On the verge of starvation, the travelers paid an exorbitant price for a dog and prepared to eat it. As Ibn Khafīf was about to eat the dog meat, he thought of the hospitable dervish, repented for embarrassing the man, and returned to ask his forgiveness.[45]

Even the redoubtable Ibn Khafīf had a lesson to learn from Junayd about satisfying his thirst. En route to pilgrimage, Ibn Khafīf failed to visit Junayd when he passed through Baghdad. Proceeding on through the desert, he took his bucket to a well, where he saw a gazelle drinking. But as Ibn Khafīf prepared to dip his bucket, he noticed that the water level sank too low to reach. He complained to God that he must surely be more important than this animal. A voice then reminded him that the animal got water because it relied on God totally.[46] Ibn Khafīf immediately discarded his bucket and traveled on, at which point the voice revealed that God was only testing him and that he could now take water from the well with his bare hands. Returning from pilgrimage, he stopped in Baghdad and encountered Junayd at Friday prayers. The storyteller takes the occasion to spotlight Junayd's clairvoyance, for Junayd chides Ibn Khafīf for his impatience: true patience would have made water bubble up at his feet.[47] Sometimes even Friends of God fail to identify the real enemy in the greater struggle.

Anecdotes occasionally suggest that God is not satisfied with the initial efforts of even the most rigorously ascetical Friend. According to the major Indian Chishtī hagiographical anthology Accounts of the Finest (Akhbār al-akhyār), Shaykh Farīd ad-Dīn maintained a demanding discipline of fasting and intake of food in general. He showed a preference for stale bread and unsalted food. One story recounts how, at the advice of his spiritual guide, he undertook an additional three-day fast to increase his austerity. When the time came to break that fast, someone brought him a bit of bread and he ate, assuming that the bread was a gift from God. But he soon became ill and vomited up the food. He went to his shaykh and asked why he had become sick, and his teacher told him the food was what a drunkard would eat. He should fast another three days and break the fast when food came from the unseen world. After three days, he waited in vain for food to appear. He spent the night in hunger, and when he became very weak, he put some pebbles in his mouth. The stones immediately turned to sugar. Three times he experienced the same phenomenon and knew then that this was food from the unseen. As a result of the experience, he acquired the nickname "Storehouse of Sugar" (Ganj-i Shakar).[48]

Unexpected reversals on the theme of fasting occasionally supply the hagiographer with an arresting narrative device. They can also demonstrate how God can work with apparent overindulgence as well as with abstemiousness. In one story, Abū Muhammad ʿAbd Allāh al-Mawrūrī, a close Andalusian associate of Abū Madyan, sits down to dinner while enjoying the hospitality of a friend in Granada. The host's son is away, and after an ample repast, Abū Muhammad offers to eat the son's portion so that the absent young man will feel satisfied, even at a distance. When the shaykh has eaten another full meal, he announces that the son cannot eat a bite more without killing himself. When the son returns, he is still carrying the food he packed that morning. He explains that earlier in the day, as he arrived at his destination, he felt as if curds and honey were flowing into his mouth and into his stomach. Even after the long walk home, the man said, he was still belching from the vast quantity of food.[49] Chapter 4 returns to the theme of the miraculous provision of sustenance.

The demands of discipline in food and drink cause many to fall short of victory in the battle. In an account of Cairo's most important places of visitation, Tādilī tells several stories about aspirants to the life of self-denial who fail to make the grade. In one, ʿAlī ibn Muhammad al-Muhalabī attempts to join a band of twelve renunciants, and after two days' travel without food or drink, he admits that he is extremely thirsty and hungry. At once, the interloper is miraculously removed and deposited at his house, clearly not up to the task at hand. In another account, a fourth-/tenth-century figure named Abū 'l-Hasan ibn al-Fuqāʿī likewise seeks to join a group of twelve renunciants. Members of the group take turns praying for food each evening, and every prayer brings a table with twelve loaves and a single fish. When the new member applies himself to the task, the result is a table with thirteen loaves and one fish. This feat is impressive, or so one would think. In turn, Abū 'l-Hasan hankers for salt, and suddenly salt appears as well. He is quite pleased with himself and tells the others that his desire for the condiment made it materialize miraculously. This admission is his undoing, however, for the renunciants will not tolerate anyone so overcome with personal desire.[50]

The mere thought of satisfying one's ego-soul with food can have deleterious effects. In one account, Central Asian Friend Abū Turāb of Nakhshab recalls an occasion on which he had an overwhelming desire for eggs and fresh bread as he traveled in the desert. When he encountered members of a tribe, they accosted him and accused him of stealing from them. As they beat the shaykh, a senior member of the tribe recognized Abū Turāb and excoriated his fellows for their unjust action. Realizing their misdeed, the assailants asked the shaykh's forgiveness. To their surprise, Abū Turāb was grateful for their rough treatment, for at last his ego-soul had received comeuppance for its wayward desires. The old Sufi who had recognized the traveler then welcomed Abū Turāb to his lodge and set fresh bread and eggs before his guest. Before the guest could protest, a voice commanded Abū Turāb to eat, for henceforth, he would experience no such desire without also receiving a beating for it. For the moment, at least, he deserved a little comfort food.[51]

Asceticism and Sexuality

Sexuality, along with the symbolism of food, is among the most common themes in the ascetical lives of God's Friends. Surprisingly, perhaps, it is far from the most important of such themes. Some conversion narratives focus on the Friend's realization that concupiscence is, or will surely become, a crucial failing. Accounts of the life of Hallāj seldom talk much about his "conversion." But according to one set of traditions, the saint had a striking experience while strolling the streets of his hometown. A shadow fell upon him from a roof terrace above, and when Hallāj glanced up, he saw a beautiful woman. Realizing his fault, he told the man accompanying him (Mūsā, the source of the account) that he knew he would pay dearly for that undisciplined look. As Hallāj was later executed, he reminded Mūsā, who was grieving among the crowd, that the forbidden glance was the reason for his execution.[52]

More than a few accounts treat the subject with a bracing dollop of humor. In one story, ʿAbd Allāh ibn al-Mubārak undergoes a kind of conversion when he realizes how inordinately attached he is to a young woman. He is so smitten that he stands in the snow below her window waiting for her to appear. Mistaking the call to dawn prayer for the night prayer, he is shocked to see the sun rise shortly thereafter. He chastises himself for being willing to stand through the night even though he would have been severely agitated if an imam in the mosque happened to recite a particularly lengthy passage of the Qurʾān. ʿAbd Allāh thereafter applies himself totally to devotion.[53]

Abū Hafs the Blacksmith lived in northeastern Persia. In one story, he falls so desperately in love with a young lady that he consults a Jewish magician for relief from his agony. The conjurer prescribes forty days totally devoid of any religious sentiment or deed of devotion. When the magician's talisman fails to take effect after the allotted time, the Jew insists that Abū Hafs must have done something good. Abū Hafs denies that he has done anything but kick aside a rock to prevent wayfarers from stumbling on it along the path. The magician cautions Abū Hafs to pay attention to any deity that would provide him such an opportunity for spiritual benefit in the face of his resolute inattentiveness. Overcome with repentance, the blacksmith transforms his already rather simple life, spending his days fasting and begging and then giving his daily wage to a poor widow. Naturally, the Jew becomes a Muslim, but Abū Hafs's conversion to a life of renunciation is not complete. One day when Abū Hafs was at his forge, a passerby recited a Qurʾānic verse in which God reminds people of an obligation they have failed to fulfill. Abū Hafs was so taken with the words that he lost his awareness of the task of forging. He forgot his tongs and reached into the forge bare-handed to retrieve a chunk of iron. He ordered his workers to continue hammering the iron, and when they yelled at him that it was already clean, he came to his senses. He realized that he had to detach himself definitively from his work, and he entered into seclusion.[54]

As in this tale of Abū Hafs, sexual attraction is often a pretext for a larger, more important point about the greater struggle. Sources do not describe Junayd as undergoing a classic "conversion," though they report that he left the glass shop he had run for some time ostensibly because he wanted more time to pray. Some stories suggest that he experienced the kind of trial and testing necessary to refine his commitment. After forty years of intense devotion in a small room attached to his uncle Sarī's house, Junayd thought he had attained the pinnacle of the spiritual quest. God had other intentions, reminding Junayd that his very existence as an individual remained a stumbling block. So the Friend rededicated himself to devotion, arousing the suspicion of the caliph because of his disruptive effects on the public. Hoping for a case against Junayd, the ruler contrived to have a beautiful slave girl seduce him with promises of love and wealth. As the girl plied her wares, Junayd inadvertently glanced at her and immediately realized that he had reason to repent. He then breathed on the slave girl, and she died instantly. Word got back to the caliph, who, we learn, was himself in love with the girl. The distraught sovereign went to pay his respects to Junayd and asked how the Friend could have killed such a lovely woman. Junayd chided the caliph for seeking to undo Junayd's forty-year quest and hinted that the caliph was responsible for his own loss.[55]

Surely one of the classic anecdotes to feature the dangers of both food and sexual lust is a story about Bāyazīd al-Bistāmī. Bāyazīd ardently wishes to ask God's protection from the "burden" of desire for food and women. But his awareness that the prophet Muhammad never made such a request prevents him from doing so. As a reward for refraining from such a self-serving prayer, God lifts his burden anyway. From then on, Bāyazīd feels so free of lust that he no longer notices the difference between a woman and a wall.[56]

EPILOGUE: RIVER OF GOLD

Stories about the Friends of God make clear that no matter how great a Friend might be, he or she never escapes the need for continual conversion and must incessantly struggle against the inward enemy in all its disguises. In fact, a virtual subgenre in the "sayings" of famous Friends underscores their recognition of frailty in the midst of effort. Friends like Bāyazīd confess that even after thirty or forty years of watchfulness over the heart, they have not purged themselves of the last vestiges of idolatry. Even the minutest distraction from perfect attentiveness to God is a reminder of the ongoing struggle to free oneself of attachments.[57]

A common story form features the possession of gold and the need to divest oneself of this and other symbols of wealth by tossing them into the great river that runs through Baghdad, the Tigris. In one story line, a would-be disciple of a famous holy person seeks instruction from the shaykh about money matters. Because possession of great wealth is a major barrier to sincere commitment to the spiritual quest, seekers must detach themselves and typically receive uncompromising instructions from their teacher about how to give perfect evidence of a change of heart.

For example, Junayd, after telling a seeker to sell his house and heave the gold into the Tigris, realizes that the aspirant needs further purification. After the man tosses the gold away, the shaykh dismisses him as though he has never met him before. Thereafter, every time the disciple returns to see him, Junayd snubs him, reminding the man that he is still attached to the fact that he has given up his wealth. Junayd finally accepts the seeker into his company when the man becomes detached from his detachment. In another story, a follower of Junayd renounces his life of comfort after experiencing an inner conversion at a session with the shaykh. Though he disposes of most of his possessions, he holds back a thousand gold coins as a contribution to Junayd, only to be told that his intended gesture is inappropriate. The seeker flings each coin separately into the Tigris. However, Junayd, after watching this process, dismisses the aspirant because his obsessive behavior suggests that he is not truly detached, and he counsels the young man to return to the mercantile life in which such calculation is acceptable.[58]

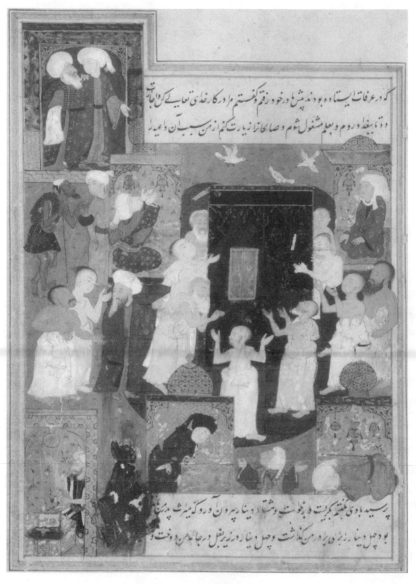

FIGURE 6.   According to Jāmī (NUJ 507–9), Shaykh Muhyī ad-dīn ʿAbd al-Qādir al-Jīlānī (d. 561/1166), dreamt or had a vision while on the roof of his house, seeing pilgrims on the plain of ʿArafāt outside of Mecca. He then asked his mother's permission to study in Baghdad and make pilgrimage. The painter has taken major liberties, first showing a scene of hajj at the Kaʿba rather than the much less iconic plain of ʿArafāt, and, more curiously, depicting the shaykh's "mother" at upper left as an old man rather than a woman. Jāmī, *Nafahāt al-uns* (Ottoman, 1003/1595), ©The Trustees of the Chester Beatty Library, Dublin T474:276r.

3. Dreams and Visions, Visitors and Voices

God in Touch with His Friends

Accounts of life-altering experiences, whether mundane and gradual or sudden and dramatic, do not tell the whole story of change in the spiritual odysseys of the great Friends of God. Hagiographical sources are full of anecdotes about the humbler course corrections that even the seekers who are most advanced along the path must make from time to time. Though these experiences are characteristically of divine origin, Friends do not always initially recognize that these relatively minor interventions come from God. A further miniconversion is usually necessary to open their eyes to the events' heavenly provenance. In one story, for example, while out on a pitch-dark desert night, Abū Turāb of Nakhshab encounters a black man "tall as a minaret." Terrified, he asks the apparition whether it is a human being or a spirit. In reply, the spectral presence asks whether Abū Turāb is a Muslim. When Abū Turāb responds that he is, the towering intruder asks whether a true Muslim would be afraid of any being other than God. At that moment, fear releases Abū Turāb from its grip, and he recognizes the visitor as a friendly reminder of his need for continual conversion.[1]

Other shared features in hagiographical accounts function as descriptions of the nature and intensity of a Friend's relationship to God. Rarely do the sources speak of an individual's interface with the divine as complete and perfect. They reflect profound awareness of the surprising variety of ways in which God seeks to fine-tune the sensitivities of his most intimate acquaintances. In this chapter, I explore the principal ways in which God communicates and Friends respond. Chapter 5 considers more directly the lapses in communication that result from the human frailty of God's Friends.

In many stories, divine contact with prophets is a paradigm for God's dealings with his other Friends. An important aspect of this theme is the concept of genealogical continuity, both within the fraternity of prophets and between prophets and Friends, the latter to present Friends as exemplars of the divine-human connection. Accounts of dreams and visions, which I discuss from a theoretical perspective in chapter 11, are among the most common narrative devices in Islamic hagiography. They offer important insights into the nature of that connection. The subjects of these spiritual communications include God (but only rarely), angels, Muhammad and other prophets, many Friends of God, and spiritual visits to major holy places (particularly Mecca).

An aural equivalent to dreams and visions is the mysterious, disembodied "caller" whose voice from offstage provides essential information and reminders for the sometimes-bemused listener. Of a slightly different character are "visits" from figures who are either deceased or known to reside a great distance from the main character in the story. Because Friends of God are only human, their relationships with God are occasionally subject to the evil intentions of Satan and his minions. Finally, we take a brief look at the Friends' role as intercessor in facilitating their followers' relationships with God.

FRIENDS OF GOD, HEIRS OF THE PROPHETS

One of the dominant concepts legitimating the sanctity and authority of God's Friends is the notion that Friends are direct spiritual descendants of the prophets. Many sources demonstrate "genetic" links among prophets as a class and suggest parallels between Friends and one or more specific prophets. Stories of prophets typically show them receiving their formal commission at the age of forty. Idrīs, for example, is sent at the age of forty to the sons of Cain and inherits the book of Seth and Adam's coffer.[2] Ilyās (Elijah), too, experiences a visitation from Gabriel, who charges him to speak truth to tyrants. Ilyās cringes at the prospect of confronting the mightiest of the earth, but the angel assures him that he will have the strength of seventy prophets.[3] One might see a rough analogy in the forty years of asceticism that many Friends of God undergo.

Uways al-Qaranī was noted for his unique personal relationship to the Prophet. Though Uways never personally met Muhammad, the Prophet remarked that he had encountered Uways spiritually as "a breath of the Merciful from Yemen." Hagiographers often comment on Uways's favored status: he alone was directly formed in the spirit of the prophets, without the aid of a mediating spiritual teacher. The spirit of prophethood sustained Uways in truth.[4] Most importantly, knowledge and humility count for more than the gift of miracles in establishing a Friend's connection to the prophets. According to ʿAttār, even though Habīb al-ʿAjamī could work marvels, he was lower in rank than Hasan of Basra, who could not. He explains that whereas miraculous powers rank only fourteenth as a station on the road to God, special knowledge merits eighteenth place: secret knowledge presupposes profound contemplation, whereas marvels require only advanced piety. ʿAttār notes that Hasan's knowledge was so great that he belongs in the company of no less than the prophets Solomon and Moses, whose advanced knowledge allowed them to do much more than perform miracles.[5] In a similar vein, the tenth-/sixteenth-century Egyptian hagiographer Shaʿrānī cites a saying of Muhammad that no human being is more sincere than his early Companion Abū Dharr, and anyone who desires to emulate the humility of Jesus should observe him.[6]

Some stories corroborate a Friend's authority through prophetic presence and approbation. Ibn ʿArabī records a dream that he experienced after visiting Abū Muhammad Makhlūf al-Qabāʾilī of Cordoba. In the dream, Ibn ʿArabī sees a vast assembly descending from heaven, some astride thundering steeds and others walking. Among them is a tall man, who explains that he is the prophet Hūd and that his companions are all the other prophets. They have come to be with Abū Muhammad and comfort him in his illness. (Ibn ʿArabī learns the next day that the shaykh has indeed been overtaken by a fatal malady.)[7]

Genealogical Links: The Unbroken Chain of Divine Providence

Metaphor is the stock-in-trade of good storytellers and is an essential ingredient in any story's magic spell. Several features in the tales of the prophets link the various divine envoys symbolically. One example is the birth of Abraham in the same "cave of light" in which Noah and Idrīs entered this world. Hagiographers also use various objects to construct a lineage of sanctity and spiritual authority that unites the fellowship of the prophets. Such emblems of historical continuity are a critical ingredient in the story of the divine-human connection. Islamic traditional sources often mention hereditary symbols, sacred heirlooms that not only bridge the generations of prophets and Friends of God but represent signature spiritual qualities of major characters. On his departure from the Garden, Adam carries a staff that will eventually become a gift from the prophet Shuʿayb to his son-in-law Moses. Kisāʾī tells of the 313 prophets' staffs that Noah loaded on to the ark in Adam's coffer. When Moses accepts the hand of Zipporah in marriage, her father, Jethro, allows Moses to select a staff from the large cache he keeps in his house. Moses selects the red one carved from a tree in Paradise and first used by Adam. It has been passed down through Abel, Seth, Enoch, Noah, Hūd, Sālih, Abraham, Ismāʿīl, Ishāq, and Yaʿqūb (Jacob, father of Joseph). The same source offers a list of important prophetic heirlooms that

God gives to Abraham and that Abraham then passes on to Joseph. They include the "turban of prophethood," the "girdle of victory," the "coat of friendship," and the "ring of prophethood," in addition to the "staff of light."[8]

The coat of chain mail fashioned by David eventually becomes part of Muhammad's armament. Solomon's seal ring becomes an emblem of prophetic hereditary wisdom. The prophet Muhammad bequeathes his twin-tipped magical sword, Dhū 'l-Faqār, to ʿAlī. ʿAlī in turn hands it down through generations of Shīʿī martyr-imams, along with ʿAlī's robe, turban, and standard. Muhammad's heroic uncle Hamza happens upon a garden that once belonged to Solomon, where he discovers the horse and saddle of Ishaq. Jaʿfar as-Sādiq, the sixth Shīʿī imam, reportedly boasted that among the symbols of his legitimacy were Muhammad's sword, armor, and standard; Moses's tablets, sacrificial tray, and staff; and Solomon's ring. He likened possession of these heirlooms, particularly the Prophet's weapons, to the Israelites' possession of the ark.[9]

Prophets, Dreams, and Visions

Another common link among prophets is their access to divine truth through dreams and visions. Though earlier prophets reportedly experienced a variety of mysterious communications, Joseph is the paragon of dreaming and dream interpretation. When he was very young—about four, according to Kisāʾī, or seven, according to Thaʿlabī, he reported to his father a dream in which he saw a staff planted, branch out, and grow skyward, far outstripping the planted staffs of his brothers. Some four years later, his father, Jacob, dreamt that wolves attacked and threw Joseph into a well, where he stayed for three days. Jacob never disclosed the dream to anyone but seems to have had a premonition as a result of it. Then, in Joseph's twelfth year, came the boy's signature dream, of the heavenly lights doing him homage. Suspecting that the dream augured no good for Joseph, Jacob warned him not to divulge it to his brothers. Joseph's siblings nevertheless got wind of it and dismissed the boy as a "dreamer." The young prophet's enduring reputation as a wise figure rests on his interpretation of others' dreams, first those of his fellow prisoners in Pharaoh's jail and later those of the ruler himself. Joseph's skill in unfolding the meaning of Pharaoh's dreams won him release from incarceration and a high place at court.[10]

Hagiographers often hint at symbolic connections between individual Friends of God and specific prophets. A particularly striking example is an extended parallel between two Josephs. A story of Yūsuf ibn al-Husayn of Rayy (near present-day Tehran, Iran) combines dream imagery, in the context of a conversion account, with Yūsuf's spiritual kinship with his prophetic namesake, Joseph. Yūsuf, like the prophet Joseph, was very attractive, and an emir's daughter became smitten with him at first sight. When she made a play for him (as Zulaykhā, the wife of Pharaoh's minister, had done), he retreated, even forsaking his native tribe. That night, Yūsuf dreamed (as Joseph had) of an assembly of people wearing green and standing before a throne. Yūsuf eagerly rushes in to find out who these people are. They are angels, they tell him, paying homage there to the prophet Joseph who had come to visit the younger Yūsuf. Yūsuf is deeply moved (still in dreamtime) to think that a prophet would come to see him, and suddenly Joseph descends and brings Yūsuf to the throne. The prophet explains that he has noticed that Yūsuf is intent only on intimacy with God and thus has guarded himself against the advances of the young woman. At that moment of renunciation, God had called Yūsuf to the attention of Joseph and made an example of him. Indeed, the prophet explains to his namesake, God has noted that Yūsuf's intentions are even purer than Joseph's. The prophet then tells Yūsuf he should seek further confirmation of his status from the "sign of the age," Dhū 'n-Nūn of Egypt, who knows the ultimate name of God.

Yūsuf awoke from the dream and set out for Egypt. For three years, Dhū 'n-Nūn refused to tell him that greatest name, for the seeker was not yet ready to bear it. Finally, Dhū 'n-Nūn decided to test the young man. He gave him a covered bowl and told him to deliver it to a shaykh across the Nile. Overcome by curiosity, Yūsuf removed the cover, only to have a mouse skitter out. When he found the unnamed shaykh and confessed his misdeeds, the shaykh explained that Yūsuf still was not ready: if he could not handle a mere mouse, he surely could not handle the divine name. Yūsuf returned to Dhū 'n-Nūn for further instruction. Dhū 'n-Nūn told the student he must forget everything he had learned to be ready for the name. Yūsuf insisted that he couldn't erase his learning in that way. Then forget your teacher entirely, Dhū 'n-Nūn commanded, for citing authority is all arrogance and egotism. Yūsuf knew he couldn't forget his teacher either. So the teacher ordered him to preach repentance to all and sundry. Vowing to do so, Yūsuf went back home to Persia. At first, he was a celebrity and attracted throngs. But little by little, he evoked criticism from every quarter, until on one occasion he found no one waiting at the appointed place for his sermon. As he left in discouragement, an old woman reminded him that he had vowed to preach regardless of human affirmation, so for the next fifty years, he preached without regard for his surroundings or his audience.[11] ʿAttār's story is one of the longest and most detailed of its kind, and it puts forth a theme of spiritual consanguinity that is an important concern of many hagiographers.

Seeing Muhammad and the Prophets

Muhammad once observed, "A veracious dream is one fourth of prophecy." Reportedly, he also said, "Whoever has seen me in a dream has seen me." According to tradition, Muhammad made a distinction between dreams "of vision" and dreams "of confusion," attributing the former to God and the latter to Satan.[12] Many hagiographers and Sufi theorists interpret this statement to mean that divine communication to human beings continues in the post-Prophetic age, only under another guise. Friends experience dreams for a host of reasons, from corroborating earthly experience to revealing mysteries or receiving chastisement from God for presumptuousness or hypocrisy. The content of dreams is often rather generic, in that no one important figure takes center stage. But in many dream accounts, prophets or famous Friends are the featured players, delivering the essential message either forthrightly or in cryptic allusions.

One narrative device that links Friends of God with the prophets is the dream account in which a prophet delivers an important message to, and about, the Friend (as in the above story of Yūsuf ibn al-Husayn). Dreams of Muhammad play a prominent role in many stories and personal accounts of religious experience. Some reports incorporate dream narratives as structural elements in stories of conversion, such as the story of the celebrated theologian Abū 'l-Hasan al-Ashʿarī. One of his "biographers," Ibn ʿAsākir, includes several versions of a series of dreams that Ashʿarī experienced during the first, second, and last thirds of the fasting month of Ramadan. In the dreams, the Prophet confronts the dreamer about his beliefs and his practice of systematic theological inquiry (*kalām*), thus precipitating Ashʿarī's intellectual and spiritual conversion.[13] This story is one of countless examples of the widespread belief in dreams of this kind. Such reports are by no means limited to formal hagiography. Some of the great Friends were privileged often with the presence of the Prophet. Rūzbihān Baqlī notes in his "diary" that he "saw" the Prophet "more than a thousand times." On one occasion, the Prophet even gave him dates to eat.[14] Most Friends, however, encountered Muhammad in dreams less frequently, although not necessarily less spectacularly.

Abu Bakr al-Kattānī reported that he saw Muhammad in dreams every Monday and Thursday night. He took the opportunities to ask the Prophet whatever questions came to his mind. One night, however, he dreamt that Muhammad was coming toward him in the company of four other men. Muhammad asked the dreamer if he could identify each of the men. Kattānī responded correctly that the first three men were Abū Bakr, ʿUmar, and

ʿUthmān, but he hesitated to identify ʿAlī as the fourth. After Muhammad had asked the man's identity three times without response, he thumped Kattānī on the chest and told him the fourth man was ʿAlī, and the dreamer repeated the name. ʿAlī then took Kattānī's hand and told him to get up and go to Safā.[15] Just then, the dreamer awoke to find himself at that spot.[16]

Muhammad's appearance in dreams and visions nearly always functions as proof of a claim to authority and legitimacy. Some dreams are attributed to figures widely admired for their knowledge. Occasionally, the dreamer explains that Muhammad's purpose in the dream encounter is to shore up the status of a third individual whose spiritual acumen the dreamer has underestimated. In one of the more arresting encounters of this sort, the redoubtable jurist and theologian Ibn Taymīya describes how a dream changed his opinion about a woman named Fātima bint ʿAbbās of Baghdad. Fātima was an adherent of the Sunnī legal school of Ahmad ibn Hanbal and a renowned scholar, jurist, judge, and ascetic in her own right. She taught a group of women and sometimes ascended the *minbar* to preach to the people. Ibn Taymīya wrote that even though he acknowledged Fātima's competence and intelligence, he was irked to see her sermonize in public and was looking for a way to prevent her from doing so. One night Muhammad appeared to him in a dream and chided him. Fātima, the Prophet reminded him, was an upright woman engaged in good and important work.[17]

Less unusual accounts of dream visions of the Prophet aim to legitimate the sanctity and authority of Friends of God who did not have to overcome the social marginality of Fātima's gender. Bishr the Barefoot dreamt that Muhammad asked him if he knew why God had bestowed such spiritual preference on him. He did not, he admitted, whereupon the Prophet explained that this favor was because he taught the importance of following the Prophet's example.[18]

Some pilgrims in Mecca once told Sadafī about a dream in which Muhammad affirmed Sadafī's contemporary Abū Muhammad at-Tamīmī as one of his Companions—the highest possible accolade.[19] Ibn ʿArabī reports that a shaykh of his, Muhammad ibn Qassūm, always uttered a particular invocation to conclude his study and prayer sessions. Later Ibn ʿArabī made pilgrimage and performed his rituals at the Kaʿba. There he dreamed that someone read to the Prophet a prayer from Bukhārī's collection of hadith. When the reader finished, the Prophet recited the prayer, asking God for the gift of seeing and hearing only the good and requesting forgiveness. Thereafter, the dreamer frequently repeated his supplication, convinced that his shaykh's practice now enjoyed the ultimate seal of approval.[20] In another account, Ibn ʿArabī reports a "vision" in which he saw that his shaykh, Abū

ʿImrān Mūsā of Mertola (in Spain), was progressing to a more advanced stage of spiritual development. He reported this dream to the shaykh, who appreciated the confirmation. Some days later, Ibn ʿArabī learned that the shaykh had indeed risen to that higher station.[21] (On a related theme, see Fig. 6.)

Dreams sometimes correct the dreamer's unfounded suspicions about another person. One account reports that ʿAbd Allāh ibn al-Mubārak had a servant who was rumored to be supplying his master from funds he obtained by grave robbing. ʿAbd Allāh decides to spy on the servant. When the servant enters a grave, the master sees him begin to pray and to perform austerities before a prayer niche within the tomb. ʿAbd Allāh weeps at the thought that he suspected his servant of crimes. After a whole night in prayer, the servant emerges from the tomb and goes to pray at the mosque, asking God to supply a silver coin to give his master. As a light shines before him, the servant finds a coin in his hand. ʿAbd Allāh, still observing from a distance, breaks his silence and lauds the servant. But the servant, realizing that he can no longer worship God in secret, asks God to let him die, and so he dies. After the master inters the servant in the tomb that had been his secret devotional refuge, he dreams that Muhammad and Abraham are riding toward him on horseback. They ask why ʿAbd Allāh buried "our friend" in penitential garb, suggesting that the servant's special rank eliminated the need to shroud him in a sinner's vesture.[22]

Some apparitions of the Prophet carry a quasi-sectarian message, evidently seeking to redress slights to segments of the Muslim community. In one account, a poor boy descended from ʿAlī confronts ʿAbd Allāh ibn al-Mubārak as the latter exits a mosque. How could such a man be so wealthy and famous when a child of the Prophet's line must scrape and labor for the barest survival needs? ʿAbd Allāh chides the boy for failing to live up to Muhammad's spiritual legacy. That night, a chagrined Prophet comes to ʿAbd Allāh in a dream and takes him to task for criticizing his descendant. ʿAbd Allāh gets up immediately and departs, intending to apologize to the child. Meanwhile, the child, too, receives a dream visitation from Muhammad, who tells the boy that if he were truly living up to his heritage, ʿAbd Allāh would have no cause for criticism. At once, the lad arises, intending to apologize to ʿAbd Allāh. When the two encounter each other that night, they reflect on their experiences and express their need for forgiveness.[23]

Sometimes Muhammad's function in dreams is to be an exalted messenger. In the following story, the Prophet's appearance is corroborated by a dream in which God explains why he has sent Muhammad. Sarī as-Saqatī tells his nephew Junayd that he should preach about the divine intervention in his life.

Junayd demurs, saying that his place is not to preach to anyone who is more spiritually advanced than he. Then he dreams that the Prophet wants him to preach. Junayd awakes to find Sarī waiting for him. Sarī explains that even if his own exhortation to preach has not persuaded Junayd, surely he cannot ignore the Prophet's injunction to do so. Junayd is astonished that Sarī knows of his dream. Sarī explains that God informed him in a dream that he had sent the Prophet to deliver that message.[24] (See Fig. 7.)

Egyptian Friend ʿAlī al-Wafāʾ describes an important early encounter with Muhammad when ʿAlī was experiencing difficulty in his Qurʾān lessons. Muhammad appeared to the boy in a white cotton shirt, which mysteriously transferred to the dreamer, and instructed him to "Recite"—much as Gabriel had instructed Muhammad himself in his initial revelation of the Qurʾān. The youth then recited Sura 93, a text often interpreted as the earliest revelation in the sacred text. Later in his life, ʿAlī recounts, Muhammad appeared to him when he was praying at his father's tomb. The Prophet embraced the young man and told him that the Lord blessed him. ʿAlī explains that, from then on, he became the very "tongue" of the Prophet.[25]

Muhammad also appears in the role of hospitable, and miraculous, host. Abū ʿAbd Allāh ibn al-Jallāʾ describes a visit he made to the tomb of the Prophet in Medina when he was in dire need. After greeting Muhammad, Abū Bakr, and ʿUmar (all buried in close proximity there, according to tradition), he declared himself the Prophet's guest. He went to sleep between the pulpit and the tomb and dreamed that the Prophet gave him a loaf of bread. Still in the dream, the pilgrim ate half of the loaf, and when he awakened, he found he still had the other half.[26]

Teaching devout Muslims the most efficacious prayers, and bestirring them when they show signs of tiring of the spiritual quest, are also important dream-tasks of Muhammad. In Sadafī's account of Abū ʿAbd Allāh al-Masālī, the author says he heard his subject asking God for protection all around and subsequently asked where he had learned that prayer. Masālī told him he received it from Muhammad in a dream after he confessed to the Prophet that he was afraid he might be overcome with complacency while traveling in the desert. The Prophet said that he would bestow a gift that Gabriel had originally bestowed on him during the Battle of the Ditch, and he instructed him in this new prayer.[27]

In a story with a similar theme, an Egyptian man sees Muhammad in a dream and complains that despite his efforts to make the king act in a just manner, nothing has changed. The Prophet tells him to persist in his efforts, explaining that when God wants someone to act well, he sends a "vizier" to remind him of that destiny.[28] Ibn Khafīf has a dream in which the Prophet

FIGURE 7.   A young Junayd (d. 298/910) on a *minbar* preaches to a crowd of
leading early Sufis, including (clockwise and identified by names written in
turbans or elsewhere) his uncle Sarī (to the right and peering out), Muḥāsibī,
Shiblī, and Abū 'l-ʿAbbās (with cane); at center beneath the *minbar* is Abū Bakr
al-Warrāq; Abū Turāb of Naskshab; Abū Hafs Haddād; and Ruwaym (just left of
minbar). The image is a veritable Who's Who of Friends in third-/ninth-century
Baghdad. Junayd had dreamt that Muhammad commanded him to preach, and his
uncle Sarī had experienced a corroborating dream. A young Christian moved to
conversion by Junayd's words appears bare-headed and tearing his garment at
upper right. Jāmī, *Nafaḥāt al-uns* (Ottoman, 1003/1595), ©The Trustees of the
Chester Beatty Library, Dublin, T474:42r.

nudges him awake with his foot and chides him. He reminds Ibn Khafīf that God pesters incessantly any person who embarks on the road to God and then pauses to rest. In another story, Ibn Khafīf, avidly seeking to follow the Prophet's example, sets out to perform two cycles of the ritual prayer on tiptoe as Muhammad had done. He falls sleep after succeeding in only one cycle, and the Prophet appears in a dream to discourage Ibn Khafīf from attempting to emulate his unique manner of prayer.[29]

Even children occasionally encounter the Prophet in dreams. Abū ʿAbd Allāh al-Kutāmī reported to Sadafī that Muhammad appeared to him in a dream when he was seven years old. The Prophet embraced the boy, touching his mouth with his right hand and his breast with the left as he recited two Qurʾānic verses (87:6, 54:17) in which God promises to facilitate memorization of the Qurʾān. Muhammad then gave the boy a drink of water, and from that time on, the child had little trouble memorizing even large portions of the scripture after hearing it recited only three times. This memorization occurred during his dreams.[30]

Poets, too, are sometimes the beneficiaries of Muhammad's inspiration and healing presence. Egyptian Friend of God and mystical poet extraordinaire Ibn al-Fārid is in the midst of composing an ode on the spiritual path when Muhammad appears to him in a dream and inquires about the poem's title. Too fancy, Muhammad replies; "Order of Progress" would do nicely, he says, and the poet complies. Another Egyptian, legendary for his poem in praise of Muhammad, is al-Busīrī. Once during a serious illness, Busīrī dreamt that the Prophet cured him by spreading his mantle (*burda*) over the poet. During that illness, Busīrī was inspired to compose the celebrated panegyric of Muhammad, the *Burda*.[31]

Encounters with God in Dreams and Visions

Reports about dreaming of God are relatively rare, for reasons that I discuss in chapter 11. But one occasionally finds striking accounts of this kind, of varying length and complexity. A report by Yahyā ibn Saʿīd al-Qattān is touching in its immediacy. Envisioning his Lord in a dream, he pleads that despite his countless entreaties, God has yet to answer him. His Lord replies simply that he loves the sound of Yahyā's voice.[32] Some stories deliver a more subtle message. In one, Dhu 'n-Nūn weeps when he recalls a dream in which God reminds him that he showed creation to the ten divisions of humankind, and nine of them preferred the world over the Creator. God then divided the tenth division into ten parts, and when he showed them heaven, 90 percent opted for heaven. Again God divided the remaining tenth into ten parts, and nine fled from hell when he revealed it to them. Of all humankind, only a small remnant was not fooled by the world or eager for heaven or terrified of hell. These few individuals God called his servants. When he asked what they sought, they acknowledged that God taught them what to desire and knew what they wanted.[33]

Some dreamers have difficulty getting over the beauty of their dream experiences. Shāh Shujāʿ of Kerman strove for forty years to fight off sleep, even rubbing salt in his eyes to keep them open. Falling asleep at last, he dreamt of God and prayed in gratitude for experiencing in sleep what he had hoped to gain by remaining sleepless. God replied that his wakefulness was what made so grand a dream possible. Still, in love with the pleasure of the dream, Shāh Shujāʿ carried a pillow with him in hopes that he could re-create the experience by falling asleep again.[34]

One story describes the possibility of a kind of vicarious experience of the divine in a dream vision. A teacher advises a student of Abū Turāb of Nakhshab who is gifted with mystical visionary experiences to consult with Bāyazīd about his visions. When the student asks what good this meeting would do, his mentor explains that to experience a vision of God in Bāyazīd's presence would be to see the Lord through the mystic's greater capacity. As the teacher and student approach Bāyazīd, his glance meets that of the disciple, and the young man falls dead. Bayazīd explains that the student was not prepared for the revelatory experience, just as the women invited to Zulaykhā's feast were not prepared to meet the beautiful Joseph and cut their hands in utter distraction.[35] In a thematically related story, Sarī as-Saqatī dreams of Jacob and asks the prophet why, given that he already enjoys God's love, he made such a scene about the apparent loss of his son Joseph. Just then Joseph becomes manifest to him, and Sarī is overcome with bewilderment at the prophet's beauty. Thirteen days later, a voice warns Sarī to think twice before criticizing lovers of God.[36]

Dreams and Visions of Angels

One unusual account uses the device of multiple mediations of divine communication. The case is striking because the mediator between God and Muhammad is a humble serving maid. As early a source as the hadith tells of the amazing experience of Zayda, a woman who served ʿUmar, a Companion of Muhammad. Zayda visits Muhammad one day and tells him that while she was gathering firewood, having just placed a bundle of sticks on a rock, a messenger rode down from the heavens on a magnificent steed. He instructed Zayda to tell the Prophet that the angel Ridwān sent word that the Prophet's community contained three types of people: those going straight to heaven without judgment, those who would be judged mercifully, and those who would enjoy Muhammad's intercession. Upon hearing her message, Muhammad instructs Zayda to command the rock to bear the load of wood to ʿUmar's residence. She does so, and the rock fulfills its marvelous mission. Muhammad thanks God for sending a message through the angel Riḍwān and for raising a lowly woman of his community to the status of Mary during his own lifetime.[37]

Other dream-inspired mediations are of a slightly simpler nature but nonetheless present arresting messages. In one story, ʿAbd Allāh ibn al-Mubārak has a dream visitation by two angels who chat about that year's pilgrimage participants. Though six hundred thousand people have made the journey, none of their pilgrimages is spiritually acceptable, they note. ʿAbd Allāh is taken aback and wonders at all the wasted effort, but an angel informs him that a certain shoemaker in Damascus has made no hajj that year and yet God credited him spiritually with a pilgrimage, as a result of which all sinners have been forgiven. When he awakes, ʿAbd Allāh decides to visit the cobbler. After a brief conversation, the cobbler asks who his visitor is and promptly faints at the revelation. Returning to consciousness, the man explains that he has long wanted to make the hajj, and had saved enough money to go, but an encounter with a truly destitute woman convinced him that he should exchange his pilgrimage savings for her greater needs.[38]

Some dreams seem designed to nudge the dreamer away from potential spiritual complacency. Explaining one intriguing dream experience, ʿAṭṭār observes that seekers must first experience despair to arrive at hope. Ibrāhīm ibn Adham has a dream in which Gabriel visits him bearing a piece of paper. Asked the meaning of this delivery, the angel explains that he is taking down the names of God's Friends. Ibrāhīm inquires whether he will make the list, and the angel tells him he will not. Ibrāhīm insists that he has at least loved God's Friends, even if he is not one of them. Gabriel then reveals that he has been told to list Ibrāhīm at the top.[39] Bāyazīd reports a dream in which angels from the lowest heavenly sphere came to awaken him to remember God. When he insists in the dream that he has not the tongue to do so, the angels from the next level arrive, and so on until the seventh rank of angels come down. The angels ask when he will be ready to remember God, and he replies that he is ready to march round the throne calling God's name.[40]

Finally, angels sometimes appear in dreams incognito to protect a Friend. In one story, a devout man has a dream of the Resurrection in which angels carrying fiery hooks climb down a ladder to earth. As they approach a village intent on destroying all the oppressors who live there, another angel emerges from the earth to caution the attackers that Abū ʿAbd Allāh al-Qalānisī lives in the village. Such a Friend of God is surely not meant for their mission. They thank the earth angel for the warning, for he has preserved them from God's wrath. When the dreamer reports his dream to Qalānisī, the shaykh counsels him to keep the dream to himself, perhaps to avoid bringing undue attention to Qalānisī's exalted status.[41]

Friends Appearing to Their Followers

Friends of God often appear, just after their own deaths, in the dreams of people among whom they once lived. In some stories, mourners are summoned through dreams—either their own dreams or those of others who pass the word—to attend the obsequies of Friends of God.[42] More typically, dream visitations function as teaching devices, seeking both to validate the life choices of the Friend and to encourage the bereaved in a certain course of behavior.[43] One dominant theme is a living person's questioning of the Friend: How did he or she deal with the challenges that confront a Muslim immediately after death (the interrogating angels, the confinement of the tomb, the crossing of the narrow bridge)? How is God treating the Friend in the next life?[44] This genre is akin to the story line in which two friends make a pact that the first to die will appear in a dream to inform the other about his or her experiences after death. Dream accounts of this kind seem to function as repositories of a community's collective beliefs and fears of the unknown. The authority of dream narratives that deliver messages about the next life is naturally enhanced when the messenger is a beloved Friend of God.[45]

In an often-told tale about Rābiʿa, she appears in a dream shortly after her own death. The dreamer asks her to recount her experience of the two interrogating angels, Munkar and Nakīr, characters generally regarded as intimidating and a cause for anxiety at death. She replies that when those "two fine young gentlemen" confronted her by asking "Who is your Lord?" she sent them packing to remind God that he needn't treat this completely devoted old woman in such a heavy-handed manner. In another story on the same theme, a seeker sees the deceased Bāyazīd in a dream and asks his former teacher how he managed to get by Munkar and Nakīr unscathed. He replies that he caught "those sweet youngsters" off guard by telling them that only God can answer truly who is Bāyazīd's Lord: let them ask God about it! In another story, Junayd reports that when the two angels approached him menacingly and asked whom he worshipped, he laughed at them. He reminded the angels that because he had affirmed directly the sultan's absolute Lordship along with all other unborn children of Adam on the Day of the Covenant, he need not respond to this query from the sultan's slave boys. After Sufyān ath-Thawrī died, he appeared in the dreams of people who asked him how he survived the constriction of the tomb, an experience believed to cause suffering both through a sense of confinement and the anxiety of undergoing interrogation by the angels. Sufyān replied that God had transformed his grave into an expansive meadow.[46]

A variation on the theme depicts a dreamer asking a Friend how God dealt with him after his death. In one account, Bishr the Barefoot replies that his Lord chided him for being afraid of the Generous One during his life. In another, God tells Bishr he is forgiven and that after a life of fasting, he may now eat and drink at will. Another time, God gives Bishr half of the Garden and reminds him to be grateful that God has made Bishr beloved to God's other servants. And in another version, God tells Bishr that when his life came to an end, he was among God's most beloved servants. In one account, a follower of Bāyazīd asks the shaykh the same question. Bāyazīd replies that when God asked him about his spiritual condition, the Friend replied that he was not worthy to be near God, but at least he had purified himself of all traces of idolatry. God reminded him of the night he gave in to hunger and drank some milk. Bāyazīd tells the dreamer that he then explained to himself that *his* stomach had begun to hurt immediately after *he* had drunk the milk, momentarily seeing himself as a separate entity and thus slipping into unbelief in the sole agency of God. This moment was the equivalent of "associating" (*shirk*) a created being with God.[47]

Qushayrī describes a man's dream about the deceased Mansūr ibn ʿAmmār, in which the dreamer asks how God has treated the Friend. Mansūr tells the dreamer that God asked him whether he was the Mansūr who had exhorted people to renounce the world while he himself went on desiring it. The Friend admitted that he was that Mansūr, but he insisted that he had always begun his public sessions by praising God and blessing the Prophet. Thus, God ordered that a pulpit be set up for Mansūr in heaven, from which he could continue to praise God with the angels.[48]

Other dreams of Friends communicate general forms of spiritual advice or legitimate the status of individuals. One dreamer asks Bāyazīd (when he appears in a dream) for some last instructions. The Friend describes life as an eternal ocean in which seekers must swim tirelessly toward a distant vessel that alone can rescue the body from the waves. Some dreams present a context for a major teacher's definition of Sufism, such as Bāyazīd's capsule comment about shutting the door of comfort and sitting with one's arms around the knees of self-denial. In one story, a famous woman, the wife of the Sufi Ahmad-i Khidrūya, attends the burial of Bāyazīd and asks those present whether they truly knew the deceased man. They reply that she is better informed than they, and she proceeds to tell them about a dream she has had. After performing her ritual at the Kaʿba, she slept and dreamed she traveled to God's throne, beneath which spread a vast desert abloom with herbage. Every flower petal was inscribed with the message that Bāyazīd was God's Friend. In a similar vein, dream accounts of deceased Friends can confirm the appropriateness and legitimacy of the dreamer's own pious practices. Sadafī records his dreams about Ibn Abī Saʿd during a period in which he (Sadafī) was staying at Shāfiʿī's tomb in Cairo. In one dream, Ibn Abī Saʿd laments that people do not pray with him any more, and the dreamer asks him what he had found most helpful as his soul departed him in the grave. Proclaiming that there is no deity but God, the shaykh answers. Ibn Abī Saʿd then tells Sadafī that the person he knew to be closest to God was Ahmad an-Najjār, because he had lived the last years of his life in the sacred precincts of Mecca and Medina.[49]

Friends of God often dream of their own deceased spiritual guides, describing the object of the encounter in terms clearly meant to reinforce the departed teacher's authority. Ibn ʿArabī recalls seeing his shaykh Abū Yaʿqūb Yūsuf ibn Yakhlaf in a dream. The shaykh's split breast emitted a light as bright as the sun. Summoned to approach, the dreamer brought forward empty bowls, which the shaykh quickly filled with milk, a symbol of knowledge and wisdom. The dreamer drank one bowl after another as fast as he could.[50] Sometimes a still-living Friend appears. An assistant to Abū Madyan dreamed that his shaykh was brilliant as the sun when he preached but became like the moon when he did not. When the assistant relates the dream to Abū Madyan, the latter responds gratefully and says he aspires to be like the sun.[51]

Some dreams of deceased saints demonstrate the saint's ongoing provision of certain salutary acts, often deeds for which followers had besought the Friend in life. Sadafī reports that a poor man who had begged from Ibn Abī Saʿd fell asleep on the shaykh's grave. The Friend appeared in a dream, lamenting that he had nothing to give the beggar just then and instructing the man to return the next day. As the beggar sat down at the grave, he prayed for God's mercy on the shaykh, and there before him were two gold coins on a rock.[52] Other stories use dreams as the vehicles by which followers of a particular Friend receive information about the Friend's death many miles distant, as in the dream in which someone sees Dāwūd at-Ṭāʾī flying and proclaiming his freedom from captivity.[53]

Occasionally, a Friend appears in a dream to deliver an apparently mundane rebuke to a disciple. A story from West Java, Indonesia, tells the tale of a certain ʿAbd al-Muhyī, a follower of the great mystical teacher ʿAbd ar-Raʾūf of Singkel, who frequented a cave where he meditated with the long-deceased ʿAbd al-Qādir al-Jīlānī. People believed that ʿAbd al-Muhyī used a mysterious tunnel from that cave to travel all the way to Mecca at miraculous speed to attend Friday prayers and then to return to Java the same day. One Friday, he came late to prayer, huffing and puffing after the long run. ʿAbd al-Qādir manifested himself to ʿAbd al-Muhyī and chided him: but for his nasty smoking habit, he would have arrived on time. Ever since that revelation, the cave or tunnel near ʿAbd al-Muhyī's tomb in Pamijahan, Java, has been a nonsmoking area.[54]

A LITTLE BIRDIE TOLD ME: INFORMANTS FROM ANOTHER REALM

Friends of God and prophets enjoy a special connection with the unseen world through various kinds of privileged (though typically one-way) communication. These sources of connection with the divine can take the form of voices or somewhat more amorphous "thoughts" from within the self, and distinguishing between the two phenomena is not always easy. One common visual metaphor in modern Senegalese imagery, for example, is a dove (Gabriel in disguise, apparently) that delivers a tiny document in its beak.[55] The communicative gift to the holy person is typically an envelope, which presumably contains a letter, but sometimes a book. Friends of God (and less exalted folk on occasion) also frequently benefit from special disclosures from offstage, as it were. Otherwise unidentified "speakers" provide an indirect form of divine communication. In addition, certain saintly or prophetic figures sometimes stop by for surprise visits, which hagiographical sources frequently distinguish from dreams or visions.

Voices from the Unseen and Unbidden Thoughts

One of the most common themes in Islamic hagiographical narratives is that of the "caller" (*hātif*). The ethereal voice pipes up as an all-purpose revelatory source when a story does not use other specific characters to fill that role. Auditory interventions can respond to virtually any need, reminding, cautioning, correcting, reprimanding, instructing, giving news of the death of an important person, or simply commenting on the passing scene. Some scholars attribute the prevalence of the "folk" phenomenon to the need for connection in the desert's vast, empty silence.

Whatever the origin of this intriguing feature, it underscores one of the essential attributes of traditional Islam: the understanding of all creation as replete with divine "signs," *āyāt*, an Arabic term that also describes the "verses" of the revealed scripture, the Qurʾān. Many Sufi authors refer to "the tongue of one's spiritual state" (*lisān al-ḥāl*), which is perhaps a somewhat more sophisticated counterpart to the "voice calling." To discern one's spiritual progress, the seeker needs to attend to the messages of every inward movement of soul. In most hagiographical narratives, however, the voice comes as a fairly straightforward messenger of essential but disembodied information.

The phenomenon is significant enough to merit three short chapters in Kalābādhī's manual of spirituality: one on voices as such, one on "insight" (*firāsa*), and one on more generic "thoughts," with the latter two not always clearly distinguished from voices. In some of Kalābādhī's anecdotes, the voice functions as a spiritual conscience, articulating various kinds of spiritual insight or the phenomenon that Sufi theorists call "transitory thoughts" (*khawātir*). Sometimes the voice chides the Friend with a gentle reminder that he or she has perhaps not been as vigilant or faithful as he or she would like to think. In some instances, the hearer is aware of a directional quality in the auditory experience, typically identifying the source as the environs of the Ka'ba. Accounts occasionally identify the voice as that of a specific Friend of God who is dead or otherwise physically distant from the hearer. And in some instances, a person perceives an inner thought as the voice of God; in others, the voice speaks when the individual is asleep.[56]

Some stories depict Friends speaking from within their tombs to those nearby. For example, Bībī Fātima Sām, in the Indian hagiography *Accounts of the Finest (Akbār al-akhyār)* by 'Abd al-Haqq Muhaddith of Delhi, speaks to a devotee from her grave and recounts her experience in the next world on her way to meet God. She reports that as she moved along, a group of angels chastised her for stepping so jauntily. In response, she swore she would go no further until God called her. Even when Muhammad's wife Khadīja and his daughter Fātima Zahrā' came to get her, she held her ground. At length, she heard God's personal invitation to advance and did so.[57]

Visitors from the Unseen: When Khidr and Others Stop By

Friends of God, as well as lesser persons in their stories, sometimes encounter mysterious and often unidentified figures. These individuals are apparently human and not angelic, but they seem to come from another dimension of existence. Although Khidr is arguably the most significant of these characters, a variety of others belong to various ranks of the celestial hierarchy or come from otherwise undifferentiated groups of Friends, such as the *abdāl*.[58] Some storytellers identify the mysterious visitors, if they identify them at all, as "men of the unseen realm" (*rijāl al-ghayb*).[59]

Khidr appears in some of the tales of the prophets and in the story of Moses, he plays his most important part in Islamic traditional lore. Sura 18,

The Cave, describes a shadowy unnamed character who appears to guide Moses in his quest for the Confluence of the Two Seas. Identified by most exegetes as Khidr, the enigmatic figure tries to fend off Moses's requests that Khidr show him the way to his goal. Khidr is convinced that Moses will be unable to contain himself if Khidr performs actions that are inwardly salvific though perhaps outwardly indefensible. Moses agrees to Khidr's condition that if he cannot refrain from questioning his guide, the two will part company. Indeed, after Khidr scuttles a ship and ensures the death of a boy, Moses lets his questions fly, and Khidr leaves him to fend for himself. Traditional sources often identify Khidr as a Friend of God to whom God granted a higher form of knowledge than he gave even to Moses. In hagiographical literature, one of Khidr's main functions is to visit those in need of guidance and spiritual initiation into a Sufi order outside of the ordinary process.[60] The "Green One's" first appearance in "Islamic" times was at Muhammad's funeral. When a voice proclaimed that the Prophet was already pure and therefore did not need to be washed before burial, another identified the first voice as that of the lying Iblīs. ʿAlī asked who the second speaker was, and Khidr identified himself.[61] Most Khidr sightings, however, occur in tales of God's Friends.

Though people might ask the mysterious visitor to intercede for them, Khidr, too, acknowledges his need for help. In one story, Abū Muhammad al-Bāghī prays one night in the *ribāt* where he is staying in Andalusia. Suddenly a light suffuses the place and he realizes he has a visitor, who announces that he is Khidr. Bāghī tells his visitor he would like to know where he resides, so that he might visit him when he feels the need. But Khidr explains that he is a placeless wanderer, appearing wherever individuals bring him to mind to ask about the progress of devout seekers. Bāghī reports several visits by Khidr. During pilgrimage, Khidr drops in, asking to be remembered at the holy places. Another time, he stops by to see if Bāghī needs anything; the latter asks Khidr to implore forgiveness from God, whereupon Khidr confesses that he, too, needs prayers. He explains to a very surprised Bāghī that Muslims are enjoined to beseech blessings even on Muhammad himself.[62]

Initiation into the Sufi Path is among Khidr's most frequent functions. Ibn ʿArabī recalls a visit to ʿAlī ibn ʿAbd Allāh ibn Jāmiʿ during which his host asked him to sit in a specific place. The shaykh explained that Khidr had occupied that place when he came to initiate him as a Sufi. At first, Khidr gave him only the skullcap of cotton, but then Khidr asked ʿAlī if he wanted to receive the patched cloak (*khirqa*) as well. (The skullcap and cloak are symbolic of initiation into a Sufi order, but the garb is usually invested by a living shaykh.) ʿAlī replied that he was not the one to make that judgment, and Khidr again placed the cap on ʿAlī's head. At that point, Ibn ʿArabī asked his host to do the same for him.[63]

An intriguing class of characters called the *abdāl* (substitutes, a category of figures in Sufi cosmology) sometimes visit, either on their own or in collaboration with Khidr. In a curious hybrid account, Sadafī reports that a certain Abū 'l-Hasan al-Bukhārī regularly enjoyed visitation of the *abdāl* during special religious feasts. While he was on pilgrimage near Mecca in the valley of ʿArafāt, two of them appeared, showing signs of self-denial similar to the shaykh's. They brought a greeting from Khidr, who had informed them that he would make his annual visit to pilgrims in the vicinity of ʿArafāt.[64] Another of Sadafī's reports tells of a man in the mosque of Qina, Egypt, who saw three *abdāl* performing their evening prayer there. The man performed his *salāt* (ritual prayer) behind them and then followed them outside, only to have them disappear from sight. When he tried to reenter the city, he found the gate locked and had to wait outside until morning. The marvel is that the gate had been locked even when he and the *abdāl* passed through it and had opened miraculously to accommodate them.[65] In a story on the same theme, a stranger enters the room where ʿAbd al-Majīd ibn Salma, a servant of Shams of Marchena, is praying at night. In a fright, the servant assails the intruder, who then identifies himself as an imperturbable intimate Friend of God. ʿAbd al-Majīd asks the visitor how the *abdāl* attained their rank, and the man says that the keys are hunger, vigilance, silence and seclusion. The visitor then takes the servant on a whirlwind tour of the world and has him back by dawn. Ibn ʿArabī's account identifies the visitor as Muʿādh ibn Ashras, one of the *abdāl*, and notes that he made these nocturnal visitations occasionally to ʿAbd al-Majīd.[66] Hagiographic accounts typically emphasize that those who enjoy visitations from individuals of the rank of *qutb* or *abdāl* should not divulge the visitors' identity to anyone.[67] Once such a figure's identity becomes known, he almost always leaves the region, never to return.[68]

Finally, some mysterious visitors come and go in stories without ever being clearly identified. Ghazālī tells a beautiful story about an apparent visitation from the unseen realm. A poor woman's husband dies, and she faces considerable difficulty arranging his funeral and burial. Her fellow Basrans had

FIGURE 8. *(opposite)* Moses approaches the Burning Bush, from which the voice of God emanated. His intimate encounter with God earned Moses the name *Kalīm*, "he who conversed" with God. Juwayrī, *Qisas al-anbiyāʾ*, Columbia University Rare Book and Manuscript Library, X 829.8 Q1/Q (1574–75), 79a.

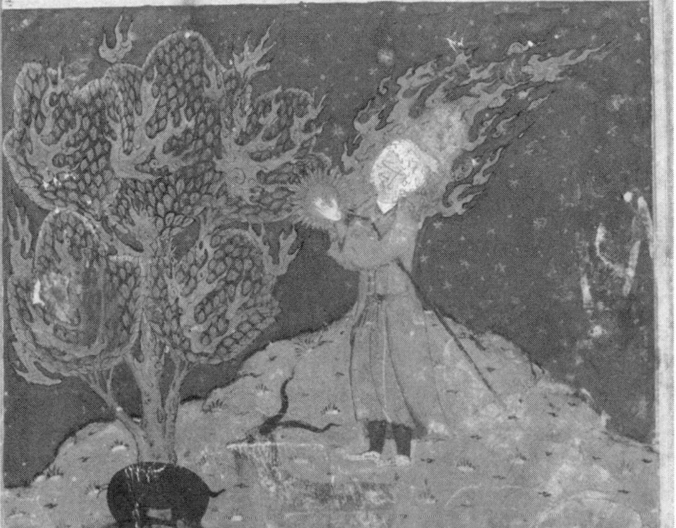

known the man as a shiftless drunk and shunned his family. His widow has
to hire people to carry his body to the place of prayer, where not a soul has
come to pray for him, and then to carry him into the desert for burial. On a
nearby mountain, the burial party sees "one of the great ascetics," who seems
to be waiting for a funeral. The mysterious figure comes and prays for the
deceased, to the surprise and even scandal of the townsfolk who learn about
his presence. The visitor explains that a dream instructed him to "descend"
to a place where he would attend the funeral of a man who had been forgiven.
Amazed at the negative responses of the townspeople, the mystery man visits the widow and asks her to tell him her husband's life story. He asks her if
she can think of anything positive in the man's life. Three things come to her
mind. Each day, drunk as he had been the night before, he would freshen up,
purify himself ritually, and pray the dawn prayer before going to the tavern.
Second, her husband always looked after an orphan or two with great kindness. Finally, he awoke every night in tears and asked God which part of hell
he would occupy. Satisfied that the dead man had indeed been forgiven, the
mysterious visitor departs.[69]

Assuming that a Friend heeds God's manifold communications and responds
appropriately, what do the traditional sources suggest about the ultimate goal
of such a saintly trajectory? Many accounts of God's Friends, scholarly and
popular alike, identify these extraordinary individuals as "mystics" whose
experience of "ecstasy" is virtually the sole important feature of their relationships with God. One effect of this treatment has been to ignore the many
aspects of Friends' lives that do not fit neatly into "mystical" categories.
Nevertheless, the intimate union that many sources suggest that God
bestowed on Friends is a significant aspect of their relationship. Hagiographical sources portray Friends of God in various relational roles, especially as servants, seekers along the path, and lovers of the truth.

According to much "mainstream" Islamic thought, no human being can
aspire to a loftier station than that of servant of God, ʿAbd Allāh. But hagiographical sources suggest that some aspirants, or seekers, on the way of God
have enjoyed a particularly intense experience of union with their Lord. Here,
as in so many other instances, prophets set the pattern. Abraham was God's
"intimate associate" (khalīl), Moses was granted intimate conversation
(called God's kalīm; see Fig. 8), and Muhammad was permitted access to the
very throne of God, where even Gabriel was not allowed to approach. As
chapter 6 reveals in detail, Friends of God function in many other equally
important dimensions. Self-absorbed they most definitely are not.

Because God's Friends are privileged with such radical intimacy with God, many Muslims believe in the *Ahl al-ighātha:* a group of Friends of God who function as intercessors and whose marvels are the principal medium of the divine mercy that believers receive. The title "Assistance" (*Ghawth*) was often conferred on individuals credited with the greatest potency. Sometimes the mere proximity of a Friend is sufficient to transform the fate of someone in need of divine forgiveness. In one account, for example, the day after a murderer meets his fate with a hangman's noose, people report seeing him in their dreams enjoying the pleasures of paradise. When the dreamers inquire, in their dreams' dialogues, how such a reprobate can enjoy such a happy fate, the murderer explains that as the trapdoor sprung, Habīb al-ʿAjamī walked by and gave him a sidelong glance.[70] Such is the power of a Friend to effect significant, if not always immediately visible, transformations. Chapter 4 shows how divine power at work in prophets and Friends of God can bring about far more spectacular changes as well.

FIGURE 9.   Ahmad-i Jām (d. 536/1141) rides a lion, using serpents as whip and reins, in a genre nature-marvel scene that is repeated in many stories of other famous Friends. The Nasser D. Khalili Collection of Islamic Art, *Fālnāma*, Golconda, c. 1610–20, MSS 979: 17b.

4. Miracles and Marvels

God Working through His Friends

Signs of divine power manifested through human beings are ubiquitous in hagiographical accounts. Chapter 11 discusses various technical theological aspects of this subject. Here I explore some of the ways in which prophetic miracles and saintly marvels play out in narratives of prophets and Friends of God. Three categories can help structure this vast subject: scope of action, type of action, and subject or theme. Because one cannot draw a tidy line between categories, some overlap exists. In the first category, scope of action, we can make a useful distinction between reflexive and transitive miracles. The former are those that redound to the benefit of the Friend, and the latter are those that benefit others.[1] In the latter type, we can further distinguish three types of relationships: among human beings; between human beings and nature; and between the seen and unseen worlds.[2]

The second category, type of action, divides wondrous deeds according to the nature of the prerogatives the marvels require. Two major subtypes are knowledge, or epistemological, marvels and power marvels. Stories of epistemological marvels emphasize works that depend primarily on the agent's extraordinary insight, awareness, and access to arcane truths. These wondrous deeds are generally transitive in scope and effect relationships between seen and unseen worlds. Epistemological marvels include the ability to discern others' thoughts (*mukāshafat adh-dhikr*), the ability to predict the future (*firāsa*), knowledge of mysteries (*basīra*), and guidance in dreams or visions of Muhammad or Khidr. Chapter 3 discussed this last form of marvelous event, along with the phenomenon of announcements from unseen voices. Power miracles are likewise transitive and typically affect relationships among persons and between human and natural realms. They feature the agent's control over wild and often dangerous natural forces, mastery of time and space, access to hidden sources of assistance, control of positive and negative spiritual energies, and the ability to intervene in life-threatening circumstances. Preference for one or the other of these types of marvels appears to vary from one region to another as well as from one hagiographer to another. In Moroccan hagiographical literature, for example, knowledge marvels far outnumber power wonders, suggesting that hagiographers in Morocco assigned greater importance to knowledge in Friends of God than to power. As we shall see, the balance tips the other way in other historical and cultural contexts.[3]

Categorizing marvels according to subject or theme allows one to elaborate on the abilities conferred by special knowledge or outward power. So, for example, control over natural forces includes divine protection from all manner of dangers and threats, such as the abilities to turn back storms at sea and tame ravenous beasts. Mastery of time and space encompasses the ability to travel great distances instantaneously, walk on water, levitate, or fly through the air. Access to hidden sources of aid include, for example, having the jinn at one's beck and call, dispatching negative spiritual powers, and the ability to effect reflexive marvels as needed for superhuman feats of self-denial. Intervention in threatening circumstances includes such power marvels as healing the sick, bringing forth food from nowhere, restoring life to the dead, and such knowledge miracles as discovering water in time of thirst and recovering hidden treasure to purchase the means of survival. This chapter blends these three ways of categorizing wondrous deeds. We begin with a brief look at some important prophetic miracles as a backdrop for understanding the marvels effected by Friends of God.[4]

PROPHETS AND SAINTS, POWER AND BLESSING
Prophetic Miracles

Prophetic narratives—whether in the Qurʾān, hadith, exegetical texts, or tales of the prophets—often feature spectacular deeds wrought by God at a prophet's behest, typically in response to a community's rejection of the divine message. Prophetic or "evidentiary" miracles (*muʿjizāt*) predominantly manifest divine power rather than knowledge bestowed on the prophet. A notable exception is the story of Khidr, especially his relationship with Moses. Sura 18, *Sūrat al-Kahf* (The Cave) and its associated exegesis and traditional lore, indicates that God bestowed a higher type of knowledge on Khidr than on Moses, who sets the scene for the story to follow with his claim to being the most knowledgeable of all prophets.[5]

Prophets frequently cause the destruction of a people's ancient idols. In some stories, all of creation expresses its outrage. The earth itself, as well as birds and a host of other animals, shout their complaints to God about the violence and disbelief of those who have rejected the prophets. In the story of Noah, even the ark speaks, proclaiming the profession of faith and declaring that only those who embark on this vessel of faith will be saved. The ship turns tour guide, informing Noah about the places over which they sail. In another story, Hūd mediates the destruction of the people of ʿĀd by an overwhelming desert wind. In yet another, Sālih restores to life a family of those who believe in his message. When the people accuse him of mere sorcery, God allows the prophet to produce a living camel out of the mountainside—and the camel speaks of God. After the unbelievers slay the wondrous camel, they pay with their lives, with Gabriel emitting a shout so horrific that they all burn to cinders.[6]

Abraham transforms a bag of sand into grains of wheat the size of pistachios, and God rescues him from the bonfire of the evil Nimrod. When Abraham prepares to sacrifice his son (Ishāq/Isaac in some stories, Ismāʿīl/Ishmael in others), the sacrificial dagger speaks up in protest and refuses to go near the boy's throat. Moses performs several miracles also described in the Bible, albeit in slightly different terms from those in the Qurʾān. For example, he transforms his staff into a serpent (or, more often in Islamic sources, into a dragon) that devours the staff-serpents of the Egyptian sorcerers, summons various plagues, and parts the Red Sea. To David, God gave the gift of magical song and the power to soften iron and knit chain mail. Solomon was known for his concourse with nature, including his ability to understand the languages of all living things and his power to harness the winds for swift travel on his carpet.[7]

Thaʿlabī includes an extended account of miracles attributed to Jesus. Thaʿlabī notes that when, as a child, Jesus breathed life into lumps of clay and made them fly, the creatures flew only until they were out of sight of onlookers, at which point they dropped dead. In this way, Thaʿlabī distinguishes human efforts from divine acts and proves to the reader that only God's work is perfect. Thaʿlabī observes that the "birds" Jesus fashioned were, in fact, bats, for bats are the most highly developed of the birds (made more perfect by possessing the attributes of mammals). Later in his life, Jesus's simple wooden bowl never lacked for food, and he miraculously provided a table full of sustenance from heaven for his followers and multiplied existing sources of food. He could cure the sick and people who were blind from birth, restore life to the dead (Thaʿlabī tells of his raising of Lazarus, of the son of an old widow, and of Ezra), walk on water, and reveal hidden secrets (see Fig. 10). On several occasions, Jesus slaughtered an animal for needed food, then raised it to life again and set it free.[8]

Islamic tradition holds that Muhammad, the seal of the prophets, performed, and claimed, only one miracle: the Qurʾān. But popular lore, including the

FIGURE 10.   Jesus raises the dead son of the old woman beseeching him (very likely after the New Testament story of the widow of Nain in the Gospel of Luke 7:11–17). The Nasser D. Khalili Collection of Islamic Art, *Fālnāma*, Golconda, c. 1610–30, MSS 979: l7b.

Prophet's sayings and deeds as enshrined in the canonical collections of hadith, attributes a variety of amazing feats to Muhammad. "Splitting of the moon" (alluded to in Qur'ān 54:1) was his most celebrated feat, sometimes likened to Moses's splitting of the sea.[9] The first major hagiographical account of Muhammad's life, Ibn Ishāq's *Life of God's Messenger,* contains several intriguing reports. In one of the more unusual tales, Muhammad invites the strongest member of the Quraysh tribe to accept the message of Islam. The leader, Rukāna, says that if he can have proof of Muhammad's veracity, he will convert. Muhammad asks whether he would believe if Muhammad could throw him in a wrestling match, and Rukāna says he would. The Prophet easily tosses the man, who insists on a repeat performance. When Muhammad floors his opponent again without breaking a sweat, Rukāna expresses his amazement. But, says the Prophet, it would be even more amazing if I called that tree and it came to me. Rukāna asks Muhammad to call the tree, and it comes forward. And when the Prophet orders the tree to return to its place, it complies. Rukāna nevertheless seems to have persisted in his belief that these deeds were merely high-level sorcery.[10]

Islamic theological writings have long maintained a careful distinction between "evidentiary miracles" (*mu'jizāt*) performed by and for prophets as proof of their divine mandate and the "marvels" (*karāmāt*) allowed to Friends of God as signs of God's power working through them. Major theologians, such as a prominent systematician of the Ash'arī school, Bāqillānī, have written extensively about the differences between "miracle" and "magic." Bāqillānī's concern is first to distinguish between the works performed by prophets and the ostensibly similar deeds managed by such negative figures as the magicians of Pharaoh. Ironically, the unbelieving people typically accuse the prophet of mere sorcery.[11] What is most important to bear in mind in the present context is the central hagiographical notion of continuity between prophetic miracles and saintly marvels. Aflākī, for example, says of "the miraculous gifts of the Friends of God" that they are "what have succeeded the evidentiary miracles of the prophets."[12] The chief distinction between prophetic "miracles" and saintly "marvels" is, therefore, purpose or intent rather than immediate cause. Chapter 11 discusses the theological distinctions in greater detail. Before looking at the types of marvels ascribed to Friends of God, let us explore how hagiographical sources have sought to maintain the continuity between prophets and Friends.

Friends of God and the Prophetic Connection

Among the contexts in which Friends are frequently compared to Prophets, perhaps the most important is that of the miracle story. These stories take three forms: first, Muhammad's own recounting of marvels; second, explicit hagiographical efforts to relate marvels of Friends to prophetic counterparts; and third, brief anecdotes that explicitly connect a Friend's marvel to prophetic prerogatives.

As we have seen, even the hadith literature contains a surprising number of phenomena that later sources generally categorize as saintly marvels. One such intriguing account in the first category of marvels is the hadith of the Cave. Once upon a time, Muhammad recounted, three men took refuge from the cold in a cave. Overnight, a boulder fell and blocked the entrance. The terrified trio agreed that their only recourse was intense prayer for deliverance. The first man told the Lord about how he had seen to the needs of his elderly parents, preparing their food daily and attending them through the night. Suddenly the boulder budged enough to admit a shaft of light. Then the second man spoke, recalling that he had fought off inappropriate feelings for his beautiful daughter and eventually sent her off with funds to keep her safe. At that admission, the boulder slid further to the side, but not quite enough for the men to escape. In earnest entreaty, the third man told a story about one of his former workers who failed to show up for his pay. He used the laborer's wage to buy a goat, which later gave birth to a kid. After a few years, his investment had multiplied into a small herd, and then, out of nowhere, the missing worker appeared asking to be paid. The employer gave the worker the whole flock because it was the result of the worker's delayed wages. In response, God nudged the boulder again, and the three were liberated.[13]

In the second category, important hagiographical sources have provided context for Friends' working of wonders by alluding to prophetic counterparts. Ibn ʿArabī, for example, talks in general terms about the phenomenon of wonders as he describes the marvelous deeds of a particularly influential friend of his. In his account of Shaykh Abū ʿImrān Mūsā ibn ʿImrān of Mertola, Ibn ʿArabī lists among possible marvels of Friends walking on water or in thin air, traveling across great distances in impossibly short times, surviving without food or water, and performing feats of clairvoyance. He mentions these possibilities in a story about how he won over a preacher skeptical of the power of marvels. He first secured the skeptic's agreement that the Prophet had made reference in several hadiths to the certainty of God's fulfilling the "trust" of some servants who might call on God. He then argued that this divine activity included a range of "miraculous" deeds.[14]

Ibn ʿArabī also discusses on several occasions the common problem of establishing the credibility of claims about saintly marvels. In one account, he notes that he habitually challenged skeptical jurists when they expressed reservations about such claims, chalking them up to mere superstition. He bases his challenges on the idea that "whoever sets out to rebuke the saints generally or specifically and whoever, not having associated with them, attacks one who does, that person demonstrates his ignorance and will never gain salvation." On one occasion, he took to task a skeptical judge whom he met on pilgrimage, demonstrating how foolish the judge must be. Though the judge had traveled little, he still claimed broad knowledge of the far-flung Muslim community and asserted categorically that not a single individual could honestly claim special gifts from God.[15]

In two stories about Bāyazīd, ʿAttār brings up an important aspect of the Friend's gift of working miracles—namely, awareness of a certain ambiguity or even danger to his spiritual integrity. In the first story, Bāyazīd is walking in the desert when an old woman approaches and asks that he carry a bag of flour for her. He is in a weakened state and summons a lion to bear the burden. Concerned about his "image," he asks the woman what she will tell her friends back in town. She will, she replies, tell them that she has met a nasty show-off. Taken aback, Bāyazīd admits that his treatment of the lion was unkind and that his desire to have people think that the lion followed his commands was indeed arrogant. From that day on, Bāyazīd asks God to offer a special sign to show his presence in every marvel. Thereafter, God sends down a light inscribed with the names of five witnessing prophets (Muhammad, Noah, Abraham, Moses, and Jesus) each time Bāyazīd performs a marvel, until at length the Friend no longer needs confirmation.[16] In the second brief account, as Bāyazīd approaches the Tigris River, the water rolls away for him to cross miraculously, recalling Moses's parting of the sea. But the Friend prefers to pay a nominal fee to a boatman rather than squander his spiritual capital for such a mundane purpose. He implies that he is loath to exercise blithely a power for which he has spent thirty years preparing.[17]

In the third category of accounts, authors more explicitly associate the marvels of a Friend with the miraculous powers of a prophet. One such anecdote describes a nighttime visit by Hasan of Basra to Rābiʿa. Rābiʿa has no lamp, so she breathes on her fingertips, and her hand emits light until dawn. ʿAttār explains that the marvel is reminiscent of the time that Moses's hand turned luminously white with leprosy. Friends of God are granted the power and blessing of marvels precisely because they follow prophets.[18]

Rūmī's disciples considered him "the Moses of the era and the Jesus of the age."[19] According to hagiographer Aflākī, when Rūmī took care of his son Sultān Walad, he would give his own nipple to the crying child and milk would flow. The hagiographer parallels this marvel to that of Abraham's sucking pure milk from his fingertip after being weaned and left alone in a cave. Aflākī also likens the marvel to water springing from Muhammad's fingertips and to the transformation of Abū Bakr's saliva into fuel to light the Prophet's mosque.[20] The same source makes an extended series of parallels between Chalabī Amīr ʿĀrif (a grandson of Rūmī) and several prophets. ʿĀrif walked one day on the Kor River in Iraq "like a column gliding on the surface," and Aflākī likens the marvel to God's causing Solomon to ride on air as though on a royal throne. He then alludes to Moses's control of the Red Sea, God's causing Nimrod's fire to become a garden for Abraham, and Hūd's control over the destroying wind released against the unbelievers.[21] In more recent times, Senegalese shaykh Amadou Bamba has often been depicted in reverse-glass painting scenes that clearly seek to echo events in the life of Abraham, such as Abraham's survival amid Nimrod's bonfire.[22]

MARVELS OF DIVINE POWER AND PROTECTION

Human beings often face great odds in the struggle to survive and keep faith on their journey from birth back to the source of their life. Even God's Friends cannot always go it alone, but more often, lesser mortals seek the assistance of Friends in time of trouble. Some stories feature God's intervention on behalf of his Friends, whereas others emphasize a Friend's protection of people unable to fend for themselves.[23]

God Protecting His Friends

Friends of God invariably have the protection of divine power, which is often revealed in relatively mundane settings. In one delightful story, a thief enters Rābiʿa's room intent on making off with her mantle. Attempting to exit, the thief can no longer find the door. He puts down the garment and again sees the way out. Seven times he attempts unsuccessfully to make his getaway, but a voice informs him that he is wasting his time, for even Satan does not dare to test the divine protection around this woman.[24] A fascinating variant on the theme appears in Ibn ʿArabī's account of Abū 'l-Hajjāj Yūsuf of Shubarbul in Andalusia. Burglars enter the shaykh's house one night while he is engrossed in prayer. Gathering up some loot, the intruders try to flee but cannot find the door. When they put down the shaykh's belongings, the door reappears. In a bid to outsmart the delusion, they leave a comrade at the door while his henchmen return to collect their goods. Alas, though their lookout assures them he had not moved, the door's location again eludes them. Failing at several attempts to find a solution, the intruders leave, empty-handed and penitent. Ibn ʿArabī claims he heard the account from one of the burglars.[25] Two thematically similar stories show how God prevented Nūrī's clothes from being stolen while he bathed. Both are also thematically related to the story of the thief who attempts to purloin Rābiʿa's clothes as she sleeps. In one tale, a thief returns the clothes at the moment Nūrī emerges from the water, but the thief's hand is suddenly paralyzed. Nūrī prays that the man's hand be restored in the same way that his clothing has been returned. In a parallel version, when Nūrī notices his clothes are missing, he prays that they be returned, and the contrite thief soon reappears.[26] In a South Asian variant on the theme, a story in *Fawāʾid al-Fuʾād* features the devout mother of Bābā Farīd, the third great Chishtī shaykh. Qarsūm Bībī is praying one night when a thief breaks into her home. He is immediately blinded by the light radiating from her and pleads with the woman to intercede with God so that he might regain his sight. She responds, he converts to Islam, and he lives a model life thereafter.[27]

Some situations in which Friends find themselves are far more threatening. A burglar attacks Abū 'l-ʿAlāʾ al-Kindī with a sword while the shaykh is praying. When Abū 'l-ʿAlāʾ yells at the assailant, the attacker is unable to move his hand until he repents of his misdeed. God's protection makes Kindī so invulnerable that he wins the nickname "Bundle of Thorns." In another story, someone attacks Abū Jaʿfar al-ʿUryanī with a knife and tries to kill him. The shaykh simply bares his neck to the assailant and orders his attendants not to restrain the thug. As the man lunges with his dagger, God twists the weapon in his hand, causing him to drop it in fear and promptly repent before the shaykh. Angels sometimes function as instruments of divine protection for Friends in such situations. In one account, Abū ʿAbd Allāh ibn Muhammad al-Mujāhid senses that he is being followed on his way home from praying at a mosque. He confronts the stranger as he approaches his door, but the man says he wants nothing from the shaykh. The shaykh enters his home and locks his door behind him, only to find the stranger inside. Confronted again, the stranger announces that he is an angel whom God has ordered to guard Abū ʿAbd Allāh at all times. And so the angel provides protection until the shaykh's death.[28]

Peril on the seas is another common story setting. Impending danger can come either from natural powers or human enemies, as the following accounts illustrate. Traveling in a boat with Ibrāhīm ibn Adham, a companion expresses his fear that a high wind will surely sink the vessel. Then a voice announces that no harm can befall anyone in Ibrāhīm's company, and the wind abates. In a similar tale, as the wind buffets his vessel, Ibrāhīm spots a floating plank with a text of Qurʾān stuck to it. Ibrāhīm asks how God can let him and his companions perish with his sacred word so near, and the wind ceases. In a variation on the theme of danger at sea, the boat of Abū Muhammad Ibn ʿĪsar of Egypt begins to founder as he travels on the Nile.

Unable to swim, the shaykh begins to recite a verse from the Qurʾān about God's command over the elements (22:65). At that moment, a plank buoys the saint up and carries him until another boat arrives to rescue him. In another story of rescue, Abū 'l-ʿAbbās al-Gharīb is swept overboard by a swinging rope as he attempts to perform his ablutions on a ship. Fortunately, he lands on a rock. His shipmates eventually discover him clinging to the side of the ship, safe and dry. The rock has apparently materialized to protect the shaykh and has conveyed him to the vessel and attached him to its gunwale before disappearing again.[29]

An important subtheme is God's ongoing defense of his Friends against attacks by Christians, and occasionally by members of other religious communities. In the following examples, peril on the sea is again a key setting. Abū Muhammad Ibn ʿĪsar of Egypt told Sadafī that Christians once attacked the ship on which he was sailing from North Africa to Mecca. The marauders imprisoned him and his family and headed for Syria. But when God stilled the winds and becalmed the ship, the Christians realized they were in trouble and left their captives on shore. They were then able to make off with the plundered vessel. Similarly, Abū 'l-Hasan al-Bukhārī was en route to pilgrimage in Mecca when several shiploads of Christians waylaid his vessel. Alerted to the peril, the shaykh prayed, and God caused the Christian ships to stop as though they had run aground. The attackers swore that if the holy person who had brought about this situation would reverse it, they would let the pilgrims go in peace. Suddenly the Christian vessels dispersed as though shot from a bow, and the Muslims proceeded unmolested. In a variation on the themes of attack by Christians and shipboard experiences, some Christians set upon Abū ʿAbd Allāh ash-Sharafī and a companion as they are picking olives in Andalusia and haul them away in chains. Because God promised the shaykh that he would never set foot in the territory of unbelievers, he softens their shackles and the captives escape. God's protection of Sharafī goes further: whenever a wrongdoer manages to board the ship with which Sharafī makes his livelihood, the vessel encounters serious turbulence, alerting the captain that the last-boarded passengers must be left ashore.[30]

Friends Defending the Defenseless

Friends often depend directly on God for help, but many stories emphasize the Friend's more immediate exercise of marvelous power in aid of those to whom God sends them. For example, as Fanakī made his circumambulation of the Kaʿba during pilgrimage, he saw an attendant treating a woman rudely. He asked God to distract the man from this poor woman, at which point a scorpion stung the man's foot and he died. Another pilgrim asked Fanakī to pray to God for him after he had lost some money. The shaykh did so and took a further step. He revealed the problem to a judge, whose assistant then reported that a lost item had been turned in. After providing an accurate description of the item, the pilgrim got his money back, and Fanakī proceeded to preach to a crowd on the importance of taking care of others. He explained that such faith-inspired altruism is in fact far greater than other pious deeds.[31]

Friends are occasionally called to rescue someone under attack by answering violence with violence. Abū 'l-Walīd ash-Shātibī of Andalusia once encountered a man in the desert about to rape a woman. When the shaykh intervened, the brigand attempted to draw his sword but could not free it from its scabbard. Holding the case against his chest, he yanked again, only to have the blade come loose and slice the veins in his neck, killing him instantly. More often than not, however, Friends do not require conventional force to alleviate suffering. Sharafī once interceded before an emir for an individual who needed justice, but the emir dismissed him. Sharafī asked God to punish the official by cutting off his food supply and making him unspeakably ugly. Shortly afterward, the emir was stripped of his authority and began to shrink until, when he died, he was no larger than a seven-year-old child. In another tale, Abū ʿAbd Allāh al-Arkushī was in a city of Andalusia that suddenly came under siege from Christian attackers. He stood on the battlements as the Christians swarmed the defenders below, while from within the citizens cried out to Arkushī to intervene. Mounting a tower, the shaykh waved his cloak and demanded that the enemy disperse. It did so immediately.[32]

SUSTAINING AND HEALING

Friends of God miraculously provide a host of needed services to a wide spectrum of people, from the destitute to the wealthy, to both women and men, and even to non Muslims (who rarely continue their misguided ways for long). This category of power marvels encompasses a variety of situations, including the provision of needed sustenance from out of nowhere, assistance for people suffering from illness, and, less often, death or near-death experiences.

Unexpected Sustenance and the Alleviation of Poverty

Story settings vary widely. Mecca and Medina head the list of urban contexts, whereas sea and desert scenes offer natural settings for stories of food and water shortage. In one story, as Abū ʿAbd Allāh ar-Rammād walks toward the seashore, apparently intent on performing his ablutions for prayer, he instead walks across the water. He spreads out his prayer rug on a rock and utters something. After one fish jumps onto the rug, the shaykh says that one fish is not enough, whereupon nine more fish surrender themselves one at a time—and then another three jump onto the rug. As the shaykh prepares to return to shore, one of his disciples suddenly appears behind him. Rammād asks how the man found him there, and the follower explains that he merely traced the leader's steps. For the sake of the disciple, the shaykh explains, God provided three more fish than usual. The disciple then tells a surprised Rammād that he will accept only cooked fish. Though the shaykh finds the demand audacious, he assures the disciple that God will respond. Soon another disciple appears at the first follower's house with three cooked fish.[33]

Stories in which a Friend's disciple effects a marvel are relatively rare, but a second example exists in which Shaykh Saʿīd of Maykhurān pays a visit to Bāyazīd. Bāyazīd sends the shaykh off to see a disciple named Abū Saʿīd the Shepherd, saying that he (Bāyazīd) has given the disciple a unique gift of miraculous power. The visitor finds the shepherd praying after having entrusted his sheep to a pack of wolves. When the shepherd asks Abū Saʿīd what he wants, the shaykh asks for grapes and warm bread. The shepherd takes a piece of wood, breaks it, and puts the pieces on the ground nearby. The piece near the shepherd blossoms with white grapes, whereas the piece near his visitor produces black grapes. Shaykh Saʿīd asks about this peculiar result, and the shepherd explains that he knew his desire would be granted, whereas the visitor had simply been testing him.[34]

By contrast, another story about divine provision of sustenance highlights the disciple's inability to create miraculous results on his own. One of Rammād's followers finds him eating drippings from a certain willow tree in a garden. The shaykh invites the disciple to taste the marvelous substance. He explains that the tree is known as the "Host of God's Friends." He recalls that he once discovered a man there who had vowed never to live anywhere but Mecca and Medina and who had received food from the tree as a reward for his choice. When the disciple later returns alone, he cannot find the wondrous food.[35]

One of the most common scenarios finds a Friend supplying food to people in dire need. On a desert sojourn, Hallāj and four hundred companions had nothing to eat. The crowd asked the shaykh for a lamb's head, whereupon he produced a roast head for each, along with two loaves of bread. When the people asked for ripe dates, Hallāj instructed them to throw him heavenward, and a shower of dates came down. Thereafter, every thorn bush Hallāj leaned upon produced ripe dates. Abū 'l-Hasan al-Bukhārī was once in Medina during a famine, and the city's people asked him to intervene to ease their economic hardship. He told them they would find food on ships that had just arrived at the port of Yanbūʿ. The provisions were so abundant that the goods not only ended the famine but also revived trade in the city.[36]

Sometimes marvel stories focus less on the special deed than on the reluctance of a subordinate character to respond with generosity. Two tales recall chapter 2's theme of detachment from wealth. In one, a poor person approaches Abū 'l-ʿAbbās al-Fāʾida as he is preaching and asks the preacher for clothing. Abū 'l-ʿAbbās orders a listener to grant the request and be assured that God will repay him in the next life. As the listener prepares to give the beggar a donation, he says with a hint of sarcasm that people like the preacher usually go right to God! Suddenly Abū 'l-ʿAbbās changes his mind and tells the beggar to visit him the next day. That night, the preacher asks God to make the gift possible, whereupon a visitor supplies him with money for the clothing. The next day when the beggar arrives, the shaykh takes him to the market to purchase a nice robe. With a twist of spite, he then instructs the poor person to find the listener and tell him that God has indeed taken care of the matter, whereupon the listener feels abundantly guilty that he has passed up such an opportunity.[37]

In the second tale of detachment from wealth, the hagiographer Sadafi is at his home near Cairo talking with a Friend of God named Ibn Abī Saʿd when a poor beggar comes by. Sadafi makes a move to give the man some money, but the shaykh prefers to hear the pauper's story first. After the man recites his troubles, the shaykh asks God to help the beggar and assures Sadafi that if God intervenes, it will signal that Sadafi deserved to keep his money. Soon thereafter, a wealthy politician comes to chat with Ibn Abī Saʿd. As the visitor is about to leave, he whispers something to the shaykh and points to a nearby prayer rug. Retrieving a coin purse from beneath the carpet, the shaykh tells the beggar that God has answered his prayers.[38]

God's Friendly Physicians

Friends of God often enjoy the ability to alleviate physical suffering, from difficult childbirth to blindness and immobility. Abū 'l-ʿAlāʾ al-Kindī's power was such that when women who were about to give birth grasped his walking staff, they experienced easier labor and delivery.[39] Abū 'l-ʿAbbās al-Gharīb was blind and immobile and asked his wife to take him to the mosque to pray. A youth named Hudhayl asked the cause of Gharīb's malady, and the shaykh attributed it to the divine will. Hudhayl called for Gharīb's wife to bring water for ablution. After purifying himself, Hudhayl took the collected drippings and cleansed Gharīb. When the shaykh asked to return home, he was suddenly able to walk, and upon returning home, his sight was restored. Hudhayl visited the shaykh the next Friday, and Gharīb's wife asked him to pray for her as well. The young man did so and vanished. Healing of blindness or other maladies of the eyes is especially common in marvel stories. In one such account, a man suffering from a severe ocular ailment beseeches Abū 'l-Hajjāj Yūsuf of Shubarbul (near Seville, in Spain) for relief from his pain. The shaykh simply places his hand on the man's eyes, whereupon the supplicant at first lies on his back as though dead and then arises fully healed.[40]

Some healing stories include elements from other story themes, including the symbolic importance of money and various types of clairvoyance. Ibn ʿArabī reports that Shaykh Abū ʿAbd Allāh Muhammad ibn Ashraf of Ronda once gave him three silver coins when he set off on a journey. As Ibn ʿArabī made his way through a dangerous place, he heard a commotion. A group traveling with an ailing man was nearby. Ibn ʿArabī had heard that applying a genuine silver piece could heal pain, so he placed the coin on the man, and the man's suffering abated. The man's companions asked Ibn ʿArabī to leave the coin with them, and he did so. When he returned to Seville, the two brothers with whom he shared quarters told him they lacked the wherewithal to feed him. Knowing clairvoyantly what had transpired on his trip, they asked him for the two remaining coins to cover their expenses.[41]

Specialization in healing powers has been common in many regions, as the stories of some South Asian Friends show. Makhdūm Faqīh banishes hysteria, whereas treatment of depression is the province of Shaykh Saddu, and exorcism is the specialty of Makhdūm Sāhib and Sakhī Sarwar. Pīr Bukhārī has power over venereal diseases; Shāh Sufayd heals intractable coughs; and Shāh Mādar and Guga Pīr cure snakebite. Manghō Pīr handles rheumatism, and miscellaneous dermatological ailments, whereas Ghāzī Miyān and Pīr Janāniyā are among the preferred recourses of lepers. Mahkdūm-i Jahāniyān Jahāngasht relieves hemorrhoids, and people suffering from eye ailments often seek help from Sakhī Sarwar. Such belief in specialization often goes hand in hand with the conviction that Friends can inflict the same maladies that they can cure.[42]

Death and Near-Death Experiences

Accounts of restoring life to the dead are rare, but occasionally someone dies as a result of an encounter with a Friend (see Fig. 11). One day when Junayd was preaching, a listener exclaimed aloud. Junayd warned him not to repeat his outburst, but the man could not contain himself and died on the spot, leaving only a pile of ashes under his clothes. A similar episode involves one

FIGURE 11.   Murra is miraculously cut in half after intruding into ʿAlī's (d. 40/661) tomb. The Friend's two fingers emerge from the tomb in a fiery nimbus to cleave the invader as onlookers express their amazement. The Nasser D. Khalili Collection of Islamic Art, *Fālnāma*, Golconda, c. 1610–30, MSS 979:29b.

of Junayd's followers who had succumbed to a momentary failure of propriety and severed his connections with Junayd. When the shaykh happened by and glanced at the former disciple, the disciple fell, hitting his head and bleeding profusely. Each drop spelled out "Allāh," and Junayd accused the man of grandstanding in the hope that others would conclude he had attained a high level of spiritual attainment with this stunt. After the man died, someone saw him in a dream and asked how things had turned out for him. The man said that at last he had become aware of the subtle deceptions of his lack of faith.[43]

Some stories feature the reversal of apparent near-death experiences. In one tale, a holy man of Cairo who has been gravely ill appears to die. During the preparation of his body for burial, the washer begins to purify the cadaver with water and notices that the man is beginning to move. When the man's family arrives, he insists that they put him back in bed. He then recounts that while they were grieving his loss, he saw a vision of throngs heading for Judgment. The crowds had escorted him to the gates of heaven and were told that his time is yet a week off. Next Thursday, he tells his family, he will surely die, but meanwhile he has time for more prayerful preparation.[44]

Miracle accounts occasionally leave matters tantalizingly ambiguous. Jāmī tells the story of a follower of Sarī as-Saqatī named Umm Muhammad. Umm Muhammad entrusts her son to a teacher, and while in the teacher's care, the youth apparently drowns in a millstream. When the teacher and Sarī go to break the news to Umm Muhammad, they attempt to console her with exhortations to patience and resignation to God's design. She refuses to believe that God would do such a thing to her and heads for the millstream. After the teacher indicates the place where the boy drowned, Umm Muhammad calls to her son; he responds, and she takes him home. Sarī later consults with his nephew Junayd about how such a thing could have happened. Junayd explains that when an individual meticulously fulfills every religious duty, God will inflict nothing upon her without informing her ahead of time. Umm Muhammad sensed this condition and because God had not apprised her of the situation, she was convinced that her son could not have drowned. She had simply acted on that conviction when she summoned the boy from the water.[45]

MARVELS OF POWER OVER NATURE

Among the more striking varieties of power marvels are those that reverse, subdue, or neutralize natural processes. Some tell of less spectacular events, including those whose results are not immediately evident and require a pointed inquiry to ascertain. Abū ʿAbd Allāh, from the Iberian town of Ghilliza, was walking one day when prayer time arrived. Because he had not performed his ablutions, he approached a man who was urinating at the roadside and performed his ablutions with the man's urine. His astonished companions examined the traces of the urine and found that it had transformed into pure water. Among people whose lives still revolve almost entirely around agricultural and other natural cycles, some Friends are able to bring rain and crops under dire circumstances. Most nature-power accounts, however, tend toward more dramatic encounters and transformations. Below are examples of Friends who tame the elements, confront and communicate with formidable forces in the animal world (including both natural and mythical beasts), and enlist the services of creation's more docile denizens.[46]

Controlling the Forces of Nature

The ability to control specific natural powers is an important theme, with wind and water at the top of the list. In one story, Habīb al-ʿAjamī is on his way to the butcher to buy meat when a wind suddenly picks him up and a voice instructs the wind to return the boy to his house. In recounting this tale, ʿAttār explains that this occurrence was not new or surprising, for the wind had once been Solomon's ride. On another occasion, Habīb meets his teacher Hasan al-Basrī standing by the shore of the Tigris River and asks him why he has stopped there. When Hasan replies that he is waiting for a boat, Habīb reminds him of a lesson he taught Habīb long ago: if he would truly renounce the world and depend on God, he could walk on the water. Habīb then models the desired miraculous behavior. After Hasan recovers from a fainting spell, he tells his companions that Habīb had been able to walk across the water largely thanks to Hasan, for Habīb had, after all, learned from Hasan. Encountering Habīb later, Hasan asks how the younger man had achieved such a spiritual status. Habīb explains that while he was occupied with whitening his own heart, Hasan had been blackening paper with his scholar's ink. ʿAttār takes the occasion to discuss the relationship between knowledge and the power to work marvels. Appearances notwithstanding, Hasan still outranks Habīb, for knowledge outranks marvels. Though Solomon worked countless wonders, he nevertheless was a disciple of Moses, to whom God revealed knowledge of all mysteries.[47]

A story about Abū 'l-Walīd ash-Shātibī expands the repertoire of natural forces to include the power of the sea. The shaykh observes a Christian ship near the shore that is carrying Muslim prisoners captured in a naval battle. The shaykh calls to the ship to approach the shore, and the wind drives the vessel so quickly inward that the crew drops the sails. When the ship runs aground, Muslims board the vessel, free the captives, and deal harshly with the Christians.[48] Another story of sea travel adds the transformation of natural objects. On one occasion, Ibrāhīm ibn Adham lacks the gold coin required for passage on a ship. After he performs his ritual prayer, the sand on the beach where he stands is transformed into gold. For his fare, the shaykh gives the boatman a handful of dinars. In another water-related account, Ibrāhīm is patching his frock with a needle as he sits by the Tigris when someone asks him what recompense he has received for forsaking his kingdom. Just then, Ibrāhīm loses his needle in the river and gestures to the fish, signaling that he wants his needle returned. A thousand fish emerge with golden needles in their mouths, but he insists that only his old needle will do. After a tiny fish retrieves the right needle, Ibrāhīm explains that such occurrences are the least of his rewards.[49]

Sometimes Friends are in need of the most basic means of survival, with the need for water foremost in the minds of travelers. In one story, Ibrāhīm lowers a dipper only to have it come back filled with gold and pearls. He prays to God to supply only water for his ablutions, for he will not be swayed by wealth. En route to Mecca in another account, Ibrāhīm's companions complain that none of them have animals or supplies. He counsels them that strong faith and trust can turn even a tree into gold, and indeed all the nearby trees turn to gold. On a desert journey, Abū Turāb of Nakhshab's disciples experience thirst and want to purify themselves for ritual prayer. After the shaykh draws a line in the sand, a spring appears. In a related account by Abū 'l-ʿAbbās, the shaykh stomps the sand with his foot and causes water to bubble up. When a companion asks for a drinking vessel, the shaykh pounds the ground with his hand and extracts a crystal goblet. When Abū Turāb asked Abū 'l-ʿAbbās how his friends responded to such marvels from God, the shaykh replied that most were skeptical. Abū Turāb pronounced the skeptics unbelievers.[50]

Finally, some accounts combine the miraculous provision of sustenance with apparent mastery over the animal kingdom. The tale that follows provides a bridge to our next major theme. When Ibrāhīm ibn Adham was on a journey with other Sufis, the travelers came to a fortification that had an ample supply of firewood. That night as they ate bread, Ibrāhīm prayed. One dervish wished for some ritually pure meat to barbecue, so Ibrāhīm prayed for such a meal. Suddenly a lion dragged a wild ass before them and watched as they slaughtered and ate it.[51] (On a related theme, see Fig. 12.)

FIGURE 12. Abū 'l-Adyān walks on burning embers to prove to a group of Zoroastrians that fire exerts its force only by God's command rather than by its inherent nature, thereby converting his witnesses to Islam. Jāmī, *Nafaḥāt al-uns* (Ottoman, 1003/1595), ©The Trustees of the Chester Beatty Library, Dublin, T474:116a.

Mastery over Jinn and Beasts

An important subcategory of tales of marvels comprises stories in which God's power allows a prophet or Friend to command the allegiance and super-human capabilities of creatures of smokeless fire called jinn (from which the more common term *genie* derives). The royal prophet Solomon had the extraordinary ability of speaking the languages of the birds and of all other living beings. But he could also domesticate the sometimes rambunctious jinn, pressing them into service in raising his magnificent temple. Ibn ʿArabi indirectly associates one of his favorite shaykhas, Nūnā bint Fātima of Seville, with Solomon. Nūnā handled jinn who desired to enjoy her companionship publicly by reminding them of the words of the prophet Muhammad. When he exposed the wiles of a troublesome jinn, Muhammad said that he recalled the words of his brother prophet, Solomon, as he disciplined the jinn to build his temple, and thus kept the jinn in check.[52]

Among mythic beasts, none presents a greater apparent danger than the dragon. One winter's night, Ibrāhīm ibn Adham settled down for a long prayer vigil in the cave where he had lived for nine years. Come the dawn, he feared for his survival in the bitter cold, but he felt a fur pelt mysteriously giving warmth to his back. When he awoke after sleeping for several hours, he discovered to his horror that the warm skin was that of a dragon. As he prayed in fear, the beast nuzzled the dust before him and disappeared from the cave. In another story, someone of little faith asks Bāyazīd an impossible question about God to test him. Discerning the man's insincerity, the shaykh sends him off to a mountain cave to consult with a "friend" of his staying there. When the questioner discovers that the friend is a dragon, he is terrified and flees in such a panic that he soils his clothes and forgets his shoes. Repenting of his skepticism, the man returns to Bāyazīd. The shaykh observes that if confronting a mere creature, however awesome, so discombobulated the man, the man is surely in no condition to handle the answer to his original query about the Creator.[53]

Most stories featuring denizens of the animal kingdom, however, tell of encounters with less fearsome, if still potentially dangerous, creatures. Serpents are the light version of their scalier big brother, the dragon. One day a follower of Egyptian friend Ibn Abī Saʿd sees the shaykh giving a poisonous snake a drink from a cup. The shaykh asks the observer to say nothing about the event. Another common trope has an otherwise potentially deadly serpent sheltering or fanning a Friend of God by waving a stalk of narcissus in its mouth.[54] Countless stories enlist the cooperation of less dangerous, more docile creatures, especially birds and dogs.

Birds appear with noteworthy frequency in miracle stories. Qushayrī tells a story, from ʿUthmān ibn Abī 'l-Atīka, about a cohort sent to raid against the Byzantines. When a contingent that is supposed to rejoin the main group fails to reappear at the designated time and place, a soldier begins to write prayers in the dirt with his spear. Suddenly a bird lands on the spear and declares that the detachment is safe and will soon rejoin the main party. Asked to identify itself, the bird says that its task is to banish sadness from believers' hearts. Just as the bird has predicted, the detachment appears. In another story, as Samnūn preaches one day about love, a bird descends to his head, then to his hand and breast, before falling to the ground so hard that it dies on the spot. Such is the power of the shaykh's message; the bird functions as a metaphor of the lover fatally smitten. In another account, Sufyān ath-Thawrī spots a caged bird in the market, and, out of care for it, he purchases it and releases it. Thereafter, the bird visits Sufyān nightly and lights upon him as he prays. When the shaykh dies, the bird grieves as it perches on his coffin. After Sufyān is buried, the bird hurls itself at the tomb repeatedly until it dies. A voice explains that because the shaykh has shown kindness to a small creature, God will be merciful to him.[55]

Dogs run a close second to birds as featured characters, and occasionally dogs share the stage with birds. Maʿrūf al-Karkhī was once allowing a dog to eat its lunch out of his bowl, when his uncle passed by and wondered why Maʿrūf was not ashamed of such behavior. Maʿrūf explained that in fact shame had led him to share his food with the animal in the first place. At a gesture from the shaykh, a bird descended to his hand and raised its wings before its eyes, suggesting to Maʿrūf that all creation shared his shame. In another story, a dog approaches Bāyazīd one day as he walks along, and the shaykh lifts his cloak. The dog then explains that if he (the dog) is dry, the shaykh need not fear for his garment; if he is wet, a simple washing will solve the problem. Merely pulling his clothes away avails him nothing. The shaykh replies that his impurity is internal whereas the dog's is external, so perhaps if they join forces, they might both be purified entirely. But the dog spurns the suggestion, explaining that though everyone rejects him and he has been unable to store bones away, everyone honors the shaykh, who has a barrel of grain laid by. Chastened, Bāyazīd realizes that if he is not worthy to associate with such a dog, the company of God is surely far beyond him. In telling this story, ʿAttār points out how marvelous it is that a Friend of God can learn from the lowliest of creatures.[56]

Gazelles and donkeys also appear frequently, and often in desert settings. In one such story, as Abū Hafs preaches in the desert to a group of companions, a gazelle approaches and places its head on the shaykh's lap. The shaykh slaps his own face, and the animal flees as Abū Hafs recovers from ecstasy. Abū Hafs explains to his friends that he had wished for a sheep to slaughter for a meal to keep his companions around for the night, when the gazelle offered itself. Why, then, they ask, did he shout and slap himself and chase off the gift? He replies that getting one's passing wish fulfilled so easily is spiritually perilous, for it is equivalent to God's removing a human being from the divine power. In a number of other stories, donkeys die in the desert, just when their owners are most desperate for their services, and are then resurrected. For example, Rābiʿa's beast of burden expires suddenly as she travels toward Mecca. Her companions offer to haul her meager belongings for her, but she waves them on, insisting that she needs to trust in God. She asks God why he, a king, is so harsh to a woman with so few resources. After all, God called her on this pilgrimage. The donkey immediately rises, and she continues the journey. ʿAttār notes that his source reported seeing the beast later for sale in the market.[57]

MARVELS OF KNOWLEDGE

An important type of saintly marvel is the mysterious, if not always superficially spectacular, feat that requires access to arcane knowledge. The various regional hagiographical traditions place varying emphasis on such feats, with a noticeably greater preference for them in North African sources, for example. Stories of these marvels often link lofty knowledge with clairvoyance and sometimes with the ability to travel instantly across great distances.

Clairvoyance and Long-Distance Connections

Clairvoyance is a significant theme in the story genre dealing with *faḍāʾil*, virtues or excellent qualities, of the Companions of the Prophet. Even so sober an author on the spiritual life as Abū Tālib al-Makkī, who talks relatively little about miracles, is not the least bit reticent to discuss numerous examples of clairvoyance among the various forms of special knowledge. Ghazālī, also rather cautious and not prone to tossing out miracle stories recklessly, tells the following famous story (from the hadith originally) about the second caliph. ʿUmar becomes miraculously aware of a faraway problem. Commanding a Muslim army, the general Sāriya is about to be overwhelmed. At that moment, ʿUmar, leading the people in prayer back in Medina, shouts, "Sāriya, the mountain, the mountain" (i.e., keep the mountain at your back). A messenger later returns from the engagement and reports that the troops had mysteriously heard a voice shouting that warning to them.[58]

Shāfiʿī, an eponymous founder of one of the four principal Sunnī law schools and one of Egypt's most popular Friends of God, was celebrated for his gifts of clairvoyance. He reportedly apprised some of his students of the fate that awaited each after death. Another early Egyptian Friend, Abū ʿAbd Allāh al-Qurashī, announced that Egypt would soon suffer a devastating epidemic, warning his followers to escape with their lives. As chapter 1 suggests, even unborn Friends have been credited with miraculous forms of knowledge. For example, Sīdī ʿAdīy ibn Musāfir was born under unusual circumstances: his father dreamt that if he returned to his wife after thirty years of wandering, the couple would conceive a special child. During his wife's seventh month, two men came by while she was drawing water. One told the other to pay his respects to the unborn Friend in her womb, and both saluted the saintly fetus. Seven years later, the same two men happened by when the child was out playing. The boy returned their greeting not once but twice, explaining that he owed them one for the time they greeted him when he was still in utero and unable to respond appropriately.[59]

Clairvoyance often figures prominently when skeptics try to get the better of a Friend or harbor secret negative thoughts about him. A Maghribī saint named Abū Yaʿazzā once received a visit from a man suspicious of the shaykh's reputed miraculous powers. After the man had stayed for the traditional three days' hospitality, he asked to take his leave, but the shaykh insisted that he stay. When the man left, the shaykh had people pursue him, for he knew the visitor would soon encounter a snake at a certain place. By the time the emissaries found the man, a snake had indeed coiled around him, and they used the shaykh's staff to free him from the serpent. The doubter then returned to Abū Yaʿazzā and admitted that God must indeed confer unusual abilities on certain people.[60]

Abū Isḥāq Ibrāhīm of Herat once expressed surprise at an excellent meal being served to Bāyazīd. Reading Ibrāhīm's hypercritical thoughts, Bāyazīd miraculously opened a wall to reveal a vast ocean and invited Ibrāhīm to plunge in with him. Ibrāhīm balked because he feared he was not ready for such an advanced mystical state. Bāyazīd explained that the bread Ibrāhīm had been eating before he arrived was made of grain chewed and spat out by grazing animals. He made this comment to underscore Ibrāhīm's lack of knowledge. Shocked by this disclosure, Ibrāhīm sought forgiveness for his critical, petty thoughts.[61]

People in need often seek help from Friends who are famous for knowing the thoughts of others or being mysteriously aware of events occurring at a great distance. A mother once besought Junayd to pray for the return of her missing son. Several times, the woman went off to wait patiently as the shaykh instructed, but at length she reported to Junayd that she could wait no longer. Junayd told her that her son had already come back, and when the mother returned home, she found her son there. Another account reports that Junayd knew through clairvoyance that some of his followers envied his favor for a certain disciple. He instructed that twenty students each to take a bird to a place beyond anyone's view, kill it, and return. All but the favored disciple brought back a dead bird. Questioned about his failure to act, the disciple explained that he could not find a place where God could not see him. Junayd thus showed his jealous students the injustice of their envy.[62]

While walking through a desert, Abū 'l-ʿAbbās al-Gharīb once encountered a group that sought a blessing from him. When he obliged, they offered to replace his rags with a new garment, but he ran to town without accepting their gift. Sadafī, the narrator of the tale, reports that when he met Gharīb after this event, he bought a cotton robe at the shaykh's request. Gharīb exclaimed that God had rescued him from temptation and promised to explain later. After two days, the people from the desert encounter showed up with a complete outfit of clothing, but Gharīb instructed them to give the gift to someone truly in need. Shortly thereafter, Sadafī reports, he discovered that the people had stolen the clothes after attacking a man. Sadafī follows up with a second story about clothing and clairvoyance. Gharīb sends a messenger to tell one of his disciples to bring a garment to the disciple's father, who will be in a garden. The student does as he is told and finds that his father has been shipwrecked and washed ashore naked. When the beneficiaries of Gharīb's clairvoyance asked about the source of his knowledge, the shaykh attributes it to a "passing thought" (*khatra*). Sadafī recounts another set of tales about Gharīb's clairvoyance, this time on the subject of books. In one of these stories, a disciple who is on his way to sell some of the shaykh's books and give the money to the poor is ambushed by bandits intent on carrying off as many books as they can. Though all the books together weigh well under each robber's capacity, they become heavier than iron and lead whenever the bandits attempt to hoist them. Thus, in the end, the disciple is able to accomplish his good work and aid the poor.[63]

One of Ibn ʿArabī's shaykhs, ʿAbd Allāh al-Mawrūrī, had the power to summon persons from a great distance without actual contact. Once a shaykha of Ibn ʿArabī's named Shams mentioned to Mawrūrī that she would like a certain Abū 'l-Hasan ibn Qaytūn to come by. She instructed Mawrūrī to write and invite him. But Mawrūrī insisted that he could contact Abū 'l-Hasan spiritually and deliver him by the next day. The next day came, and no visitor appeared. Mawrūrī said that he had had a lapse in concentration and would fix the problem. By noon that day, the visitor arrived. Abū 'l-Hasan explained that he had heard a voice instructing him to visit Shams in Marchena and had immediately cancelled Qurʾān class for the next day. But on the morrow, he no longer had the desire to make the visit, which was the moment Mawrūrī became absentminded. When the students came to school—that is, after the teacher had changed his plans—the teacher again heard the voice, at which point Mawrūrī had regained his concentration. Shams had a similar power. When Ibn ʿArabī and Mawrūrī were visiting her, she suddenly called out, "ʿAlī, go back and retrieve the kerchief." When her guests inquired about this strange outburst, she explained that, on his way to visit her, ʿAlī had taken a break for lunch and had left a kerchief behind.[64]

Some acts of clairvoyance occur during attacks on Muslims by Christians, typically in the Iberian peninsula. According to Ibn ʿArabī, Abū Jaʿfar al-ʿUryanī one day predicted that his caravan would run afoul of Christian brigands the next day. When he proved prescient indeed, his captors extended him respect and agreed to let him be ransomed for five hundred gold pieces, setting him free in advance of the payment. He later insisted that his captors solicit the ransom money from as many people as possible, rather than from only two or three of the wealthiest, arguing that his liberation should reflect positively on the whole community.[65]

Knowledge and the Gift of Instantaneous Travel

Another prominent type of marvel story that relies on Friends' privileged access to knowledge and the wellsprings of power features the miraculous ability to traverse great distances instantaneously. Chapter 3's story about the magical tunnel from Java to Mecca is a good example of the collapsing of space and time that traditional sources call "folding the earth." I include these tales in this chapter not only because special knowledge is so often the factor that makes marvelous travel possible but because increased knowledge often results as well.

In one story, Ibn ʿArabī is performing the evening ritual prayer at home in Seville and has a longing to visit with the great Moroccan Friend Abū Madyan, who lives more than a six weeks' journey away in North Africa. As he finishes praying, a companion of Abū Madyan, Mūsā Abū ʿImrān as-Sadrānī, suddenly appears and tells Ibn ʿArabī that he has just been praying with Abū Madyan and that the shaykh sends him a message: the two are not destined to meet in this life, but God's mercy brings security for both. Then the visitor disappears and returns to Bugia on the North African coast (in present-day Algeria).[66] Maghribī saint Mūsā Abū ʿImrān reportedly traveled as far as the mystic clime of Mount Qāf, the distant mountain range encircling the earth. Though the distance to the mountain's summit was a three-hundred-year journey, Mūsā prayed the late morning prayer at its base and the late afternoon prayer at the summit. When he spoke to the serpent that surrounded the mountain (grasping its tail in its mouth), the creature asked about Mūsā's shaykh, Abū Madyan. When Mūsā asked how the serpent knew of Abū Madyan, it expressed its surprise, for all of creation knew and loved that Friend.[67]

Ibn al-Hakīm al-Kahhāl of Tunis used to signal the time for the call to prayer by coughing softly. One night, however, the assembled crowd waited long for the authoritative cough. Meanwhile, a mosque attendant who was in the courtyard felt something hit him from above: the preacher had fallen from the sky and gone swiftly into the mosque to deliver the belated cough. Ibn al-Hakīm cautioned the attendant to keep quiet about the story he was about to tell him: he had been circumambulating the Kaʿba in far-distant Mecca when the time for prayer came, and he had to complete the ritual in Mecca before returning.[68] Many important Friends of God cited for such gifts cautioned their followers not to be too impressed by such powers. Even Satan can travel to Mecca and back in the twinkling of an eye. The dawning of faith in the heart is a far more important marvel.

EPILOGUE: MORE MARVELOUS THAN THOU

Not only the bad guys suffer the negative consequences of a Friend's wondrous gifts. A curious and entertaining theme in hagiographical accounts of marvels is the often unseemly competition among Friends to work the most spectacular wonder. Sources use the term *munāqara* (quarrel or contest) to describe stories in which one Friend puts another to a test, forcing the other to prove his authenticity. In one such story, Shiblī hurls another Friend into the Tigris, saying that if the man is sincere, he will, like Moses, emerge unhurt; otherwise, like Pharaoh, he has no hope. Sometimes the contest is a more forthright competition in wonder-working skills. Some stories are relatively simple in plot, as when rival Friend Mahmūd Hayrān shows up mounted on a lion, and Hajjī Bektāsh upstages him by speeding about astride a stone wall. Others are a bit more complex. One story tells of a North African Friend who visits another riding on a lion. His host tells him to quarter his mount in the stable with his cow. Entering the house, the visitor discovers that the host is being entertained by a bevy of dancing girls. On the following day, he discovers to his horror that the cow has eaten his lion. In another tale, told by ʿAttār, Hasan throws his carpet on the river and invites Rābiʿa to pray with him on it. She then throws her carpet into the air, chiding him for wanting to pray where people can see him. Better to go where prayer is beyond human gaze, she announces, and in any case, the real point of prayer is to do what neither fish nor fly can do.[69] The purpose of these curious tales is arguably to question whether the power of marvels is truly a positive gift or perhaps a stumbling block, even for the greatest of God's Friends.

The temptation to misuse power, hinted at indirectly in tales about the contest of marvels, is a fine reminder of the simple humanity of God's Friends. Chapter 5 explores further implications of the human condition shared even by people on the most intimate terms with God.

FIGURE 13.   Hallāj (d. 309/922) stands on the gallows as executioners prepare to cut off his hands. Various famous Sufis among the observers are identified by names on turbans (including Shiblī, Ibn ʿAtāʾ, and Junayd [who actually predeceased Hallāj]). Jāmī, *Nafaḥāt al-uns* (Ottoman, 1003/1595), ©The Trustees of the Chester Beatty Library, Dublin, T474:79r.

5.   Mere Mortals

Friends and the Human Condition

Islamic traditions about prophets and saints are replete with stories that showcase the individual's extraordinary attributes and abilities. These traditions also include abundant reminders of the frail, flawed creaturely status of even the most exalted of God's messengers and Friends. As previous chapters have hinted, Friends have often been involved in the sufferings and needs of other people as intercessory advocates. But Friends of God can be just as needy as the people who look to them for strength and guidance. Only human after all, prophets and saints occasionally rouse the divine pique, sometimes model less-than-exemplary relational habits, give sporadic hints of susceptibility to diabolical innuendo, and, with a couple of notable exceptions, they die. Islamic hagiographers have dealt with the foibles and faults of God's favorite people through a variety of common themes.

WHEN GOD CHIDES PROPHETS AND FRIENDS

Even the noblest of God's creatures walk on feet of clay. As we shall see in greater detail later, Muslim authors have sometimes debated the degree to which prophets are immune to sinful tendencies and the wiles of Satan. In any case, traditional sources supply many accounts in which the greatest of the great fall short of perfection. Moses murdered an Egyptian in anger, intending to defend a Hebrew. Had the man worshiped the true deity, God would have punished Moses severely. David succumbed to the "bird of temptation" when it appeared in his window and drew his attention to Uriah's wife, Bathsheba. His dalliance with her merited the divine displeasure. Solomon temporarily lost all his powers and kingdom, when one of the rebellious demonlike creatures, Sakhr, disguised himself as the king. Solomon entrusted the seal ring to his handmaiden, but the impostor fooled her and took the ring, and for a time the jinn ruled his realm.[1] The role of such diabolical temptation in the lives of both prophets and Friends is a major theme in the traditional accounts.

Satan and the Prophets

Chapter 2 alludes briefly to the barriers on the path between God and his elect, his prophets and Friends. Here we revisit the theme, looking at the "mere" humanity of these paragons of the spiritual and moral life. Kisāʾī cites a saying of Ibn ʿAbbās that prophets are too exalted for the devil to be allowed to put them to the test in a direct confrontation. But the majority opinion seems to be that most of the prophets have nevertheless had to deal with the devil's disruptive skullduggery and pervasive negative influences.[2] Adam is arguably the most prominent example of a prophet who confronts Iblīs's temptations directly and personally.[3] In general, the devil insinuates himself into the affairs of prophets more obliquely than he does with Adam. Iblīs manages, for example, to sneak onto Noah's ark by hanging on to a donkey's tail, and he commandeers the helm for a time. God allowed the devil free reign over Job's body but not over his soul.[4]

When the devious king Nimrod was looking for a way to get Abraham into a roaring fire, Iblīs, disguised as an old man, counseled the king's minions to use a catapult. Then angels held down the machine and prevented it from working. But Iblīs again intervened, advising Nimrod's people that they could drive the angels away by having ten naked women dance before them. In his lengthy section on Adam and his sons Cain and Abel, Thaʿlabī describes the role of the tempter in great detail, and even looks into the prophetic "future" of "those to whom Iblīs appeared." Major figures include Pharaoh, Solomon, and John the Baptist. Thaʿlabī, however, has Satan play a much more active role in the episode of Abraham's intended sacrifice of his son than he appears to play in attempts to undermine other prophets.[5]

Someone once asked Rūmī why Satan did not shrink from trying to tempt Muhammad but ran in a panic from the very shadow of the Prophet's Companion ʿUmar. Rūmī replied that Muhammad was a vast sea, whereas ʿUmar was merely a cupful of water: the ocean does not need protection from a dog, for a dog poses no threat to it. But because a dog can do great damage to a cup of water and pollute it with its tongue, one needs to protect the cup.[6]

Putting God's Friends to the Test

In contrast to his experiences with the prophets, Iblīs enjoys relatively unfettered access to God's Friends, and he seizes every opportunity to exploit their human weaknesses. Many Muslim authors have addressed the problem of human susceptibility to Satan's guiles. Few have addressed the topic so exhaustively as Ibn al-Jawzī does in *The Devil's Deception (Talbīs Iblīs)*. The noted Baghdadi preacher is also the author of a less famous work on story-telling in which he points out the dangers in popular traditions of oral hagiography.[7] In his overview of the disastrous successes of Satan in the history of humankind, Ibn al-Jawzī documents in narrative profusion the stratagems the devil has employed against rank unbelievers of various kinds as well as against Jews and Christians. He then turns his attention to several groups within the Muslim community, assembling dozens of examples of Satan's ability to dupe even ascetics, devotees, and Sufis in particular. Iblīs scores his most devastating blows by convincing sincere ascetics that extreme behavior is the way to go, when in fact avoiding lawful behavior and abandoning society are an abdication of one's fundamental ethical responsibility to set a Prophet-inspired example for the public.

Ibn al-Jawzī argues that Friends of God are particularly vulnerable to the hypocrisy of renunciation for the sake of display. Those who take advantage of their ability to perform saintly marvels are an especially large target for Ibn al-Jawzī, for their behavior represents the nadir of hypocrisy. Marvels worked for the purpose of drawing attention to a Friend of God are manifestly not of divine origin but a triumph for the devil. Satan "has led many a weak devotee astray by showing him something resembling a miracle wrought in his honour, in consequence of which the man has claimed prophethood." Ibn al-Jawzī does not by any means write off all Friends of God as deluded charlatans. He does, however, take a very narrow view of the ingredients of authentic saintly demeanor and cautions that the very characteristics many people identify as the hallmarks of sanctity are in fact carefully crafted diabolical ruses.[8]

God's closest Friends have met their match and found cause for repentance in a variety of other circumstances as well. Stories sometimes depict the holy person as potential prey to the same enticements that pose a spiritual threat to all ordinary mortals. Among the more frequently described temptations are dealings with women and looking at attractive individuals. For example, Abū ʿAlī Hasan the Tanner, from Seville, belonged to a much-maligned socioeconomic class. In the popular vernacular, the technical term for "tanner" (*shakkāz*) carried the meaning of "sissy," referring to men who were as soft as the animal skins they cured. One day as Hasan spread materials to dry by the river, a local woman decided to taunt him. She greeted him, and he replied appropriately, interrupting his state of recollection. When she pressed him to divulge his occupation, hoping he would disgrace himself by uttering the "sh-word" (i.e., *shakkāz*), he cleverly responded with a series of circumlocutions.⁹

In one account, Abū ʿAbd Allāh ibn al-Jallāʾ looks intently at a handsome young Christian man and is transfixed by his beauty. Just then, Junayd happens by, and Abū ʿAbd Allāh asks him whether such a handsome individual is destined for hell. Junayd replies that the questioner has clearly been gazing with inappropriate intent and has been snookered by the devil. Abū ʿAbd Allāh should rather have seen signs of the divine creativity in that person. Shortly thereafter, Abū ʿAbd Allāh suffers the punishment of forgetting the Qurʾān, and not until years later does his repentance merit his recovery of the sacred word in memory. He stops viewing created beings as "mere objects."¹⁰

HOLINESS AND ORDINARINESS

Friends of God share so many of the frailties and failings of the general run of humankind that they remain, paradoxically, rather ordinary even in the face of their uniquely favored relationships with God. The hagiographers accounted for this intriguing combination by spinning stories with which many of their readers and listeners could identify.

Friends Forgiven: When the Great Ones Falter

In his manual of spirituality, Kalābādhī makes important observations about the possibility and actuality of sin and the need for forgiveness in prophets and Friends of God. He begins, as usual, by referring to prophets and to Muhammad's Companions as touchstones of sanctity. Prophets are kept safe from "major sins," and, according to some, from lesser sins as well. Friends of God, in contrast, are not so protected, but they find repentance easier than other people when they do fall into sin. Friends are altogether human in that they enjoy all the natural pleasures of eating, sleeping, and religiously legitimate sexual life; but when they lose their balance, they more readily than other people seek to regain it by renewing their total reliance on God.

Muhammad's observation that ten of his Companions would be among the inhabitants of paradise did not exempt those paragons of virtue from the persistent fear that they might sin against God. Kalābādhī is quick to note, however, that the Companions were less fearful of the prospect of punishment than of shortcomings in the awe and solemnity they experience in God's presence. By avoiding major sins, the Companions were virtually assured of forgiveness for their minor sins. If a Companion lapsed into major sin, the gift of swift repentance was his. Friends of God likewise were made aware of their future place in paradise, but they know their fate through the inward message that God discloses to their hearts. As with the Companions, such knowledge in no way exempts Friends from a keen sense of their sinful proclivities and the all-too-human possibility of offense against God. Yūsuf ibn al-Husayn asked God to consider his attentiveness to the needs of others as compensation for his lapses into ego-centeredness. Abū Hafs likewise asked forgiveness for all his faults, acknowledging that one can come before God only in awareness of absolute poverty. Friends feel the need to repent for wayward thoughts perhaps more often than they do for more obvious misdeeds. Bāyazīd remembered a day when he entertained the notion that he must surely be the spiritual paragon of his time. As he realized his arrogance, he headed down the road and stopped in a residence, vowing to wait there for a divine messenger who might restore him to true self-awareness. On the fourth day, a one-eyed camel rider who had traveled from afar approached. When the rider came to a stop, he asked whether Bāyazīd had made him come all this way to open his blind eye and shut the sighted one and "drown the citizens of Bistām [Bāyazīd's home] with him." The Friend was stunned as the visitor warned him to be vigilant over his heart and then departed.[11]

Even with these lapses, the conviction that Friends of God are not entirely at fault for apparent sinfulness remains a recurrent theme, as in a tale that ʿAttār tells about Tirmidhī. A comely maiden offers herself to the Friend, but he rebuffs her advance. Not to be rejected, the woman later hears that Tirmidhī is resting in a nearby garden and resolves to seduce him. The Friend runs from her and vaults over the garden wall as she shouts that he is actually after her. Years later, the aged Tirmidhī thinks back on his long life and recalls that day. He muses wistfully that he might as well have satisfied the woman's urgent desires and asked forgiveness later. Suddenly he realizes the sinfulness of his second thoughts and berates his ego-soul for regretting a missed opportunity to sin. After mourning his lapse for three days, Tirmidhī dreams that the Prophet consoles him and assures him that he is not entirely at fault. The Prophet tells the Friend that his apparent backsliding resulted instead from the passage of another forty years since Muhammad's departure from the earth. With the waning of the Prophet's spiritual presence, even the greatest Friends can expect to see their commitment diminish.[12]

The Perils of Domesticity: Family Lives of Friends

One oft-mentioned source of soul-threatening distraction is family life, with accounts typically focusing on problems posed by wives and children. The resulting picture will strike many readers as far less life affirming than one might expect. Certainly, on balance, hagiographical accounts list heavily toward disapproval of domestic life and marital sexuality.

Stories of God's Friends run hot and cold on the subject of human companionship generally, and on marriage and family life in particular. On the one hand, Muhammad recommended marriage and extolled the companionship of a good woman. In addition, various proverbs warn against solitude, for the devil can more easily have his way with lonely souls. Those who avoid marriage therefore miss a chance to act on the example of Muhammad and risk sinning as a result of unanswered lust. On the other hand, stories of Friends often emphasize that one must concentrate solely on one's relationship with God. Those who marry risk losing that concentration and can scarcely avoid leading the body astray with legitimate sensual delights. Some sources cite a saying, which they attribute to the Prophet, that a time will come when spiritual values will be so hard to find that those who have neither wife nor offspring will be the most spiritually nimble and adaptable to difficulties. According to the hagiographical literature, more than a few spouses maintained nonsexual relationships throughout their lives together.

Various authorities on the Sufi Path recommend celibacy. But some argue that one ought to strive to favor neither marriage nor celibacy, allowing God's preference to become apparent. Those who are led to celibacy ought to emulate the prophet Joseph, who declined to satisfy his lust with Zulaykhā (the wife of Pharaoh's minister). Married men should take Abraham as their model, for his trust in God was such that he surrendered his wife Sarah entirely to God. When Sarah expressed jealousy of his slave girl, Hagar, Abraham deposited Hagar in God's care in the desert (here the emphasis is on Abraham's perfect trust, not on his apparent willingness to dispose of a wife). Sarrāj notes, however, that this situation should be the exception. One ought to follow Abraham's example strictly only if one's wife and offspring share the father's level of spiritual attainment.[13] In the end, married persons need to maintain their devotions assiduously while seeing always to a wife's needs and expenses. For celibates, the key is to be ever vigilant against straying thoughts and eyes and to refuse to accept Satan's blandishments as an excuse for backsliding.[14]

Some Friends have left first-person accounts of their marital experiences. Eighteenth-century Sufi Ahmad ibn ʿAjība includes a prominent chapter in his "autobiography" entitled "Regarding Women We Have Married and the Children That Have Resulted from These Marriages." Ibn ʿAjība begins with the customary citation of Qurʾān and hadith, emphasizing the Prophet's preference for marriage, even though he was the "master of renunciants." He even recommends concubines for men who are not married, as a protection against the devil's enticements. But a more important purpose for marriage than assuaging lust lawfully is the hope of bearing and raising a "virtuous child." One ought not to seek social status or wealth through marriage but should marry a poor, humble woman, lest his partner's prestige become a cause of arrogance. Ibn ʿAjība goes into surprising detail in his mini marriage manual. Eventually, he returns to his own experience of marrying a total of six women, who bore him thirty-one children. He concludes the chapter by reflecting briefly on the fact that he has already suffered the deaths of twenty-two of those children. He takes consolation in Muhammad's saying that anyone who loses three preadolescent children will see them blocking the road to hell for him after his death.[15] Many of God's male Friends had families, and sources record a variety of stories about the often-difficult fate of their children and wives.

Betrothal stories are important in this context. A woman named Fātima invited Ahmad Khidrūya to ask for her hand in marriage, and the two shared a life of spiritual renunciation. In fact, Fātima enjoyed a more spiritually intimate relationship with her teacher Bāyazīd than did her husband. But even Bāyazīd once took inappropriate notice of her, and she announced that she could no longer remain in the company of the exalted shaykh. Later, after the couple had traveled to Nishapur, Yahyā ibn Muʿādh came to the city, and Ahmad asked Fātima to throw a party for him. She required not only the usual cattle and sheep but also twenty donkeys to feed to the dogs that had every right to attend when a shaykh of Yahyā's stature was in town. Bāyazīd apparently made an observation that partially explains why the sources give Fātima such coverage: anyone looking for a man in woman's clothing need only meet Fātima![16] Such backhanded compliments of women are not unusual in hagiographical lore.

A more conventional element of tension in the process of matchmaking is the father's disapproval of a daughter's most likely prospects. Shāh Shujāʿ of Kerman rejected a local ruler's request to marry his remarkable daughter, deciding instead to look for a poor dervish in search of a spouse. He was convinced that his daughter's ability to recite Qurʾān would surely make her more attractive to such a suitor. He found a man who could afford a dowry of only three silver dirhams and made the arrangements. When the young woman entered the dervish's house, she asked the man why a scrap of stale bread was sitting on the water bottle. He explained that it remained from the previous night and that he had saved it. Suddenly she announced that she would leave him, explaining that he clearly did not trust God enough, holding on to the crust that way. The dervish asked her what he could do to change her mind, and she told him he had his choice: her or the crust. ʿAttār does not reveal the suitor's response to the dilemma.[17]

A more common conflict arises from the perceived incompatibility between love for God and attachment to God's creatures. One day when Fudayl ibn ʿIyād showed particular affection for his little boy, the toddler asked whether his father loved him. Fudayl confirmed that he did, and the boy inquired whether his father also loved God. When Fudayl affirmed that he loved God as well, the precocious tot asked how he could love two beings if he had only one heart. Fudayl complemented the child on his effective preaching but then ceased lavishing his attention on him. Fudayl later prayed that a malady of the child's urinary tract be healed, and his prayer was swiftly answered. But when the boy died, Fudayl smiled, explaining that because God was pleased to take the boy to himself, Fudayl could only concur. He also had two daughters, and when his death approached, Fudayl told his wife to take the children to a high mountain. She was to ask God to take care of them now that Fudayl no longer could. After Fudayl's funeral, his wife honored his wishes, and as she prayed, a wealthy ruler with two sons happened by and arranged on the spot for a splendid double marriage.[18]

Children can pose problems for their saintly parents. In some instances, God helps out by removing the obstacle. Samnūn had a daughter to whom he was quite attached. On her third birthday, he dreamed of an assembled throng at the Resurrection and asked who owned a light-emitting banner he saw there. When he learned that it belonged to people who love God and whom God loves, he decided that he belonged with them. Alas, the feeling was not mutual. They rejected him, explaining that he was clearly too devoted to his daughter to join their company. Though he was called "the Lover," they said, he no longer lived up to the name. Still asleep, Samnūn asked God to remove all obstacles from his path to God. When he awoke, he heard that his child had died in a fall from the roof of the house.[19] Abū 'l-ʿAbbās al-Fāʾida had seven children, but because his poverty made life very difficult, he asked God to unburden him of the children. All seven died before the next month had passed, and life became less straitened for the couple.[20]

Sarrāj offers a theological explanation for the prevalence of this apparently sad state of affairs in the lives of so many Friends. He recounts an anecdote in which God reproves Fath al-Mawsilī for showering affection on his son and perhaps diluting the father's love of God. In his commentary on the story, Sarrāj points out that Muhammad could express tenderness for his children only because of his extraordinary spiritual status. God had no need to be jealous of the Prophet's affections, whereas lesser individuals give God cause for concern when they turn their attention elsewhere.[21]

Some Friends confess—even boast—that they contracted marriage and fathered children by reflex. Abū ʿAlāʾ al-Kindī made clear that his three children were the result of only three sexual contacts with women. One was "for the sake of God," responding to the Qurʾān's injunction to marry; one was for the sake of the Prophet, who had enjoined Muslims to marry and reproduce so that the community would be a source of pride for him; and one was for his own sake, in response to the Prophet's saying that individuals leave only three legacies when they die: a charitable gift, knowledge that lives on in others, and a good child to pray for the deceased father.[22]

Occasionally, a story gives us a curious glimpse of overall "family dynamics." In one such story, ʿAbd Allāh ibn al-Mubārak's wife becomes angry with him because he regularly gives sustenance to the needy, so he divorces her. Soon thereafter, the daughter of a family of influence notices ʿAbd Allāh at one of his devotional sessions and asks her father to betroth her to the shaykh. He does so, offering a dowry of fifty thousand gold coins. ʿAbd Allāh later learns in a dream that because he earlier divorced out of love for God, God is now rewarding his commitment.[23]

One of the lengthier family narratives is that of Ibrāhīm ibn Adham. Sarrāj cites Ibrāhīm's observation that marriage is akin to setting out on a voyage and that having a child is certain to cause a shipwreck.[24] Ibrāhīm lived accordingly. In a major variant of his "conversion" story, he leaves his infant son behind in the palace; an important and intriguing Malay interpretation of the story softens some of the harsher aspects, reporting that only after Ibrāhīm left his wife did she learn that she was pregnant. The child's mother tells him that his father is gone but might be in Mecca. Thus begins the boy's quest for his father.

ʿAttār's sparsely detailed version of the tale reports that the youth embarked on pilgrimage at the head of a throng of four thousand. In Mecca, he encountered a poor old man whom he sensed must be his father. Ibrāhīm, for his part, spotted a young man whom he was sure must be his son. The boy remained noncommittal until one day Ibrāhīm sought out the caravan from Balkh and found his son there. Instead of approaching the boy, Ibrāhīm sent a companion to ask his identity. The boy admitted tearfully that he was the shaykh's son, and his mother, who was traveling with him, went with the lad to find Ibrāhīm. When father and son embraced, Ibrāhīm heard a voice warning that he could not love two. Even in the Malay version, Ibrāhīm sends his son away somewhat callously for fear that he will jeopardize his own relationship to God. ʿAttār observes, however, that this behavior is not so strange:

one need only consider Abraham's willingness to sacrifice his son. The Malay version dedicates the whole last section of the tale to the return journey of Ibrāhīm's son.[25]

Finally, the story of Ibn Khafīf provides a striking alternative narrative, turning many of the persistent family themes topsy-turvy. Most of God's Friends who married did not do so remarkably often. Ibn Khafīf was a notable exception. He began by asking for the daughter of a servant, but after she had a miscarriage, Ibn Khafīf gave the wife permission to seek a divorce. He had dreamed that Muhammad was surrounded by throngs of people drowning in their own perspiration. Then a little child led his father out of the crowd and across the bridge to the next world. As a result of the dream, he decided that since he now had a child who might do the same for him after his death, he was satisfied. Many women sought him out, and he eventually contracted four hundred marriages. Only one wife stayed a long time, and he never consummated any of the unions, evidently regarding them only as occasions for a higher exercise of self-denial.[26]

BENEATH THE SURFACE: FRIENDS, FEELINGS, AND RELIGIOUS EXPERIENCE

Expressions of saintly affect, as well as the responses of people in various relationships with Friends, often serve the larger ends of hagiographic development of images of God's Friends in all their flawed perfection. Relatively few scholarly studies delve explicitly into the affective life of God's Friends and their constituents. Hagiographical literature over the centuries has, nonetheless, given more than a little attention to various aspects of this crucial feature of the Friends' full humanity. Feelings offer important insight into Friends' relationships to other human beings, as well as to God. By contemporary standards, traditional accounts can seem quite stylized in dealing with matters of feeling. Even so, they help us see the great Friends as genuine individuals rather than as mere cardboard cutouts. These remarkable people are not simply gossamer embodiments of sanctity but individuals with distinctive personalities.

In many narrative accounts, authors link certain affective responses of Friends with faith, repentance, longing for God, fear, hope, and, ultimately, an elevated experience of the divine. Sufi theorists such as Sarrāj, Kalābādhī, Qushayrī, and Hujwīrī (to name only a few of the earlier major authors) have laid out intricate, subtle, and psychologically insightful models of spiritual growth. Many of the "stations" (*maqāmāt*) and "states" (*ahwāl*) they describe have an unmistakable affective component, and hagiographical narratives have a marvelous way of putting flesh on those theoretical bones. The emotive responses of Friends of God, and of their followers and acquaintances, often reflect these deeper spiritual conditions.[27]

Not surprisingly, the language of affect in hagiographical accounts is as beholden to metaphor as are poetic expressions of feeling. We can see such metaphor at work in the story of a seven-year-old boy who sits in the company of an elder Friend as the older man is fasting. He reports that as the elder meditates next to him, his own young heart is "saying Allāh." The older man promises that if the boy becomes his student, his heart will talk that way all the time.[28] One typically has to look beneath exclamations that, if taken literally, suggest a miraculous event to discover their authentic affective import. For example, a fairly common expression is that an "eyewitness" to the life of a Friend of God hears every hair on someone's head praising God. This expression invites the reader or listener to appreciate the intensity and extraordinary nature of the experience of ineffable holiness, rather than to take the words at face value. The same caveat applies in interpreting particularly striking descriptions of emotional responses by Friends of God and by the people to whom they relate.

Expressions of emotion are often quite subtle. Friends of God sometimes teach and instruct seekers with a simple smile that affirms a disciple's appropriate response to the master's tutelage. An enigmatic smile at the performance of a miraculous event, for example, may be all that a seeker needs to confirm that he or she has caught a critical insight. But the responses of the beneficiaries of a saintly marvel are also important. An effusive claim such as "I saw it with my own eyes!" communicates a significant affective message, suggesting a personal and immediate experience rather than mere intellectual assent to an abstract truth. In other words, high emotion and the sense that one is in the presence of a greater-than-human power go hand in glove. Just as people are frequently unable to describe precisely how they feel, so they cannot find adequate words to characterize a remarkable occurrence.

Tears and laughter are perhaps the most obvious expressions of emotion in hagiographical accounts. People who repent and experience conversion shed tears of compunction, of course. But Friends of God weep copiously for a host of other reasons, as do their followers. Pilgrims who first glimpse the Ka῾ba, preachers and their audiences who are deeply moved by a beautiful delivery, and mystics who arrive at a higher truth all receive the gift of consoling tears. Friends of God laugh at the absurdities of worldly attachments and at the follies of God's enemies, and often enough even laugh at themselves, but they usually do not laugh at the foibles of the well intentioned.

Intimately related to affectivity in general are attitudes and convictions about the human body. Pervasive renunciation of this world and a variety of ascetical practices that seek to subdue the "jackass of the body" play an important role in many hagiographical narratives. One might expect that the emphasis on self-denial would result in images of transparent, even disembodied characters. On the contrary, however much God's Friends might seem to cherish the Shakespearean wish that "this too solid flesh would melt," they appear before the reader's imagination clothed in the shared envelope of all humankind.[29] In the hagiographical literature, illnesses of every type come in for considerable and often detailed description and are interpreted variously as divine recompense, calls to repent, and occasions for the display of God's power through a Friend. Diverse conditions make the body a frequent venue and vehicle for marvelous works. Women's bodies can be reminders both of the dangers of temptation and of the divine beauty. Even men's bodies, in the instances of the prophets Joseph and Muhammad, can betoken the latter. Finally, as chapter 7 discusses further, the mortal remains of Friends of God continue to generate a full spectrum of emotion in devotees.[30]

CONFRONTATIONS WITH ILLNESS AND DEATH

With a few rare exceptions, all of God's earthly creatures suffer the ravages of finitude. All face the prospect of death and accountability for their lives in this world. This section offers stories about how great prophets and Friends have dealt with the harsh reality of mortality. We begin with stories of prophets, look briefly at the final days of major Shīʿī martyr-imams, and conclude with the deaths and obsequies of God's Friends.

Death and the Prophets

Stories of prophets' deaths are quite varied, with the great ones' final moments ranging from quiet and barely noticeable to fairly spectacular. Kisāʾī cites the following observation by Ibn ʿAbbās: "There was not a single prophet or apostle who did not hate the cup of death except our Prophet Muhammad, who said, 'How blessed is he who is reverted to my Lord and Paradise and the Sublime Place and the Prepared Cup.'" Four notable exceptions to ordinary mortality among the prophets are Idrīs, Khidr, Elijah, and Jesus. When Elijah completed God's work and appointed Elisha as his successor, God supplied the prophet with a steed that flew on flaming, multicolored wings. Elijah was free to ride the mount at will, for the prophet was now both an earthly human and a heavenly angelic being. In Islamic lore, Jesus was not crucified but was taken up to heaven alive after a look-alike took his place on the cross.[31] Numerous stories about the more convention-ally mortal prophets recount how they flinched, and even hedged their bets, at the prospect of death.

One of the more unusual narratives of a prophetic death is that of Abraham, who prayed that God would allow him to choose the moment of his demise. The angel of death entered the prophet's life disguised as a frail old man, playing on Abraham's fabled tendency to extend hospitality to all comers. Spotting the elder traveling toward him, Abraham provided a don-key to carry the man the remaining distance. When the prophet supplied food to the visitor, the old man tried unsuccessfully to put the food into his mouth, hitting his eye and ear instead. When at last he found his mouth, he instantly excreted the food. Abraham grew suspicious. He asked the man why he was having so much trouble eating, and the man responded that his problem was the result of his advanced years. But when Abraham ascertained the man's age, he realized he himself was only two years younger than the visitor. Abraham asked whether he too should expect to suffer such difficulties two years hence, and the man replied that he would indeed. The two-hundred-year-old Abraham immediately implored God to take him in advance of such suffering, and his visitor facilitated his request.[32] (See Fig. 14.)

Moses also was less than resigned to his mortality, and God contrived to change his attitude. He prompted Joshua to visit Moses morning and evening. During each visit, Moses asked what God was up to with Joshua. Moses thought that Joshua owed him an explanation, but the younger man refused to disclose God's ways with him. Eventually, Moses became so annoyed with Joshua's pes-tering that he began to wish for death. Before Moses's change of heart was complete, however, the Angel of Death appeared. Moses sent the angel pack-ing with a clout to the eye, and the angel complained to God. After God repaired the gouged eye, he sent the angel back to tell Moses how he might extend his life a bit. Moses should place his hand on a bull's back and count the hairs under the space of the hand: he would live that many more years. But Moses decided that waiting for a known interval would be intolerable, so he asked the angel to take him on the spot. After losing an eye to the irate prophet, the Angel of Death was understandably reluctant to approach people openly, and he ful-filled his task gingerly from then on. Another version of Moses's death takes a very different tack. One day when Moses steps aside to relieve himself, he spots a group of angels digging a particularly splendid grave. When he asks them for whom the grave is intended, they explains that it is for a favored ser-vant of God. Moses praises the beautiful resting place, and the angels ask Moses

FIGURE 14. Abraham, threatened but escaping death, is catapulted into the fire, as his nemesis King Nimrod, counseled by Iblīs, attempts unsuccessfully to do away with the prophet. Angels prepare to minister to Abraham by converting the fire to a pleasant garden. Page from unidentified manuscript, c. 1600, Turkey. Los Angeles County Museum of Art, The Edwin Binney, 3rd, Collection of Turkish Art at the Los Angeles County Museum of Art. M.85.237.35. Photo © 2005 Museum Associates/LACMA.

if he would like to be that favored servant. He would, Moses responds, and the angels instruct him to recline in the grave. There he takes his last breath and the angels bury him.[33]

Among the finest reflections on the deaths of Muhammad and his closest Companions are those by Abū Hāmid al-Ghazālī in the fortieth and final book of his masterwork of pastoral and mystical theology, *The Revitalization of the Religious Disciplines (Ihyā' ᶜulūm ad-dīn)*. Ghazālī begins the book *The Remembrance of Death and the Afterlife* by noting that God showed Muhammad no favoritism when the time of death arrived, even though the Prophet's body was "immaculate." Ghazālī insists that the simple mortality of so exalted a figure should give ample cause for reflection on one's personal accountability. He assembles reports about Muhammad's interactions with a variety of deathbed visitors. Amid tears shed by many, including by the Prophet himself, Muhammad conferred his final exhortations on his closest relatives and associates.

One extraordinarily dramatic moment occurs in an account by the Prophet's wife ᶜĀ'isha. Muhammad senses the presence of the Angel of Death, who has requested the Prophet's permission to enter, but the Prophet asks him to hold off until Gabriel has visited one last time. Gabriel and Muhammad converse about the Prophet's experience of impending death. Gabriel explains that the Angel of Death has never before asked permission to enter and that in spite of God's intense longing to welcome Muhammad, God has decided to honor the Prophet one more time in this extraordinary way. Gabriel then takes his leave, saying that his mission among humankind is now finished—a turn of events that makes this Prophetic demise unique.

As high lamentation overcomes those present at the moment of Muhammad's death, a mysterious figure appears at the door and admonishes the mourners to put all their trust in God. They stop grieving momentarily, but when the speaker vanishes, they resume. Another voice calls out with a similar message of divine consolation in loss. Abū Bakr then explains to those assembled that the unexpected visitors are the prophets Khidr and Ilyās. When they prepare to wash Muhammad's body, sleep overcomes the washers and a voice instructs them not to remove the Prophet's clothes as they ordinarily would with a body. As they wash the Prophet's body, his limbs move mysteriously, without any effort on their part, to make their job easier.[34]

Muhammad's Companions and the Shīᶜī Imams

Muhammad's Companions include his immediate successors to leadership of the young Muslim community. Stories of the deaths of the first "Rightly

Guided Caliphs," Abū Bakr and ʿUmar, are understandably briefer and much less spectacular than accounts of prophetic deaths. According to Ghazālī, when Abū Bakr's time came, his daughter ʿĀʾisha was again the principal interlocutor at the scene. The chief features of the account are his choice of ʿUmar as his successor, his exhortation to ʿUmar, a reflection on the last things, and his final prayer for divine mercy. ʿUmar's final hours commenced when an enemy stabbed him as he led the ritual prayer. ʿUmar knew the blow would be fatal. Mourners came praising his good fortune for having been a Companion of Muhammad. ʿUmar requested that all his debts be paid from his family funds. Again ʿĀʾisha plays a crucial role in the story. ʿUmar asks to be buried next to Abū Bakr and Muhammad, and ʿĀʾisha agrees to surrender to ʿUmar her hoped-for burial place there. After a brief exhortation to whomever would become his successor, ʿUmar dies. ʿAlī enters the scene and praises ʿUmar for the blessing of his having been an intimate friend of Abū Bakr and Muhammad.[35]

In addition to his role as the fourth Rightly Guided Caliph in Sunnī tradition, ʿAlī ranks as the first imam, spiritual successor to the Prophet, in Shīʿī tradition. His murder by partisans of his predecessor caliph, ʿUthmān, figures prominently in that tradition's history of redemptive suffering and martyrdom. ʿAlī reportedly encouraged his constituents to "go forward into battle and do not shrink away since there is no escape from death. Even if you are not killed, you will die. By God . . . a thousand sword blows on the head is easier than death in bed."[36] To be sure, the redemptive deaths of all the imams feature prominently in Shīʿī lore. But the most important story is that of Husayn, the "protomartyr." The following is a sketchy outline of the story. In the year 61/680, Yazīd ascended the throne as the second Umayyad caliph. In his concern to deal with restive elements in the realm, he resolved to dispense with ʿAlī's son Husayn and his small band of supporters unless they vowed allegiance to the throne. Husayn refused to cower in the face of vastly superior force and advanced to meet the royal foe at a place in south-central Iraq called Karbalāʾ. In an outright slaughter, Husayn's band of warriors, women, and children was virtually obliterated. Ancient sources recount this tale at length and in stunning detail, and it is still reenacted annually in "passion plays" (*taʿziya*) in Twelver Shīʿī communities, especially in the Middle East and South Asia. Observance of Husayn's martyrdom occurs at the beginning of the first lunar month, Muharram, and culminates on ʿĀshūrāʾ, the tenth of the month.[37] Martyrs are part of the broader community of God's Friends. None of their stories, however, have either merited as much narrative attention or assumed the communal centrality of the Shīʿī story of Husayn.

The Mortality of God's Friends

Ghazālī includes important sections on the sayings of famous holy people as they approached death or attended the funerals of others. At the end of the first section, he notes that his subjects' words as they faced their own deaths "differed only in accordance with the discrepancy between the states of those that pronounced them. For some men are dominated by fear, others by hope and still others by love and yearning; each man speaks in accordance with his state, and all of them, within the context of their states, are correct."[38] In other words, one can learn from observing how someone faces mortality, as long as one is aware of disparity in their inward conditions. Ghazālī follows that section with observations that underscore the teaching value of funerals, especially comments by some major Friends of God. Let their comments, he advises, teach the reader the appropriate response to the certainty of death.[39]

Relatively few hagiographical anthologies include accounts of the deaths of God's Friends. This omission is in part because of the brevity of many accounts in the works of authors like Qushayrī and Hujwīrī. These writers are, not surprisingly, primarily interested in offering a smattering of each Friend's words and deeds in the short space available in their chosen literary form: manuals of spirituality with only a brief hagiographical component. Works like those of Abū Nuʿaym al-Isfahānī, ʿAttār, and Jāmī—which seek to tell complete life stories—are more likely to encompass accounts of Friends' deaths. Qushayrī is one of several authors of theoretical treatises who devotes a significant separate chapter to stories of saintly deaths. Kalābādhī has a chapter entitled "God's graces granted during and after dying" but curiously mentions prominently the deaths of only one anonymous figure and another little-known character among Muhammad's Followers (second-generation Muslims). In both cases, the focus is on actions by the corpse during preparations for burial.[40] Among the narratives of the final hours of important Friends, the following offer a good sample of the themes and concerns arising from their holy deaths.

Friends sometimes die in peculiar circumstances and from mysterious causes. Nūrī's sudden death was reportedly precipitated by a curious encounter with a blind man who repeatedly called the name of God. Nūrī cautioned the man that genuine knowledge of God would kill him. At that point, Nūrī became disoriented, wandered into a field of sugarcane, and sustained countless wounds while whirling about. As Nūrī bled to death, the people who had come to take him home saw the name of God in each drop of the blood that he shed.[41] Abū Turāb of Nakhshab died alone in a remote place in southern Iraq, and years passed before travelers discovered his body. There he stood, quite intact and unmolested by predators, holding his walking stick, and facing in the direction of Mecca. On the ground in front of him was a water bag.[42]

Important hagiographical accounts of the mystical poet Ibn al-Fārid describe the Friend's departure from this life in some detail. One describes the poetic ecstasy that immediately preceded his demise. In that account, the saint's nephew ʿAlī draws a parallel between physical and mystical death. Ibn al-Fārid one day passes a fuller who is shredding a piece of cloth and knows instantly that he must overcome his ego if he is to die well. The author of a more extended narrative reports that he was moved by an apparition to travel from Iraq to Egypt, where Ibn al-Fārid was in his final hours. The dying man hailed the visitor as one of the Friends, for Ibn al-Fārid had asked God to send saintly mourners for his obsequies. In his narrative, the visitor says that Ibn al-Fārid's color changed as he received a vision of heaven. Enjoining his visitor to attend his grave for three days, the saint died smiling. After the burial, the visitor had a vision in which Muhammad, the other prophets, and all the angels and Friends joined him in prayer for Ibn al-Fārid.[43]

A key account of the death of Chalabī Amīr ʿĀrif, one of Rūmī's grandsons, shows several special features. Chalabī began to feel ill on a Friday and visited his father's tomb. After praying and reciting poetry, he lay down on the spot within the mausoleum where he would be buried. For twenty-five days, his illness progressed, and at the end, the earth quaked for three days. After he died, the mourners discovered that his coffin was so short that Chalabī's feet would not fit. As the mourners fell into great wailing, his legs miraculously shrank to the point that the attendants could close the coffin.[44]

The most extended account of unusual circumstances, which comprises many smaller reports and observations, is that of the martyr Hallāj. As Hallāj's executioners engaged in their grim task, his servant and his son asked for a word of final advice. He cautioned them to distract the ego-soul and to occupy themselves totally with knowledge of the ultimate truth. As he went to his gallows, he danced in his chains, for he knew his liberation was at hand. Again his disciples asked for a final word. He shocked them by castigating those preoccupied with his goodness, saying that his persecutors would enjoy double the reward, for they acted out of a unity rooted in the law. With each cruel act in the protracted execution, ʿAttar reports a new exchange between Hallāj and the assembled followers. He explains, for example, that with the blood of his amputated hands, the martyr performed ablutions for his final ritual prayer. As his executioners were about to cut out his tongue, Hallāj asked for a moment to speak his last, and he prayed that his torturers be forgiven. Every one of his severed limbs shouted his union with God, and after he was cremated, so did the ashes as they were poured into the Tigris.[45]

Stories of Friends' final hours often underscore the great person's sense of connection with the prophets. On her deathbed, Rābiʿa made a final request. She asked that those gathered to see her off allow her to face death alone "for the sake of the Lord's prophets." As the assembled mourners stood outside the room, they heard a voice within reciting a Qurʾānic verse welcoming Rābiʿa to paradise (89: 27–31). When they no longer heard the voice, the mourners entered and found her dead, and they summed up her life by observing that she never once presumed that God "owed" her even the tiniest benefit.[46] Fudayl likewise made a reference to the prophets during his final moments. He observed that one need not envy them, for they, too, had to endure the rigors of the last things: the constriction of the grave, resurrection, hell, and the "narrow bridge." More surprisingly, perhaps, he also reminded mourners that the angels must suffer even greater terror, for unlike humans, angels can find no relief from their pain.[47]

One of the more striking end-of-life tales in this context is that of Central Asian Friend Ahmad Yasawī. Hagiographic accounts report that, in his desire to emulate the Prophet's death at age sixty-three, he entered into a subterranean chamber at that age and symbolically passed into another world. No less a pair than the prophets Ilyās and Khidr had supervised the excavation, allowing the Friend to enact the Prophetic injunction, "Die before your (actual) death." But this underground chamber was no mere pit. It included a tunnel leading in the direction of Mecca, at the end of which was a domed burial chamber with an interment niche. The hagiographers claim that the saint remained in permanent hibernation for as many years as he had lived aboveground. One account says that Yasawī never missed his Friday congregational mosque prayers, however, for his ability to tunnel great distances through the earth at light speed allowed him to attend prayer times in such distant places as Mecca or Cairo.[48]

Final wishes and parting advice are important features of many death accounts. Junayd went to visit his uncle Sarī when he was at the point of death, and he used a fan to cool the suffering shaykh. Sarī told Junayd that he was only fanning the flames of destruction. In response to Junayd's request for some final wisdom, Sarī advised him never to let human companionship turn him from companionship with God. Junayd himself desired to die listening to his disciples enjoying a meal together. As death rapidly approached, he asked to be prepared for ritual prayer. When his assistants neglected to pour water over his hands and beard during the prescribed ablution, Junayd wept over the omission. Much to his companions' surprise, he then began to recite Qur'ān. He explained that reciting the sacred text was the best way to prepare for the moment at which his destiny would hang in the balance. He died clutching his prayer beads, and when the body washer tried to open his hand for purification, a voice informed him that only God's order would again loose those fingers. A dove perched on Junayd's coffin and explained to the mourners that it would stay there permanently out of love, and it even chided the shaykh's followers, telling them that their grief was delaying Junayd's final release.[49]

Another important theme in death stories is the final divestment of all earthly treasure as a fitting conclusion to a life of ascetical renunciation. To the very end, Bishr maintained his rigorous self-denial, even giving away his shirt to a poor person, which required him to be buried in a borrowed garment. During his life, not a single animal relieved itself in the city of Baghdad, out of deference for Bishr's practice of going barefoot. The first time an animal did befoul the streets of the city, people knew the Friend had died. ʿAbd Allāh ibn Mubārak, too, was resolved to depart this life relying only on God, dispensing the last of his possessions to the needy. Asked why he did not leave his estate to his three daughters, he assured the questioner that his children would be better off with God alone looking after them. In keeping with the mysteriously detached way in which he had lived, Ibrāhīm ibn Adham simply disappeared at death, so that even the whereabouts of his grave remain uncertain. His passing meant the demise of peace in the world.[50]

Sufyān ath-Thawrī asked a disciple to "buy death" for him if he should encounter it on his journey. In this way, he sought to take initiative in dealing with the inevitable. He prepared himself for death often, meditating on it intensely and never feeling sure that he was destined for heaven. Still, when his time came, he admitted that his final days put him to the test. He endured his final illness in a stable and insisted on repeatedly purifying himself lest he meet death in a state of ritual uncleanness. Mourners gathered, informed in their dreams of his imminent departure. The shaykh instructed them to distribute a thousand gold coins to the poor. In a reversal on this theme, Ahmad Khidrūya approached his onrushing demise in a state of debt, owing seven hundred gold coins to various creditors as a result of his generosity to the poor and wayfarers. With his creditors gathered in his room, Ahmad prayed that God would make good his debts. Just then, an anonymous individual came to the door and repaid all of the shaykh's debts, after which he died.[51]

Some accounts include details of the obsequies as well as of the Friend's death. Ibn ʿArabī recalls that after the death of his houseguest ʿAbd Allāh Badr al-Habashī, he had intended to wash the man's body himself. But early the next day, crowds arrived to pay their respects before he could perform the ritual. One of the mourners was a jurist and Sufi named Kamāl ad-Dīn Muzaffar. When Ibn ʿArabī explained the predicament, Kamāl related that he had the day before heard a voice tell him three times to purify himself; the third time, the voice instructed him to be prepared to wash the body of one of God's Friends. After Kamāl had washed ʿAbd Allāh's body, Ibn ʿArabī asked him to lead the funeral prayer. Kamāl then disclosed that as he was washing the body and feeling unworthy, ʿAbd Allāh had opened his eyes momentarily and smiled. Ibn ʿArabī explains that after the burial, the shaykh spoke clearly to him from the grave, responding to a concern that Ibn ʿArabī had expressed to him. People thereafter reported seeing a light reaching to the heavens from that grave.[52]

Dhū 'n- Nūn's death followed a serious illness, during which he expressed a wish that he be allowed to know God, however briefly, before he departed this life. He advised his followers at the end to keep the company of people who teach about God by their very presence. On Dhū 'n- Nūn's forehead, grieving disciples observed an inscription in green, identifying the shaykh as God's beloved and a martyr slain by the divine love. Birds flew over his body en route to the cemetery, shielding it from the torrid sun, and at the call to prayer, the shaykh pointed a finger skyward. The mourners buried him with his hand frozen in that gesture.[53]

Bāyazīd died as he had lived, with the name of God on his tongue, keenly aware that he had often called that name with less than full awareness. One of his closest associates (Abū Mūsā), who was not present at the shaykh's death, reported a dream in which he bore the celestial throne on his own head. The next day he headed off to tell Bāyazīd of the dream, only to find that his mentor had already died. Because Abū Mūsā did not have enough room to support a corner of the coffin in the funeral procession, he stood underneath it and lifted it with his head. Then Bāyazīd appeared to him in a dream, explaining that Abū Mūsā's earlier dream had foreshadowed his carrying the shaykh's body in that way.[54]

The great Egyptian mystical poet Ibn al-Fārid wrote that his own ailing shaykh summoned him to pay his last respects. He instructed Ibn al-Fārid to arrange for his funeral and caused an image of his burial plot, near Moses's Place of Prostration by the Muqattam Hills south of Cairo, to appear to his student. Ibn al-Fārid was to take the shaykh's body to that spot and wait for a visitor from the mountain. Suddenly, like a bird, the visitor descended and instructed Ibn al-Fārid to lead the prayers. As he did, rows of green and white birds gathered, and a huge green bird swooped down, ate the shaykh's body, and rejoined the flock. The visitor explained that this action illustrated the saying that the souls of martyrs, whether of war or of love, are in the crops of green birds that fly freely in paradise. He himself, the man explained further, had once been a martyr of love until he "made a slip" and lost his privileged position. Ibn al-Fārid was later buried in that place.[55]

A story about the death of Rūmī's dear friend Burhān ad-Dīn raises the important issue of whether a holy person's grave ought to be especially memorialized. Another of Rūmī's companions, Shams ad-Dīn, saw to the funeral arrangements and erected a building over the burial site. Several days later, the structure fell apart, and it was replaced by a more elaborate dome; but that memorial, too, collapsed. Then Shams ad-Dīn had a dream in which Burhān forbade him to construct a monument over his grave.[56]

Aflākī names Rūmī's wife Kirā Khātūn a "Friend of God on earth." When her funeral procession passed a certain gate of the city of Konya, the bier suddenly stopped and could not be carried beyond that spot. Rūmī's son began a Sufi *samāʿ* with his fellow dervishes, and when the mourners were through praying, they were able to carry the bier to the lady's tomb. After her interment, the tomb began to glow with such a light that many mourners swooned. Later that evening, Kirā Khātūn appeared to someone who asked the apparition why her bier had stopped by the gate. Kirā explained that a couple accused of adultery had been stoned just the day before at that spot, and she had stopped to pray for the couple to be delivered into God's mercy.[57]

Friends of God are so like the rest of us, and yet so different. Their links with the prophets underscore both their similarity and their uniqueness. Above all, the hagiographical accounts I discuss in this chapter raise important questions about the historical and literary functions that Friends of God have fulfilled in Islamicate societies. To the degree that Friends share the ordinary humanity of those who seek wisdom and consolation from their stories, they are models to emulate. Insofar as they are paragons of truly extraordinary gifts and achievement, mere mortals can only stand back in admiration. Chapter 6 and subsequent chapters of part 2 explore these and other roles that God's Friends have played in multiple contexts.

PART II

Friends of God in Context

.   .   .   .   .

The five chapters of part 1 laid out the great hagiographical themes that are common to so many holy lives. My purpose there was not to suggest that the lives of Friends of God fall into a predictable pattern but to propose a way of reading their life stories with an eye for shared literary motifs and subgenres. These story settings and types have been a way to introduce many of the great Friends. Part 2 discusses the social, institutional, ritual, and cultural settings in which Friends of God have acted historically or in which Muslims remember them today.

Chapter 6 investigates the social role of Friends of God—as examples of ethical values and as models of engagement for the benefit of their communities. It emphasizes the importance of the Friends whose chosen behavior or gender differences rendered them marginal. In chapter 7, the patrons and founders of major social and religious institutions take center stage. These institutional foundations leave markers that allow us to trace, in chapter 8, the outlines of the "sacred geographies" that make up the wider world of God's Friends. Chapter 9 concludes our thematic overview by exploring how the various traditions about God's Friends have survived and how they find expression in recent times. Through these chapters, the narrative elements so prominent in part 1 yield increasingly to more theoretical concepts and distinctions.

FIGURE 15.   Shaykh Najm ad-Dīn Kubrā (d. 617/1220) defends the central Asian
fortress of Khwārazm against Mongol attack, demonstrating one of the more
active roles played by some Friends of God. Jāmī, *Nafaḥāt al-uns* (Ottoman,
1003/1595), ©The Trustees of the Chester Beatty Library, Dublin, T474:225v.

6. Friends and Their People

Society and Service to Communities

Many Friends of God have recommended flight from humankind as the only way to avoid losing their spiritual focus. Even the most austere and reclusive of renunciants, however, have found cause to tend to the obvious needs of their constituents. Dozens of major figures, including prophets and Companions of Muhammad as well as later saintly characters, have opted to wade into the hurly-burly of mundane affairs, seemingly unconcerned that they might be engulfed in a sea of humanity. Gregariousness and holiness are not mutually exclusive.

Several thematic threads run through Friends' responses to their communities. Saintly example in general and the moral uprightness of so many Friends are the broadest categories that emerge from the traditional sources. Hagiographers' acknowledgment of such qualities does not mean, however, that these writers regard their subjects as worthy of imitation in every detail of their often-eccentric lives. Just beneath the surface of even the quirkiest behavior lie core ethical values and a pervasive orientation to justice. After a look at this broad theme of ethical modeling, I focus on Friends' roles as counselors and confidants, warriors and martyrs for the faith, and advocates for the socially and economically marginalized. This chapter's final segment explores two other aspects of social marginality: the saintly liminality of "fools for God" and questions of gender.

Two more theoretically oriented themes run just below the surface of this and subsequent chapters. One is a distinction, maintained in a number of classic hagiographical sources, between urban and rural Friends. Some sources link city saints with a more extroverted approach to life in general, particularly in their willingness to engage the powers that be. Others associate authentic power with freedom from the trappings of external authority, which is available only to Friends who cultivate the quieter life of the countryside or desert.[1] The urban-rural dichotomy does not impose impermeable barriers, for city folk often headed for the hinterlands precisely to contact Friends who lived off the beaten track. Another thematic dyad is that of admiration and imitation. As earlier chapters suggest, many of the deeds of God's Friends inspire admiration and wonder but are clearly beyond the reach of even the most advanced spiritual seeker. Much of this chapter concerns matters generally within the reach of ordinary folk seeking to emulate the deeds of the great ones.

PUBLIC VIRTUE, MORAL EXAMPLE, AND SERVICE TO OTHERS

Even the most reclusive Friends of God cannot avoid publicity altogether. They represent value and aspiration in a way that serious religious seekers find both appealing and challenging. Ordinary people may have little chance of emulating such exemplary people in detail, but Friends are nonetheless beacons of virtue and ethical conduct.[2] Beginning as early as the sections of the hadith literature dealing with the "excellent qualities" (*fadāʾil*) of Muhammad and his Companions, Islamic hagiographical sources have consistently evidenced interest in the relationships between sanctity and virtue. A strong sense of social solidarity and service to the community of believers emerges as a fundamental value, and as the context for discerning and evaluating other virtues. Altruism rooted in the basic conviction of God's sovereignty over all humankind nurtures a range of other values. Some Friends exemplify a religious rectitude founded on uncompromising detachment from the material world. But even the dourest ascetics are in general keenly aware of the social implications of the faith: God alone is truly self-sufficient; all human beings are inherently needy. The ultimate in human generosity, therefore, is sharing one's spiritual and earthly possessions in the conviction that God will supply all of one's own needs and that the Bounteous One intends the divine largesse to be shared with the neediest people.[3]

Some Friends of God attempt (not always credibly, according to their critics) to walk a fine line between preaching renunciation and enjoying the benefits and amenities lavished upon them by affluent patrons. This balancing act is particularly evident in the lives of Friends whose distinctive forms of spirituality called for the greatest involvement in civic leadership and, consequently, in matters of economic development (a topic I take up in chapter 7). In this respect, many sources evoke images of Muhammad as the ideal of involvement in public life and as one who modeled consistently a life of material simplicity and other-centered service. Social capital—often including, paradoxically, a Friend's preference for life on the margins—is a major ingredient of saintly moral authority. And many societies have associated ethical credibility directly with perceptions of fairness and honesty. Muhammad's fellow Meccans, for example, had such high regard for his even-handedness that they asked him to oversee the replacement of the Black Stone in a corner of the newly rebuilt Kaʿba. The Prophet placed the stone on a cloak and had four chiefs of the city's main tribal constituencies each lift the cloak by one of its corners; then he placed the stone into its socket, and the rebuilding proceeded upward.[4] Later in his life, Muhammad's reputation for fairness prompted the leaders of Yathrib (eventually to be renamed Medina [City]-of-the Prophet in Muhammad's honor) to invite him northward to arbitrate their city's intractable tribal disputes.

With the exception of the most eccentric among them, Friends of God are generally depicted as models of proper demeanor (*adab*) in their relationships with God and their fellow human beings. Khwāja ʿUbayd Allāh Ahrār, a major Central Asian Naqshbandī Sufi, is an excellent example. His hagiographers clearly saw their shaykh as an advocate for his people who embodied the highest ethical standards. A passion for justice marks accounts of this extroverted Friend's social presence. The shaykh was not only a major founding figure but was also a prominent voice of conscience and care for the needy. He and many other major Friends derived their moral authority from their perceived spiritual commitment. The social implications of their commitment have played out in a variety of important ways.[5]

FRIENDS ENGAGED

First and foremost, Friends of God teach by example as well as by the often pithy and engaging sayings attributed to them. One important consequence of moral and spiritual authority is that some Friends of God attract the inquiries and confidences of the people among whom they live and work. In a number of accounts, paragons of holiness and devotion find themselves bound by inescapable conviction to take up arms in the quest for justice. Stories of warrior-Friends often place the central figure in the forefront of outward combat as an example of courage and, sometimes, superhuman physical prowess. But the jihad of the great ones more characteristically assumes the less spectacular form of representing the needs of the poor, the socially marginal, and the politically disenfranchised, in the public square and in the corridors of power. The following section explores Friends' engagement as confidants and guides, warriors, and advocates for their people.

Confidants and Patrons

In hagiographical accounts, disciples of famous Friends of God benefit regularly from their teachers' sage advice and often regard them as the most trusted confidants. Some spiritual conversations occur in informal settings and spontaneous encounters; others take the more organized shape of formal spiritual direction. Some soul-meetings feature an individual seeker with a Friend; others occur in groups, with the teacher responding to the inquiries of members of an assembly. Group interactions typically occur either in mosque sessions or at meetings of a Sufi order. Whatever the venue or occasion, such exchanges are examples of the "science of hearts" in action. Sources frequently depict Friends guiding the wayward. The Friends are not always gentle in their counsel, particularly when they detect hypocrisy or self-pity. But the experienced confidant and guide invariably appears to dispense just the right message—or, perhaps more to the point, to facilitate the seeker's discovery of the solution.

Many of the stories I have already told depict Friends as confidants and guides. Virtually any exchange between a saint and a disciple—or even a chance acquaintance—can turn into an occasion for offering advice. Sometimes the Friend is the one who learns the most from the encounter. This first dimension of social engagement is not a significant theme in stories of the prophets, suggesting an important difference between prophets and their heirs in the divine plan.

In a more broadly societal sense, many Friends of God, in various cultural contexts, have become identified as "patrons" of social and economic groups or trades. In South Asia, for example, Bahāʾ ad-Dīn Zakarīya of Multan and Shāh Jalāl of Bengal are patrons of boatmen and fishermen. Boatmen in India look to Qādir Walī Sāhib (in the south) and Maʿlūm-i Yār (in the north) for help. Pīr Badr protects sailors, and the mysterious Khidr generally aids people who make their living on or with water. Shāh Mūsā Lohar is the guardian spirit of blacksmiths, along with the prophet David, who could knit chain mail. Oilmen seek protection from Hasan Teli, dyers turn to Pīr Alī Rangrīz, sweepers and cesspool cleaners ask help from Lāl Beg, and athletes look to Sakhī Sarwar.[6] Similar protective specializations exist in countless other regional contexts.

Warriors and Martyrs

Prominent Friends of God stand out from their peers as particularly redoubtable warriors "on the way of God." Historically, the two most common settings for stories of warrior Friends are the Muslim struggles against the Christian *reconquista* in Spain and the ongoing wars of attrition against the Byzantine Empire in the lands at the opposite end of the Mediterranean. Less-frequent settings depict Friends dislodging Crusaders already ensconced in Middle Eastern territories; attempting to fend off the Mongols as they drove westward; or pushing back the frontiers of unbelief to Islamize a region such as Indonesia (see Fig. 15).

In spite of the best intentions, not all Friends who set their course for military action achieve their desire to engage in external jihad in defense of the faith. In one story, Abū 'l-Khayr at-Tīnnātī heads off to the Byzantine frontier intent on waging both outer and inner warfare. For the former, he has equipped himself with sword, lance, and shield. For the latter, he searches for a *ribāt*, an institution that was originally an outpost to house warriors but eventually became solely a retreat for those undertaking the inward struggle of ascetical renunciation. En route, he settles in a cave and resolves to sustain himself only on food that is divinely provided each day. But when he spies a lovely piece of fruit, he succumbs to his lower desires and begins to eat it. Acknowledging his lapse, he spits out the mouthful and tosses away the fruit. At that moment, a group of soldiers spots him and hauls him off to their commander, mistaking him for one of the bandits who has been accosting travelers nearby. In fact, the commander even suspects that the shaykh is the leader of the pack, and he begins to cut off the extremities of all his prisoners. He orders Abū 'l-Khayr to put forth his hand and a soldier amputates it. When the shaykh begins to pray that he not lose his leg also, a passing soldier recognizes the Friend and intervenes just in time. This Friend ends up with war wounds inflicted, ironically and quite unnecessarily, by his own people.[7]

Several famous early Friends of God, including some who never actually took up arms, are listed among combatants in important military engagements. The ever-colorful Bāyazīd reportedly turned the tide of a battle during which Byzantine forces were on the verge of overwhelming the Muslims. Someone called to Bāyazīd for help, and from the northeast (Bāyazīd's home region) came a fire that routed the Byzantine hosts. ʿAttār reports that ʿAbd Allāh ibn al-Mubārak fought an otherwise anonymous "unbeliever." When time for prayer came, the Muslim asked leave of the infidel to go apart and pray. The Christian made the same request later, and ʿAbd Allāh reciprocated—or seemed to do so. As the infidel began to address his graven image, the Muslim decided to take him by surprise. Just then, however, a mysterious voice chided ʿAbd Allāh about living up to his word, and the Friend relented. When the Christian asked what had prevented ʿAbd Allāh from carrying out his treachery, the Muslim explained that his God had spared the unbeliever's life for the sake of integrity. Not surprisingly, the Christian confessed that he could not imagine opposing a deity so high-minded as to criticize a partisan in the interests of an enemy, and he converted to Islam.[8]

Andalusian Friend Abū Marwān al-Yahsubī was intent on fighting against the reconquering Christians and headed for a *ribāt*. He got the worst of a skirmish one day and was nabbed while trying to make his getaway. God protected him from the enemy until the Muslims could regain the advantage in battle. Communicating later through their Arabic-speaking Jewish scribe, the Christians asked how Yahsubī had secured divine protection against the Christian warriors. The Friend replied by sending them a copy of his theological work about how to refute Christian polytheists.[9]

At the eastern end of the Mediterranean, another nemesis threatened. A founder of an important Persian Sufi order, Abū Ishāq al-Kāzarūnī, was also famous as a raider (*ghāzī*) against the Byzantines, who were attempting the reconquest of Syria during the fourth/tenth century. Unfortunately, the Muslim Buyid rulers in Baghdad were not in favor of serious resistance against the Byzantines, and the Friend thought they were shirking their responsibility. Kāzarūnī therefore took up the cause and hoisted the banner against the infidels, notably supplying financial support to Muslim armies.[10]

Rūmī, associated as he is with the poetry of mystical love, is surely among the last people one might expect to have strapped on a sword. But his major hagiographer, Aflākī, includes an intriguing account by one of Rūmī's followers about the Friend's warrior exploits. Mawlānā (Rūmī's honorific title, "Our Master") kept a stable of Arabian horses. One day he asked that a particular steed be saddled and brought to him. Rūmī mounted the horse and bolted for Syria. That night, Rūmī returned exhausted at the time of evening prayer. The next morning, he departed again on a fresh horse. On the evening of the third day, he reappeared with enigmatic good news: an attacker had been vanquished, but he would say no more. A few days later, a caravan from Syria arrived with word that the citizens of Damascus had seen Rūmī there joining the fight to fend off the Mongol invaders. Aflākī tells the story primarily as evidence of Rūmī's marvelous powers—no ordinary person could travel back and forth from Konya to Damascus three times in as many days—but the account also illustrates the persistence of the theme of Friends as defenders of the faith.[11]

Not all warrior Friends survive the fray in their violent encounters, and still others give up their lives without ever taking up arms. Whatever the circumstances of their deaths, many such Friends are considered martyrs. Martyrs play a particularly important role in Shīʿī hagiography, in that martyrdom has been the shared lot of the imams. Husayn's death, at Karbalāʾ (not far to the south of Baghdad) in 61/680, was in many ways the paradigmatic saintly death. As we saw in chapter 5, he was overwhelmed by a vastly superior force when he joined battle with the unjust Umayyad tyrant, the caliph Yazīd.[12] Stories of other martyr-imams (many of them poisoned) are less well-known outside of Shīʿī circles, but all emphasize the importance of the Friends' "redemptive suffering" as a form of service to the community of believers.[13]

Sunnī Friends, too, include some important martyrs. We can recall, for example, the death of Hallāj described in chapter 5. Uways al-Qaranī died fighting alongside the fourth Rightly Guided Caliph, ʿAlī, in the battle of Siffīn (36/656), during which ʿAlī fought to a draw with Muʿāwiya, then governor of Damascus. Eight of Junayd's most promising students took a notion to support the struggle against Byzantium by taking up arms, and the shaykh concurred. Junayd joined the eight in the front lines and watched as all of his disciples fell to a single Christian warrior. Seeing a vision of nine litters in the air, Junayd wondered whether the ninth was meant for him. After Junayd returned to the fray, the Byzantine who had mowed down the disciples told Junayd that the ninth litter was actually for him rather than for Junayd. The Byzantine soldier forthwith converted to Islam, turned around and dispatched eight of his former comrades, and fell as a martyr himself. When the new convert had occupied the ninth litter, all nine vanished, and Junayd returned to continue leading his community in Baghdad.[14]

Friends in Need

Characteristically, those Friends of God who have the least (usually by choice) are most solicitous of and dedicated to the poor. Abū ʿAbd Allāh al-Khayyāt was a tailor and one of Ibn ʿArabī's shaykhs. He was particularly attentive to supplying the poor with food, shelter, and clothing. He had migrated to Egypt from Andalusia during a time of dire famine and poverty. Ibn ʿArabī visited with him there. One night, the disciple felt himself powerfully drawn to the shaykh's presence. When Ibn ʿArabī arrived at Abū ʿAbd Allāh's place, the shaykh said that he had been concentrating on him, for the younger man had something the Friend needed for a beggar who had just stopped by. Ibn ʿArabī immediately surrendered the five silver coins he had. Friends are not shy about asking their followers to put their money where they claim their faith is.[15]

Stories of advocacy for the needy and oppressed are not limited to accounts of living Friends in action. The grave is no barrier when great need is apparent. Few among the revered dead have stirred more ardent cries for help in time of trouble than the great jurist Shāfiʿī. Even his most commonly used name means "my advocate" or "intercessor." The name has usually been understood in a lawyerly sense, but the popular practice of leaving letters at his tomb in southern Cairo has lifted the quality of his counsel to a higher level. Countless visitors to his mausoleum have implored his aid by sliding heartfelt pleas under the door or tucking messages into the domed shrine's masonry. Most requests have focused on a specific matter of Islamic law (family and inheritance, for example), but here the entreaties take place in a larger spiritual framework. Many plaintiffs beg the Friend of God to take their causes to the heavenly court, at which other saints also are in solicitous attendance and might sway a judgment in their favor.[16]

Friends in High Places

Access to the powerful is an important theme in the stories of individual Friends as well as in those of representatives of major Sufi orders. The bigger the institution, the more money is necessary to sustain it, and the more it must rely on significant sources of patronage. The growth of local and regional religious organizations sometimes represents a threat to rulers. As a result, stories often describe how a Friend of God wins or escapes a confrontation with a ruler, who subsequently asks forgiveness for his effrontery and may even become a disciple of the shaykh.[17]

Khwāja ʿUbayd Allāh Ahrār was celebrated for his courage in representing the rights of his people in the corridors of power. His boldness in confronting institutional injustice took a variety of forms. When princely adversaries threatened war in the city of Samarqand (in present-day Uzbekistan, just north of Afghanistan), he made the countercase that conflict would cause dire suffering for the city's weakest citizens. Apprised that certain authorities were oppressing his associates, the shaykh promptly and miraculously did away with one of the malefactors.[18]

Ibn ʿArabī describes Abū Muhammad ʿAbd Allāh al-Qattān's fearless struggle for justice in the courts of the mighty. One sultan, determined to be rid of Abū Muhammad, had the brave man hauled before his prime minister (*wazīr*). Without batting an eye, the Friend rebuked the administrator, reminding him that the ruler was deluded in his belief that he had power over the saint's life. When the minister sent the shaykh to prison while he conferred with the sultan, the Friend declared the sultan's prison no more than a reflection of the incarceration that all people of faith experience in living amid the trappings of this world. Hailed before the sultan the following day, Abū Muhammad stood alone. In the eyes of the ruler, he was "an ugly man for whom nobody cared and whom no-one wished well, all because he spoke the truth and brought to light the faults and misdeeds of men." But when Abū Muhammad began to speak of God and recite scripture, the sultan began to change his mind and asked the Friend for his opinion of the sultan's rule. Without hesitation, the shaykh launched a withering critique of the monarch's delusions of grandeur. Abū Muhammad struck home, and the chastened sultan offered the shaykh a position at court. Abū Muhammad declined to legitimate the fraudulent reign by his presence. Even after the Friend continued with his less-than-flattering observations, the ruler pardoned him and showered him with gifts. Abū Muhammad accepted the pardon but declined the gifts, which the sultan bestowed on the shaykh's family. The outspoken Friend persisted in his public denunciation of crooked rulers and accompanied the troops who went on military campaigns against encroaching Iberian Christians.[19]

Turkish Friend Hajjī Bektāsh found himself in a confrontation with a regional governor when the ruler accused the Friend of lax religious practice. As the governor called for ritual prayer, the Friend caused the ablution water to become blood, thus rendering the very means of purification a source of further impurity. Hajjī Bektāsh followed up with an even more devastating move, predicting the governor's downfall, incarceration, and blindness, the last of which only the Friend could cure. Hajjī Bektāsh thus managed to get rid of the ruler, banishing him to resume his life elsewhere with his sight restored. Hajjī Bektāsh, bad Friend/good Friend, thereby represents the notion that government is a necessary evil whose baser aspects need to be counteracted by saintly power. Some two centuries later, another Turkish Friend, Otmān Bābā, took on no less than the sultan who had brought down the last of the Byzantine Empire by conquering Constantinople in 857/1453. Otmān Bābā accurately foretold that Sultan Mehmet "the Conqueror" would fail to take Belgrade (present-day capital of the Balkan state of Serbia). The ruler was forced to acknowledge the Friend's authority and became his disciple. The Friend fared less well against the new Ottoman capital's religious authorities, however, and was driven away with his dervish followers.[20]

Relationships between rulers and Friends are not always adversarial, however. A classic theme in hagiographical accounts, as well as in royally commissioned documents such as court histories, is a trip by the ruler or a member of the royal family to the countryside to take counsel with a famous spiritual guide. This type of story presents an interesting twist on the rural-urban typology. Rulers in many settings chose to be portrayed both in text and image as devotees of spiritually powerful Friends of God. Miniature paintings (particularly from Mughal India) often depict a richly dressed ruler, surrounded by a grand retinue complete with musical ensemble, sitting humbly at the opening of a cave or under a tree in a remote landscape, where a threadbare Friend grants an audience. Some of the most important memorials to God's

Friends are monumental tombs funded by rulers who considered themselves disciples of the saintly shaykhs. Even the exalted Mughal Indian emperor Akbar, for example, was a devotee of Chishtī shaykh Salīm. Believing that the shaykh's blessing had made possible the birth of a male heir, Akbar gratefully built a splendid tomb for Shaykh Salīm Chishtī and surrounded it with the royal palace-city of Fatehpur Sikri.[21] Akbar entrusted the royal heir, named after Salīm, to the tutelage of Chishtī spiritual guides (see Fig. 16).

FRIENDS ON THE FRINGES

Traditional sources often describe two important groups of Friends of God as socially marginal: "fools for God" and women. The former are typically individuals who have deliberately opted for a state of permanent liminality, though some have (perhaps paradoxically) banded together with others of like mind. They have always and everywhere been very much in the minority. In turn, Muslim women acknowledged for their sanctity have been on the fringe in the sense that they have been far less visible than their male counterparts in traditional hagiographical sources, though in reality, they have typically constituted a demographic majority in their given populations.

Fools for God

Friends of God have stood out from the generality of humankind, usually without attempting to do so. Some, however, have made a vocation of differentiating themselves, even going to great lengths to incur social censure— or at least to avoid actively cultivating public esteem. Such interesting characters have sometimes been dubbed "fools for God," because they care only for divine approval, even at the risk of appearing emotionally unstable or dangerous. This social-spiritual orientation has taken various forms.

One category of footloose Friends is the *malāmatīya*, a doctrinally eclectic movement related to Sufism, with roots in northeastern Iran. As the hagiographer Sulamī explains in his important *Treatise* (*Risāla*) on the tradition, the name means "those who bring blame (*malāma*) upon themselves," and it reflects the underlying principle that understating one's spiritual rank and values is preferable to garnering social and religious approval through outward display or symbolism. Hamdūn al-Qassār is widely acknowledged as the founder of the movement, albeit with the significant influence of his teacher, Abū Hafs al-Haddād, and Abū ʿUthmān al-Hīrī. According to the teachings of the movement, individuals who lived in material poverty were not to appear impoverished. Even to credit oneself privately with success in religious deeds, or to hope for a heavenly reward,

FIGURE 16.   The tomb of Shaykh Salīm Chishtī (d. 979/1571), Fatehpūr Sikrī, India, was built by Mughal Emperor Akbar to honor his own spiritual guide and the Chishtī Sufi order. Photo by John Renard.

was a spiritual failure. The tradition traces its origins to none other than the Prophet, whom the Qurʾān extols as impervious to blame (5:54).

In its more extreme forms, the tradition promoted behavior and ethics calculated explicitly to evoke disapproval and rejection. A tendency to favor withdrawal from the public in all ritual practices may have influenced, for example, the Naqshbandīya Sufi order. Some scholars point out that the tradition was, at least initially, not so much a reaction to institutional Sufism as a reaction to the overt displays of piety by the Karrāmīya of Nishapur. The movement was particularly important in Central Asia but also enjoyed considerable success in Turkey and the Balkans, as well as in portions of the Arab Middle East.

A second category of marginal Friends is the *qalandars.* The term originally meant "rough-hewn" (hence, "rube") and referred to itinerant, "antinomian," mendicant dervishes who were unattached to any institutional framework. As individuals, *qalandars* distinguished themselves by flaunting social and religious conventions in clothing as well as in behavior. Some apparently went out of their way to marginalize themselves for reasons of spiritual commitment, convinced that one ought not to seek human approval through conformity to "official" religious or social norms. Their asceticism included a decided antipathy to formal learning. In this respect, their approach sought to be less attention getting than that of the Malāmatī dervishes. Ironically, the *qalandars* soon developed their own brand of conformity by affecting common practices such as shaving the head completely (including eyebrows), wearing coarse garments and headgear, and carrying standard and drum.

Followers of the colorful Friend Hajjī Bektāsh Walī eventually formed an order called the Bektāshīya. Hajjī Bektāsh was a Khurāsānī dervish who may have moved to the west around the time that the family of Rūmī left home in advance of the Mongol invasion. Rich hagiographical accounts assert that he died in 738/1338, but 738 turns out to be the numerical equivalent of the letters of the Arabic alphabet in the name Bektāshīya. Tradition also traces the saint's spiritual pedigree to the Central Asian shaykh Ahmad Yasawī. Some scholars place Bektāsh among the *qalandars* because of his relaxed approach to ritual obligations. What is beyond dispute is his position among a small handful of "signature" Sufi saints of modern Turkey, along with, for example, Rūmī and Yūnus Emre; he was also a patron saint of the Janissary Corps in Ottoman times.

The Bektāshīya was an organization of Anatolian origin that eventually spread to the Balkans and was transplanted to parts of the central Middle East and Iran. Later Shīʿī elements influenced the hagiographic traditions connecting the order's spiritual lineage to the line of imams. Much influenced by Anatolian *qalandarī* practice, the order's ritual gradually became quite elaborate and colorful. The order also incorporated strong elements of Shīʿī ritual into its liturgical calendar, especially observance of the martyrdom of Husayn. By the tenth/sixteenth century, the order had split into celibate and noncelibate branches, and all major foundations had come under the jurisdiction of a celibate leader in Anatolia.

Finally, a category of fringe Friends especially important in South Asia are the *malangs, qalandar*-like mendicants who attach themselves sporadically to various holy places as servants of a Friend's tomb-shrine. Popular usage seems on the whole to restrict the term *qalandar* to individuals with specifically Sufi connections, whereas *malang* refers more generically to religiously motivated beggars. Some *malangs,* of course, are considered charlatans, but many are popularly regarded as spiritually potent, if socially marginal. Female *malangs* are rare but not unheard of. The word, which carries connotations of deviation from social norms in Malay, has gradually taken on the extended meaning of "unfortunate" or "star-crossed" and has become associated with poverty in Southeast Asia, and hence with asceticism; but it does not appear to be a common term there for Sufis as such.[22]

Engendering Friends: Female Models of Holiness and Devotion

Stories of saintly women of ancient times have long been part of the Islamic hagiographical tradition, but rarely do these stories feature these women as important figures in their own right.[23] Several women's stories are intimately related with those of major prophets. Women also appear in narratives of many post-Prophetic Friends. As often as not, their sanctity is largely a reflected glow from the light cast by the male Friends in their lives—their husbands, brothers, sons, spiritual advisors, and chance acquaintances. A number of female Friends emerge as characters in their own right, but these individuals are generally women who, like their liminal male counterparts, have opted for lives of renunciation and difference.

Hagiographers have expressed a variety of attitudes toward women. ʿAttār, for example, makes several pointed observations about his inclusion of an extended account of Rābiʿa. Often acknowledged as Islam's first "mystic," Rābiʿa is the only woman with an individual entry in ʿAttār's anthology, and the author seems to think he needs to defend his decision to include her. He takes his cue from Muhammad's observation that God is not concerned with the outer forms of people but with inward intention. He notes that because Muhammad's wife ʿĀʾisha was responsible for handing on "two-thirds" of the tradition, the decision to pay attention to a woman who was a maidservant of ʿĀʾisha surely makes sense. Besides, he continues with a backhanded compliment, a woman engaged in the way of God is in effect a man, so Rābiʿa's inclusion in the company of men is a moot point. He adds, quoting ʿAbbāsa (a saintly woman of Tūs in eastern Persia), that at Judgment, when the "men" are summoned to come forth, Jesus's mother, Mary, will be the first to join their ranks, for the realm of union with God makes no distinction of individuality, let alone gender.[24]

Ibn al-Jawzī criticizes Abū Nuʿaym al-Isfahānī, author of one of the most monumental of all hagiographical anthologies, for giving women short shrift. He says that Abū Nuʿaym ignores women, "even though it is well known that given women's apparent shortcomings, failing to mention female devotees causes men to ignore women in general." Ibn al-Jawzī reminds his readers that no less a teacher than Hasan of Basra was a disciple of Rābiʿa.[25] Out of 278 biographical sketches in *Glimpses of the People of Sufism*, Tādilī gives separate accounts of only 5 women, and 3 of them remain anonymous.[26] Persian hagiographer Jāmī makes an indirect statement about his views on female Friends by clustering entries on some three dozen saintly women at the end of his anthology, *Warm Breezes of Intimacy*. These generally brief entries have the heading, "A remembrance of the women endowed with experiential knowledge who have attained to the ranks of men."[27] Munāwī's extensive Arabic hagiographical anthology, *Shining Stars of the Biographies of the Masters of Sufism*, contains entries on nearly three dozen women, without noteworthy comment about his rationale for including them.[28]

Early Islamic tradition accorded four women a particularly elevated status. The four "perfect" women are the martyred wife of a pharaoh in the time of Moses, Āsiya; Mary, mother of Jesus; Khadīja, Muhammad's first wife; and Fātima, Muhammad's most prominent daughter, wife of ʿAlī, and mother of the second and third Shīʿī martyr-imams. One tradition holds that Āsiya's servants were the ones who discovered the infant Moses floating in the river. More importantly, she suffered martyrdom when she confronted Pharaoh for his stubborn unbelief.[29]

Mary models saintly virtue in equally important, if less dramatic, ways. Chapter 1 recounts the tale of her mother's desire to dedicate Mary to divine service. When the infant Mary is presented to the thirty temple priests, they vie for custody of the "dedicated girl." In a miraculous casting of lots, Zakariya (father of John the Baptist) wins custody. Under his guardianship, Mary appears to produce a miracle, for whenever Zakariya seeks to attend to her needs, he discovers that God has already supplied her more than ample provisions. Along with her son, Jesus, Mary is preserved from Satan's "stab in the side" that renders all other humans sinful. Her courage through the difficulties of her unusual (and apparently suspicious) pregnancy and in the social embarrassments following Jesus's birth set Mary apart as a model.[30]

The two most famous women in Muhammad's life, wife Khadīja and daughter Fātima, model their own exemplary qualities. Muhammad's first wife was known as "the pure woman" and was her husband's earliest and principal supporter during his initially troubled experiences of revelation. In spite of the increasing stress and hardship attendant to the Prophet's rejection by many Meccans, Khadīja was steadfast in embracing Islam. Fātima, known as "the resplendent woman," was Khadīja's youngest daughter.[31] She, too, was a model of courage during times of social upheaval and conflict that made family life difficult. Shīʿī sources often liken the mother of martyr-imams Hasan and Husayn to Mary and elevate her as the progenitrix of that branch of Islamic tradition. Fātima survived her father by only six months.[32]

Women who play prominent parts in the lives of Friends of God appear in a wide variety of guises and relationships. Whether the women are explicitly identified as Friends, sources describe them in a number of relational roles.

They are wives, mothers and grandmothers, sisters, confidants, strangers encountered serendipitously, individuals with a more or less independent existence, and symbols of (frequently negative) spiritual qualities. Many female Friends in hagiographical stories are destitute either because of longstanding socioeconomic circumstance or because of a deliberate choice of radical renunciation. Some of the most celebrated women, however, hail from the other end of the social spectrum, representing either a religious elite or royalty.

Some wives of God's Friends attain a measure of spiritual status derivatively rather than in their own right. In a Malay narrative of the famous Ibrāhīm ibn Adham, wife Sitī Sāliha suffers deeply when her undomesticated husband departs on pilgrimage, leaving her alone to raise their infant son. The narrative, which I touch on in chapter 5 but which merits revisiting here to illuminate the role of gender, uses the wife and mother as a device for describing how truly devout women should behave in the face of hardship, even when the difficulty results from a spouse's exclusive dedication to God. As Sitī Sāliha's son grows into young adulthood, he tells his mother he must set out for Mecca to find his long-lost father. After a long search, the boy believes he has come across his father, though he cannot be absolutely sure. In a touching scene reminiscent of the emotionally fraught reunions of ancient epic traditions, the boy cajoles his father into acknowledging his identity. Despite the young man's agonized entreaties, Ibrāhīm tells his son he cannot return to see his wife, for that action would vitiate all his service to God. When the heartbroken son returns to tell his mother the sad tale, Sitī Saliha utters a prayer of surrender, asking only that she be reunited with her husband in the hereafter. The author of the narrative then observes, "That is how women who love their husbands behave. If Sitī Saliha was like this, how much the more should we women believers be devoted to our husbands, in the hope that we shall obtain the mercy of God the Exalted in the hereafter. O you my sisters! Emulate what is described in this tale so that you may be secure in this world and the next."[33]

A number of the women in Rūmī's circle experience amazing events and are forthrightly acknowledged as Friends of God. In one story, Rūmī's second wife, Kirā Khātūn, visits the house of her husband's former confidant Chalabī Husām ad-Dīn, and her son Sultān Walad also happens by. The lady reports a dream in which Rūmī appeared to her as the mythical bird of paradise called the ʿAnqā, which no human eye had ever seen. The bird enveloped his son Sultān Walad in his wings. Her host, upon hearing about this dream in which he has no role, immediately conceives a jealousy of Sultān Walad.[34]

Other mothers, and grandmothers, occasionally figure prominently in hagiographical accounts. Amadou Bamba's saintly mother, Mame Diarra

Bousso, is so revered in Senegal that she is often compared to Mary, mother of the second-last prophet. Mame Diarra is a primary role model for countless Senegalese women. She learned Qurʾān by the age of ten, was an accomplished religious scholar by the age of nineteen, and is credited with many marvels. Her mother, Amadou's grandmother, often dressed in male clothing and is also celebrated for her holiness.[35] The twelfth-/eighteenth-century Moroccan Sufi Ahmad ibn ʿAjība tells a series of marvelous stories about his great-grandmother, Sayyida Fātima, in discussing his genealogy. He describes her as "a well-known Friend of God to whom the invisible was unveiled" and as one of the "people of assistance," a class of intercessory Friends at the top of the saintly hierarchy. She reportedly worked great marvels and was often sought out for her holy counsel. She once pushed to safe port a ship in danger of being overtaken by Christian assailants, was gifted with clairvoyance, and once even dispatched her deceased father on an errand of mercy to her son-in-law. Fātima was a redoubtable foe to anyone who conspired to cheat her or any other trusting soul.[36]

Sisters of God's Friends appear fairly often in hagiographical accounts, typically functioning as foils to their brothers and acting as elaborate props in a narrative whose real subject is the male Friend. Bishr "the Barefoot's" sister once boldly approached the renowned legal scholar Ahmad ibn Hanbal with a question. She told him she made a living by spinning yarn on her roof at night, with light shed only by the ruler's torches, and she wondered whether her practice was legally acceptable. Ahmad asked why she should be so scrupulous, and when she announced that she was Bishr's sister, he wept at the devotion of this family. Her spinning by borrowed light, he admitted ruefully, was not an acceptable practice. She must follow the meticulous ways of her brother to the point that if she were tempted to spin under another's light, her hand would refuse to comply. Sarī "the Huckster's" sister one day asked if she could clean out his house for him. He refused, saying that his life was too worthless for such an offering. But sometime later his sister arrived to find an old woman sweeping up. The sister berated her brother for turning her away and enlisting a stranger to do the job. Sarī told her not to worry, for the old woman cleaning up was "the world" that had asked for his affections and whom he had rebuffed. Because the world had persisted in its quest for involvement in the Friend's life, God had permitted it this menial task.[37]

Women function quite often as the spiritual teachers of male Friends. Ibn ʿArabī's two short hagiographical remembrances of the important Friends in his life include accounts of four shaykhas whose spiritual acumen he regarded highly. Of Shams, known as "mother of the poor," the shaykh observed that "her spiritual state was characterized chiefly by her fear of God and His good pleasure in her, the combination of the two at the same time in one person being extremely rare among us." Ibn ʿArabī reports that he met Nūna bint Fāṭima when she was ninety-six years old. One day a distraught woman came to see the shaykha, saying that she feared that her husband had traveled to another town to marry another wife. Nūna summoned the first chapter of the Qurʾān to follow the man and lead him back. When the man returned on the third day, he reported that a sense of anxiety had beset him just as he was heading for the wedding ceremony. He was not sure why he had returned to his wife.[38]

Major male Friends sometimes encounter by chance holy women with whom they have had no prior relationship. Principal settings for such meetings are Mecca (in the context of pilgrimage), the desert or a mountain, and miscellaneous nondescript roadside or riverside settings. Most such locales help define the character's liminality, as does the apparent insanity of some female Friends. In other words, some of God's favorite fools are women. Storytellers sometimes foreground the women's "otherness" by describing them as black, or otherwise ethnically unusual given the story's provenance (for example, as Turkish amid a non-Turkic population), or as slaves.

Dhū 'n- Nūn is among the male Friends who frequently encounter women in stories that raise questions about women's religious and social status. Many of the stories illustrate the sanctity of anonymous women by having the more prestigious male Friend learn from their example. According to ʿAṭṭār, Dhū 'n-Nūn's otherwise-unnamed sister became a mystic through service to her brother. Her spiritual status was sufficient to accord her the gift of at least one marvel. After reading a text of the Qurʾān about God's provision of manna and quail to the people of Moses, she insisted that she would not relent in prayer until God rained manna and quail on her. When she got her wish, she bolted from her house and disappeared permanently into the desert.[39]

Most of the other women of Dhū 'n-Nūn's acquaintance, however, were apparently wise enough in their own right to turn the tables on the more-celebrated male Friend. Dhū 'n-Nūn reportedly told many of the relevant stories himself. The mystery women Dhū 'n-Nūn encounters serendipitously embody a wide range of truths and spiritual insights. They tell the famous Friend a lot about himself, sometimes in surprisingly blunt speech, sometimes through symbolic actions. In at least one instance, Dhū 'n-Nūn deliberately seeks out the advice of a woman with a reputation for intense devotion. Sometimes Dhū 'n-Nūn tries to test the women, only to have them reverse the dynamic and cause him a twinge of spiritual embarrassment. If he were truly a spiritually advanced person, the woman might observe, he would have been oblivious of any woman in his vicinity and would not have addressed her in the first place. His only rejoinder to such otherwise-justifiable criticism is that he is so struck by some spiritual quality that he is genuinely unaware of the woman's gender. Surely the most striking feature of these accounts is the brutal honesty with which the women address and respond to this celebrated Friend. They call him a lazy ne'er-do-well and label him inept, spiritually backward, vain, hypocritical, and downright dishonest. Dhū 'n-Nūn never flinches in the face of such criticism and doggedly pursues the deep wisdom he knows these women command. In one unusual account, Dhū 'n-Nūn hears a supplicant voice while wandering through the mountains near Jerusalem and discovers a woman "thin as a stick of incense." She knows his identity because God has revealed it to her. Dhū 'n-Nūn bids her resume her prayers, and God responds by taking her life as the male Friend looks on. Just then, a much older woman who looks like the deceased woman appears and thanks God for his kindness. Dhū 'n-Nūn asks the identity of the dead woman, and the older woman identifies the dead woman as her daughter, Zahrāʾ the God-Intoxicated.[40]

Among the female Friends who appear in stories as individuals in their own right, Rābiʿa stands out; but the issue of her gender is rarely far beneath the surface. ʿAttār reports that several people once visited Rābiʿa in order to question her about her gender. Because God had granted virtue, nobility, magnanimity and prophecy only to men, they argued, surely nothing of real spiritual value remained for her. She replied that they were of course correct in their assertions about the glories of the male gender. She could not, alas, resist adding that no woman had been guilty of egotistical claims, arrogance, or pederasty. Rābiʿa often plays opposite men in stories designed to demonstrate her capability and wit. In one story, Hasan al-Basrī, Mālik ibn Anas, and Shaqīq of Balkh confront her with bold assertions about the nature of spiritual sincerity. She replies in turn to each of their three definitions of sincerity, each of which turns around an affliction sent by God. She insists that sincerity really entails forgetting the affliction altogether, even as the women of Egypt (Qurʾān 12:50) were quite oblivious to the fact that they had sliced their hands in astonishment at the beauty of Joseph.[41]

Several women who have lives of their own, so to speak, appear in Aflākī's hagiography and belonged to Rūmī's circle. Fakhr an-Nisāʾ (Pride of Womankind) was a Friend of God who lived in Konya in the later seventh/thirteenth century. She was a close friend of Rūmī and a member of a social elite. Aflākī calls her "a perfect person," alluding to a concept typically associated with male Friends. She was a "Rābiʿa of Creation" who enjoyed the support of the influential and spiritually advanced of her time and was gifted with miraculous powers. A companion of Fakhr an-Nisāʾ, Nizām Khātūn, also merited Aflākī's explicit characterization as a Friend of God. She was particularly poor and owned only a single cloth that she was saving for her burial shroud. But her desire to provide a *samāʿ* session ("audition," a prayer/recollection ritual that typically includes recitation, music, and rhythmic movement) for Rūmī led her to ask her attendants to sell the garment and use the proceeds for the ceremonies' expenses. The next day, the shaykh told her not to sell the garment, for he had come to attend *samāʿ* in her presence instead. A three-day audition session followed in the lady's home.[42]

Kirā Mānā was the nurse of Rūmī's son Sultān Walad and was celebrated for her marvelous deeds. As she prepared a meal for her master, she had a vision of angels calling her to God. She declined to depart, saying she was busy just now and was grieving her distance from Sultān Walad's father. The angels returned later and informed her she had no choice but to go with them. She instructed her eyes, tongue, and hand to go on weeping, lamenting, and working until she returned, and so they did. When she reappeared from her trip to the next world, she gladly rejoined her bodily limbs as they continued obediently doing her bidding.[43]

Aflākī describes another female Friend of God on earth, Khush-liqāʾ of Konya, as a "religious scholar and knower of God [i.e. a mystic]." Many male disciples in the towns of eastern Anatolia sought her counsel. She reported standing up to Nāsir ad-Dīn the preacher when he made disparaging remarks about Rūmī's grandson, Amīr ʿĀrif Chalabī. Her boldness made the preacher so irate that he left town, only to be forced by an injury to return the following Friday. In fact, he had been injured by ʿĀrif Chalabī himself, who rode his horse into the mosque while Nāsir ad-Dīn was preaching and wounded him with his spear. The preacher became a disciple of ʿĀrif Chalabī and died of his wounds three days later. Khush-liqāʾ recalled that she asked Chalabī tearfully what had become of the preacher. He replied that he had liberated the man and then went to visit his grave.[44]

Several important female Friends of medieval days have enjoyed unusual staying power and continue to attract significant local or even regional constituencies today. One such figure is Sayyida Manūbīya of Tunisia, a nation-state often noted for its reformist tendencies. This Friend's two holy sites—one in the capital city of Tunis and another in the nearby village of Manūba—attract large numbers of visitors every day of the week. But the principal gatherings are once-weekly sessions on Sunday in Manūba and Monday in Tunis. The afternoon *hadra* ("presence") rituals attract mostly women, whereas evening *dhikr* ("recollection") ceremonies draw mostly men. Sayyida Manūbīya is one of very few female Friends of God to inspire a full-scale hagiography shortly after her death. In fact, this holy woman has retained such popularity that as recently as 1418/1997, an official government publication on Tunisian women through the ages included a ten-page article on her.

Devotion to Sayyida Manūbīya has played out at both a rural site (in her home village of Manūba, about four miles from Tunis) and an urban *zāwiya* in Tunis, with the present structures at these sites dating from the first half of the nineteenth century. According to local traditions, her body lies in Tunis, but her spirit is alive in Manūba. These traditions also number this woman among the forty disciples of Abū 'l-Hasan ash-Shādhilī, eponym of the Shādhilīya Sufi order. Though such a relationship seems unlikely, Sayyida Manūbīya may well have been distantly connected to the founder through one or more of his followers, and the weekly evening rituals at her two sanctuaries are those of Shādhilī and are frequented by members of the Shādhilīya. For her male devotees, therefore, the lady recalls the great Sufi order, whereas for her female visitors, she is the ecstatic mystic who embodies concern for everyday problems.

Most distinctively, however, Sayyida Manūbīya is a favorite of young women desirous of finding a husband. For the newly married, her sanctuaries are the sites of the rite of passage from girlhood into womanhood. And when new parents celebrate the birth of their first child, they often do so in the presence of the lady, whose blessings they seek. Among the lady's other most ardent devotees are widows and women who have never married, as well as those whose marriages have been a source of suffering. Her compassion for all such women is a hallmark. But Sayyida Manūbīya is above all the patroness of Tunisia's women at large, who celebrate her as the truly liberated woman whose "daughters" constitute her spiritual retinue. The order of the day in her sanctuaries is "come as you are" and "express whatever you are experiencing," which provides a uniquely open atmosphere among the venues of Tunisia's Friends of God.[45]

In less positive treatments of the female gender, a relatively common theme in traditional hagiographical accounts casts a woman as the temptation-prone ego-soul (*nafs*). In a story from Sadafī, a man often overhears his neighbor apparently arguing loudly with a woman and even assaulting her, yet, to his surprise, he never hears a sound from the woman. Even when the neighbor speaks tenderly to her, she seems to make no response. Other neighbors also notice these odd occurrences. When the listening neighbor's pregnant wife goes into labor, he goes next door to get help from the ever-silent wife, but the man there insists that he lives alone. Then why, the visitor inquires, do people hear him engaging with "someone" they are sure is a woman? That woman, the man replies, is his ego-soul, and he deals with it according to its moods. Sadafī concludes that his vocal neighbor clearly shows that he is a Friend of God by providing just the remedy to relieve his inquiring neighbor's wife in her difficult childbirth.[46]

Finally, hagiographical accounts do not always present gender themes conventionally and straightforwardly. Some accounts raise fascinating questions about the construction of gender. One story from Aflākī describes in striking terms Rūmī's motherly qualities in nurturing his son Sultān Walad. Before the baby was weaned, Rūmī often held him while he slept. But Rūmī was in the habit of keeping night vigil, and Sultān Walad cried loudly whenever his father tried to put him down while he prayed. Ever the devoted father, Rūmī picked up the baby each time; and when the infant continued to cry for his mother's milk, Rūmī would put his own nipple in the baby's mouth. Employing a common pun, Aflākī reports that Sultān Walad sated himself on pure milk (*shīr*) from "that lion (*shīr*) of higher meaning," Rūmī. The hagiographer compares this marvel with the infant Abraham's ability to suck milk from his own finger in the cave, the emergence of water from Muhammad's fingertips; and the transformation of Abū Bakr's saliva into oil to light the Prophet's mosque one dark night.[47]

FIGURE 17. Making *ziyāra*, Mughal Emperor Akbar (d. 1014/1605) kneels at the tomb of the great Chishtī Friend Shaykh Farīd ad-Dīn Ganj-i Shakar (d. 664/1265) in Ajodhan (now Pakpattan in Pakistani Panjab), in 986/1578. Mughal, *Farhang-i Jahāngīrī*, ©The Trustees of the Chester Beatty Library, Dublin, IN 61.9.

7. Founding Friends

Authority, Institutions, and the
Economics of Intentional Community

Some of the social relationships and networks that we saw among Friends of God in chapter 6 developed into more formal socioreligious structures and organizations. These institutional dimensions of the lives of God's Friends are diverse and complex. A Friend of God's relationship to the larger community of Muslims is often embodied in related institutions. Moreover, a Friend's relationship with his or her community depends on perceptions of the Friend's authority and of his or her qualifications to teach the tradition or represent one of its many constituencies. Since societal institutions can flourish only where sources of funding are readily available, even "world-renouncing" Friends can wield immense economic power in their communities. In return for sage counsel, well-heeled seekers often underwrite the Friends financially. Patronage of God's Friends by rulers and other well-placed public figures is indeed a critical ingredient of the larger story of saints and their public. Many important Friends of God have founded major Sufi orders, and numerous sub-foundations have spun off from foundations typically linked to the founding Friend's tomb. This chapter explores some of these institutional implications of sanctity. A persistent theme, and one that offers a good starting point for this chapter, is the desire to establish the religious authority of the more socially engaged Friends by emphasizing their knowledge and solid foundation in the traditional religious sciences.

KNOWLEDGE, AUTHORITY, AND THE RELIGIOUS ESTABLISHMENT

Quite a few celebrated Friends of God have been as much admired for their expertise in the intricacies of Islamic religious disciplines as for their spiritual acumen. Biohagiographical accounts of the most influential Sufis

165

nearly always provide specific information about their subject's formal education in the traditional religious sciences. These areas of mastery include Qurʾān and the exegetical classics, hadith criticism, religious law (*fiqh*, sharia), and in some cases, even the sometimes-controversial discipline of *kalām*, or systematic theology. Critics of Sufism, and of orders that have acclaimed certain individuals as Friends of God, have occasionally leveled accusations that some Friends showed flagrant disregard for the Revealed Law. But accounts of the same Friends of God invariably point out their credentials in specific "schools" (or legal methodologies) of Sunnī Islamic law. For example, to cite only a few affiliations, Muhāsibī, Ibn Khafīf, Sulamī, Ghazālī, Ibn al-Fārid, and Qushayrī belonged to the Shāfiʿī school; Jurayrī, Kalābādhī, Ahmad-i Jām, and Hujwīrī, to the Hanafī; Ibn ʿAtāʾ, Abū Tālib al-Makkī, and Ansārī, to the Hanbalī; and Shiblī, Tirmidhī and Ibn ʿAbbād of Ronda, to the Mālikī. Bearing these connections in mind can help us appreciate the larger institutional context in which the lives of many Friends of God played out. Sources that set out to describe a saintly figure as a religious scofflaw are decidedly in the minority, and are typically ones that focus on the socially marginal figures I describe in chapter 6.

Friends and Higher Knowledge

To a great extent, the spiritual authority of God's Friends is intimately connected with their privileged access to higher forms of knowledge. For example, medieval documents from the archives of the North African city of Qayrawan (in present-day Tunisia) offer important insights into the essential relationships among holiness, knowledge, and spiritual authority. In the medieval Maghrib, dominated historically by the relatively conservative Mālikī law school, sanctity is largely unimaginable in the absence of strict adherence to traditional constraints of religious law. Scholar-saints are a major category among Maghribī Friends of God. As the cornerstone of Qayrawan's saintly community, one of the Companions of the Prophet supplies an unmistakable link to the ultimate human source of higher knowledge and authority, Muhammad himself. Late-medieval Qayrawan is but one of many settings in which key Friends of God derived their authenticity and credibility from their integration into the larger context of institutional religious legitimacy.[1]

In other words, many traditional sources cite knowledge as the primary credential for saintly authority. Above all, Friends of God represent the quest for a kind of knowledge that builds on the "exoteric" religious disciplines of scripture, prophetic tradition, and law. Their reason for being is to practice unyielding intellectual and emotional honesty in the search for the ultimate truths. As Friends teach in word and deed, one cannot own, manipulate, or take for granted these elusive realities. One can only try to foster a climate in which dedicated seekers can give themselves over to the quest and thus to facilitate an open-ended process of discovery that transcends any formal system of academic accreditation. To that end, a number of important Friends embroiled themselves in the less-than-contemplative enterprise of building communities of inquiry that seek experiential knowledge (*ma'rifa*) to build on knowledge acquired through the traditional religious sciences (*'ilm*). A wide range of foundations are credited to Friends of God, ranging from fairly small single-purpose establishments to extensive complexes that serve multiple functions. The latter institutions include ritual spaces such as mosques and oratories; educational facilities, from more basic Qur'ān and hadith schools to more advanced madrasas; residential facilities for members of orders and miscellaneous visitors and travelers; facilities that provide social services, such as soup kitchens and even medical clinics; libraries; and funerary facilities.

One of the most celebrated and best-documented founding Friends is Naqshbandī Shaykh Khāwja 'Ubayd Allāh Ahrār. We know of his extensive community-building efforts thanks to a series of *waqf* (pious endowment) documents that provide considerable detail about his deeds and intentions. Ahrār was a major mover and shaker in the Central Asian cities of Samarkand, Bukhara, and Tashkent (in present-day Uzbekistan). The shaykh endowed several large foundations, including an important madrasa in Samarkand in 875/1470. Exercising great practical savvy, the founder set up an extensive network of shops and other mercantile concerns to fund the various "nonprofit" elements of the religious complex centered on the college of law and theology. Some of Ahrār's critics accused him of unseemly self-interest when he stipulated that control of the endowment's funds must remain in the hands of his heirs.[2]

On the other side of the question of knowledge and authority, some Friends of God have roused the formal censure of religious scholars. Specialists in Qur'ānic exegesis, hadith scholarship, and religious law have often looked askance at the pursuit of esoteric knowledge. For God's Friends, such experiential knowledge is not a threat to the traditional religious disciplines but an absolute concomitant of an intimate relationship with God. Lovers of God take the greatest risks of all and can run afoul of the strictures of religious propriety—or worse—when they voice their souls' passion. A critical feature of Friends' relationships to God is their willingness to risk the charge of blasphemy by making statements that appear to suggest a metaphysical identity with God. To be more precise, these Friends are not so much "willing" to speak bluntly about God as they are constrained to do so. Among the more celebrated examples are Bāyazīd and Hallāj. Bāyazīd is perhaps most famous for his outburst "Glory be to me!" and Hallāj was executed ostensibly for his claim "I am the Truth." These two Friends are not alone in their claims to knowledge that threatens the bounds of institutional control.

Dangerous Knowledge

One unusual category of martyrs is that of prominent Friends suspected of infidelity to the core teachings of Islam. Some of these individuals were accused of claiming more intimate knowledge of God than a mere mortal has any right to claim. Hallāj of Baghdad was the prototypical "martyr-mystic," and ʿAyn al-Qudāt of Hamadhān was another famous member of this class of Friends, who were sometimes identified as "heretical" because they divulged dangerous secrets of unity with God. Their heresy was, ultimately, not a question of what they knew but of what they refused to keep to themselves.[3] Hagiographical records of these martyrs for divine knowledge rarely, however, treat the political contexts and motivations so essential to a deeper understanding of the events.

From Indonesia come some of the more striking stories of Friends suffering martyrdom because they refused to repudiate their intimacy with God. The twelfth-/eighteenth-century Javanese *Book of Cabolek* describes how several important Friends of God met their deaths in the kingdoms of early modern Java (the central large island in the Indonesian archipelago). At least two of their stories are clearly patterned after that of Hallāj, and one of thee men died at the hands of others whose names are listed among Indonesia's premier Nine Friends of God, the Wali Songo.

Shaykh Siti Jenar was so focused on union with God that he parted company with the other eight Walis and taught the secrets of friendship with God to disciples who were not ready for such powerful knowledge. Sunan Kalijaga, one of the Nine Friends, cut off Siti Jenar's head; the martyr's blood first flowed red but then turned a fragrant white and proclaimed the profession of faith. At that point, both body and blood disappeared, but Siti Jenar's voice continued to be heard proclaiming the centrality of union with God. Sunan Pangung was similarly condemned to die for his refusal to keep silent, but in this story, the Friend was burnt to death. Sunan Pangung walked into the flames carrying writing materials and composed a work on the path toward union with God. Before dying, he emerged to present the book to the sultan who had executed him.[4] Stories of this kind represent a variety of underlying motives. Some, for example, underscore the spiritual irresponsibility of the one executed, indicating that the execution was thus justifiable; others point out the folly of those bent on shoring up the rigid formalism of exoteric religious disciplines with no awareness of higher values.[5]

Knowledge is at least as significant an ingredient in the authority of the great founding Friends as the reputation for working marvels. The working of wonders attracts more attention, but privileged knowledge promises more lasting results and can provide a critical focus for communities within the greater community of Islam.

FOUNDING INTENTIONAL COMMUNITIES OF SEEKERS

Several important aspects of the founding activities of major Friends of God offer insight into the critical social function of community building. The most prominent of these features are the organizational history of Sufi orders, the specific social services provided by the orders and their related institutional structures, and the stories that enshrine communities' conviction that their foundations are the result of a divine mandate or commission.

Sufi Orders and Their Institutional Structures

Many of the confraternities generically known as Sufi orders have historical ties with important Friends of God. Some of these *tariqas* (ways or paths) resulted from the specific intentions of Friends long identified as their founders. Other organizations came into being as formal structures after the deaths of Friends, in which instances the "founders" are, more precisely, "eponyms" (people who gave their names to the organizations). But long before any of the various "paths" took the form of highly structured organizations, famous Friends of God were rallying points for more fluid gatherings of spiritual seekers. Convening at the residences of shaykhs and shaykhas renowned locally and regionally for their sagacity and piety, devout Muslims availed themselves of the Friends' advice and living examples.

As the reputation of a Friend grew, devotees would arrive in greater numbers, and from farther away, to benefit from the charisma and *baraka* (blessing, hence also power) of the teacher. A Friend's private space would in time prove inadequate, so followers would be forced to seek out more ample venues for their gatherings. Mosques and madrasas, often quite large and with spaces for multiple simultaneous gatherings, supplied the need in some instances. But the increasingly advanced nature of the teaching, along with more exclusivity in admitting members to the community, eventually gave rise to brick-and-mortar institutions designed specifically for the needs of Friends and their students. From Morocco to Malaysia, several important architectural forms emerged to serve the needs of these communities. The structures had to provide spaces for communal ritual gatherings and teaching sessions with the Friend; residential facilities for core members of a community, as well as for longer-term affiliates and occasional pilgrims from abroad; funerary facilities, from small, simple tomb-shrines of local holy persons to grander mausolea of founding figures and their successors to leadership; outreach facilities, such as soup kitchens, medical clinics, libraries, and educational facilities for children; and, in connection with the larger complexes, a variety of mercantile facilities to provide income for the upkeep of the larger institution. Physical evidence suggests that the number of occasional residents must have equaled, if not exceeded, the number of permanent residents at some of these institutions.[6]

Technical terms for the various institutional forms and functions differ regionally, but some of the more common terms follow. *Zāwiya* (plural *zawāyā*), which originally meant the "corner" in which a Friend of God lived, came to refer variously to relatively small tombs, mosques, or centers of devotional activity, and in North Africa, even to larger complexes of Sufi organizations. A *khān[a]qāh* (Arabic-Persian) is primarily a residential facility for core members of a community or may be a whole complex, roughly synonymous with the Arabic-Persian term *jamāʿat-khāna* (assembly hall). *Dār as-siyāda* (house of descendants of the Prophet), *dār as-sulahāʾ* (house of the upright ones), and *duwayra* (small circle) can also refer generically to community facilities. The term *ribāt* originally designated a fortified refuge for warriors on the frontier, but eventually its metaphorical meaning of a "place of attachment" took over, and warriors of the spirit replaced fighters seeking to expand the boundaries of Islamdom. In North Africa, the cognate *rābita* (hermitage) referred to an institution associated with Friends of local influence. However, both of the latter terms gave way to *zāwiya* during the 800s/1400s. In South Asia especially, *dargāh* (Persian for door-place, hence court) referred variously to residential facilities, major tombs, or simple shrines of Friends, whereas in Turkey, the term *buqʿa* (place) fulfilled a similar function. Retreat or withdrawal for particularly intense periods of spiritual discipline occurred in a *chilla khāna* (house of forty [days]) or *khalwa* (solitude). Terms for exclusively funerary functions include *qubba* (dome), *turba* (earth), *imāmzāda* (Persian, descendant of the imam), and *mazār* (place of visitation).[7] Of the two most important types of residential facilities, the *khanqāh* was typically for members of a single Sufi order, whereas the *dargāh* was often at the disposal of more than one lineage.

Beneath the Brick and Mortar

Behind the proliferation of brick-and-mortar construction was the evolution of organizations claiming the authority and spirit of specific Friends of God. Like their material settings, these "orders" or "ways" *tarīqa* (plural *turuq*) became increasingly complex. As circles of disciples grew, so, gradually, did the need for organizational structures that could accommodate larger and more diverse groups in more focused communities of purpose. Abū Saʿīd ibn Abī 'l-Khayr of northeastern Iran is often credited with drafting the first formal rule or charter for the regulation of community life, but the organization was limited to a single foundation. One of the first organizations of regional significance was that of Abū Ishāq al-Kāzarūnī of Iran. During the first half of the sixth/twelfth century, early major orders gained transregional importance under the leadership of ʿAbd al-Qādir al-Jīlānī of Baghdad, Ahmad ar-Rifāʿī of Iraq, and Abū 'n-Najīb ʿAbd al-Qāhir as-Suhrawardī of Iran, and his nephew Abū Hafs ʿUmar as-Suhrawardī. Some of the orders had close ties to guildlike *futūwa*, or chivalry-oriented, organizations. Many orders grew so expansively that they spawned branch foundations or "suborders" (sometimes referred to as *tawāʾif*, singular *tāʾifa*, party, faction).

Among other prominent Friends of God whose names are associated with major organizations are (in roughly chronological order) Najm ad-Dīn Kubrā of Central Asia, Muʿīn ad-Dīn Chishtī of South Asia, Ahmad al-Yasawī of Central Asia, Abū 'l-Hasan ash-Shādhilī of Morocco, Hajjī Bektāsh of Central Asia/Turkey, Jalāl ad-Dīn Rūmī of Turkey (the Mawlawīya order took its name from Rūmī's honorific, Mawlānā, which means "our master"; see Fig. 18), Ahmad al-Badawī of Egypt, Burhān ad-Dīn ad-Dasūqī of Egypt, Bahāʾ ad-Dīn Naqshband of Central Asia, Shāh Niʿmat Allāh Walī of Persia, Muhammad Sayyid Nūrbakhsh of Persia, Ahmad at-Tījānī of North Africa, Mulay al-ʿArabī ad-Darqāwī of North Africa, Muhammad ibn ʿAlī as-Sanūsī of North Africa, and Amadou Bamba of Senegal.

Practices and internal structures varied from one order to another. Among the common distinguishing attributes were modes of livelihood, degrees of political activism, social integration or preference for isolation, relative emphasis on daily communal life, and styles of prayer and ritual. Organizational structures and principles guided the establishment, functioning, and spread of Sufi orders and related institutions. They sought to enshrine and perpetuate the charisma of the founding Friend while facilitating the day-to-day maintenance of the community. The oldest historical records of formal organization are *silsilas*, genealogies tracing the spiritual lineages or pedigrees of prominent individual Sufis who identified themselves with a particular organization. Expanded versions of these "chains" eventually became the basis of hagiographical texts. The earliest attempts to organize institutional structures were in the form of rules authored (often allegedly) by founding Friends of God. Organizational concerns grew more complex as the orders expanded locally and, in many instances, spread regionally and

FIGURE 18.   Rūmī and early followers, who came to be known as the Mevlevi dervishes, engage in a variation on their famed "whirling" style of paraliturgical dance. Jāmī, *Nafaḥāt al-uns* (Ottoman, 1003/1595), ©The Trustees of the Chester Beatty Library, Dublin, T474:248v.

transregionally by founding new branches. In general, the larger the institution, the more elaborate became its methods of regulating communal life and delegating authority.

Some original foundations have insisted on maintaining centralized control over their branches, whereas others have allowed considerable autonomy in derivative foundations. Local foundations assigned different daily duties to members of various ranks. Organizations varied in their acceptance of members outside the core of an order. These affiliates—sometimes known as *awlād at-tarīqa*, children of the Path; *muhibb*, lover; *mutashabbih*, one who emulates; *muntasib*, "one who seeks a connection" (in the Bektāshīya)—participated in a limited number of the organization's activities and often played a supporting role. An analogy in the Christian tradition is the so-called third order organizations such as the Franciscans. Early gatherings centered on shaykhs whose authority derived from their spiritual attainment and piety. As the organizations grew into more formal institutional structures with multiple foundations, systems for maintaining the organizations naturally grew more complex.

As is so often the case in the evolution of religious institutions, if a founding Friend of God were to revisit the organization that has taken his or her name generations later, he or she might be surprised at the changes that have taken place. Administration of these intentional communities has historically reflected diverse theories and structures of authority. Intentional communities run the gamut from very loosely structured organizations to intricately hierarchical ones. Those with the most detailed and complex "organization charts" have the greatest degree of internal division of labor, with one superior delegating varying levels of authority to assistants. Most organizations have developed stable procedures for establishing successorship to a founder and subsequent shaykhs. Some orders maintained a high level of centralization even with the addition of new branches or suborders, whereas others have allowed new to remain quite independent. Many organizations have evolved distinctive ranks and titles, such as *nā'ib* (deputy shaykh), *khādim* (servant, assistant), and *muqaddam* (leader of a group within a local organization).

One Friend who is legendary for his founding activities is Abū Ishāq al-Kāzarūnī. One of southwest Persia's most famous preachers of his day, the shaykh first constructed a mosque to be the focal point of Kāzarūn, not far from the city of Shīrāz. In a town where Zoroastrianism remained a potent presence, Abū Ishāq's founding instincts were critical in fostering local Muslim identity. The Friend likened his building efforts to Abraham's construction of the Ka'ba. After the shaykh was buried in his mosque, the site continued to be a place of refuge for his many followers and converts to Islam. But more important than the mosque Kāzarūnī founded was the multifaceted community he fostered by constructing and funding a reported sixty-five *ribāts* in the region. The network became famous for its hospitality to the poor and to hungry travelers. Well into the later Middle Ages, members of the organization—known variously as the Kāzarūnīya, the Ishāqīya (after Abū Ishāq), and the Murshidīya (after a term that means "spiritual guide")— kept alive the spirit of the founder in their communities and traveled abroad to spread the shaykh's message.[8]

Many other important Friends of God endowed communal institutions. In his "autobiographical" account, ʿAlāʾ ad-Dawla as-Simnānī records in some detail his founding activities in the north-central Persian city of Simnān. After living for some time in a Sufi hospice (*khānqāh*) associated with important local religious leaders of previous generations, Simnānī decided to endow several new residential facilities. He describes the intense satisfaction he derived from setting up a number of pious foundations in the form of *khānqāhs*. Indeed, his gifts to these endowments were twice the inheritance he left to his widow and son. He notes that he was careful to avoid appointing any family members or descendants as officials or beneficiaries of the endowments, thereby minimizing the appearance of conflict of interest. Simnānī also stipulated that no children of officials of the endowment be allowed to assume the offices of their fathers, lest impure intention creep into the administration of the funds. In his account, he associates his founding largesse and attention to such details with his personal decision to renounce the world and his concern to make facilities available to others who seek to pursue a similar course.[9]

Founding Revelations: Divine Sanction of Institutions

Dreams, visions, and other divine communications sometimes command a Friend of God, or a saint's followers, to found an institution on a particular site. These communications enhance the religious legitimacy and spiritual authority of a wide range of foundations, especially mosques, madrasas, Sufi residential facilities, and tomb-shrines. In some visual renditions of the theme, an angel (typically Gabriel) appears to deliver a building to the holy person. One of the classic paintings shows Gabriel bringing a large architectural complex (which could even represent a whole city) to Muhammad. A more modern version shows Gabriel hovering over Amadou Bamba with a remarkably realistic rendition of the mosque of Touba, where the saint was to be buried and which he founded.[10] More important are images, for example, of Amadou Bamba that depict a dove visiting him with the divine command that he construct the monumental mosque that became the center of his birthday pilgrimage at Touba.[11] Even patrons not otherwise known for their piety have sometimes declared a divine origin for their decisions to endow major religious foundations.[12] Mausoleums, which so often become the nucleus of an expanding organizational complex, are especially important in this respect.

Famed Central Asian Friend Sayyid ʿAlī Hamadānī is said to have dreamt that the prophet Muhammad enjoined him to pick out a gravesite for himself in a local forest. On the following day, he took a group of people to the place and explained that he would occupy the tomb three years and a day hence. As the group was gathered at the site, wild animals from the woods came forward and bowed to Sayyid ʿAlī, immediately allaying the fears of his companions. Instructing his followers to make visitation to the place, the Friend of God completed the circle of essential ingredients in the initial founding of a sacred site.[13]

One of the better examples of a major mausoleum's evolution is the story of the founding of Rūmī's tomb. Stories about intimations of the siting of a tomb are sometimes very simple and unspectacular. Some accounts explain that the individual chose the site for his own burial place. Rūmī's father, Bahāʾ ad-Dīn Walad, rode his mule to a spot outside the walls of the central Anatolian city of Konya and sat looking at a small mound. He then declared that he and his sons would be buried in that spot. The place soon became famous for its unusual powers. After his father's death, Rūmī visited the tomb to meditate on vexing questions, and a voice from within would provide a response to his dilemmas. One day a rider raced past at a disrespectful speed, prompting Rūmī to comment that the rider should have known that the place was suffused with Bahāʾ ad-Dīn's spiritual presence. The failure to acknowledge this sanctity caused the horse to unseat its rider and drag him till his body disintegrated. The punishment sought to ensure that "those with bad manners on the road and those deluded by their status [this rider was a courtier of the sultan] take heed . . . of the jealous anger of the Friends of God and not act with presumption and boldness. . . ." Even the sultan prayed at the tomb, once seeking strength to overcome an approaching rival army. That night, Bahāʾ ad-Dīn appeared to the sultan in a dream, urging him to move against the enemy. When the sultan continued to doze, the Friend whacked the bed with his staff and poked the sultan in the chest. Thanks to this saintly intervention, the sultan went on to victory. Associates of Rūmī often reported dreams featuring the tomb. One described a light that emerged from it and engulfed his house and eventually lit the entire town and the world itself. The hagiographer, Aflākī, explains that the dream indicated the cosmic significance of this family institution.[14]

Aflākī devotes significant attention to the evolution of this "sepulchral shrine" into a "rare mausoleum." When a follower of Rūmī decided to advance the project, he told Rūmī's son Sultān Walad how much money was available. Sultān Walad asked how he could possibly proceed with so little cash, and the man replied that he would seek advice from Rūmī himself. The arrow of his sincere prayer reached the target of acceptance and caused God to move the heart of those in power so that money began to pour in. One especially intriguing episode in the unfolding saga of the sepulchral shrine's institutionalization associates it with the coffin of Abraham. An anonymous dervish came from Syria to pay his respects to Rūmī's grave. He had once lived in Jerusalem as a *mujāwir* (devoted resident) at the Al-Aqsā mosque and at the tomb of Abraham in Hebron. Aflākī, who was present during this episode, reports that after the community gave the visitor hospitality, the man dreamed about Abraham's tomb. He envisioned four bearers carrying the coffin of Abraham into Rūmī's mausoleum. God had instructed them to reinter Abraham in this new site. He interpreted his dream to mean that *everyone*—even the great prophets—sooner or later made visitation to this exalted sepulchral shrine. During the years after Rūmī's death, the power of the shrine would keep the city safe from all dangers, so long as its citizens continued to honor the tomb.[15]

This theme, of course, has another side, though this version seems less often told. In legends from South Asia, the tombs of several Friends of God collapse spectacularly when their inhabitants caused them to crumble out of embarrassment at having a grand structure built over their remains. Stories of this sort feature such notables as Ibn Hanbal in Baghdad, Bahāʾ ad-Dīn Naqshband in Bukhara, and Lāl Shāhbāz Qalandar in Sehwan, India.[16]

AUTHORITY, SHRINES, AND THE "CULT" OF GOD'S FRIENDS

Building a foundation in memory of a Friend of God is one thing. Ensuring its survival and growth is another. In general, the entombed presence of an individual known for holiness shed an aura of prestige and sanctity on the institution linked to the tomb. However, in some instances, the opposite was true. Some persons buried within the precincts of a dervish lodge, for example, enjoyed a higher level of respectability than their achievements and reputation warranted. The public sometimes simply assumed that because such institutions were on sacred ground, the people buried there must have equally holy status. Then, as later generations of Sufis, often members of well-established orders, took over the sites, they adopted the entombed individuals into their orders' hierarchies of sanctity. Funerary chambers tended to be among the most publicly accessible parts of a dervish lodge (at least in Anatolia), with sizable windows on the main street that allowed passersby to make a symbolic "visit" to the tomb and listen in on ritual sounds emanating from within. This accessibility clearly distinguished tombs in dervish institutions from the more-sequestered funerary chambers of other institutions, such as mosques and madrasas. Further, this openness to the outward world fostered the celebrity of certain saints as travelers took their stories to other cities.[17]

For the religious "establishment," tomb-shrines have often been a source of contention. The most common reason for "official" resistance has been the theological argument that Islamic revelation does not countenance a mediating role for human beings. In a more general sense, many Muslims have articulated serious reservations about participating in rituals at tombs or other shrine sites, because they assume that such rituals require them to pray to, rather than for, the individual memorialized at the site.[18]

Shrines and Spiritual Authority

What confers shrine status on a burial place? What do pilgrims to these places want to gain from their visits? And why does popular practice so often seem to thrive in the face of official disapproval? The *dargāh* of Nizām ad-Dīn Awliyāʾ in Delhi is one of South Asia's most intriguing Muslim sites and offers a fine example of the link between such institutions and religious or spiritual authority. The great Chishtī Friend's shrine consists of a large courtyard with his tomb at its center. Within the larger courtyard are various smaller ones. Subordinate structures play a variety of roles, from housing the operations of the shrine staff (both Chishtī Sufis and lay officials) to providing space for rituals such as purification for prayer and curative bathing (a large pool) and preserving the patrimony of the Chishtī order (library and archive facilities). The officiating personnel of this and other major shrines include the leading specialists in the cult's regular ritual observances—typically either descendants of the Friend or religious scholars; a category of lesser officiants often known as the Friend's "neighbors" (*mujāwir*), who are responsible for perform ritual cleaning services of a devotional sort (as distinct from ordinary maintenance tasks generally left to lower-caste individuals); and individuals and groups who provide a host of other services, most prominently musicians and singers who facilitate communal rituals.[19]

Accounts of contemporary pilgrim experiences at Nizām ad-Dīn's shrine provide an instructive case study in this context. Many visitors to the *dargāh* come on pilgrimage from all over India, hoping to gain some special benefit. But most devotees are more local folk who stop in several times a day, not to acquire a blessing but to give thanks for a cure or gift. Though their first visit may have been prompted by desperation, they continue to come because of the sense of pervasive spiritual care that makes the place holy. Pilgrims report the unshakable conviction that the Friend is not truly dead but is living in their midst as they gather; though the Friend is veiled from their sight, he is accessible to those who come with the appropriate disposition. Some visitors report dreams and visions of Nizām ad-Dīn within the shrine precincts. Whatever the mode of encounter, repeat visitors above all experience a consoling, sustaining presence. To be sure, visitors still report cures and marvels. But above all, this place offers seekers respite from the outer world's stresses and the freedom to remove their masks and pretenses and to surrender themselves without artifice to the compassionate response of the Friend.[20] Chapter 8 describes further how such shrines have functioned as ritual venues for pilgrims. For the present, let us look at how such foundations came to be integrated into the larger institutional frameworks surrounding Friends of God.

Pilgrim Guides and the Etiquette of Ziyāra

Among the important sources of hagiographical information is a genre of literature, the "pilgrim guide," that developed in medieval cultures. The guide evolved for both practical and educational reasons. Travelers intent on making visitation to sacred sites needed help in getting there, often from great distances. Not surprisingly, the most widely known guides focus on the universally acknowledged sacred cities, principally Mecca and Medina (see the frontispiece) but sometimes Jerusalem as well. These guides not only provide detailed descriptions of the various precincts within the larger areas that are "forbidden" or off-limits to any but genuine pilgrims but also sometimes included elegant illustrations of the sites. A further development of the genre catered to pilgrims who wanted to journey to institutional sites associated with favorite Friends of God. One famous seventh-/thirteenth-century work is a fine example of a relatively simple, austere overview of a sacred geography as understood in the Arab Middle East during the era of the Crusades. This *Book of References to the Knowledge of Visitation* lists the burial places of scores of individuals but does not go into detail about their lives. The Syrian author notes that he wrote the guide in response to requests from pious friends that he document places that he has visited. He is happy to describe some of the "amazing things, monuments, buildings, and structures" he has witnessed in his extensive peregrinations. The sites include tombs of some of the prophets, and he explicitly mentions "righteous persons, *abdāl*, Friends of God, and religious scholars" who lived and died in Syria, Egypt, Iraq, and the Arabian Peninsula.[21]

One factor that determines how founding Friends make their mark on the religious life of millions of Muslims is the way in which their constituents choose to acknowledge the Friend's ongoing presence among them. Tombs and shrines, like that of Nizām ad-Dīn in Delhi, are focal points in the religious practice of many local and regional communities. Uniquely revered resting places call for uniquely reverent symbols and rituals. Some pilgrim guides function as catalogs of important tomb-shrines and related sites that pilgrims should include in their religious travel plans; some offer detailed instructions for the ritual practices appropriate to specific shrines; and some combine aspects of the travel guide with visitation etiquette.

Sources combine detailed instruction on visitation etiquette with specific tour-guide information on the most important sites in a region or locality. Egyptian author Ibn ʿUthmān's *Guide for Pilgrims on Visitation* lays out a set of specific directives for proper conduct before and during a visitation. He begins with purity of intention, characterized by a wish to perform the visitation entirely out of desire for God and repentance. Any vestige of desire to gain respect or reputation vitiates the act. Friday is the optimum day for a visit, for on that day that Muhammad visited, but because God created light on a Wednesday, that day is an acceptable alternative. Pilgrims should avoid stepping or resting on graves. Ibn ʿUthmān recommends visiting the burial places of prophets and relatives and Companions of Muhammad. Pilgrims ought to approach the front of the tomb and talk as if speaking with a living human being, but they must resist the temptation, and undue familiarity, of kissing graves or applying the dust to their bodies. However, he recommends recitation of Qurʾān and supplicatory prayer addressed to the deceased, as well as prayer for Muhammad. Supplication for oneself is allowed, but one must also be mindful of the deceased person's noblest attributes. Visiting deceased family members is often recommended, but visitors are advised to moderate their expressions grief and avoid wailing or self-mutilating behavior. Friends and family members may sit near the tombs, and reciting Qurʾān for the benefit of the departed is recommended. But when passing the graves of enemies, pilgrims must overcome the temptation to gloat over their departures from this life. In general, visitors should avoid laughter and should not perform ritual prayer near graves. [22]

Documents that help devotees find their Friends' shrines and tell them how to behave once they arrive are part of the larger category of literature called hagiography. Many hagiographical works originate within the institutions dedicated to the veneration of Friends and are shaped by their ideologies and politics.

CULTIC CENTERS AND HAGIOGRAPHICAL SOURCES

The relationships between the devotional centers associated with Friends of God and the hagiographical sources that inform us about them are complex. Chapter 10 takes up questions about the functions of the texts themselves. Here I suggest some ways of understanding how cultic centers, with their unique cultural, social, and political contexts, influence the production of hagiographical accounts.

Some Friends have gained reputations for founding important institutions. More frequently, however, the institutions founded by their followers or by political leaders who are eager to capitalize on the Friend's local prestige have expanded Friends' fame and power. To create such institutions, of course, Sufi organizations have had to cultivate sources of significant funding, which often has required a rapprochement with political authorities. Sheila Blair distinguishes between the monumental scale of mausoleum-centered institutions in the "grand tradition of saints like Imam al-Shāfiʿī" and the more modest scale of tombs for Friends of more regional stature.

Not all Friends of God founded institutions, even on a local or regional scale. But a significant number left legacies far beyond the cities and lands of their origin, most notably in the form of enduring and influential Sufi orders. Many major hagiographical works have arisen from within the ranks of particular orders, typically telling the stories of the organization's founder and his family or of successors to leadership of the order. Such accounts frequently focus on the glory and charisma of the *tarīqa*'s earliest generations, describing their marvelous deeds and divinely sanctioned choices in laying the group's foundations and directing its pristine unfolding. Two examples illustrate how scholars are beginning to gather and arrange the pieces of an intricate puzzle. The emerging picture provides insight into the institutional contexts in which some major Friends of God have had their origins and derived their authority and fame. One combines the study of architecture and urban planning with the evolution of hagiographical sources. The other examines further the purposes of institutionally generated hagiographies.

Foundations and Texts in the Age of Rūmī

Recent research on the medieval eastern Anatolian foundations of Sufi organizations offers important insights into the relationships between institutions and the evolution of hagiographical sources. Sara Wolper suggests that members of dervish lodges gathered the material that became the substance of hagiographic narratives, which in turn shaped the communal identities of subsequent members of their organizations. The lodges thus became local archives that enshrined an order's collective memory. Wolper uses an interdisciplinary approach to study how the dervish lodges reshaped local religious and cultural forces by changing the "hierarchy of spaces" in an urban setting. They did so by a deliberate transformation of urban planning, through purposeful placement, orientation, and structuring of their lodges. She draws her data from three medieval cities in eastern Anatolia and analyzes the ways the lodges helped mediate religious, spiritual, and political authority. Wolper argues that architectural visibility informs one's perception and experience of the world; thus, changes in "visual hierarchy" change one's behavior and worldview.

Wolper examines how dervish lodges promoted the reshaping of religious communities in medieval Anatolia during the years that Rūmī lived in the Saljūqid capital at Konya. She argues that the Bābā Rasūl revolt against the rule of the Saljūqid dynasty in eastern Anatolia in 638/1240 politicized the lodges after Bābā Rasūl's followers took to meeting in them regularly. This development in turn gave rise to new sources of patronage from within the Saljūqid administration, generating new interest in endowing lodges and tomb-shrines and thus shifting interest away from the madrasa, the more traditional beneficiary of Saljūqid patronage.

In the dervish lodges, members of the orders assembled hagiographic lore that would shore up the authority of founding figures. They did so by portraying formal relationships between Friends of God and the officials of the ruling Saljūqid dynasty. They even featured some of their political patrons in the narratives, thereby increasing the likelihood of receiving continuing financial and political support from the royal court. The followers of a given Friend of God also benefited if the Friend counted important political figures among his or her spiritual followers. Rulers enhanced the authority of the Friend's institutional descendants by submitting themselves to their tutelage.

Two main types of written sources contribute to Wolper's conclusions: foundational documents called *waqfs* and Sufi hagiographies. But buildings also played a critical role in conferring religious authority and prestige. Real estate—what Wolper calls "visible turf"—communicated power and status. Lodges were the least costly foundations to endow, because they required more modest initial investments, were smaller, required less upkeep, allowed lower salaries, and required less supporting funding than, say, madrasas, and were thus most attractive to donors. Two kinds of institutional symbolism converged and reinforced each other: the symbolic location of the lodges in the "literal space" of their urban contexts and the "literary space" of hagiography.

Wolper documents changes in urban space through foundational texts as well as physical sites, noting that before 638/1240, the organization of public spaces in the three target cities was "grafted" onto Byzantine structures. After 638/1240, Muslim authorities began adapting Byzantine spaces more actively, giving greater prominence to distinctively Muslim architectural functions such as those of the madrasa, caravanserai, and tomb-shrine. Sufi orders located dervish lodges strategically along heavily traveled pedestrian thoroughfares, affording them heightened visibility and easy access. Later location of tombs near major lodges further enhanced their prestige and allowed the lodges to become increasingly influential in determining social and economic patterns in the lives of the cities.

Lodges gradually made inroads into the "more restrictive" authority of madrasas and mosques that were under the control of religious scholars rather than the more independent Sufi leaders. By their placement outside the Saljūqid dynastic city centers and nearer the city gates, the lodges also caught the attention of visitors immediately and siphoned off economic activity from the citadels, because the carefully chosen location of the lodges melded the market place with the religious space of the Sufi organization. Though lodges generally were not massively imposing structures, their facades were sufficiently ornate and iconic to capture attention. Lodges were often at the center of architectural complexes, and the wide range of services they offered (including food for the poor as well as attractive ritual ceremonies and venues for intellectual discussion) made them natural focal points for a broad spectrum of the populace.[23]

FIGURE 19. *(opposite)* Workers at the upper left carry roofing materials to repair the shrine of an Indian Friend of God, with various religious officials in animated interchange in the courtyard. Jāmī, *Nafaḥāt al-uns,* attributed to Laʿl (Mughal 1604/5), ©The Trustees of the Chester Beatty Library, Dublin, IN 61.5.

Texts and Foundations in Medieval Central Asia

Some hagiographical works that have emerged from Sufi organizations focus on a specific institutional purpose. They seek to legitimize and aggrandize the order's leadership and history over all others—in a mode that Devin DeWeese calls "*tarīqa*-consciousness." Hagiographic accounts often hint at competition between and among orders through literary upstaging, handing the "lesser" competitor a serious dose of criticism for its doctrinal, juridical, or ritual inferiority. In such texts, the stories of individual leading figures in the order are vehicles for highlighting the order's inherent strengths. The leading Friend might, for example, have a dream in which the Prophet approves of the saint's choice of a certain kind of prescribed prayer for members of the order.

DeWeese makes a useful distinction between the public and private features of institutions connected with Friends of God. For nearly five hundred years, the Central Asian shrine of Ahmad Yasawī, in present-day Kazakhstan, had a wide variety of public functions. It functioned politically as a source of legitimacy, economically as a source of many supporting endowments and multilevel patronage, and ritually as part of a network of shrines in a pilgrimage visitation circuit. Equally important, but harder to detect, are the more private aspects of the institutional life of a Friend's inner circle. Yasawī's shrine functioned hagiographically as a clearinghouse for narratives about the "founder" of the Yasawīya order. It was a place where members of the order constructed—or reconstructed—their institutional identity by "re-spiritualizing" accounts of the Friend that had previously evolved more publicly and "popularly."

Sources that seek to articulate and consolidate the more private features of institutional life in Sufi orders typically underscore concerns about authority and spiritual legitimacy in the leadership, as well as suggest methods for the formation, discipline, and identity development of members. In the rather unusual case of Ahmad Yasawī, the "private" sources emphasize the Friend's spectacular ability to generate marvels on an epic scale. The preponderance of such accounts about Yasawī suggests that the stories originated within more public contexts and sought to grip the popular imagination. When the members of the order began to generate their own hagiographical identity, using the material already widely known outside Sufi circles, they did so apparently in response to a parallel development in the rival Naqshbandīya order.[24]

Many Friends of God have never had an explicit association with institutional developments. Indeed, accounts of some important figures might leave the impression that an authentic Friend would not dream of getting involved in the mercantile and political aspects of institutional life. Founding Friends have nevertheless made an important contribution to the lives of Muslims across the globe for many centuries. Their story would be incomplete without some accounting for their works and for stories about their founding activities. We turn now to the role of institutions, from the humblest local shrines to the most extensive religious foundations, in creating a global geography of revered sites and ritual settings.

FIGURE 20.   Pilgrims pray at the Jannat-i Darvāza, in the *dargāh* of celebrated Chishtī Friend Khwāja Muʿīn ad-dīn (d. 633/1236), Ajmer, India, October 2001. Photo by Anna Bigelow.

8. Where God's Friends Walked

Revered Sites and Ritual Settings

One could lay out a detailed map of Islamdom, from Morocco to Malaysia and from Albania to Zanzibar, just by plotting out sites made holy and famous by Friends of God. Connected by routes that pilgrims have used over many centuries, these destinations form an expansive network of devotion, social interaction, and trade. Islam's prophets and Friends of God collectively represent as cogent a force for way-finding and sacralization as one is likely to encounter in a major religious tradition. Their lives and stories invariably evoke a sense of place—whether a city or towns, desert or mountain, seashore or hinterland. Muslims of every age have come to associate the important events of their own communal history, as well as events in their individual life stories, with the lore of those who have modeled holiness and devotion for them. Much of Muslim religious life, so bound to a sacred terrain by the "mystic chords of memory," is colored by ritual associations with this geography of faith.[1]

Whenever Muslims enact their five-times-daily ritual prayer (*salāt*), they face Mecca. When they make the hajj or *ʿUmra*, "the greater" or "lesser" pilgrimages,[2] respectively, they go to Mecca, as well as (typically) to the Prophet's mosque in Medina, where Muhammad is buried. A third major sacred site is Jerusalem. The ancient city is most prominently associated in Muslim lore with Muhammad's Ascension and with previous prophets, especially Abraham, David, and Solomon, but it has also become increasingly important politically as well as religiously for Muslims, Jews, and Christians alike.

In addition, countless less-celebrated cities and towns feature spiritual centers, many of which are anchored by ancient institutions linked to local paragons of sanctity. One historian suggests that "Islamic cities" share in holiness in three ways: by the power and blessing (*baraka*) of a prophetic or saintly tomb or shrine, or of the tombs of an exceptionally large number of descendants or Companions of Muhammad; by their role in the larger narrative of salvation; or by their function in religious cosmology.[3] An important genre of literature focuses on the *fadāʾil*, merits or fine features, of major holy sites or of individuals such as the Companions of the prophet Muhammad. Data culled from works in the genre have in turn supplied important themes in visitation guides for pilgrims that offer detailed tours of cemeteries and individual shrines in countless sacred sites.[4] This chapter examines a variety of sacred settings and looks at some of the many ways in which the memory of prophets and Friends of God has constructed a world for millions of Muslims. We begin with the three cities that stand at the center of the spiritual world for all Muslims (Mecca, Medina, and Jerusalem) and expand into an abbreviated global tour from North Africa to Southeast Asia, with brief stops at prime sites at the centers of regional and local "sacred geographies."

THE PIVOTAL HOLY PLACES

Holy places reside in two kinds of overlapping sacred geography: global/universal and local/regional. Muslims have always been keenly aware of living in a global religious setting whose center is the Arabian city of Mecca. There a shrinelike sacred place called a *haram* (from an Arabic root connoting forbiddenness and therefore restricted access) features a roughly cube-shaped structure called the Kaʿba (from an Arabic root meaning "to dice into cubes"). The structure existed during the lifetime of Muhammad, and Islamic lore reports, variously, that it came into being in the time of Adam and that God commanded Abraham and his son Ismaʿil to rebuild it, or that Abraham initiated the structure. Either way, the Kaʿba symbolizes many centuries of spiritual questing and reconnoitering, for it was a destination for pilgrims long before Muhammad's time.

The Prophetic Origins of the Kaʿba's Sanctity

Mecca's sacred precincts are perhaps the most prominent settings for tales of the prophets, as well as for stories of Friends of God. After Adam, the first prophet, repented of his primal disobedience, God assured him of forgiveness and called him "truly my friend." Adam and Eve had been temporarily separated, but God sent Gabriel to tell Adam that he and Eve would be reunited at the site of Mecca, where Adam was to build Mecca and God's House, the Kaʿba, after its celestial prototype, the "Frequented House" (*al-bayt al-maʿmūr*). Adam and his descendants were then to circumambulate the House seven times and become the primordial pilgrims in this place that would be the first town on earth. Kisāʾī gives considerable detail associating Adam and Eve with sites within the pilgrimage precincts, beginning with the two hills Safā and Marwā and the sacred spring of Zamzam, which would later play a central role in the life of Abraham's wife Hagar and their son Ismāʿīl. In that place, on a Friday's eve, Adam's wife conceived her first child. Thaʿlabī's version is briefer than Kisāʾī's but further links the couple with ritually important sites outside Mecca, Mina and ʿArafāt.[5]

Noah's journey in the ark took him around the world in six months. When Noah arrived at length above the site of the Kaʿba, he circumnavigated the site for seven days in a waterborne equivalent of pilgrim circumambulation (Thaʿlabī). Kisāʾī reports that Noah had asked God's permission to make pilgrimage before the flood, and while Noah was at Mecca, God protected the ark by having angels lift it heavenward until Noah had completed the rituals. At this point, the ark becomes an actor in the story. After the earth floods, the ark takes Noah first to Jerusalem, where it speaks to inform Noah of the future importance of this place for his prophetic descendants. Proceeding to Mecca, the ark circumnavigates the Kaʿba seven times, thus foreshadowing the pilgrim ritual of circumambulation. The ship then takes Noah on a tour of sacred sites, telling him about each place's significance in the history of faith.[6] (See Fig. 21.)

Abraham's connections with Mecca arguably have the greatest symbolic importance among Friends for Islamic tradition as a whole. The prophet, Intimate Friend of the Merciful (*khalīl ar-rahmān*), as he is still commonly known, went with his wife Hagar to Mecca and took up residence not far from the Kaʿba, which lay in ruins as a result of Noah's flood. There he left her with the infant Ismāʿīl and returned to his wife Sarah. During his absence, Hagar's experience of near panic in her need for water caused her to run frantically back and forth between the two hills Safā and Marwā. Gabriel descended with assistance, and Ismaʿil scratched the earth to bring forth the spring of Zamzam. When the boy reached his majority, Hagar died.

Three times in subsequent years, Abraham's desire to see his son prompted God to send Gabriel with a heavenly steed (some say it was Burāq) to bring the prophet to Mecca. During the first two journeys, Abraham did not find his son at home and so departed, leaving a message with his son's wife. On the third journey, Abraham finally reunited with his son, and God commanded the two men to rebuild the Kaʿba. After father and son had completed the task, Gabriel conducted them to all the sacred sites within the larger area now associated with pilgrimage rituals.[7] Just a few feet from the door of the Kaʿba today stands a small cupola that marks the "station of Abraham"

FIGURE 21. Noah and his family stand on the ark, which is possibly circumnavigating above the Kaʿba. At lower left, a man tries to escape the rising water. At lower right, an enigmatic element (variations of which occur in a number of scenes of this event) appears to show a man meditating in a vaulted or bell-like structure; this image may reflect the notion in some Muslim societies that the mysterious water-dwelling Khidr is a patron of seafarers. Naysābūrī *Qisas al-anbiyāʾ*, 1580, Spencer Collection, The New York Public Library, Astor, Lenox and Tilden Foundations; Psnypl_spn_575, MS 46:19a.

(*maqām Ibrāhīm*). Within its reliquary is a stone on which Abraham is said to have stood, next to his son, after completing the Ka'ba. According to tradition, God caused the stone to soften like wax, so that the footprints of Abraham would remain there permanently for devotional reverence by generations of pilgrims.

According to Tha'labī, Solomon once journeyed to Mecca to make pilgrimage. When he entered the precincts of the Ka'ba, he was saddened by the numerous idols there and moved on. Even God's House itself grieved, moving God to inquire about the cause of its tears. The Ka'ba replied that God's prophets and saints, like Solomon, did not even stop there momentarily, let alone mention God's name or engage in prayer within its walls. God consoled the House and promised that it would soon be the focus of a new spiritual vitality under the leadership of God's favorite prophet (Muhammad, of course). God then enjoined Solomon to worship at the Ka'ba by offering up twenty thousand ewes and five thousand cattle. He then foretold the coming of Muhammad. Solomon later returned there on the wings of the wind to make pilgrimage.[8]

The next prophet with major links to Mecca in the traditional accounts is Muhammad. He was born there and lived in Mecca for over fifty years, before migrating northward to Medina with the young Muslim community in the Hijra, 1/622. During Muhammad's early life, the Ka'ba had already long been the center of Meccan life. It was one of a number of similar structures at the heart of sacred sites throughout the Arabian Peninsula. The rather plain building reportedly housed some 360 images of pre-Islamic deities. A black stone, perhaps of meteoric origin, mounted in one of the Ka'ba's corners was an ancient symbol of the place's sacredness.

Early in the first/seventh century, thieves made off with treasures from the roofless Ka'ba. The leading tribesmen of the Quraysh proposed to rebuild the structure and needed a way to include the city's various constituencies symbolically in the renewal. Muhammad was granted the honor of replacing the black stone. Tradition holds that he laid down his cloak, placed the stone in the middle, and asked respected local tribal leaders to raise it together before he reinstalled it. Muhammad was then thirty-five and had not yet received his inaugural prophetic commission. After the initial revelations, traditionally dated to 610, Muhammad began to preach his new message, and before long, the Quraysh came to perceive him as a threat to their hegemony. For the next twelve years, the Prophet's relationship to the holy site was tenuous at best, for the Quraysh sought to ban him from its sacred precincts. Some eight years after the Hijra, Muhammad and his supporters returned to reclaim Mecca for the Muslim community and performed a ritual cleansing of the Kaʿba. Traditional accounts say that during that visit in 9/630, he destroyed the idols housed there. During his "farewell pilgrimage" shortly before his death, in 11/632, Muhammad completed the reclamation of the Kaʿba as the premier Islamic ritual site.[9]

Friends of God and the Kaʿba

Against the backdrop of prophetic associations with Mecca and its sacred precincts, one can understand why stories of so many latter-day Friends of God prominently feature Mecca, the Kaʿba, and pilgrimage. Journey to Mecca is one of the most common story lines in traditional hagiography. One of the principal themes in these accounts is the Friend's intense desire to make pilgrimage and his or her willingness to undergo great hardship in the process. A related theme turns on various forms of reversal, in which either the Friend's intention is subverted or the Friend becomes the goal of the journey rather than the journeyer.

En route to Mecca via the desert, Rābiʿa saw the Kaʿba advancing to meet her. She insisted that she sought the Lord of the House, not the House itself. As beautiful as the Kaʿba may be, she went on, she wanted to see the approach of her Lord. A related account includes Ibrāhīm ibn Adham in this story. After fourteen years' journey, Ibrāhīm finally arrives at Mecca, only to find that the Kaʿba is not there. A voice informs him that, indeed, the Kaʿba has departed to welcome Rābiʿa on the last leg of her journey. As she comes hobbling into town, suddenly the Kaʿba reappears in its accustomed location. Ibrāhīm berates the old woman for causing such a stir. Having none of his abuse, Rābiʿa counters that he was the one making a scene by taking so long to get to Mecca! He merely spent extra time in prayer en route, he explains in his defense.

Rābiʿa returns to her home city of Basra and again resolves to go on pilgrimage. But this time she plans to beat the Kaʿba at the welcoming game. For seven years, she crawls across the desert. Upon her arrival at ʿArafāt in the valley outside Mecca, a disembodied voice asks her what she wants. If her desire is to encounter God, the voice warns, she should know that she would only be obliterated by the encounter. Rābiʿa responds that all she wants is to experience a "drop of poverty" in her spiritual thirst. The voice answers that the seeker is still too engrossed in her own life to experience her wish. Then she sees in the air before her an ocean of blood. The voice explains that this blood is all that remains of other seekers who have wanted union with God. When Rābiʿa asks to know one feature of their lot, the voice replies that they all began with seven years of arduous questing. Hearing this answer, she realizes that she is not worthy of seeing the House, let alone the Lord of the House. And she returns home to Basra to pray.[10]

One of the more striking examples of metaphorical imagination in stories of God's Friends is the use of imagery in which the Friend represents the Ka'ba. For example, an individual might approach a Friend to announce his or her intent to make pilgrimage and to ask how to take maximum spiritual advantage of the opportunity. The Friend responds that the would-be pilgrim would be better off circumambulating the Friend. One variant has the Friend supersede the Ka'ba directly; another explains that because the Ka'ba has in fact come to the Friend (as in the first story of Rāb'īa above), the pilgrim need not travel all the way to Mecca. Aflākī tells a story about Fakhr an-Nisā', a woman of Rūmī's circle, who desired to visit the Ka'ba. She resolved first to consult with Rūmī to see if he concurred with her decision to make the journey. Before she could give voice to her concern, he told her that her intention was good and that he hoped they might attain that blessed goal together. That night, as Rūmī performed his devotions on the roof, he called Fakhr an-Nisā' in excitement to come to the roof. There he pointed out to her that the Ka'ba had actually come to them and was circling above them—in a reversal of the usual ritual in which pilgrims ritually circumambulate the shrine. Fakhr an-Nisā' immediately relinquished her desire to make the trip and surrendered to God.[11]

Some stories focus on the pilgrim's intent, reporting that he or she needs to refine the motive for pilgrimage through lengthy suffering. After living in a cave for a spell, Ibrāhīm ibn Adham hit the road for Mecca. Along the way, a stranger taught him God's highest name. When Ibrāhīm invoked God with that name, Khidr materialized before him and explained that the prophet Ilyās (Elijah) had disclosed the name to him. Ibrāhīm continued his journey and encountered a band of seventy Sufis who were nearly dead from devotion. One of them warned Ibrāhīm that he should be wary of the God who slays pilgrims mercilessly. Khidr had visited them as well, as they reached Mecca, but when the seekers seemed to take the slightest hint of credit for their success, a voice reprimanded them for their hypocrisy. They had lost track of the true goal and were satisfied with less than God, and they had to pay the ultimate price. The young man explained to Ibrāhīm that he was still spiritually "raw" but would survive if he ripened. Ibrāhīm took fourteen years to complete this journey. As his caravan approached Mecca, he raced ahead and met a group from the city who asked if Ibrāhīm were in the group, for the Meccan elders wanted to meet him. Ibrāhīm asked why they would care about such an unbeliever, and they began to pummel him, accusing him of being the unbeliever. Right they were, he admitted. He then berated his ego-soul for coveting the adulation of the shaykhs of Mecca in the first place.

Ibrāhīm spent his days in Mecca working for everything he needed, even hauling wood and gardening.[12]

In another sort of narrative reversal, Friends of God sometimes teach a truth about pilgrimage that their listeners find hard to swallow. Making the hajj itself can provide a sense of personal satisfaction, so the pilgrim must be willing to give precedence over feeling good to more immediate and altruistic material and spiritual needs. Some friends once visited Bishr the Barefoot and invited him to accompany them on pilgrimage. He agreed to go so long as they took nothing, asked for nothing, and accepted nothing offered. They agreed only on the first two conditions, and he replied that they were not fully trusting in God. Another time, a man told Bishr that he had two thousand silver dirhams and intended to make pilgrimage. Bishr said that if the man truly wanted to honor God, he should instead support an orphan or a family; otherwise his proposed trip would be no more than sightseeing. When the man insisted that the pilgrimage was uppermost in his mind, Bishr told him that he thought so only because he had come by the money dishonestly and was looking for a way to assuage his guilt.[13]

Even the most advanced Friends occasionally perform the right devotions for the wrong reasons. Sometimes Ibrāhīm visited the Kaʿba by night, hoping to have the place to himself. His plan rarely turned out that way, but one night a torrential rain thinned out the usual crowd. All alone, Ibrāhīm knocked on the door of the House and asked for freedom from sinfulness. A voice replied that everyone asked for the same thing, but freedom from sin would only render God's infinite forgiveness and mercy useless. And when Ibrāhīm asked for forgiveness of his sins, the voice answered that he would do better to ask forgiveness for others and have them return the favor.[14]

Bāyazīd, too, yearned for privacy during one of his visits to the holy places and went to even greater lengths to achieve it. Like Ibrāhīm, Bāyazīd spent a surprisingly long time getting to Mecca. The journey took him twelve years because, also like Ibrāhīm, he stopped every few paces to pray two cycles of ritual prostration. He spent a full year in Mecca before returning home, postponing a visit to Medina in the hopes of later making a separate trip there. He separated the two aspects of his pilgrimage out of respect for the Prophet, for he did not want his visit to Medina to seem like a mere afterthought. As he approached Medina (see the frontispiece), a throng of pilgrims joined him on the road. He did not want to be distracted by a host of companions on his visit, so he decided to drive them off by making an arresting statement that sounded like outright blasphemy: "I am God and there is none other beside me; adore me." Taking him for a lunatic, the crowd dispersed. ʿAttār, in his account of this story, is quick to add, however, that the shaykh was not referring to himself but was speaking "with God's tongue." His reported experience of pilgrimage parallels an important feature of similar stories about Rābiʿa. Bāyazīd recalled that during his first trip to Mecca, he saw the House; during his second, he saw the Lord of the House; and during the third, he saw neither the House nor its Lord, because he was so immersed in God that he was unaware of anything in particular. Bāyazīd was famous for observing, to people who came looking for him, that he had been doing likewise for thirty years without success.[15]

Desire to be free of the demands of the public while in the holy place can drive a Friend to apparently harsh behavior. Not every Friend's behavior on hajj is worthy of emulation. One account about Fudayl ibn ʿIyād states that he used the Kaʿba as a pulpit for delivering his spiritual message. He made a pilgrimage to Mecca along with his wife, and the couple stayed for a while so that he could study. Eventually, the local people began to seek him out for advice and counsel. But when family members traveled to Mecca to see him, he refused to speak to them and they refused to leave. So Fudayl mounted the Kaʿba and warned them that they had too much time on their hands. All who heard him were reduced to tears, but even after his family departed, Fudayl stayed atop the shrine. This Friend did not always react so negatively to the presence of throngs of ordinary folk. On another occasion, Fudayl was performing the usual hajj rituals at ʿArafāt. He marveled at how easily God could forgive the assembled throng of penitents and prayed for that result. Some pilgrims asked Fudayl his opinion of the crowd, and he replied that, but for his presence, the assembled group would surely receive God's pardon. But how, they asked, did he discern their fears? He replied that only a fearful or mournful person recognizes others of his kind.[16]

Ibrāhīm, like other prominent Friends, occasionally needed to learn a lesson from an unlikely teacher. Still desiring to have the holy site to himself, Ibrāhīm reported that he once rolled himself into a reed mat to hide from the custodians of the Kaʿba. After one watch of the night, an elderly ascetic and forty companions entered the holy place. When the old man finished his prayer, a companion announced the presence of someone not of their group. The old gentleman disclosed that the stranger was Ibrāhīm, who had been unable to feel consoled in his prayer. At that point, Ibrāhīm popped out and asked the elder to explain why he could not find peace. The man explained that one day when Ibrāhīm purchased some dates in Basra, he had picked up a fallen date and assumed that it was his. After that revelation of his misdeed, Ibrāhīm returned to the shopkeeper and asked pardon. The merchant was so impressed that he quit his business and eventually became one of the *abdāl*.[17] Some stories emphasize the miraculous quality of a Friend's mere presence in the holy place. Yet another time, Ibrāhīm napped under a pomegranate tree after praying near the Kaʿba. The tree spoke and invited the pilgrim to have some of its fruit, but Ibrāhīm declined. After the third invitation from the tree, the Friend plucked two pomegranates and gave one to a companion, but the fruit was sour. The companion returned later and found that the tree now bore sweet fruit, a change that the local folk attributed to Ibrāhīm's having napped in its shade.[18]

Even Friends sometimes need help to make pilgrimage, and sometimes the help arrives from most unexpected sources. One year, during the official pilgrimage season, ʿAbd Allāh ibn al-Mubārak resolved to observe the standard hajj rituals even though he was not able to get to Mecca. As he engaged in the observances, a decrepit elderly woman approached and remarked that she could see how badly he wanted to make the hajj. She announced that she would be his way to Mecca, but he expressed his doubts that they could make the trip in the three days left in the hajj season. She said that she could traverse great distances quickly, and he agreed to set out with her. At each body of water, the old woman instructed him to blink, and, behold, they crossed the obstacle. After the two had performed the hajj rituals, the woman asked ʿAbd Allāh to accompany her to a cave in which her renunciant son lived. There the son told his mother he was about to die and asked her to help him get ready. When the young man died, the two travelers buried him, and the woman told ʿAbd Allāh that she intended to remain thereafter at her son's grave. She sent him off, assuring him that when he returned the following year for hajj, she would be gone.[19]

God may provide a powerful traveling companion at any time. When Sadafi was on his way to make pilgrimage, he met an old man too poor to care about. As the ship took on passengers to the point of overcrowding, the passengers put the old man in a rowboat alongside. Sadafi watched with trepidation as the wind-whipped waves threatened to swamp the dinghy, so he lifted the man back onto the ship and became his protector. As the men slept in a hostel that night, a voice called the elder's name, and he arose to keep prayerful vigil all night. When Sadafi asked the man who had called him, his companion replied that he wasn't sure; but the voice always reminded him of his duty to pray his litanies. In Mecca, Sadafi asked the old man to recount his experience of marvels. The old pilgrim told him that on one of his fourteen pilgrimages, he had become separated from his caravan. Wandering the desert desperate for food, he encountered a sheep that provided him with milk, and when the man awoke next day, the sheep was still there and stayed with him until he rediscovered the caravan. Later, as he circumambulated the Kaʿba, Sadafi saw the old man and learned that he had been a date-palm climber and had once fallen from a great height without injury.[20] Sadafi intimated that one ought never take for granted another person's spiritual status.

Special gifts and favors sometimes result from a Friend's ritual observances on pilgrimage, especially for Friends who circumambulate the Kaʿba. When Abū Hafs al-Haddād arrived in Mecca, he encountered a band of destitute folk sweltering in the heat. The Friend grabbed a stone and attempted to blackmail God by threatening to destroy the sanctuary's lamps if God did not supply the needs of these poor people. As he circumambulated God's House, a stranger came forth with a sack of dinars for him to spend on the impoverished pilgrims.[21]

Jerusalem and Vicinity

Jerusalem first appears prominently in the Islamic tradition as the original *qibla*, the point of orientation of daily ritual prayer. Shortly after the Hijra, Muhammad received a revelatory injunction (2:144) to change the *qibla* to Mecca. But Jerusalem continued to gain importance in Islamic lore through its association with the narrative of Muhammad's night journey and Ascension. According to traditional interpretations of 17:1, God carried Muhammad by night from Mecca to the "farthest mosque" (*al-masjid al-aqsā*), which appears to refer to a structure originally constructed in 97/715 in Jerusalem that stands at the southwestern corner of the site that Muslims call the Noble Sanctuary and Jews call the Temple Mount. Traditional narratives report that Gabriel then guided Muhammad on a journey of ascension through the levels of heaven, eventually arriving at the throne of God. A widely accepted interpretation is that the Ascension began on the site now occupied by the Dome of the Rock (completed in 73/692) at the center of the Noble Sanctuary, a place traditionally identified with the site of Solomon's Temple and with Abraham's intended sacrifice of his son (see Fig. 22).

Many of the major prophets are linked with Jerusalem, both in stories of their individual lives and in the narrative of Muhammad's night journey. Numerous features of the city dating to medieval times associate specific sites with individual prophets and have historically been part of traditional circuits of visitation recommended to pilgrims. The site of Solomon's temple is where Muhammad reportedly met various earlier prophets, who asked him to lead them in the ritual prayer. Tales of several pre-Islamic prophets make significant references to Jerusalem as well. David is credited, in Jewish and Christian tradition, with the founding of the city, but in Islamic tradition, Jerusalem has a timeless quality. As we have seen, the story of Noah puts forth the traditional view that Jerusalem existed even at the time of the flood. When God orders David's son Solomon to construct a temple, God indicates

FIGURE 22.   The Dome of the Rock in Jerusalem (c. 73/692) is associated with Abraham, Solomon, and Muhammad in Islamic lore, and it was a site of visitation by many famous Friends of God during medieval times. Photo by John Renard.

that he is to build it at the "Rock of the Ascension," referring to an important event in Muhammad's life that was then more than fifteen hundred years in the future. Tales of the prophets indicate that Jerusalem was the hometown of Jonah's family. Joseph fled from there to Egypt with Mary and Jesus. Solomon's Chair is a stone in the area around the Dome of the Rock, near the Dome of Jacob, and some post-Crusade sources speak of a "Dome of Solomon" as well. Some medieval commentators also locate in Jerusalem the "Niche of Mary (or Zakarīya)," in which she was miraculously supplied with food, and the "Cradle of Jesus," in which he spoke as a newborn.[22]

David and his son Solomon are said to be buried in Jerusalem. A number of sites in the greater environs of Jerusalem remain important for Muslims as the burial places of earlier major prophets. About twenty miles south of Jerusalem, Hebron, or Kiriath-arbah, is home to a mosque that enshrines a site that is believed to be the Cave of Machpelah. According to the biblical account (Genesis 23), Abraham purchased the site as a burial place for his wife Sarah, who died in Hebron. Abraham was later buried there, as were

FIGURE 23. The mosque/tomb of Abraham stands in Hebron, Palestine (occupied West Bank), known in Arabic as al-Khalīl (Abraham's title as "Intimate Friend [of God]." The site also encompasses the graves of Sarah, Isaac and Rebecca, Jacob and Leah, and Joseph, as well as a "footprint of Adam." The sanctuary structure evolved over several centuries, with earlier portions dating to Herodian and Byzantine times. Large- scale expansions and refurbishments took place through late antiquity and the middle ages well into the ninth/fifteenth century. Photo by John Renard.

Isaac, Rebekah, Leah, and Jacob. Hebron was also the first capital of David's kingdom. One unusual tradition even brings Lake Tiberias (the Sea of Galilee) into the orbit of sanctity by claiming that the Ark of the Covenant and Rod of Moses were consigned to the waters and will be rediscovered just prior to the final resurrection.[23] (See. Fig. 23.)

Near Jericho, just off the road to Jerusalem, the shrine of the prophet Moses has long attracted pilgrims for an annual celebration. Usually coinciding with Greek Orthodox Holy Week, the Muslim festivities begin the Friday before Holy Week and end on Good Friday. One feature of the observances is a massive procession from Jerusalem to the site traditionally identified as Moses's tomb. The tomb complex includes two mosques, a cemetery, and a hostel for pilgrims. A group of celebrants from four prominent local families, known as servants of the prophet, are responsible for key organizational aspects of the procession and festivities. The procession ends by returning to Jerusalem early on Good Friday.[24]

Some Friends of God, including a number of women, also have connections with Jerusalem and related sites. Friends have been among the many pilgrims to Jerusalem and surrounding holy places. Such pilgrims often remained for extended periods as devoted residents (*mujāwir*) at shrines such as the tomb of Abraham in Hebron.[25] One of Muhammad's most famous Companions, Abū 'd-Dardāʾ, reportedly was among the earliest Muslim visitors to Jerusalem. Tradition holds that he then invited another devout Companion, the Prophet's barber, Salmān the Persian, to join him there. At least one late-medieval pilgrim guide lists a site sometimes identified as Salmān's tomb in Jerusalem as an important destination but suggests that another unnamed holy person is actually buried there.[26] Dhū 'n-Nūn met and sought the spiritual guidance of Fātima of Nishapur in Jerusalem, and nearby he met Zahrā, as well as two other anonymous women who had important spiritual teachings for him. One source notes that Rābiʿa al-ʿAdawīya was buried at the peak of the Mount of Olives. And a "second" Rābiʿa, a holy woman from Syria, is also said to be buried on the Mount of Olives, across the Kidron Valley from the site of the Temple. Another Syrian woman Friend of God, Umm Hārūn, used to walk from Damascus to Jerusalem and back each month. A woman of Basra named Fakhrīya once stood for forty days waiting for the Jerusalem mosque to open its gates to her. Another female Friend, Lubāba al-Mutaʿabbida, was a permanent resident of Jerusalem.[27] The presence of such women in Jerusalem is not an earth-shaking revelation in itself, but it counters the common assumption that solitary women typically could not move around on their own.

BEYOND THE CENTRAL HOLY PLACES

Many important Friends of God have sanctified local and regional geographies by their lives and deaths. They account for hundreds of important sites, and considerations of space unfortunately require hard choices in selecting ones for this discussion. Beginning in North Africa and moving eastward, this section focuses on some of the saints and sites whose stories continue to be integral features of a number of largely Muslim societies.

Northwest Africa

Fez (Fās) is arguably Morocco's holiest city, thanks to its relationship to Mawlay Idrīs. Histories say that this celebrated ancestor of North African

Sufism founded the city, and he is buried in a sacred enclosure outside of Fez. Mawlay Idrīs is considered a major descendant of the prophet Muhammad and is likely the only Friend of God credited with founding an important "sacred" city. Fez (actually two cities linked inextricably by centuries of growth) and its immediate environs have become something of an extended necropolis. For generations, local residents have attributed countless marvels to Friends of God buried here. During the middle ages, Fez was home to many famous members of the Shādhilīya and Darqāwīya Sufi orders. Iberian-born Abū Madyan, a spiritual ancestor of the Shādhilīya, and Shādhilī teacher Ibn ʿAbbād of Ronda both spent parts of their lives in Fez after emigrating from Andalusia. In more recent times, an extension of the Shādhilī tradition, called the Darqāwīya, grew out of the teaching of Mawlay al-ʿArabī ad-Darqāwī. Like Ibn ʿAbbād, this teacher was an honorary citizen of Fez, and he is buried nearby in a tomb that still attracts pilgrims from the region.[28]

To the southwest of Morocco, the much smaller nation of Senegal remains one of the most vibrantly saintly regions in the world. Shaykh Amadou Bamba founded the Murīdīya Sufi order in 1323/1905 and lives on in the popular culture of Senegal. The Senegalese especially associate him with the city of Touba (from the Arabic *tūbā*, refers both to a cosmic tree that grows in the celestial garden and to a state of happiness and prosperity), where he lived from 1305/1887 to 1313/1895 and where he is buried. The mystical meanings of the name are enhanced by numerical symbolism: its Arabic letters have a combined numerical value of twenty-eight, which is the number of letters in the alphabet as well as the number of days in a lunar month and the number of words in the Qurʾān's opening chapter.[29] The saint's presence suffuses the city and is evident throughout Senegal in images that associate Amadou Bamba with the central holy site, Mecca's Kaʿba. Touba became a major center of regional visitation very soon after the shaykh's death, and pilgrims circumambulate his tomb throughout the year as well as during Amadou's birthday celebration. The popular belief is that when pilgrims assemble, the Kaʿba travels from Mecca to Touba, the destination of pilgrim followers of Bamba. In addition, accounts suggest that Amadou miraculously brought forth the "Spring of Mercy," which most scholars see as a sacred parallel to Mecca's Well of Zamzam.[30]

The Central Middle East

No Middle Eastern city boasts more sacred vestiges than Cairo, which is perhaps best known for its pharaonic tombs. Cairo and its environs have never held universal religious interest for Muslims. Nevertheless, regional lore has legitimated the place, particularly the area southeast of the city near the Muqattam hills, by associating it with the prophets. According to these traditions, Noah's descendants settled here before founding the first major Egyptian city, Memphis. Jacob dwelt here at one time, and Joseph was initially buried beneath the Muqattam cliffs. Joseph's remains were moved to Giza and ultimately to the Nile island of Rawda, because vegetation grew only on the south of the original grave and only on the northern side of the second. Joseph's body remained in Egypt for three centuries, until Moses finally removed it during the Exodus. Even Jesus lent an aura of sanctity to the city by telling Mary that Muhammad's followers would eventually be buried below the Muqattam hills. One medieval legend holds that God gave the Muqattam hills their sacred status. After the Revealer announced that he would allow Moses to hear the divine voice on a mountain, only Sinai hesitated to promote itself for the high blessing, out of deference. Then God ordered every other mountain to offer up something dear to it. Each presented one great treasure, but the Muqattam mountain surrendered every sign of fertility and willingly subjected itself to abject barrenness. God then compensated the Muqattam hills for their selflessness by promising that celestial seedlings, the remains of Muhammad's beloved Companions, would soon be planted in the valley below.[31]

Mausoleums of dozens of Muslim Friends are sprinkled amid the graves of several sprawling Cairene cemeteries of medieval vintage. In the Qarāfa cemetery, believers identify an otherwise nondescript cluster of seven tombs with the seven *abdāl*.[32] The saintly individuals whose burial places have attracted visitors over the centuries represent a wide range of backgrounds, from Muhammad ibn Idrīs ash-Shāfiʿī, a famed jurist, to Ibn al-Fārid, one of the finest Arabic mystical poets.

Shāfiʿī was a major legal scholar who taught mostly in Baghdad and Egypt and who wrote one of the most influential early treatises on Islamic jurisprudence. After construction of a mausoleum over his grave, the site began to attract devotional visitation, especially from local pilgrims. Around 576/1180, the famed hero of the "anti-Crusade" Salāh ad-Dīn (Saladin) built a commemorative madrasa complex dedicated to Shāfiʿī not far from his tomb. The site is in the southern part of Cairo near the Muqattam hills, whose cliffs border the city to the east. Some thirty years later (608/1211), one of Saladin's successors constructed a monumental mausoleum over the tomb, with a dome nearly fifty feet high. One of Cairo's largest cemeteries eventually developed around these two structures.[33] Today, the great jurist's tomb remains an important site for visitation. Supplicants bring concerns of every kind and leave touching petitions on scraps of paper, pleading for the Friend's aid for relief from poverty, sickness, infertility, and hunger.

Ibn al-Fārid, an adherent of the Shāfiʿī law school, is justly celebrated for his original lyric poetry of mystical love. He frequently creates arresting imagery of pilgrimage and of the Kaʿba as a symbol of the divine beauty. The Ayyubid sultan who raised the grand mausoleum of Shāfiʿī, al-Mālik al-Kāmil, offered to build a similar memorial to Ibn al-Fārid, but the mystic wanted no part of it. Nonetheless, his tomb near the Muqattam hills, not far from Shāfiʿī's mausoleum, became a magnet for visitation soon after his death.[34] Over subsequent centuries, the grave of the famed mystic attracted by turns lavish funding and official controversy. But as recently as 1402/ 1981, the Egyptian government granted the Rifāʿīya Sufi order permission to renew public festivities celebrating the saint's *mawlid*.[35]

Two other famous sites in Cairo honor female Friends Sayyida Zaynab and Sayyida Nafīsa. Sayyida Zaynab, one of the granddaughters of Muhammad, is celebrated in an annual weeklong *mawlid* in Cairo, and seekers traditionally visit her grave on Fridays. Zaynab may never have set foot in Egypt, but Egyptians, though virtually all Sunnī, celebrate her heroism during and after the battle of Karbalāʾ. People seek out Sayyida Zaynab, who was a champion of justice for the oppressed, to obtain relief from eye ailments and to gain access to the heavenly council of Friends who are believed to converge on her shrine. Sunnī Muslims care most about her close relationship to Muhammad. Sayyida Nafīsa was the great-granddaughter of ʿAlī's son Hasan (the second Shīʿī imam). Her fame rests largely on her miraculous deed of causing the Nile to rise by casting her veil upon its waters. Though the burial chamber is open to the public only on her *mawlid*, Qurʾān recitation occurs at her tomb complex every Sunday, her "visiting day."[36]

Just to the north of Cairo in the Nile delta, the city of Tanta remains an important center for devotees of the major Sufi founder Ahmad al-Badawī. Ahmad was of Iraqi origin but has long been intensely beloved by countless Egyptians, who celebrate his principal *mawlid* every autumn. Visitors to his tomb complex in Tanta spend over a week in a carnival atmosphere, with ceremonies heavily oriented toward fertility and fecundity in every aspect of creation. Pilgrims express a vivid sense of the saint's presence and a belief that he is aware even of their conversations about him. His *mawlid* has drawn more than a million and a half pilgrims.[37] The ancient city of Luxor, south of Cairo, deserves special mention. Though most visitors know it as the site

of the Valley of the Kings and the Temple of Karnak, Luxor is more important for local Muslims because of its associations with the life and death of
Shaykh Yūsuf Abū 'l-Hajjāj. The Friend, whose tomb now occupies the center of the ruined Temple of Luxor, takes a back seat only to Ahmad al-Badawī
among Egypt's major Friends of God.[38]

Due north of Egypt and across the Mediterranean, in west-central
Anatolia, lies the Turkish city of Konya. During the early sixth/twelfth
century, Konya had a major political role as the capital of the Saljuqid
Sultanate of Rūm (eastern "Rome"). But by the end of that century, as the
sultanate faded into eclipse, Konya was gaining celebrity status as the burial place of the great Friend Rūmī and several of his associates and family
members. We saw in chapter 7 how Rūmī's burial place evolved into a place
of spiritual grace and power. As a goal of pilgrim visitation to a Friend's tomb,
Konya is largely of regional importance. Its reputation turns almost exclusively on the mausoleum dedicated to Rūmī's family and followers in the
Mawlawīya order. But its continuing ability to draw pilgrims, even in the
heart of an avowedly secular state, qualifies Konya as a noteworthy sacred
place. Also buried not far from Rūmī's mausoleum is the Friend credited
with inspiring much of the poet's lyric verse, Shams of Tabrīz.

Damascus, Syria, is the next major city toward the east with significant
necropolises and shrines. Much of the aura of sanctity here, as so often elsewhere, derives from sometimes legendary or folkloric associations of place
with individuals who established the Islamic tradition. One tradition holds
that Cain killed Abel there; another, that Abraham's presence sanctified a
nearby mountain. Most prominent among the prophetic connections is the
shrine of the head of John the Baptist now housed in the Umayyad mosque
in the center of Damascus. That congregational mosque also embraces associations with other prophetic figures. Some say the prophet Hūd constructed
one of Damascus's walls and is buried in the vicinity. Other stories associate the enigmatic Khidr with a spot near the city, where he reportedly
prayed. Yet another tradition identifies one of the mosque's minarets as the
site to which Jesus will return. Two large cemeteries (one in the city and
another just outside the ancient walls) contain the graves of many of
Muhammad's Companions, including that of the celebrated ascetic Abū'd-
Dardāʾ and two attributed to Muhammad's first muezzin (mosque official
who announces the call to prayer), Bilāl the Abyssinian. Perhaps the most
famous saintly figure interred in the Damascus area is Ibn ʿArabī, whose
grave remains a significant goal both for local pilgrims and for visitors from
distant lands.[39]

Every Land Is Karbalāʾ: Sites Sanctified by Shīʿī Martyrs' Blood

Since the grim day in 61/680 when ʿAlī's son Husayn and his band were slaughtered in the area that is now south-central Iraq, Shīʿī Muslims have sanctified and revered over a dozen Middle Eastern sites. Wherever the imams and their families and supporters suffered martyrdom, shrines commemorating their witness have arisen and become centers of visitation. But Husayn's sacrifice was the event that gave rise to the proverbial saying, "Every day is ʿĀshūra [the tenth day of Muharram, the first Islamic lunar month], and every land is Karbalāʾ [a city southwest of Baghdad]."

Shīʿī Islam's sacred geography began to unfold in southern Iraq with the establishment of ʿAlī's power base at Kufa. Like Iraq's second-largest city, Basra, Kufa developed from a military encampment that Muslim armies set up as they rolled out of the Arabian Peninsula in conquest of the central Middle East. Kufa was ʿAlī's caliphal capital from 36/656 to 41/661. After ʿAlī was assassinated in the Kufa mosque, he was buried in a tomb that soon became the central shrine of the city of Najaf, just west of Kufa. Six of the twelve imams of the so-called Twelver branch of Shīʿism are buried in various Iraqi cities, including Samarra and Kazimayn. Samarra is reportedly the place where the twelfth imam, Muhammad al-Mahdī, went into "concealment" (*ghayba*). Twelver Shias believe that the last imam did not die but has been in concealment since 260/872 and will return to usher in an age of justice at the end of time. Various accounts say that Muhammad al-Mahdī communicated with his community through a series of four "deputies" (*wakīl*), or representatives, between the time of his initial disappearance and the death of the last representative in 329/940 (beginning the "greater concealment"); all four representatives are buried in Baghdad.[40] Sadly, Samarra's main Shīʿī shrine was nearly destroyed in sectarian attacks in 2006 and 2007.

In addition, a score or more of the various imams' family members are buried at Iraqi sites. The remaining five imams and their families are buried outside of Iraq, most significantly in Iran, where the most famous destination of Shīʿī pilgrims is the tomb of the eighth imam, Rizāʾ, at Mashhad in northeastern Iran. But Cairo is also home to shrines of the "people of the house" (*ahl al-bayt*), members of the family of the Prophet. Sayyida Zaynab's (see above) brother Husayn, the third imam and protomartyr of Shīʿī Islam, is also enshrined in Cairo, at the crossroads of the old Fatimid walled city's main intersecting pathways. Annual *mawlid* festivities for

Husayn center on a site that many believe is the final resting place of the martyr's severed head.[41] In addition, his mosque hosts regular *dhikr* (recollection) gatherings of Sufi organizations that convene to bathe in the imam's spiritual illumination.

South and Southeast Asia

South Asia is home to about a quarter of the world's Muslims. Its principal present-day nation-states, Pakistan, India, and Bangladesh, are also home to scores of important major sites associated with Friends of God. The region deserves more attention than space permits here. In the south-central Indian region called the Deccan lies Khuldābād, "abode of eternity." The city's vast necropolis embraces the resting places of scores of Friends of God who have played important roles in South Asian Islam. Many of these prominent figures were influential members of the Chishtīya, a dominant Sufi order in the region. Khuldābād was the first major Muslim pilgrimage center and Sufi shrine in the Deccan. The necropolises of Gulbarga, also in the Deccan, and Makli Hill, in Sind (present-day Pakistan), are perhaps the two other most important South Asian sites of this kind.[42]

One of South Asia's premier shrines is that of Mu'īn ad-Dīn Chishtī in the central Indian city of Ajmer. The city lies near a major Hindu pilgrimage center at Pushkar, and its congregational mosque was built on the site of a Jain monastery that formerly sat at the base of Forbidding Hill (*ajay meru*). Mu'īn ad-Dīn's shrine became a center of pilgrim visitation in the eighth/fourteenth century and reached its pilgrim peak under the emperor Akbar. A major hagiographical work about the shaykh, *Accounts of the Finest* (*Akhbār al-akhyār*), provides only a brief description of the construction of that premier tomb-shrine, preferring to pass along the master's sayings and stories. Other sources, however, combine to offer considerable detail on the history, design, and ritual life of the site. Pilgrimage to Ajmer on a large scale began about a century after Mu'īn ad-Dīn's death in 633/1236. Pilgrims took inspiration from major political figures. Some two centuries later, under the early sovereigns of the Mughal dynasty, embellishment of the shrine reached its peak. The emperor Akbar made fourteen pilgrimages to the shrine and made massive contributions to its beautification and expansion. Akbar's son Jahāngīr, grandson Shāh Jahān, and great-granddaughter Jahān Ārā Begūm, were also fervent devotees of Ajmer's preeminent Friend of God. Though the shrine's fortunes waxed and waned during early modern times, the site survived lean times and continued as central India's major Friend's tomb. It still attracts a large number of visitors from all over South Asia in particular, but it draws Muslims from farther abroad as well, particularly those with South Asian roots.[43]

About one-sixth of the world's Muslims live in the Southeast Asian nation of Indonesia, where a different kind of sacred topography, perhaps uniquely Southeast Asian, developed. During the centuries when much of the archipelago was "Islamized," countless sites became associated with "Muslim" saints, many of whom are nameless and thus "Muslim" in a rather generic sense. Indonesian tradition calls these hallowed places *kramat,* adapting the Arabic term for "marvel" or "saintly miracle" and applying it to virtually every object or place associated with Friends of God as well as to a host of sacred items with little or no connection to Islam. Some burial sites are Islamized places that were once for the worship of indigenous guardian spirits (such pre-Islamic sites are known as *pundhen*). Visitation to individual sites for various ritual purposes is common in Indonesia, and countless villages boast holy graves. Many ritual places, however, are not graves at all but sites of monuments (some even of Hindu or Buddhist origin) or places that saintly figures visited. One striking feature of the sacred topographies of Indonesia is the relative paucity of sites associated with prophets and founders of Sufi orders. And some regional traditions regard departed Friends of God as less powerful than dead rulers, because the Friends once lived under a monarch's sovereignty (this view may be a residue of medieval Hindu and Buddhist beliefs in the divinity of kings).

In addition, as in other regions of the world, some pilgrimage or visitation "circuits" encompass multiple sites. If one can speak of a network of sacred sites, the tombs of the Nine Friends of God (Wali Songo) arguably represent such a regional geography for pilgrims from across Indonesia and throughout the year. One or more of the Wali Songos' tombs might be part of a circuit tour, along with the graves of less celebrated regional or local Friends. Sites other than the tombs of the Nine Friends have also joined the network of visitation places, either as individual destinations or as a group. The unusual dynamics behind this appropriation of revered real estate deserve a closer look here.

Brawijaya is said to have been the last king of the Hindu realm of Majapahit in Java. Legends about him highlight important aspects of the creation of sacred geographies in premodern Indonesia. After Muslim invaders ran him out of his land in 934/1527, the king fled to the south and met Sunan Kali Jaga (one of the Wali Songo, who was also known as "Seal of the Friends of God"). After Brawijaya changed his name to Pandan Arang, Kali Jaga continued to visit him, in disguise, in hopes of converting him to

Islam. Pandan Arang first renounced his wealth and the power of the governorship he had been granted. He traveled to the cosmic mountain range that girds the earth, Jabal Qāf, and thereafter converted many Hindus after winning a competition in miraculous power. Pandan Arang then took to a retreat on Tembayat Hill, where Kali Jaga initiated him into the mystical sciences. Proclaimed a *walī*, Pandan Arang continued to convert inhabitants of the region through his miraculous works. Accounts report that he was buried on Mount Gunung Malang, one of the foothills of Jabal Qāf—clearly situating Pandan Arang on a cosmically potent site. The most important aspect of the legend of Pandan Arang is his formation of a *mandala*, a religious community centered on a major religious figure.[44] Tembayat's hill was likely the center of a pre-Islamic sacred site, and the story of Pandan Arang's appropriation of the site effectively claimed the holy place in the name of Islam. The resulting *mandala* was but one of many such religiously significant sites.[45] Chapter 9 revisits the role of Friends in Indonesia.[46]

MARKING SACRED TIMES AT THE SACRED PLACES

Time and place intersect in important ways in the beliefs and practices of all religious traditions. Formal pilgrimage to Mecca, like other major features of Muslim ritual and devotional life, is inextricable from Islam's lunar calendar. On a somewhat smaller scale, every place that reveres a Friend of God has its own ritual life, typically following a calendar linked to the life story of the patron Friend. Although some accounts of ritual feature extraordinary ecstatic behavior at shrines (see Fig. 24), most shrine activities are more orderly and reserved. For example, the *dargāh* of Muʿīn ad-Dīn Chishtī at Ajmer, India, follows a liturgical calendar that calls for performing rituals at the site in daily, weekly, monthly, and annual cycles. Twice each day, the predawn and midafternoon *khidmat* (service) rituals, performed exclusively by officials called *khādims*, begin with a recitation of the call to prayer and religious greetings, after which the officiants enter the shrine. Behind closed doors, the *khādims* ritually rearrange the various adornments to the tomb(s),

FIGURE 24. *(opposite)* Friend of God Jahm Raqqī carries a younger devotee. In one of his shortest entries, Persian hagiographer Jāmī explains that Jahm was responding to another man's ecstatic dancing and eventually fell unconscious himself after carrying his heavy load around the courtyard. Jāmī, *Nafaḥāt al-uns*, attributed to Laʿl (Mughal 1604/5), ©The Trustees of the Chester Beatty Library, Dublin, IN 61.3.

sweep up fading flowers, clean the burial places thoroughly, place new garlands and decorative cloths, and distribute the old floral pieces to pilgrims outside. During the afternoon service, the officiants allow a few male pilgrims to enter the shrine as silent onlookers. Ordinary pilgrims are allowed to enter during intervening times, assisted by the *khādims.*

A second regular daily ritual called "illumination" (*roshnī*) occurs at dusk just before sunset ritual prayer. A *khādim* brings in a tray of scented woods, while four others enter the tomb and take up candles in its corners. Walking to a drumbeat, three other *khādims* carrying candles begin to move toward the tomb, passing through two rows of pilgrims. Entering the shrine's eastern portal, they recite poetry honoring the entombed Friend and are joined within by male participants. Inside the tomb, the first *khādim* lights his candle, the second gives unlit candles to the four officiants in the corners, and the third supplies candles for the candlesticks that surround the tomb. After the first *khādim* lights the four corner candles, he recites Persian lyrics in praise of the Friend, and the four corner officiants carry their candlesticks outside to the outer corners of the enclosure, blessing the pilgrims as they go.

At the end of each day, the *Karka* ceremony closes the shrine late in the evening. Pilgrims stand in rows outside the tomb as the *khādims* emerge one at a time. The officiants move toward a bin, where they place all materials they have cleaned from the tomb. *Qawwālī* singers intone verses that are specifically for the closing ceremony as the doors of the shrine shut for the night.

Every Thursday and Friday, people gather in the eastern courtyard of the shrine, where the main officials sit in places of honor. *Qawwālīs* begin to sing devotional lyrics in honor of Shaykh Muʿīn ad-Dīn. In addition, celebrants observe the death anniversary of the Friend on the sixth day of every lunar month with special Qurʾān recitation in which many reciters complete the whole text in about an hour. Various death anniversaries of other Friends fill other days throughout the year. The ʿurs (wedding to God) of Shaykh Muʿīn ad-Dīn is the liturgical peak of the year, occupying largely the first week of the seventh lunar month. Pilgrims arrive from all over the subcontinent, and a group of virtually marathon *qawwālīs* camp out at the shrine. The festivities include multiple cleansings and re-adornments of the tomb, overseen by the *khādims* and accompanied by many hours of musical celebration and prayer. A small door to the shrine, kept closed throughout the year except for a handful of special days, remains open for the first six days of the month. The shrine is closed to pilgrims on the sixth day, when the *khādims* again perform the final rituals. The chief official of the shrine, called the *dīwān*, at last enters the tomb through the small "door of paradise" to pay his respects with other top officials. After the party emerges from the tomb, the *khādims* send the pilgrims on their return journeys.[47]

Such a breezy survey of so vast a topic can barely suggest the richness and variety of the smaller worlds that comprise the larger world of God's Friends. As I suggest in chapter 9, this global sacred geography is not simply of antiquarian interest. Countless twenty-first-century towns and villages in scores of regions across the globe continue to identify specific places as uniquely blessed and to celebrate their blessings ritually.

FIGURE 25.   Devotees follow a model of the tomb of Husayn (d. 61/680 at Karbalāʾ in Iraq) in a procession commemorating the death of the Shīʿī protomartyr, Rawalpindi, Pakistan, 1980s. Photo by David Edwards.

9. Friends in Our World

Much of the data available to us about Friends of God are historic and often quite ancient. Some of the most engaging stories of holy lives come to us from "classic" sources, both literary and visual. And many of the most important places associated with Friends of God—from sprawling cemeteries with their often grand and imposing mausolea to large medieval complexes founded by Friends long-since deceased and humbler wayside shrines—can easily strike one as oversize relics of antiquarian interest. But Friends of God have remained an important and immensely vibrant feature in the faith and practice of hundreds of millions of Muslims through the leanest of times and right up to the present. Muslims the world over continue to acknowledge the enduring significance of paragons of holiness and devotion, from prophets to Companions of Muhammad, and from Muslims of long ago celebrated for their commitment to God to contemporary figures whose faith inspires countless seekers. A wide range of contemporary contexts testify to the extraordinary resilience of individual Friends and their stories, as well as to their larger institutional and devotional significance.

Recent print and electronic publishing in the Americas and abroad reveal ongoing interest in the holy people of Islam. Some might suggest that "resurgence of interest" is a better word choice than "ongoing interest," but that phrase implies that stories of God's Friends have undergone a historical hiatus of popularity. Anthropological studies, however, indicate that many largely Muslim early-modern and contemporary societies have continued to delight in recounting these tales, even when the production of written versions has fallen off. But recently their stories have taken on a different cast and have found new media, new venues, and new and more inclusive audiences. This final chapter of part 2 explores four features of contemporary Islamic hagiography: the major individual saintly figures who still enjoy popularity around the globe; significant trends in recent hagiographical literature and in both traditional and more novel forms of visual hagiography, including the use of "new media" to communicate hagiographical material; the functions of Friends of God in contemporary contexts; and the multiple dynamics that continue to generate "new Friends." An epilogue acknowledges the importance of continued interest in Friends celebrated for their literary and spiritual achievements.

POPULAR FRIENDS FROM MOROCCO TO MALAYSIA

This chapter takes a sampling of Friends of God who command continued respect and followings in various parts of the world, and who therefore deserve recognition for their contemporary importance, regardless of their historical origins. First come Friends of local and regional repute, and then we look at those with devotees across a much broader spectrum, from several larger regions or nation-states to virtually the whole of Islamdom.

Local and Regional Friends

Friends of God too numerous to count remain important symbolic and spiritual presences in thousands of towns and villages, especially in nations with significant Muslim populations. Particularly in the more traditional social contexts, paraliturgical rituals as well as more expansive community celebrations still revolve around the tomb-shrines of hometown Friends. Birthdays and anniversaries of death, which celebrate the "wedding" of the Friend's soul to the divine, are quintessential occasions for gatherings of devotees. Many local economies continue to depend to some extent on such festivities, with pilgrims from surrounding towns and villages arriving for the appointed days and bringing a small but much-needed infusion of commerce.

Local Friends are a diverse lot and include a greater proportion of women than do the wider orbits of saintly repute. Tunisia's Sayyida Manūbīya, who appeared in chapter 6, arguably belongs to the category of local Friends, as does Sīdī ʿAmr al-Fayyāsh, whom we meet later in this chapter. One could categorize Munawwar Shāh, who also appears later in this chapter, as either a local or a regional Friend. Countless other figures who are very important in villages and towns from Morocco to Malaysia remain beneath the radar of the broad survey I undertake here.

Some Friends' names and fame have spread beyond the immediate environs of their native or adopted homes. Such regional figures are sometimes "ethnic" Friends (I use the term loosely here), perhaps claimed by speakers of a particular language, such as Sindhi or Panjabi. Some populations of Muslims have suffered geopolitical bisection as politicians and victorious warriors have drawn new lines on a map, which, from a religious perspective at least, are often arbitrary. The ancient traditional regions of Sind and Panjab, therefore, are now divided between Pakistan and India. Several Friends of God arguably deserve the label "pan-Indian," if one identifies India by its pre-1367/1947 boundaries and thus includes present-day Pakistan and Bangladesh. Hujwīrī and Farīd ad-Dīn Ganj-i Shakar Chishtī are in this group, as are the variable members of the "Five Pīrs" of South Asia.

Some Friends have become "national" patrons in that they are more or less exclusively claimed by, say, Moroccan or Chinese or Indonesian Muslims. Egyptian Shaykh Ahmad Radwān, possibly Pakistani Friend Munawwar Shāh, and Indonesia's Shaykh Yūsuf of Makasar (all described later in this chapter) are Friends of regional fame who arguably have "national" identification as well. Senegal's Amadou Bamba, too, is a saint of largely national repute. Friends who bring Islam to a region also frequently grow into regional celebrities. Many Muslims who now find themselves within the geopolitical sphere of China, for example, honor Muhammad's Companion Saᶜd ibn Abī Waqqās as the person who introduced Islam there. One might say the same of Indonesia's Wali Songo, who will return later.

We know of many regionally important Friends from hagiographical sources written explicitly to memorialize Friends of God whom the authors knew personally (or nearly so). Stories from Iberian-born Ibn ᶜArabī's two short hagiographies, as well as Sadafī's recollections of his Maghribī acquaintances and Egyptian Safī ad-Dīn's anthology of the lives of his teachers, all fit into this category. Another important source of information about regional Friends are histories of individual Sufi orders that developed in specific regions. Aflākī's account of the early Mawlawīya order, for example, includes stories of over a dozen Friends who played important roles in Turkey and surrounding areas. None of the order's supporting cast attained the wider renown of its central figure, Jalāl ad-Dīn Rūmī. Other order-specific hagiographical sources provide extensive material on Central Asian regional Friends, such as Ahmad Yasawī and Bahāʾ ad-Dīn Naqshband, as well as major members of the South Asian Chishtī order, such as Muᶜīn ad-Dīn Chishtī.

The constituencies of some Friends of regional scope can cross ethnic and linguistic lines, particularly in countries with large populations and geographic expanses. In India, for example, with its scores of regional vernaculars, the shrines of regional Friends draw pilgrims from half a dozen or more of India's culturally diverse states, attracting many non-Muslims as well. Another category of regional Friends is descendants of Muhammad, who enjoy a place of honor in the ritual lives of Sunnī Muslims, especially in the central Middle East. In this group are some of the widely revered female Friends, members of Muhammad's family such as Sayyida Zaynab and Sayyida Nafīsa.

Friends of Broader Fame: Transregional and Global Figures

A number of important Friends have inspired devoted followings in more than one region. Areas of a transregional Friend's popularity are often, but not always, contiguous. One regional population might, for example, claim a Friend as a native son or daughter, whereas another region some distance away might own the saint because he visited their land—and perhaps died and was buried there. Bāyazīd al-Bistāmī thus "belongs" to Iran, where he was born, and to both the central Middle East, where he lived several years, and Bangladesh, where some say (inaccurately) he paid a visit. Martyr-mystic Hallāj has also assumed the stature of a transregional, perhaps even global, Friend by virtue of his rather spectacular story.

An elite corps of Friends commands nearly global acclaim. Perhaps the most widely beloved of the post-Prophetic Friends (excluding prophets as well as Muhammad's family and immediate successors) is ʿAbd al-Qādir al-Jīlānī. Born in north-central Iran, ʿAbd al-Qādir studied and preached in Baghdad, lived an ascetical life for twenty-five years in Syria, and was buried in Baghdad. But his circle of popularity encompasses the globe, nearly wherever traditional communities of Muslims reside. As with a number of other global Friends, the extent of ʿAbd al-Qādir's renown and influence has had a great deal to do with the spread of the Sufi order that bears his name, the Qādirīya. That organization set down roots in North Africa, the central Middle East (including Arabic, Persian, and Turkic areas), Central Asia (including present-day western China), and the Panjab as well as other parts of India. In West and sub-Saharan Africa, too, ʿAbd al-Qādir has often figured in accounts of later important figures (such as ʿUthmān dan Fodio), many of whom reportedly met the great Friend in dreams and visions. Even in places in which the order never enjoyed a dominant or leading institutional presence, ʿAbd al-Qādir projected a surprisingly vibrant persona. In Indonesia and other parts of Southeast Asia, for example, this Friend remains nearly as popular and widely acclaimed as the uniquely Indonesian regional Friends, the Wali Songo.[1] Not all transregional or global Friends attained their extended fame because of the far-flung spread of their orders. Central Asians claim Jalāl ad-Dīn Rūmī, for example, because he was born in present-day Afghanistan; Iranians, because he wrote in Persian; and Turks, because he lived most of his life in Anatolia. But Rūmī's truly global repute has come largely because of the immense popularity of his poetry.

Though many prophets and Prophet-related figures have continued to enjoy global importance, few of them have given rise to the type of "cultic" practices that have grown up around many post-Prophetic Friends. So, for example, though Abū Bakr is held in the highest esteem, no central venue draws crowds to celebrate his birthday or death. Some regional populations of Muslims do, however, claim to possess the tombs of prophets, and some of these locations do function as the focal points of recurring ritual observances.[2] In chapter 8, we learned that a host of such sites exist in the Middle East. Even more such sites house the tomb-shrines of members of Muhammad's family. That extended group includes not only ʿAlī and Fātima and their sons, Hasan and Husayn, but other prophet-descendants among the Shīʿī imams, who are of global importance to the 10 percent or so of the world population of Muslims who are Shīʿī believers. (See Fig. 25.)

Various other Friends of global renown comprise a special category. Hagiographical anthologies by authors such as Sulamī, Hujwīrī, Abū Nuʿaym al-Isfahānī, Qushayrī, ʿAttār, and Jāmī have been widely influential in many parts of the world for centuries. Occasionally translated from their original Arabic and Persian, these and similar works have contributed to the global fame of scores of early Friends with important roles in the history of Sufism. Characters such as Maʿrūf al-Karkhī, Habīb al-ʿAjamī, Junayd, and Sarī as-Saqatī have rarely been "claimed" by regional or national constituencies, and their fame does not rest definitively on traditions surrounding their tombs and associated pilgrimage and related rituals. Even so, Muslims the world over have heard of these colorful figures and acknowledge them as important Friends. Finally, in a category all his own is the ubiquitous and mysterious Khidr, whose unexpected visits I described in chapter 3. Because he founded no order, he has no institutional constituency. Because he did not live and die as other Friends have, no particular locale claims possession of his tomb as a pilgrim goal. Nevertheless, few of God's Friends enjoy greater fame than Khidr.

CONTEMPORARY HAGIOGRAPHIC COMMUNICATION

Muslims across the world continue to produce hagiographic communications in a wide variety of forms and media, including a striking profusion of works in print for both general readers and scholars. In addition, several important forms of nontextual communication are popular.

Literature and Scholarship

"Classic" works of hagiography in Arabic, Persian, Turkish, and a host of other regional languages, are not hard to come by today. Publishing houses in the

Middle East and across the globe continue to produce beautifully printed versions of the great books in Islamic religious literature. Abū Nuʿaym al-Isfahānī's monumental Arabic *Ornament of the Friends of God and Generations of the Purest*, for example, is readily available in handsomely bound sets. A Beirut publishing house whose name suggests a "renaissance of the Arabic heritage" put out a ten-volume version of the classic as recently as 2001, and dozens of similar examples exist. In Iran, a late twentieth-century edition of ʿAttār's Persian *Remembrances of the Friends of God* is readily available in affordable cloth binding, in its fourteenth printing, in shopping-mall bookstores in Tehran—much more elevated fare than most Americans could hope to find in their neighborhood mall.[3] While the ready availability of such volumes will catch the interest of a relatively small number of specialists in Islamic studies and native readers of Arabic and Persian, it documents an important fact about Islamic hagiography. Publishers still print thousand-year-old works because people still want to buy them, and stories of holiness and devotion continue to interest enough readers to constitute a market niche.

However, interest in hagiographical works is not limited to the classics. Muslim authors in many parts of the world continue to produce varied forms of literature in dozens of languages. A cursory glance through mail-order catalogs from half a dozen Islamic-book suppliers in the United States reveals a host of English-language works for readers of every age. Though these works typically appear under such headings as "*Sīra*" and "biography" and even "history," they often fit into one or more of the subcategories of hagiography that I have defined in earlier chapters. They generally identify their subjects as prophets, the Prophet and his family members or Companions, and "Islamic heroes," rather than Friends of God, though this last term occasionally appears in titles of individual works (especially translations). Books that seek to educate children about the exemplars of devotion and ethical values are very much in evidence. And no shortage exists of references to "amazing" deeds wrought by and through these extraordinary individuals, even when the aim is evidently to downplay the miraculous and emphasize the "mere humanity" of the subject. Booksellers clearly find ample readership among English-reading Muslims to offer a substantial array of options.

Retellings of the lives of long-deceased Friends of God are also a significant index of hagiographical vitality. Works of this kind include individual bio-hagiographies as well as the contemporary equivalent of hagiographical anthologies. Most individualized accounts feature stories of regional or national figures as told by one of the featured Friend's modern-day fellow citizens, and are typically published in the Friend's actual or adoptive "homeland."[4] Anthologized works generally evidence broader interest, both in their geographical spread and in the historic significance of the highlighted figures. Most recent examples I have surveyed include leading figures in Muslim history and across the globe, and they embrace leaders noted more for their civic and intellectual achievements than for their personal piety, as well as those more celebrated for their spiritual acumen. A three-volume Indian publication entitled *Saviours of Islamic Spirit*, for example, includes in the first two categories (in volume 1 alone) the caliph, ʿUmar ibn ʿAbd al-ʿAzīz; Nūr ad-Dīn Zangī and Salāh ad-Dīn al-Ayyūbī (a.k.a. Saladin); scholars of hadith as a class; legal scholar Ahmad ibn Hanbal; and pioneering theologian Abū 'l-Hasan al-Ashʿarī. Among the individuals one would find in more traditional hagiographies are Hasan al-Basrī, Abū Hāmid al-Ghazālī, ʿAbd al-Qādir al-Jīlānī, Ibn al-Jawzī (himself the author of an important hagiographical anthology), and Jalāl ad-Dīn Rūmī. In his preface, author ʿAlī Nadwī gives several reasons for producing his multivolume work. He wants to inform Muslims about the sweeping historic contributions of dozens of outstanding individuals (given that, in his view, many people think such figures are rare exceptions). He bemoans the scarcity of balanced accounts of spiritual leaders in works that tend to focus on "Kings and Emperors" and warns that only inclusion of people who have worked for "the renovation and regeneration of Islamic faith and practice" can give Muslims a sense of "the innate vitality of Islam." An accurate assessment of the impact of such individuals, he insists, depends on an understanding of their historical and cultural contexts, so only credible historical criticism can bring out the true impact of these "masters."[5]

In addition to such general-interest or "popular" books, a fair number of works of scholarly intent have been produced of late by Muslim specialists in hagiography. A search with the terms *biography, Muslim saints, Java,* and *Indonesia* in a global online library database, for example, turns up several dozen works in Indonesian that have been published in the past twenty years. Many, if not most, of these publications are on the famous Nine Friends of God (Wali Songo) of Indonesia, focusing on both "biography" and "legend," often in the context of the "Islamization" of Java. More recent Indonesian figures, such as Shaykh Yusuf of Makasar, are also represented. Studies of specific themes, such as twentieth-century Egyptian scholar Yūsuf an-Nabhānī's *Compendium of Marvels* (*Jāmiʿ al-karāmāt*), also provide important insights into the persistence of hagiographical interest.[6]

Hagiographic Narrative beyond the Printed Page

Evidence of the persistence of hagiographical interest in many Islamicate societies is not limited to written sources. Sound recordings (CDs and audiocassettes) are an increasingly popular variation on contemporary hagiographical texts. *The Life Story [sīra] of Muhammad* is the most popular audio title, followed closely by spoken versions of stories about the Prophet's wives and Companions and about influential early religious leaders like Abū Hanīfa (founder of one of the four extant Sunnī schools of religious law). Such materials increase the accessibility of hagiographical accounts. Some of them are retellings from the classic sources, and some are fresh examples of an "oral tradition" whose purpose is to instill love for Muhammad and admiration for Islam's ancestors in faith.[7]

Chapter 10 offers further historical examples of classic—or "primary"—oral hagiography. In some social and cultural contexts, genuine oral tradition (as distinct from the "secondary" oral accounts in audio recordings) has continued unabated. In present-day Senegal, for example, devotees of the Friend of God Amadou Bamba continue to refine the narrative of Amadou's life. Of the 286 "trials" of the shaykh's life (286 is also the number of verses in the Qurʾān's second sura), devotees select several signal events, and the selection remains a living, fluid process. These "stations" in Amadou Bamba's life story function rather like the great feasts by which Christians and Buddhists canonize the lives of Jesus and the Buddha. The story of Amadou Bamba is therefore a living reality, an organic treasury offering vast possibilities to reshape and adapt the meaning of the Friend to fit the needs of individuals and the community. Through this editing process, storytellers can use specific episodes to sum up the meaning of the Friend's life for a particular community. For example, the celebrated scene in which Amadou Bamba prays on the water while "colonials" look on in amazement from a passing ship and fish dance around the shaykh to gain his blessing has become a kind of signature miracle.[8]

Friends in Contemporary Popular Visual Media

Another type of "living" hagiography appears in a variety of pictorial forms. Visual hagiography can communicate in ways not possible with the written or spoken word alone. Perhaps the most significant effect of using visual media is to convey a Friend's contemporaneity. Textual and oral narratives are largely limited to recounting the lives of important Friends of God diachronically, in a linear fashion. Pictorial images, however, can collapse time by including multiple characters and episodes in a single frame. They can distill an entire narrative by juxtaposing key symbols that viewers will readily associate with essential moments in a Friend's life story. In many instances, the visual image condenses an already familiar narrative. So, for example, an image might depict the Friend meeting with another famous figure who lived centuries earlier or, if contemporary, lived many miles distant. Other images might make more startling statements by portraying a regionally or locally celebrated Friend in the company of other famous people whom the Friend clearly never met, suggesting a general parity or similarity that is apart from existing stories. (For example, Amadou Bamba might appear in the same picture with Mahatma Gandhi.)

One can conclude that the artist of such abstract images does not intend the viewer to take the work literally, but to consider it at a deeper symbolic level. All of the imagery, however anachronistic or historically improbable, aims to place the greatness and holiness of the Friend in sharp focus. The spiritual quality of the subject is all that matters; specific historical details fade to a soft-focus background.[9] Among the more widespread traditional techniques evident in recent visual hagiography, two types stand out. Some feature a multiframe device to suggest a sequential narrative content. This device is common in illustrated children's stories, the equivalent of "graphic novels" of Friends' lives, and coloring books of such perennial charmers as ʿAbd al-Qādir al-Jīlānī. Single-frame nonnarrative images predominate in calendar art, devotional prints, miscellaneous posters, and reverse-painted glass panels to be hung on windows. These usually colorful images function typically as either generic reminders of the Friend's presence in the world or visual synopses of a signal event in the great one's life. Let us look briefly at four of the more common types of hagiography in two dimensions: calendar art, reverse-glass painting, posters, and murals.

Calendar art and devotional prints are easy to produce and inexpensive. They are a significant medium for communicating hagiographical themes in various regions, especially in South Asia. Images of Friends of God engaged in various works or preaching to their followers, as well as those of tomb-shrines and other sacred sites associated with the Prophet and important Friends, are among the most popular subjects. Stylized depictions of the Kaʿba in Mecca, the green dome over the Prophet's grave in Medina (see the frontispiece), and Jerusalem's Dome of the Rock (see Fig. 22) are easily recognizable symbols of key aspects of Muhammad's life. Images of the tomb-shrines of Muʿīn ad-Dīn Chishtī, perhaps India's best-known regional friend, and ʿAbd al-Qādir al-Jīlānī, a Friend with a global following, are the most common reminders of post-Prophetic personalities. Devotional prints of South Asian provenance typically present Friends in one of four iconographic configurations: simple "portraits," clusters of major Friends (sometimes in the form of a family tree), images of tomb-shrine architecture symbolic of one or more Friends, and (most numerous) images of Friends standing, sitting, or praying near their tomb-shrines. Such images can function as souvenirs of visitation to the Friend's shrine, illustrations for storytellers, or aids to devotional prayer.

In the latter capacity, their use is arguably informed by the ancient Hindu concept of *darshan*, in which images facilitate the contemplative process of "seeing and being seen by" the figure depicted.[10]

A delightful genre of folk art that is widely popular in North Africa is the reverse-glass painting. Designed to be suspended in windows of homes and shops to give the impression of stained glass, these multicolored objects are a relatively recent art form and can be quite elaborate and expensive. Senegalese reverse-glass paintings include scenes from the lives of prophets such as Abraham's near sacrifice of his son and Noah's ark. From Muhammad's time come images of historical events, such as the Battle of Badr, and symbolic allusions to the Prophet's reception of revelation and his journey to the heavens, using images of Gabriel and the hybrid winged quadruped Burāq. But easily the most popular themes are taken from the life of Senegal's most important modern Friend of God, Amadou Bamba. Elsewhere in North Africa, popular subjects include ʿAlī and his martyr-sons, Hasan and Husayn, and the ubiquitous ʿAbd al-Qādir al-Jīlānī. Popular images of ʿAlī depict him vanquishing demons and dragons as symbols of evil, whereas ʿAbd al-Qādir characteristically performs the marvel of taming a lion, thereby reminding viewers of the Friend's manifestation of divine power and *baraka*.[11]

In prerevolutionary Iran, a long-standing tradition of poster and mural painting has provided a visual record of stories of the Shīʿī martyr-imams. Portable storyboards have supplied illustrations to supplement oral performance of the master narratives of redemptive suffering. On a much larger scale, architectural murals have provided a backdrop and overall visual context for the ritual reenactment of these stories in the form of *taʿzīya*, popularly known as "passion plays."[12] Since the Iranian Revolution of 1400/1979, many of these Iranian pictorial traditions have continued, augmented by other media (such as paper currency and postage stamps) and reinterpreted through the lens of revolutionary ideology and changed perceptions of Iran's political roles in the Middle East. Ayatollah Khomeini appears as a new Moses who brings down the pharaonic shah, with the Iranian people reenacting the struggle of the martyr Husayn against a tyrannical ruler. The moral of the story often appears in a caption: "For every Pharaoh, there is a Moses." Images of Iranian soldiers fighting Iraq during a nearly decadelong conflict sometimes blend with symbolism recalling the martyr Husayn's struggle against the despotic first-/seventh-century Umayyad regime. The motto "Every day is ʿĀshūrā (10 Muharram 61/680) and every land is Karbalāʾ" epitomizes the synchronic message of this common visual imagery.[13]

Larger-scale two-dimensional imagery plays an equally important but very different role in contemporary Dakar, the capital of Senegal. "Talking walls" invariably present paradigmatic images of Amadou Bamba, standing facing the viewer and staring enigmatically over a draped headdress that veils the lower half of his face. His form reappears now and then in pictorial parades showing a host of prominent twentieth-century African and global figures, including Pope John Paul II, Nelson Mandela, Martin Luther King, Malcolm X, Jimi Hendrix, and Bob Marley (without the Wailers). The Friend's visual presence amid often unlikely clusters of world celebrities symbolizes Amadou's role in sacralizing all of reality as well as the specific local places defined by the unavoidable images. Many portraits of individual figures show a letter-carrying dove (a symbol of divine revelation and guidance) delivering the same heavenly message that the great Friend of God received, being the first in the region to do so. Such large-scale imagery embodies a distinctively Senegalese exuberance, imagination, and wit.[14]

Friends and the New Media

"New media" are in evidence in virtually every Muslim community. Websites dedicated to cyber-Friends are proliferating on the Internet, for example, and producers are packing immense quantities of information into a variety of formats that users can access on portable devices. Even a casual search for "Muslim Saints" on the Internet brings in hundreds of sites representing an amazing variety of characters, cultural contexts, and communities. Not surprisingly, data from such sources are often tendentious and generally not subject to serious critical scrutiny. Even so, the sites document a significant ongoing fascination with Friends across the globe. Some Internet sites take a negative approach to the topic, condemning all talk of "saints" as blatantly un-Islamic. But the vast majority of websites purport to inform visitors of the ongoing spiritual benefit of getting to know God's special Friends.

In addition, one can now access multimedia material about historically famous Friends on CD-ROMs and DVDs. One excellent example is a CD-ROM produced in the south-central Indian city of Ajmer that highlights the ancient but still-vibrant shrine of the eighth-/fourteenth-century Friend Muʿīn ad-Dīn Chishtī. Slickly produced, the disk offers background information on the sacred site, including detailed architectural photographs and considerable visual documentation of the rituals that animate the sanctuary. Because the Chishtī order has long been instrumental in spreading the popularity of devotional music, the disk also includes a good deal of audio, both to provide background and to offer a sampling of favorite mystical poems set to music and performed by *qawwālī* ensembles that enjoy rock-star status in much of South Asia. Although the product is as yet available only in the Urdu language, the medium could expand with relative ease into wider markets.[15]

FUNCTIONS OF FRIENDS AND SAINTHOOD IN CONTEMPORARY MUSLIM SOCIETIES

Recent oral, pictorial, and literary hagiographies and the new media naturally reflect the evolution of cultural and historical understandings of the Friends of God. In turn, Friends frequently represent condensed, crystallized versions of an Islamicate society's intimations of self-identity and place in the world. They function as representatives of independence in the face of colonialism; advocates for religious values in an increasingly secularized world; and ambassadors and bridge builders in interreligious relations. Below is a selective sample of these important functions in various political and cultural contexts.

In many regions, Friends of God remain important symbols of the struggle to overcome the residual effects of colonialism and to fend off the deleterious influences of "Western" trends toward secularization. Many of Amadou Bamba's miracles are recycled stories from earlier hagiographies that showcase his steadfast refusal to collaborate with foreign occupying powers. The Friend's fearless witness, memorialized in story and visual imagery, provides encouragement and confidence in the face of seemingly insurmountable odds. Amadou enables the powerless by his example of unfailing trust in God. In one favorite story, depicted in various visual media popular in Senegal, the colonial authorities throw the Friend into a cage with a ravenous lion in hopes of ridding themselves of this impudent pest. The beast, of course, becomes a disciple of the Friend, foiling the foreigners' evil designs.[16] In Indonesia, still-popular tales of the Wali Songo go hand in hand with widespread pilgrimage to their tombs.

Friends of God also function as symbolic levees against the perceived tide of secularization. In the postrevolutionary era of Communist China, for example, Muslim communities have continued to tend to the small institutional venues that they associate with Friends of God. Especially in the western Chinese province of Xinjiang (the Uighur Autonomous Region also known as Eastern Turkestan), Friends of three types remain significant: individuals (typically Sufis) credited with bringing Islam to the region even at the cost of martyrdom; Sufi shaykhs of subsequent centuries; and major Arab and Turkic Muslim leaders of the past. Short hagiographical works in Uighur (the language of a major ethnic Muslim group in Xinjiang), distributed illegally for the most part, provide devotional help for individuals seeking to relate to several dozen Friends of particular importance in Central Asia and China. These works focus on some prophets and Companions of Muhammad as well as later Sufis, mostly ones of the Naqshbandīya order. Owners of businesses also commonly consider certain Friends their patron saints. For example, Idrīs (who gave humankind the secret of the arts of civilization) is the patron of tailors; Noah, of carpenters; and David, of stoneworkers.

The Chinese government has recently reduced many Friends' tombs to museums, totally destroyed others, and persecuted various Muslim leaders. Devotees have, however, evidently remained undaunted. Particularly committed are those who espouse the causes of Friends best known for the purity and strength of their faith, though a few people still champion Friends who actively resisted the Communist revolution by force of arms. Not surprisingly, devotion to Friends in Xinjiang is fraught with political overtones. For many followers, this devotion is a symbol of ongoing protest against China's claim to Eastern Turkestan. Resistance to cultivating devotion to Friends of God has recently come more vociferously from Uighur intellectuals. Though often sympathetic to the Communist regime, many of them are primarily motivated by the desire to reform and purge Muslim practice of activities they consider un-Islamic innovations.

Pilgrimage to the more important shrines in Eastern Turkestan has nevertheless continued, despite government moves to restrict the meeting and movement of organized Muslim religious groups. Significant ritual times include the tenth of Muharram, which for China's largely Sunnī Muslims commemorates sacred events in the lives of several prophets, including Abraham, Joseph, and Jesus. In a uniquely Chinese adaptation of the liturgical calendar, to accommodate the fact that a major pilgrimage site is in the desert, the pilgrimage occurs on April 10 annually rather than rotating backward through the solar year like events timed with the Muslim lunar calendar. Many of the mausoleums are tended and administered by families or "honor groups," in keeping with traditions of Central Asian origin that are now unique to western China.[17]

Finally, an important social role of God's Friends is to create links between members of disparate communities of faith. Intercommunal relations in some areas turn to a great extent on transsectarian participation in rituals at shrines of Friends. This role is particularly important in several regions of South Asia in which large populations of Muslims live in close proximity to equally sizable or even larger populations of Hindus or Christians.

The regional popularity of certain Friends is so expansive that their tombs and associated institutional sites have provided venues for de facto interreligious encounters that have prompted a dramatic, if temporary, dissolution of communal boundaries.

Contemporary examples from the Indian state of Bihar provide an excellent illustration of this dynamic, particularly in the kinds of institutional contexts I discuss in chapter 7. Just over 14 percent of the current population is Muslim, and at least six Sufi orders have played historically significant roles in the region. The largely Hindu state is also home to a number of sites of great importance to the early history of Buddhism. One scholar argues that the symbolic Muslim appropriation of ancient Hindu and Buddhist sacred sites has conferred on those places greater prestige among Muslims than that claimed by other Muslim sites with no pre-Islamic faith traditions. For example, a ninth-/fifteenth-century foundation connected with a Muslim Friend is in Vaishali, where Buddhist, Hindu, and Jain traditions converge in important ways. The *dargāh* of the Shattārīya order was constructed on the site of a Buddhist reliquary structure in this town also steeped in Hindu Vashnavite and Jain devotional traditions.[18] Muslims' deliberate choice of this multireligious site long ago continues to have important repercussions in the religious lives of the local populace. Muslims and Hindus alike observe a Hindu festivity at the Friend's tomb that is inspired by belief in a female serpent deity. When Hindus hold a three-day feast there to celebrate the god Rama's birthday, a representative of the Shattārīya order comes to town for an observance at the tomb of the Friend. People of the two faith communities recite their own prayers and perform their own rituals, but they do so in concert. Similar convergences have been documented at Muslim institutional sites in Bihar that are associated with the foundation of other Sufi orders, in festivities to honor a Friend of God.[19]

CREATING NEW FRIENDS

Friends of God continue to emerge in Muslim communities across the globe. At least three distinct dynamics appear to be at work in this important phenomenon. The first is a very traditional process in which an individual is popularly acknowledged as a Friend much as in medieval times—according to classic criteria such as asceticism and *baraka*. Another dynamic is an extension of the process of Islamization, begun centuries ago in many cases but by no means complete, in which indigenous religious concepts and rituals are reconciled with prevailing "Islamic" values and practices. Individuals sometimes receive the status of Friend of God if they have played a major role in a region's Islamization. The third dynamic is a process that recognizes an individual's perceived role in liberating a community from colonial powers, as in the case of Habīb Bourguiba, former president of Tunisia.

Friends Judged by Traditional Criteria

Some Friends receive their pedigrees by meeting traditional criteria for sanctity. Two examples are the Egyptian shaykh Ahmad Radwān and a Pakistani figure named Munawwar Shāh. Hagiographical accounts praise Ahmad Radwān's asceticism and devotion, his extraordinary generosity and numerous marvels, and the vast following to whom he imparted the seeds of spiritual renewal. Most notable is his broad appeal across socioeconomic lines, with his home continuing to draw large crowds to the southern village of al-Baghdādī, near Luxor. He was a blend of his father's controlled austerity and his Khalwatīya Sufi uncle's ecstatic proclivities. His main hagiographer, Ahmad ʿAbd al-Mālik, interprets the shaykh's life as a three-stage development: from rigorous, tearful asceticism; to the acquisition of peculiar language skills and divine disclosures characteristic of an axis, and the ability to predict future events; to a more settled time in which he devoted himself to the spiritual formation of others. ʿAbd al-Mālik emphasizes the shaykh's moral virtue, but marvels of clairvoyance also figure prominently. Radwān enjoyed visions and dreams of the Prophet and the whole communion of God's Friends, and as the *ghawth* of his age, he claimed sweeping intercessory powers, but always in abject humility.

Shaykh Radwān's saintly celebrity infiltrated the realm of politics, and he had a complex relationship with the late president Gamāl ʿAbd an-Nāsir (Nasser). Nasser agreed to meet with the shaykh, at the advice of one of his ministers, recalling the long-standing function of Friends as counselors to the powerful. The president even built a railway station named after the shaykh and situated to facilitate visitation to the Friend's home. This ambivalent relationship continued, with the shaykh generally fending off the politician's attempts to co-opt him with gifts. Meanwhile, the shaykh's competitors accused him of consorting with a "communist" and dismissed him as unworthy of exalted spiritual status. Varying accounts of Radwān's relationship to Nasser during the Six Days' War in 1387/1967 suggest divergent perspectives. One insists that after counseling Nasser against warring with Israel, the shaykh returned home and died on the eve of the war. Another holds that the Friend died immediately after the war ended; still another reports that the very ill shaykh was in Cairo on the last day of the war (June 10). Although Nasser wanted to move the shaykh to a military hospital, Radwān preferred to stay and die with his friend the president. Supporters of the shaykh claimed that Radwān predicted that the war would be devastating for Egypt, whereas opponents insisted that the shaykh had encouraged Nasser to attack. Thus did the versions of this new Friend variously interpret his role in the life of Egypt. They cast him as either hero or villain, depending on their views of the proper function of a Friend of God in political affairs. Thirty years after Radwān's death, yet another hagiographical account retold his story, suggesting that his celebrity remained undiminished.[20]

From Pakistan comes a twentieth-century, still-evolving story of a new local patron Friend of God. Munawwar Shāh was a mendicant well known to the Panjabi villagers of Saidpur. Within a few years of his death, popular imagination had transformed Munawwar the *faqīr* (mendicant) into the protecting Friend whose tomb was a destination of pilgrims from the wider region. The process appears to have begun in earnest with the construction of a sanctuary over his tomb to commemorate the first anniversary of his spiritual "wedding."

For that occasion, Munawwar's nephew and a few of the Friend's disciples composed a brief written account of Munawwar's life and times. According to this narrative, the Friend was born in 1339/1920. He was one of five siblings, lost his father at a young age (a fate shared by many male Friends), married, and soon conceived a desire to become a *faqīr*. After entrusting his young wife to family members, Munawwar went so effectively into hiding that his family concluded that he was dead. About twelve years later, the ascetic resurfaced, sold his properties, became a disciple of a local Chishtī shaykh, and endowed a *khānaqāh* complex for the order, complete with mosque, school, public kitchen, and hospice for travelers.

Known as the "naked lord," Munawwar spent twelve years in the service of his spiritual guide and then departed for a village near the Pakistani city of Rawalpindi. There he lived an austere life, gradually attracting a circle of seekers who built a compound for him. He never took up residence in the new facilities, however, for his spiritual guide instructed him to depart for the village of Saidpur. Under a mango tree there, he spent the next thirty-six years of his life. Eventually displaced by a government decision to construct a Japanese garden on the site, Munawwar took up residence beneath a nearby banyan tree. He was accused of being an Indian spy, so he retreated to the jungle. There he freed himself of suspicion by exorcizing the new site of its ancient demons, gaining the esteem of Saidpur's citizens and gathering a group of *malangs* as devotees. Followers persuaded Munawwar to allow them to construct a more permanent complex for him, including accommodations for pilgrims and a structure in which his devotees could tend a symbolic fire in his honor. Sometime during the 1400s/1980s, a noted Chishtī *pīr* visited Munawwar Shāh, and the two arranged that a son of the *pīr* would keep custody of the Friend's sanctuary after Munawwar's death. In July 1409/1988, after the Friend discovered that he had cancer, he declared that he would die in seven months and instructed his followers to build him a tomb. There he was interred in January 1410/1989.

Denis Matringe's analysis offers important insights into the dynamics of Munawwar's sanctification. His hagiographical account of this contemporary Friend of God describes Munawwar's life in three stages: the years before his departure from home, the time he lived in Saidpur, and the period during which he resided on the outskirts of the village. Several variant versions of Munawwar's life insert specific features to make the account conform to classic hagiographies. They thus include, for example, the number of goats he tended for his shaykh (fifteen hundred or four thousand), his tutelage by a "mystery shaykh," his unmarried status before he chose a life of renunciation, the numbers of years he spent in various places (twenty or forty years, depending on the source), and the length of time he knew of his impending death. Stories of his miraculous powers (his exorcism of the demons and his prescience of death) were originally rather spare and unspectacular but eventually became the subjects of embellished accounts. Among the more notable variants of these stories are those attributed to a respected local police officer, presumably to enhance their credibility. For example, the officer and his wife had been unable to bear a child for fifteen years. One of the officer's colleagues took him to Munawwar Shāh, who instructed him to seek the intercession of a regional saint in Furpur, ʿAbd al-Latīf Shāh (a.k.a., Barrī Imām, "the Forest Friend" or "Jungle Saint"). The officer did so, and his wife bore a son nine months later. But the child was born seriously deficient, so the officer returned to Munawwar. The Friend gave him a band to put around the infant's neck while reciting a specific prayer, and the baby was healed.

To appreciate the meaning of these expansions of the story of Munawwar Shāh, we need to understand Saidpur's relationships with two neighboring villages, both of which boasted their own powerful Friends. Beneath Saidpur's saintly aspirations may lie a desire for greater respect in the neighborhood of villages whose patron Friends have inspired shrines of considerable prestige and grandeur. With local respect, not surprisingly, come increased government support and the economic benefits of pilgrimage traffic.[21] One could account for many similar developments in the contemporary emergence of Friends of God in other social and cultural contexts.[22] Each case and context, however, has its own ingredients, impetus, and dynamics. But the story of Munawwar Shāh more than adequately illustrates for present purposes the enduring phenomenon of "sanctification."[23]

Friends and Islamization

Contemporary Indonesia, which has the largest national population of Muslims in the world, offers examples of the second dynamic: identification with the ascendancy of Islamic faith in the region. Supernatural power is the hallmark of Friends of God in Indonesia, as in so many other Islamicate contexts. Indonesians who acknowledge the importance of a *waliala* (in Arabic, *walī Allāh*) typically do so at a place identified as the Friend's grave. In many instances, a Friend's devotees know and admit that the "grave" actually holds no remains but is instead device that confers a measure of "Islamic" respectability on reverential rituals carried out there. The "grave of the Friend" is typically a sacred site long associated with the spirits of village guardians or founding ancestors, known as *pundhen*. When such sites are Islamized, they are called *kramat*, from the Arabic term for saintly marvels, *karāmāt*.

A wide range of figures are acknowledged as Friends of God in Indonesia. Some are purely local tutelary spirits, some are characters of pre-Islamic myth and legend with connections to specific regions, and others are religious scholars of more recent times credited with Islamizing specific regions of Indonesia. Some are founding figures of Sufi orders, and others are Wali Songo, who generally receive credit for bringing Islam to the islands in the first place. Countless sacred sites for pre-Islamic practice and belief have yet to be Islamized, and the process continues.[24]

Indonesia's tribal peoples exemplify variations on the theme of Islamization. For example, the Gumai people superimpose an Islamically acceptable interpretation on pre-Islamic traditions that honor tribal ancestral spirits, who function in ways analogous to those of Friends of God.[25] Sacred ancestors of the tribal Bugis are the object of reverence for Muslims among this tribe, whose members follow Shāfiʿī legal practice for visiting graves on three major Islamic feast days: ʿĪd al-Fitr (breaking of the fast at the end of Ramadan), ʿĪd al-Adhā (sacrifice during the formal hajj), and ʿĀshūrā (the tenth of Muharram). Such visitation is considered Islamically acceptable, however, only for graves of Muslim Friends of God and not for ancestors in general. Religiously acceptable Friends include Shaykh Yūsuf, an eleventh-/seventeenth-century religious scholar celebrated for his resistance to Dutch colonization; and the three "Dato" (known only as Patimang, Bandang, and Tiro, the names of the places containing their graves), who brought Islam from Sumatra. But to facilitate official acceptance of their ritual veneration of ancestral spirits, the Bugis have taken to disguising many associated holy places as graves. Moreover, they believe that ordinary people can become *waliala*, with appropriate funerary rituals to ease their voyage in the next life. Ancestral village protectors function much like intercessory Friends, and their graves are goals of local visitation.[26]

Friends and Political Power

The survival of Friends of God in contemporary Indonesia offers still other surprising twists, including a curious story that provides a transition to the third dynamic. In chapter 8, I described the transformation of a former Hindu king named Brawijaya into the *waliala* Pandan Arang, who became the center of a sacred site in southern Java. One of the more arresting aspects of the story of Brawijaya/Pandan Arang is the claim by the people near his former kingdom of Majapahit in Eastern Java that his tomb is there. However, the people of the area acknowledge that the tomb is empty, because Brawijaya disappeared mysteriously and attained spiritual freedom. The site is maintained only as a concession to Islamic belief and practice. Believers report that his spirit returned to this spot by a circuitous route: it entered into former Indonesian president Soekarno, who, as the new Brawijaya, traveled to the site to put the saint's spirit at rest at the grave. Though the story does not claim sainthood for the president, it demonstrates that the tradition of spirit survival leaves room for such an interpretation—one that Indonesia's Muslim reformers would surely repudiate.[27]

A full-blown example of the transformation of a political figure into a hero-saint comes from North Africa. Tunisia's former president Habīb Bourguiba was known as the "Supreme Warrior" (*al-mujāhid al-akbar*), but he was more than a national secular hero. For example, one story reports that a famous woman named Wāsila ben ʿAmmār persuaded Bourguiba to go with her to visit a living local Friend of God, Sīdī ʿAmr al-Fayyāsh. The flamboyant Friend had foretold that Wāsila would wed the future leader of Tunisia. As the two headed for the Friend's place, Bourguiba suddenly insisted that the Friend should instead come to visit him, proclaiming that he would raze the "crazy" Friend's residence and have him committed to an asylum. That night, the Friend appeared to Bourguiba in a dream and informed him that he (Sīdī ʿAmr) would subvert Bourguiba's designs to destroy him. Bourguiba repented of his evil plan and set about supporting the Friend's devoted following.

The other side of the story is that Bourguiba, obviously ambivalent in his views of sainthood, gradually assumed the status of a larger-than-life religious figure. Beginning in 1381/1961, Bourguiba fasted publicly during Ramadan and endorsed the national observance of Muhammad's birthday, though he had previously eliminated many Sufi institutions (*zāwiyas*) and burial places in the interest of both urban renewal and secularization. But Bourguiba had avoided damaging the places associated with Friends with major followings, many of which he actually refurbished and enlarged. Bourguiba was careful to publicize his patronage of the tombs of the great Friends, especially those identified as patrons of villages and towns. Meanwhile, the leader began to set himself up as the patron Friend of the entire nation, becoming ironically the "patron saint" of secularization in the name of development.

Bourguiba's constituents increasingly attributed to him both the sayings and deeds of a person with the status of a Friend of God. Gradually, the ingredients of a "hagiography" of the Supreme Warrior formed a body of literature virtually synonymous with the history of the modern nation-state of Tunisia. Patterned on the biography of Muhammad, this hagiographical tradition emphasizes Bourguiba's leadership in the "greater jihad" against underdevelopment, for like the Prophet, he combated official (colonial) resistance against all odds. The leader's chief "miracle" in such accounts was his overthrow of colonial French rule, but popular esteem has also touted Bourguiba as a source of *baraka*.[28]

EPILOGUE: LITERARY FRIENDS TODAY

Many Friends of God live on today in their poetry and other literary contributions. Millions of well-educated Muslims across the globe continue to read, memorize, and share with others the wisdom of Friends, now enshrined in over a dozen major literary languages. Indeed, the literary heritage of Islam's Friends of God is arguably one of the most distinctive features of this remarkable group of human beings. Christian tradition boasts some thousands of saints, canonized over nearly two millennia. But apart from the relative handful of Johns of the Cross and Hildegards of Bingen, few Christian saints are remembered as affectionately in our day for their poetry as for their more conventionally miraculous works and intercessory powers.

Publishing houses throughout North Africa and the Middle East still produce texts of Arab poets of high literary renown who died as long as a thousand years ago. Hallāj of Baghdad, Ibn al-Fārid of Egypt, and Shushtarī of Andalusia remain accessible to a surprising number of readers in recent original-language editions. Among the Turkic-speaking people of Turkey and the Central Asian republics, the works of mystical Friends such as Yūnus

Emre remain well-known and much loved. Rūmī is often acknowledged as one of the world's premier religious poets in any language. His originally Persian didactic and lyric mystical poetry is still as popular in Turkish translation as in the original tongue throughout the Persian-speaking regions of Iran and Afghanistan. Among the so-called vernacular poets of South Asia, Sindhī and Panjabī Friends of early modern times (such as Sultān Bāhū, ʿAbd al-Latīf of Bhit, and Bullhe Shāh) retain pride of place in regional literary pantheons. The same is true of the great Friends who have written both in the former *lingua franca* of South Asia, Persian, and in the modern linguistic symbol of Muslim nationhood, Urdu. In Southeast Asia, too, religiously literate readers continue to cherish the works of Friends like Hamza Fansūrī, the first great Muslim mystical poet in the Malay tongue.

One of the truly spectacular characteristics of Islam's patrimony of Friends of God is the remarkably seamless integration of holiness and high culture, ecstasy and aesthetics, love and language. Certainly, many famous Friends have been celebrated for their populist simplicity and their opting for identification with ordinary folk rather than pursuit of the approbation of cultural and political establishments. But the world is immeasurably richer for the finely tuned verbal skills of dozens of Friends of God and for the continued appreciation by millions of readers, Muslim and non-Muslim alike, of their literary heritages.[29]

PART III

Friends in Theory

Understanding the Stories

. . . . .

In part 1, the stories of God's Friends spoke for themselves. Arranged thematically, scores of individual narratives from major hagiographical sources offered an overview of the lives and times of some of Islamdom's most colorful and influential paragons of holiness. Part 2 gradually introduced elements of theory to guide readers toward a more analytical understanding of those stories. Some of the theoretical literary and theological aspects of this vast narrative tradition have themselves become the subjects of more technical analysis in important Muslim religious texts. These analyses appear in the prefatory remarks of some major hagiographers as well as in individual works on mystical spirituality and theology.

After a brief survey of major genres of hagiographically relevant literature, chapter 10 explores how Muslim authors have developed concepts essential to interpreting the stories both as literary works and as aids to devotion and inspiration. It focuses largely on how hagiographers structure and connect their stories, and on what they tell us about their intentions in crafting tales of God's Friends.

Chapter 11 then turns to traditional Islamic discussions of the content of hagiographic tales. It shows how major Muslim theorists have analyzed such important themes as the nature of sainthood and the distinctive capabilities attributed to Friends of God. In turn, the chapter looks at how scholars have understood Friends' miracles, intercession, dreams and visions in the context of mystical spirituality, cosmology, and theology. It therefore provides theoretical underpinnings for essential themes illustrated through story in earlier chapters.

FIGURE 26. A complex has formed around Rūmī's (d. 72/1273) tomb in Konya (Turkey). The domed building to the left is Sultan Sulayman's mosque (967–970/1559–62), which commemorates the victory of the sultan's son Selim over his son Bayezit); the fluted cupola at center stands over Rūmī's burial place (replicated on the mosque's *minbar),* and the large domes to the right enclose mosque and ritual space that now functions as a museum as well as a mausoleum of generations of leaders of the Mevlevi (or Mawlawīya, "whirling dervishes") order. The site remains a goal of *ziyāra* for many in the region. Photo by John Renard.

10.   Literary Dimensions

Genre, Function, and Hermeneutics

Interpreting tales of God's Friends is as complex and challenging as it is enjoyable and rewarding. To develop a balanced understanding of the many meanings and functions of this vast treasure-house of legend and lore, one needs to reach back to the beginnings of the Islamic tradition. Islam's earliest sources, the Qurʾān and hadith, offer important insights into the phenomenon of storytelling. In the introduction to this volume, I highlighted some of the indispensable traditional written sources of Islamic hagiography. Here I expand on that brief outline with a closer look at the principal literary forms through which Muslim authors have preserved and communicated Islamic traditions. Hagiographers often preface their works with discussions of their authorial intentions and the lessons they hope readers will glean from their works. The reasons they offer for writing and reading tales of God's Friends show us the functions of the literature in Islamicate societies—as opposed to the functions of "contemporary" Friends. An appreciation of function naturally gives rise to an exploration of authors' levels of interpretation.

This chapter turns on several central questions of interpretation, which we can apply to individual texts. What do we know about the specific intentions of the author of a text? What readership did the author have in mind? Can we identify a particular literary genre, or combination of genres, in the text? What are the communicative limitations and strengths of the literary form the author has chosen? How have specialists in Islamic studies approached and interpreted the sources? In other words, what kind of information have scholars gleaned from these sources, and through what academic disciplines have scholars most often filtered the ancient sources?

STORYTELLING IN ISLAMICATE SOCIETIES

In many traditional and primarily "oral" societies, recounting stories of a people's ancestral foundations has long been an essential way to preserve the community's heritage. Memory and imagination converge as one generation hands on its patrimony to the next, highlighting the sayings and deeds of the tribe's heroes and exemplars. When a religious tradition, such as that of Islam, grows to encompass much greater cultural and ethnic diversity than it embraced at its origins, the distinctive stories of each community that adopts the new faith begin to blend with the newly introduced religious lore. As Islam expanded, many figures of major significance in the newly conquered societies were gradually "Islamized," taking on the religious characteristics of central figures in the ancient Islamic tales. For example, the great Iranian heroes of the Persian *Book of Kings* (*Shāhnāma*) by Firdawsī began to talk and act like observant Muslims, even though the characters' stories originally preserved pre-Islamic values and beliefs. Conversely, originally Islamic (including biblical) characters were gradually indigenized, taking on the manner and look of their new ethnic and cultural contexts. For example, many Iranian stories came to describe a thoroughly "Islamic" and "Arab" ʿAlī in terms more congenial to a Persian setting.[1]

Qurʾān: Fables of the Ancients?

Islam's scripture, the Qurʾān, began as a kind of oral tradition, growing out of the preaching of Muhammad. This preaching originally conveyed a message of moral responsibility and concern for social justice. Within a few years of the initial public revelation around 610, Muhammad's Qurʾānic discourse began to incorporate more illustrative material in the form of excerpts from tales about pre-Islamic prophets. Episodes from the stories of Moses and Abraham, as well as others with clear links to ancient biblical traditions, became staples in Muhammad's homiletical repertoire. But other characters arguably of extrabiblical provenance also played essential roles in the Prophet's exhortation. Qurʾānic narratives set tales of the so-called Arabian prophets Sālih and Hūd, for example, side by side with those of biblical fame. A third figure, Shuʿayb, was often included in a trio of Arabian prophets, though some scholars argue that he actually bears a similarity to the biblical Jethro of Midian, Moses's father-in-law.[2] In response to the Prophet's use of time-honored prophetic exemplars in his preaching, Muhammad's early critics repeatedly dismissed his public discourse as little more than "fables of the ancients."[3] Allusions to just over two dozen prophetic figures comprise the largest category of narrative material in the scripture. Those stories became the foundation, both in tone and content, of Islamic hagiographical lore. But in addition to providing tone and content, early Islamic tradition contributed other important ingredients to the large treasury of hagiography that I have broadly defined in this volume.

Anecdotes among the Hadith

Long before Muhammad's time, Arabs cultivated their collective memory through a sort of "oral biography" through which they documented their own genealogies, spiced with anecdotes about especially important family members. As generations passed, these brief "reports" (*khabar*, pl. *akhbār*) eventually were recited along with the names of individuals who had preserved specific accounts. Early Muslims adapted this mode of living memory to enshrine the sayings and deeds of their Prophet, gradually stitching countless disparate reports into a more or less coherent bionarrative of Muhammad. From that larger picture, specialists edited out explicitly "religious" elements, especially features judged to impinge directly on law, ritual, and belief. These elements became the basis of the body of lore, and eventually literature, called hadith.

This body of orally preserved lore about Muhammad gradually became too expansive to be entrusted entirely to memory. Muslim scholars therefore set out to commit the remembered treasures to writing. By the end of the third/ninth century, a small library of "authoritative" collections of hadith had come into being. Editors such as Bukhārī and Muslim—the two most prominent and revered early hadith scholars—organized their material in a variety of ways. For our purposes, a roughly thematic structure is the most useful and important method.

But in addition to containing the sayings and deeds of the Prophet, which are the bulk of the hadith collections, these volumes include a more narrowly focused type of material. Sprinkled throughout the dozens of topical chapters are important anecdotes that reveal specific personal, ethical, and spiritual characteristics of the Prophet, his family members, and earliest Companions. Recalling the exemplary behavior of Muhammad as well as the "excellences" or virtues of many of his contemporaries among the first Muslims, these accounts became the earliest sources of hagiographical material, in its narrower, more technical sense.[4] These usually brief accounts became the earliest model for the kinds of notices one finds, for example, in the hagiographical sections of the great fourth-/tenth-century Sufi manuals of spirituality.

Professional Raconteurs

Even after memory of the Prophetic legacy was safely ensconced in written form, storytelling in the traditional societies of early Islamdom remained an important medium of religious education, edification, and entertainment. In fact, the growth of new literary forms such as "tales of the prophets" seems to have contributed directly to the avocation of preachers and professional raconteurs. Written sources thus shored up developments in oral tradition, which in leapfrog fashion, in turn gave rise to new genres of written material.

Medieval Muslim authors paid considerable attention to the power and function of storytellers in their communities. Some observers were especially concerned about the potential pitfalls of irresponsible tale mongering. Abū Tālib of Mecca, for example, was adamantly opposed to raconteurs, whose trade he regarded as deleterious to the faith of listeners. He saw the story-tellers as peddlers of insubstantial and, worse still, misleading accounts of the spiritual models of the past—tales that were entertaining, perhaps, but unworthy of their noble subject. Abū Tālib argued that the difference between sessions dedicated to stories for their own sake (i.e., purely for entertainment) and spiritually beneficial sessions is that the latter encourage people to focus on spiritual mindfulness and remembrance of God. Stories about famous holy people are really, therefore, about the One to whom people dedicate themselves. A century and a half later, Ibn al-Jawzī's *Book of Storytellers and Professional Raconteurs* discussed in great detail the danger inherent in the public performance of sacred tradition. Like Abū Tālib, he warned that storytellers with responsibility for passing on the legacy to crowds of eager listeners must take great care not to succumb to the allure of celebrity status. They must resist the temptation to inflate their tales with elements of the spectacular that might obscure the essential ethical component of the exemplary conduct of ancestors in faith.[5] As we shall see, such warnings about the role of storytelling and the awesome responsibility of handing on traditions of the great Muslims were not lost on those who committed their stories to writing. Moreover, some major Friends, such as Rūmī and Saʿdī, though they were not hagiographers as such, rank among the premier storytellers about other Friends of God (see Figs. 26 and 27).

HAGIOGRAPHY'S PRINCIPAL LITERARY GENRES

Three major categories of literary genres provide us with the bulk of our hagiographical data, even though only the first two types are generally recognized as hagiography in the strictest sense. Around the fourth/tenth century, Arabic biographical (or perhaps biohagiographical) anthologies began to appear. Beginning a century or so later, the life stories of individual Friends of God took their place in the hagiographical library. In this category of individual life accounts, I include for organizational simplicity a genre that could have occupied its own category: students' collections of the recollections and memorable

FIGURE 27.   The tomb of Saʿdī (d. 692/1292), a major literary Friend famous for his storytelling, poetry, and "wisdom" works that blend prose and poetry, stands in Shiraz, Iran. Photo by John Renard.

sayings of their influential teachers. But in addition to these two genres, important sources include "autobiographical" accounts of major Friends.

At this point, we should understand a general technical distinction among the terms *hagiography, biohagiography,* and *hagiology.* This working distinction applies particularly to the tone and thematic content of traditional sources about paradigmatic religious figures in general, whatever the genre. *Hagiography* focuses on the uniquely spiritual and moral qualities of the subject, including in many instances elements of the miraculous or marvelous. ʿAttār's *Remembrances of the Friends of God* is the quintessential example of this approach, offering relatively sparse commentary on the stories of the Friends. *Biohagiography* adds significant information about the subject's personal, public, and political life. One example is the Indian work known as the *Naqshbandī Assemblies.*[6] This added information expands the individual's stature as a paragon of involvement in the real world. *Hagiology,* finally, includes elements of doctrine or other theoretical considerations with narratives. Tādilī and Jāmī, for example, introduce hagiological features in their anthologies and include sections on miracles in their introductions.[7]

Anthologies or Collected Lives

Four principal types of works fit in the general category of anthology or collective biography. First, some freestanding hagiographical collections arrange famous figures in organizational or institutional categories (*tabaqāt,* meaning "classifications" or "generations") rather than presenting them chronologically or grouping them geographically. Second, some larger works integrate hagiographical sections using the *tabaqāt* structure into handbooks of Sufi spirituality. Third, some works stick to recounting multiple exemplary lives, using a variety of organizational principles.[8] Finally, an important type of hagiography restricts coverage to figures who lived in a specific geographical region or were personally known to the author.[9]

One of the earliest types of "collected" works is the freestanding (*tabaqāt*) genre. This genre groups major figures according to their role in the early history of Sufism or their affiliation with a particular Sufi order. It shares the overall structural concerns of works that gather, for example, biographical sketches of major figures in other cultural categories, such as poets or specialists in religious law. Authors of these works exhibit an overriding concern for the institutional life to which their subjects contributed, though they frequently indicate that their accounts may provide a wider range of spiritual benefits as well. The earliest works of this genre include Sulamī's Arabic *Generations of the Sufis* and Ansārī's Persian volume of the same title. Material eventually written down in these works was first transmitted orally, and the written work authenticated the tales by including a list of transmitters, after the ancient pattern of hadith scholarship. Except in multivolume works such as Isfahānī's *Ornament of God's Friends,* entries are generally brief and provide basic data about the individual's circumstances, education, notable spiritual mentors, and personal qualities, along with a selection of the Friend's more famous words and deeds. Miracles generally play a secondary role in these works, as does analysis of the Friend's historical and social contexts. Authors are more interested in providing a convenient summary of figures prominent in their spiritual genealogies as a guide for readers already embarked on the religious quest.[10]

In addition, several major classical "manuals" of Sufi life and spirituality dedicate significant sections to brief sketches of the lives and sayings of personalities whom the authors judge to be of critical importance in the history of Sufism. Two authors of compendious works of this type, Qushayrī and Hujwīrī, retain some organizational or structural elements of the freestanding *tabaqāt* works. Qushayrī begins his Arabic *Treatise* with major second-/eighth- and third-/ninth-century figures, whereas Hujwīrī begins his Persian *Revelation of Realities Veiled* with the Companions of the Prophet. Both writers declare that one of their principal hagiographical concerns is to provide cause for reflecting on the ethical and spiritual examples of these great people, examples that clearly demonstrate that every one of them lived in consonance with the Revealed Law.[11]

A more generalized type of hagiographical anthology offers a not-necessarily-chronological collection of stories and sayings of pious individuals. Titles of such anthologies can include a variety of technical terms such as *tadhkira* (memorial, remembrance, recollection), *tarjama* (biographical notes on the subject's early years, education and teachers, written works, pilgrimages and travel, and miscellaneous anecdotes), *siyar* (exemplary life stories, plural of *sīra*), and *manāqib* (feats, marvelous accomplishments). The term *memorial* gained currency beginning in the sixth/twelfth century, particularly in Persian sources, and often referred to nonhagiographical accounts of poets and other famous people. *Manāqib* is now often included in the idiomatic Arabic expression for "hagiography," *adab al-manāqib* ("the literature of amazing accomplishments"). But the term also describes a lengthier hagiographical work devoted to the life of an individual Friend of God.[12] Accounts of this third type mainly seek to inspire readers by recounting more idealized holy lives and are typically unconcerned with rooting their subjects in detailed historical contexts. ʿAttār's Persian *Remembrances of the Friends of God* is the preeminent example of the "generations" format for the purpose of spiritual edification. I will return to this work shortly for a look at ʿAttār's expressed motives for composing it. All of the first three kinds of anthologies offer broad coverage in both time and space but are naturally rather limited in their coverage of individual figures.

The last type of collective hagiography includes works that recount stories of Friends of God who were either known to the author personally or lived in the author's home region. This type can provide more detailed geographical and chronological coverage, though individual life stories remain generally brief. Earlier chapters of this book recounted many stories from writings of this type by Ibn ʿArabī and Sadafī.[13] In this chapter, I take a slightly more detailed look at the author of another work of this fourth type. Like other authors of such works, Safi ad-Dīn uses geographical context as an organizational principle, in his case centering his world of sanctity around Egypt and parts of Syria and the Hijāz (the region of the northwestern Arabian Peninsula that includes Mecca and Medina). He includes some characters from farther west (North Africa and Spain) and east (especially Iran) who had some connection with the main figures in this area. Some 60 of his 155 figures hailed from Egypt, another 60 were from al-Andalus and the Maghrib.

Safi ad-Dīn lived during the later years of the Ayyūbid dynasty (565/1171–648/1250) and the beginning of Mamlūk rule (648/1250–923/1517). His work begins with accounts of his own chief teacher, Abū 'l-ʿAbbās al-Harrār, and Harrār's teacher, along with several shaykhs from his early youth. He then describes a group of spiritual guides whom he met in Fustat, a "suburb" of Cairo, after his shaykh's death. Among these guides were individuals in the Shādhilīya order, an organization especially prominent in Andalusia and North Africa. Finally, he tells of a number of shaykhs associated with the great teacher Ibn as-Sabbāgh, himself the author of an important life of Shādhilī. One of the key features in his work and in, for example, the hagiographical anthologies of Ibn ʿArabī is that the authors recount the stories of individuals known to them personally (or, in a few cases, by association). Safi ad-Dīn does provide somewhat more detailed accounts of the Friends closest to him than of other figures, but the sources that offer the greatest depth of insight into specific Friends of God are those that aim to tell a single life story.[14]

Individual Life Stories

More expansive treatments of individual holy lives naturally allow broader coverage and more intricate detail. The earliest works in this genre typically cast the featured Friend as the model of the religiously observant Muslim who strictly adheres to the prescriptions of Revealed Law (sharia). Only gradually did a greater interest in the miraculous come to the fore. On the whole, these more detailed accounts also provide much greater insight into the Friend's historical and cultural contexts than do the collective hagiographical works. The genre has two principal subtypes. In one, the followers of a Friend credited with founding a Sufi order retell the story of their leader within the city that was his spiritual home; in the other, the authors recount the role of a less well connected, and typically "rural," Friend remembered for his or her local or regional social and political influence. Authors of the former type are generally less interested in presenting miraculous accounts than in laying out an example of holiness in keeping with the well-regulated life of the Sufi organization. They thus emphasize the Friend's authority, wisdom, and leadership qualities. Stories of more local, nonurban figures tend to place more emphasis on the Friend's role as intercessor or mediator (both in the here and the hereafter) and to show how the Friend's influence extends beyond the grave.

These full-scale biohagiographies generally follow the whole course of a Friend's life. Beginning with childhood and upbringing, the accounts move through the Friend's education and the "conversion" that set him or her on a life of renunciation. Accounts often culminate in marvelous episodes and a holy death, which is sometimes followed by evidence of the Friend's continuing spiritual presence. The whole-life format evolved from about the fourth/tenth century to the ninth/fifteenth century. Some such works are also called *maqāmāt* (stations along a trajectory), because they offer a way of understanding a life story in terms of spiritual progress.[15]

A further important type of literature provides indispensable information about individual figures through gathered teachings and anecdotes. The genre known as *malfūzāt* (utterances, discourses or by extension, assemblies) presents the sayings of a single famous Friend. Typically, the Friend has delivered these words in public or semipublic gatherings of followers, and his or her trusted disciples have then written them down and edited them. An example is the eighth-/fourteenth-century Indian work *Morals for the Heart* (*Fawāʾid al-fuʾād*), described by one scholar as "preeminent among all *malfūzāt* of medieval Indian Sufism: it exemplifies the virtue of Persian prose as a simple but effective tool for communicating diverse situations, moods and thoughts. It captures the spirit of Chishtī Friend Nizām ad-Dīn Awliyāʾ's towering presence, his absolute loyalty to his *pīr*, his taste for poetry and *samāʿ* and his empathy."[16] A second example is a later eighth-/fourteenth-century work, Jaʿfar Badakhshī's *Choicest of Wonders* (*Khulasāt al-manāqib*). It contains assorted anecdotes recounted to the author by his *pīr*, Mīr Sayyid ʿAli Hamadānī, about himself and various other Sufis.[17] Friends in other cultural contexts also inspired works in the genre. In Turkey, for example, the discourses of Rūmī remain a major source of information about that remarkable individual.[18]

Autobiographical Forms

Some of the more famous Friends have left first-person accounts of their lives and experiences of spiritual quest. Claiming saintly rank for oneself may seem entirely self-serving, and doing so was in fact more the exception than the rule. Several Friends of God nevertheless authored their own self-legitimating accounts, and these works are worth considering briefly here. Not surprisingly, some are rather colorful and include expansive claims to knowledge and power, whereas others are more self-effacing. Tirmidhī penned arguably the earliest extant spiritual autobiography. Curiously, his wife's dreams play a featured role in the account.[19] Martyr-mystic ʿAyn al Quḍāt al-Hamadhānī's *Apologia* and Ghazālī's autobiographical reflections, which I describe briefly in chapter 2, are also in this category.[20] One of the more recent first-person accounts is that of Ahmad ibn ʿAjība, which I describe in chapter 5.[21]

Some first-person accounts, especially from later-medieval and early-modern North Africa, purport to be inspired by conversational encounters with Muhammad in dreams or visions. In addition to shoring up the religious authority of their subjects, these oneiric autobiographies open for us revealing windows into the aspirations of these Friends and their followers. The Friend's intercessory role in achieving salvation in the hereafter also stands out, and in these texts, individuals clearly admit to aspiring to such a role. Most importantly for present purposes, these works offer extensive descriptions of the kind of dream experiences that most frequently appear in third-person anecdotes about Friends of God—that is, about someone *else*. Only a claim that the Prophet himself had enjoined a Friend to intercede could, it seems, justify such a bold course of action.[22]

HERMENEUTICAL ISSUES: LEVELS OF INTERPRETATION

Perhaps the most fundamental question one can ask about the hagiographer's task is "how to describe through facts and words that which, by definition, is remote from (mere) speech and a quest for facts."[23] To answer that question, we can reflect on how we respond to a great work of poetry. Few thoughtful readers of e. e. cummings or Shakespeare, say, would be inclined to exclaim, "Nice sentiments; but did it *really happen?*" Sensitivity to metaphor is essential to understanding many types of verbal communication. Metaphor suffuses even the most pedestrian daily conversations in idioms like "you're pulling my leg" or "let's cut to the chase." But in recent years, American colloquial speech has evolved in ways that don't always let metaphors be metaphors. One often hears expressions like "I was *literally* scared to death," or "I had goose bumps—*literally.*" Many people find themselves caught unawares between using once-trenchant figures of speech and trying to explain them away by insisting that they refer to some "fact." But idioms and poetry, in whatever language, come into being precisely because some realities exist that we either cannot or would rather not reduce to journalistic reports. Such realities by definition transcend ordinary experience, and by extension, transcend ordinary language as well.

Hagiography has a lot in common with great poetry. Both literary forms communicate idiomatically, and both rely on the power of metaphor to hint at truths that elude verbal captivity. The same problem that occurs when one asks whether an experience described in a poem "really happened" also arises when one assumes that an apparently spectacular hagiographical account has only one level of meaning. Of course, some readers choose to believe that a "miracle" account is "true" because it describes an actual, empirically verifiable event, whereas others believe that such an account is "only a story" (that is, it's "false") about something that never occurred. Common American parlance casts "myth" in a losing battle with "fact," dismissing at a stroke much of the world's collective wisdom. Such binary thinking misses the point entirely: there is a middle ground where poetry and hagiography live. Thus, one can say truly that someone's heart was "aflame with love" without feeling the need to scrub for cardiac surgery or that someone "brought the dead to life" without immediately checking to see if the tomb is really empty.

Hagiography is not historiography. Unfortunately, neither authors nor readers always draw clear lines between the two forms. Certainly, some hagiographical accounts provide "hard data" about verifiable events in a Friend's life as well as about his or her historical and cultural milieu. But readers need to be aware that hagiographers sometimes choose not to distinguish the mundane from the marvelous in their narratives. Occasionally, they may even appear to deliberately falsify the historical record for the purpose of aggrandizing their subject. An account might, for example, stretch the truth about a Friend's influence at a royal court or the number of followers in his retinue. Such blurring of boundaries only makes it more difficult, and more imperative, to cultivate a delicate blend of critical acumen and sensitivity to the elements of mystery, power, and wonder that the author seeks to communicate.[24]

Alas, in the valley of metaphor, ambiguity is king. Some accounts suffused with the aura of the miraculous appear to ask readers to take them at face value, and one can hardly doubt that many readers have done so. Two substantial documents about the life of Shaykh Ahmad of Jām, for example, catalog hundreds of the Friend's marvels as though they are the sum and substance of his saintly career. Surely the authors assume that their readers will accept all of the episodes they recount as simple, empirically verifiable facts? In one of these accounts, Sadīd ad-Dīn of Ghaznī (in present-day Afghanistan) offers an important hermeneutical clue as he describes his intentions in compiling the work.

Sadīd ad-Dīn begins his narrative, *The Colossal Elephant and His Spiritual Feats*, by insisting that he initially went to Shaykh Ahmad's *khānqāh* "with a suspicious mind, only for the purpose of testing him."[25] Seated in the back of the assembly, the skeptical observer listened as one of the

Friend's sons finished preaching and Shaykh Ahmad ordered that a melon and a watermelon be divided among the numerous visitors. Impossible, Sadīd thought, even if the shaykh had ten melons. He decided to put the shaykh to the test, thinking to himself, "If he is a man of vision, let him give me the slice of melon which the servant put in front of him." Before Sadīd had uttered a word, Shaykh Ahmad called his name and invited him to come forward for his slice of melon. A duly embarrassed Sadīd became a disciple, for the shaykh's "spiritual power [*ahwāl*] radiated over me." Overcome by a totally new feeling, Sadīd continues, "So many were the benefits I received that it is not possible to write them all down. I decided to recall and write about a small sample of the spiritual states [*ahwāl*] . . . that it might serve as a memento for the friends, and as a consolation for his disciples . . . as well as a memento for readers and observers."[26]

Sadīd ad-Dīn then unfolds his second motive for writing. The fundamental problem, as he sees it, is that too many people have historically denied the miracles of Muhammad as well as those of God's other Friends, and he believes his duty is to refute the naysayers. Impressive as are the deeds of Shaykh Ahmad, they pale by comparison to Muhammad's works. Nevertheless, that God has given Ahmad such wondrous gifts during the "latter days" of "upheavals and tribulations we are experiencing" only proves the "prophethood and mission" of Muhammad. Sadīd enumerates "another kind of good work" of Shaykh Ahmad: one hundred eighty thousand people have repented and seven thousand non-Muslims have converted. And, he adds, "all of these show just one sort of the good deeds" Ahmad worked. Here the author provides an important clue to his personal conviction. Those who are not unmindful will know, those who are not blind will see, and those who are sincere will rejoice in his account of Ahmad. However, those not disposed to accept the evidence of Shaykh Ahmad's extension of the Prophet's mission will only persevere in their "ignorance, denial, and stupidity."[27] In short, even in a work virtually composed of the marvelous, the author makes clear that things are never only what they appear to be. One's perception of marvels presupposes openness in faith, and Sadīd ad-Dīn's avowed skepticism had clearly not been sufficient to undermine his receptive predisposition. Sadīd ad-Dīn's reflections on his authorial intent find parallels in other hagiographical works.

Before turning to evidence of the explicit intentions of some major hagiographers, let us look at a rare and striking comment that bears on the interpretation of the lives of God's Friends. Few documents address the matter as forthrightly as the twelfth-/eighteenth-century Javanese *Book of Cabolek*, much of which discusses whether and how Friends of God ought to disclose the fundamental aspects of intimacy with their Lord. A king asks his brother-in-law how a mystic, who aspires to follow in the steps of earlier Javanese martyrs, dares to speak about a "secret knowledge," interpreting a famous traditional Javanese poem almost as if he were a Buddhist! Brother-in-law Bapang replies that according to the "knowledge of ultimate reality," divulging these things is not wrong, for one must understand them metaphorically rather than view them as points of basic doctrine. He explains that many of God's Friends have adopted a metaphorical interpretation of union with the divine, thereby revealing knowledge that cannot be divulged directly. In the end, the king spares the life of Mutamakin, the one who had sought martyrdom.[28]

Authorial Intent

Many of the authors of hagiographical works offer important clues in their introductory remarks about their intentions and hopes for their literary labors.[29] Thaʿlabī wrote one of the most important versions of tales of the prophets. In his chapter on creation, he includes a list of five "insights" or "wisdoms" in store for his reader.[30] He bases his comments on the conviction that God related stories of the prophets to Muhammad so that he could pass on these same insights. First, the accounts prove that Muhammad, unlettered as he was, received an authentic revelation. Second, they encourage believers to emulate the heroic behavior of the prophets (who functioned as models for Muhammad as well) even as they warn against the conduct of unbelievers. Third, they explain that God clearly preferred Muhammad and his people over earlier peoples who endured much greater suffering. Fourth, they provide essential instruction and guidance about history and religion. Finally, the accounts keep alive the memory of the prophets and Friends of God, "so that those who do well in keeping the saints' memories alive thereby assure themselves a speedy reward in this world, in order that the saints' good renown and legacy may remain forever." This focus on memory is so, Thaʿlabī notes, because "human beings are stories," in that the mere mention of one who has died brings that individual back to life.[31] An eighth-/fourteenth-century Turkish reworking of the life of the Prophet by Mustafā Darīr goes a step further in assessing the value of Friends and heroes. He notes that these saintly individuals "would not only teach their readers gratitude, patience and the praise of God, but would in themselves be a form of prayer."[32]

As in Sadīd ad-Dīn's work on Shaykh Ahmad, authors of lives of individual Friends have often made observations about the benefits of encountering "their" Friend in their narratives. Abū 'l-Hasan ad-Daylamī wrote a biohagiography of his teacher, Ibn Khafīf of Shiraz. His portrayal emphasizes the shaykh's asceticism as an exemplary way of discovering personal peace by renouncing this world. But above all, the author emphasizes the absolute trust in God that undergirds Ibn Khafīf's Herculean self-discipline.[33] One of Ibn Khafīf's most celebrated students, Abū Ishāq al-Kāzarūnī, is also the subject of an important full-scale account. His biographer emphasizes the shaykh's active role in defending the faith as chaplain to soldiers at war with Byzantium in the later fourth/tenth and early fifth/eleventh centuries, as well as his foundation of a major Sufi community.[34]

Abū Saʿīd ibn Abi 'l-Khayr, a contemporary of Kāzarūnī, likewise features in an important biohagiographical narrative (mentioned above) written by a great-grandson. Ibn-i Munawwar notes that he was moved to write the work by the conviction that Friends of God extend prophetic presence in the world. As a link in the chain of sanctity that connects humankind to the Creator, Abū Saʿīd's life story is a reminder of the sacred context and ultimate goal of life in this world. Friends convinced Ibn-i Munawwar of the need for a written account of the shaykh's life, given aging disciples' dwindling memory of his teachings. Here the author reflects on the reality of spiritual entropy and the need to reinvigorate the spirit of religious striving: "religious science is no longer available to everyone, and pious actions are as rare as the philosopher's stone. Yet, in no less wise do the words of that outstanding man of religion, unique in his age, give delight to the ears of the true believers and provide pleasure for the hearts and souls of those who aspire to follow the mystic path."[35]

Many hagiographers report that their keen sense of the Friend's sustaining presence has encouraged them to write. In his collective hagiography about the earliest members of the Mawlawīya order, Aflākī comments tellingly on his motives for completing his work. He reports that his patron, Chalabī Amīr ʿĀrif (Rūmī's grandson), on his deathbed charged him with continuing his hagiographical project, "collecting the feats (*manāqib*) of our forefathers and ancestors and writing them down until you complete this." He must "not neglect it, so that in the presence of [Rūmī] your face will beam with honest pride, and the Friends of God will be content with you."[36]

One of the most elaborate statements of purpose in a major hagiographical work is that in ʿAttār's *Remembrances of the Friends of God*. Before enumerating his specific intentions, ʿAttār makes a series of revealing methodological observations. His purpose is to defend his decision to avoid "commentary" (*sharh*) on the anecdotes about, and sayings of, the Friends. First, he says, had he sought to explain the material in greater detail, his book would have been impossibly long. Second, detailed study and analysis (some scholars have called such study "hagiology") are available in other kinds of works. Third, he makes a particularly instructive comment about his concern for accuracy in handing on the stories. He notes that, on the one hand, he has purposely omitted the traditional chains of transmitters that earlier hagiographers retained in their works, because he believes that the stories can stand on their own. On the other hand, he insists that he has been particularly careful in introducing any amplification or abridgment. Fourth, ʿAttār does not want readers to confuse his comments with the sayings of the Friends, though he occasionally saw a need to make an observation to discourage the untrammeled imagination of those not prepared to understand these stories. Finally, he would have included prophets as well as Muhammad's Companions and family, but such a project would have required another large volume.

ʿAttār includes an intriguing variety of motives, some unabashedly self-interested, some alluding to the inherent qualities of the material, and some describing the sense of service that impels his efforts. The author is not shy in admitting that he hopes his book will make his name and reputation survive his own death. He prays that God's Friends will respond to his efforts by sending blessings and intercession his way, both in this life and in the next. He hopes also that the power of the teachings of the great Friends will rub off on him and transform him into their likeness.

ʿAttār also comments on the material at his disposal. Citing Muhammad's observation that talking about holy persons brings down mercy, ʿAttār expresses the desire to share in the bounty as he "spreads a table" of such rich fare. Following Junayd, he observes that the words of the Friends are among the divine forces with which God strengthens seekers. Those words are in fact so potent that they stiffen the resolve of those incapable of living them out fully. Even for the average person unable to plumb the immense depths of a Friend's teaching and example, stories of saintly lives are the stuff of salutary contemplation. Because the original sources of the most important early teachings exist only in Arabic, a language inaccessible to many Muslims, he is motivated to translate them into Persian. However, he insists that even passing contact with these teachings can bring about changes in people unaware of their deeper meanings—just as one who knows no Arabic can benefit from hearing the Qurʾān recited.

ʿAttār then ticks off several more motives that stem from his interpretation of the age in which he lives and the needs of his contemporaries. Because he himself has found the banquet so satisfying, he wants to invite others to share it with him. In his youth, he loved the teachings of the Friends of God, but as he has grown older, he has seen charlatans and hypocrites steal so much saintly thunder that he believes he must restore the tradition's pristine authenticity. In the absence of the great Friends, people need to reflect daily on their words and deeds, and his narratives offer contemplative substance. ʿAttār's accounts have the power to encourage believers in their struggles and revive their trust in divine mercy. Like Ibn-i Munawwar, ʿAttār believes that a postprophetic world was dark indeed and desperately in need of illuminating exemplars. He concludes that his readers can scarcely hope to find a more helpful spiritual support than his book, for it offers them access to the wellsprings of the Friends' teachings and actions.[37]

Parables, Teaching Tools, and the Role of Typification

Hagiographers often tell stories with a fairly clear pedagogical intent. Many accounts seek to communicate a parabolic message, a "moral," and thus to transcend culture, geography, and chronology. Even Friends about whom a fair amount of concrete, specific information is available can function as "types." The storyteller may exercise a certain narrative license when the need presents itself. As so many authors have suggested in prefatory remarks, the significance of God's Friends far exceeds the sum of their words and deeds. Even so, because accounts of saintly actions and aphorisms enshrine the memory of a community's *experience* of a Friend, one cannot simply dismiss reports of the Friend's words and deeds as literary contrivances. Interpretation is thus a complex balancing act for scholars.

Vincent Cornell, a specialist in North African hagiography, suggests that analyses of hagiographies need to emphasize typification rather than trope, because the former "deals with experience more than rhetoric and conveys a similar sense of the 'sedimentation of meaning' without the negative connotation of fiction or falsehood." In other words, one needs to take seriously the sayings and works attributed to a Friend by understanding them as part of a larger pattern. Cornell describes eight principal Moroccan "types," each representing one of the many ways in which Muslim communities have experienced and remembered their Friends. Each type in his interpretation is defined by a specific dimension of authority. The *sālih*, or model of "ethical authority," is the quintessential Moroccan type, followed by the *qudwa*, or "exemplary authority" after the Prophetic model. A third type is the "peg" or *watad*, who exemplifies "juridical authority" through extensive knowledge of the legal disciplines. Fourth is the *murābit* (one housed in a *ribāt*, or closely bound to a shaykh), a rural saint whose "social authority" flowed from local relationships rather than specialized knowledge. Cornell lists the *shaykh*, the fifth type, as an embodiment of "doctrinal authority," as exemplified by Abū Madyan. Symbolizing "generative authority" is the *ghawth*, or pivotal Friend most noted for "assistance" to his communities. "Religiopolitical authority" such as that of Ibn Mashīsh, is best represented by the *imam* type, though some imams were also prominent *murābit* types. Finally, at the center and summit of the saintly hierarchy, the "pole," or *qutb*, represents "inclusive authority."[38]

Another model for understanding how traditional sources characterize Friends and other exemplary religious figures looks at the use of titles and other descriptors. Frederick Denny points out that certain titles and qualities or states (especially in North African/Berber and Arab contexts) are "earned," whereas others are "bestowed or attributed." Earned titles include *shaykh* (as a general honorific), *walī* (in the Qurʾānic sense of patron or protégé), *ghāzī* (warrior), and *shahīd* (martyr). Titles bestowed or attributed by popular acclaim, or inherited, include *shaykh* (now referring to the leader of a Sufi order, for example) and *walī* (now with the more specific meaning of Friend of God). Key terms denoting earned qualities or states include *sālih* (pure, righteous), *zāhid* (renunciant), and *sālik* (one who journeys to God); terms denoting roughly parallel bestowed or attributed states include *ʿisma* (divinely granted spiritual perfection), *fitra* (a condition of innate sinlessness that removes the need for effortful renunciation), and *majdhūb* (one who is drawn to God without the individual effort required of the *sālik*).[39]

Such typologies can help us decipher the underlying meaning of hagiographical accounts. Typification is a particularly helpful concept for understanding the evident stereotyping in anecdotes about Friends' activities or suffering. The clearly formulaic similarity of reports about figures who are distant in time and space does not seek to rob Friends of their individuality. For example, shared descriptions of specific Friends as predominantly "renunciant" types emphasizes one style or pattern of spiritual development among the many possibilities. Major hagiographers are able to express diverse spiritual and theological concerns by emphasizing different kinds of saintly qualities, depending on the purpose of the work at hand. For example, Shaʿrānī's "greater" *Generations* emphasizes the lives of Friends who were larger than life and beyond the reach of ordinary people—admirable, but hardly imitable. In his "lesser" hagiography, however, Shaʿrānī focuses on the ethical aspects of some Friends, depicting them as models of the kind of uprightness, renunciation, and piety to which less theologically sophisticated folk might aspire.[40]

Recycling Narrative Forms

One of the many pleasures of working with Islam's hagiographical traditions is encountering retellings of a repertoire of basic story types in varied

ʿAttār on Mālik ibn Dīnār[41]	*ʿAttār on Dhū 'n-Nūn*[42]	*Hujwīrī on Mālik ibn Dīnār*[43]
Mālik embarks on a ship. The crew asks him for the fare, but he does not have it. The crew members beat him up and prepare to throw him overboard. Suddenly all the fish in the water put up their heads, each one holding two golden dinars in its mouth. Mālik pays the crew with the miraculous windfall, and the men fall at his feet. ʿAttār explains that this story shows how the Friend acquired the name "Mālik (Possessor) of the Dīnār." The Friend then walks on the water and vanishes.	Dhū 'n-Nūn embarks on a riverboat. A merchant onboard announces that he has lost a jewel, and the passengers unanimously accuse Dhū 'n-Nūn of stealing the gem. At once, a thousand fish pop out of the water holding jewels in their mouths. Dhū 'n-Nūn takes one of the jewels and gives it to the merchant, whereupon the passengers fall at the Friend's feet. ʿAttār explains that this story reveals the origin and meaning of the name Dhū 'n-Nūn, "Master of the Fish."	Traveling by ship, Mālik is accused of stealing a jewel. He begins to pray, and suddenly all the fish around the ship surface, holding jewels in their mouths. He takes one of the jewels, gives it to his shipmates, and then walks on water all the way to the shore.

contexts. Anecdotal narratives form the heart of Islamic hagiography, and some appreciation of the ways in which anecdotes function is essential to understanding the larger hagiographic intent of a work. Anecdotes may have become important as a subgroup of parables, with some elements of the fable occasionally in evidence. Much of their power derives from their simplicity and ability to appeal to a broad spectrum of people. Many anecdotes enshrined in Islamic hagiographical sources have enjoyed very long lives and have become the bases of standard story types, such as those we saw in part 1 (such as nativity and infancy, conversion, miracle, and death narratives), which we can further distinguish according to their specific thematic content. A full appreciation of hagiographical narratives calls for understanding their embrace of well-developed types.[44]

Some story types migrate, with minor variations, from one source to another or even recur within the same source. In many instances, a single author "recycles" a basic plot in the stories of a single Friend of God. The table above offers examples of both dynamics. In the left column is Persian author ʿAttār's version of a story of Mālik ibn Dīnār, and on the right is Hujwīrī's much-earlier and simpler Persian version of a similar anecdote. In the middle column, ʿAttār's anecdote uses a variant of the story type about Dhū 'n-Nūn. Interestingly, ʿAttār uses the anecdotes etiologically, to explain the origins and meanings of proper names by punning on them.[45]

Identifying similar story patterns in this manner is helpful in several ways. First, it provides concrete examples of the way in which written accounts of Friends spread. Second, it suggests that, even when sources appear to repeat stories from earlier sources or merely to insert a different Friend's name into a "stock" tale, minor changes allow a later author to adapt the account for his specific purposes. Finally, the formulaic use of stories and story forms shows how hagiographical sources teach through typification without reducing all Friends to cardboard cutouts.[46]

DISCERNING THE LARGER FUNCTIONS OF THE STORIES

A literary heritage of the scope and complexity I discuss here does not lend itself to a few sweeping generalizations. One can, however, suggest broad functional themes that illuminate the importance of this patrimony to the greater Islamic faith tradition. In this section, I build on earlier discussions of author's intentions and Friends' functions by describing two larger ways in which the *tales* have functioned within Islamicate societies: by preserving community traditions and by offering polemics in service of proselytization.[47]

Preserving the Tales and Traditions of Islamic Life

Beyond authorial intention, the question of a literary work's *sitz im leben* is critical to understanding how it preserves Islamic traditions. As one scholar notes, the main question is, What kind of a Friend of God does the interested public want to see portrayed in his life story? The answer lies in the organizational and institutional context in which the Friend lived.[48]

Two opposing historical/temporal dynamics can inject subjectivity into or distort hagiographical accounts. One is the tendency, evidenced in Shaʿrānī's *Greater Generations*, to describe early saintly figures in restrained, sober terms, while portraying Friends who lived closer to the author's time in more fulsome, precise language. The opposite dynamic is the tendency of hagiographers to add titles and functions to an earlier Friend whom previous sources generally described in more restrictive terms, while treating more contemporary figures more critically and even skeptically. For example, ancient sources regarded Nawawī largely as a major Traditionist and a devout ascetic who carried on the tradition of the earliest ancestors in faith. Later, Subkī classified Nawawī as an important Sufi, whereas Suyūṭī and Sakhāwī went a step further and called him the greatest of God's Friends. In addition, the latter two authors in effect competed with each other, with Sakhāwī (who wrote two years later) piling on additional titles and evidence of miracles.[49]

Proselytizing and Polemics

Many Friends of God have been credited with inspiring or actively implementing efforts leading to the Islamization of various communities. Indonesian traditions identify the Wali Songo, for example, as major "missionaries" to the central islands of the vast Southeast Asian archipelago. Another interesting regional context is the much-contested South Asian land of Kashmir. Successful proselytization was, as Devin DeWeese argues, "a tremendous source of prestige and influence both within the established Muslim community and among the newly converted groups themselves. Whether or not Sufi Shaykhs were primarily responsible for much of the conversion to Islam in this period [Central Asia, late eighth/fourteenth–early ninth/fifteenth centuries]—and they probably were—they and their followers clearly sought to highlight their role in the spread and solidification of Islam." Because many hagiographical accounts describe conversion as a communitywide event, the accounts tend to claim the Friend of God as more than just a missionary: he is the spiritual ancestor of a whole Muslim community. Kubrāwī shaykh Sayyid ʿAlī Hamadānī is the subject of a significant tradition that identifies him as the founder of Kashmīrī Islam—even though the earliest major hagiographical account of this Friend does not mention any involvement in Kashmir. One narrative attributes Sayyid ʿAlī's success in making converts to his founding a *khānaqāh*. Another tells of a dream in which Muhammad commissions the shaykh to convert a Kashmiri populace as yet totally ignorant of Islam. In a third version, Kashmir's ruler dreams that the sun will rise in the south. His interpreter tells him that a stranger will make all of his subjects Muslims, and three days later Sayyid ʿAlī arrives.[50]

EPILOGUE: HISTORICITY, IMAGINATION, AND HUMOR

Given the wide variety of expressed intentions and methodological concerns in hagiographical accounts, how should we interpret them? Certainly, these hagiographical testimonies rarely, if ever, say explicitly that the most important aspect of the lives of God's Friends is their historicity. They are not primarily interested in nailing down events and using them as "proof-texts" for a religious argument. Former American poet laureate Billy Collins's "Introduction to Poetry" offers some apposite reflections. The poet says that he encourages his students to engage the literature imaginatively: think of a poem as a color slide to be held up to the light, a hive to be held to the ear, a maze through which a mouse makes its way, a dark room in which the reader must grope about for the light switch, a lake on which to water-ski while waving to the author's name on the shore. Too often, he laments, the reader's immediate response is to strap the poem down and "torture a confession out of it" in hopes of discovering its "real meaning."[51] Hagiographical narratives likewise deserve to be liberated from the tyranny of bland facticity.

Despite the initial impression of credulousness one might take away from a casual reading of many hagiographical accounts, concern for historicity is surely not the foremost issue in interpreting this vast treasury of resources. Perhaps most people who have read these stories and spun related yarns across the world and over the centuries have found a matter-of-fact quality in the tales. But knowing whether the events actually happened has generally been far less important than the tales' ability to create a sense of connection with the larger community of believers, entertain and edify, and allow the listening and reading public to identify immediately with the characters. The products of hagiographical imagination, in its many Islamic forms and tonalities, are a treasury of sage wit that recommends not taking oneself too seriously.

What stands out above all is the authors' emphasis on the power of the stories to inspire and edify readers and listeners. If the narratives are also entertaining, well and good. But uppermost in the authors' minds is the transformative potential of their often-arresting accounts of extraordinary people. Renewing social values, uplifting drooping spirits, prodding the conscience of those who have lapsed into spiritual torpor, calling the powerful to account, restoring perspective by reminding readers of the larger picture— such are the overriding purposes of hagiographers, if one takes their claims at face value. Face value, however, yields only half the story. For the rest, one has to read between the lines, taking into account the author's subtle (and not-so-subtle) grinding of religious, cultural, and social axes.[52]

FIGURE 28.   Jonah (Yūnus) emerges from the whale, exemplifying God's miraculous power on behalf of a prophet. Nīshāpūrī, *Qisas al-anbiyāʾ*, 984/1577, Spencer Collection, The New York Public Library, Astor, Lenox and Tilden Foundations; Psnypl_spn_574, Persian MS 11: 114a.

11.   Theological Dimensions

Hagiography, Faith, and Controversy

Beneath the shelter of hagiography's engaging narrative simplicity, a host of complex questions have taken refuge. Welcome to the subtext of hagiology. As early as the second/eighth century, Muslim thinkers began to discuss potential misunderstandings about the relationships between prophets and Friends of God. Do Friends enjoy the same spiritual prerogatives as prophets? If so, might Friends seem to usurp prophetic power and authority? Are prophets and Friends equally aware of their exalted spiritual status? Does either group enjoy the assurance of entry into paradise? Are the two groups equally susceptible to the ordinary failings of pride and sinfulness? Do prophets and Friends enjoy equal access to preternatural powers?

This chapter draws on three types of traditional sources to explore some of these questions: treatises by major theorists, relevant chapters in influential Sufi manuals of spirituality, and works with a specifically theological perspective. From the third/ninth century through the seventh/thirteenth century and beyond, among the more seminal theorists who produced treatises on the theory of sainthood were Tirmidhī, Ibn ʿArabī, and Azīz-i Nasafī. During the fourth/tenth and fifth/eleventh centuries in particular, a number of influential Sufi authors published important "handbooks" of spirituality. As we saw in chapter 10, some of the manual writers incorporated compact hagiographical anthologies into their expansive works. Among those who also included theoretical sections were Kalābādhī, Sarrāj, Qushayrī, and Hujwīrī. Finally, beginning around the late third/ninth century, theological treatises also sometimes paid specific attention to issues related to Friends of God. Bāqillānī offers a good example of a major theological theorist, in that he provided a centrist interpretation of the Ashʿarī school that was a crucial contributor to Sunnī thought. Distinctively Shīʿī theological notions of miraculous power conclude our consideration of miracles and marvels. I begin with overall theories of sainthood (sometimes in relation to prophet-hood) and move then into more specific thematic issues, including miracles, dreams and visions, visitation, intercession, and impeccability/infallibility.[1]

THEORIES OF SAINTHOOD

The most common Arabic term for "saint" or Friend of God is *walī* (plural *awliyāʾ*), a noun derived from a verbal root that denotes proximity or close relationship. This term can suggest associations of either one peer to another or superior to subordinate. In the latter sense, *walī* can mean patron or protector, and the cognate nouns *wilāya* and its alternate form, *walāya*, can suggest a position of authority or guardianship. The latter occurs twice in the Qurʾān (8:72, 18:44), referring in both instances to divine protection. In some scriptural contexts, the term *walī* (found over a hundred times, along with its plural) is best rendered as "heir" or "benefactor."

These technical terms appear in various contexts in the Qurʾān and hadith, but not until the later part of the ninth century did Muslim thinkers begin to hammer out a coherent theory of "sainthood" as a parallel to the phenomenon of "prophethood." The process by which individual Muslims have been elevated to the status of Friend is very different than the conferral of sainthood in, say, the Roman Catholic tradition. Muslim *awliyāʾ* have sometimes achieved their status while still alive, whereas Catholic holy persons are not officially proclaimed saints until after death, sometimes after a very long interval. In the Islamic tradition, acknowledgment of extraordinary sanctity is almost entirely a result of popular acclaim. Roman Catholic tradition has evolved an elaborate institutional procedure that involves official advancement of an individual's cause through stages (venerable, blessed, worthy of full sainthood), during which church officials closely scrutinize evidence for specific signs and qualities.[2] Various early authors described the desired qualities of "Friends of God." In the fourth/tenth century, Abū ʿAbd Allāh as-Sālimī indicated that Friends are known by "their elegant expression, excellent conduct, docility, generosity, non-belligerent attitude, willingness to accept the disclaimers of any who offer them, as well as kindness toward all creation whether of good or ill disposition."[3] Let us now look at some of the more technical and theoretical approaches to the subject.

Al-Hakīm at-Tirmidhī, who hailed from a city just north of the border of present-day Afghanistan in Uzbekistan, penned the first extant major theoretical work on Friends of God. Unlike the various hagiographical genres I discuss in this book, Tirmidhī's *Life of the Friends of God* (*Sīrat al-awliyāʾ*, also *Khatm al-walāya*, *The Seal of Sainthood*) is long on analysis and short on narrative. Its purpose is not to edify or entertain but to situate the phenomenon of the spiritually exemplary person within the larger framework of traditional Islamic doctrine. Tirmidhī's work therefore represents early systematic thinking about the cosmological and metaphysical questions that drive a theology of sainthood. He was not the only important early figure to talk about sainthood in a generally systematic fashion, nor even the first. Hasan al-Basrī, Bāyazīd, Sahl at-Tustarī, and Junayd were at the forefront in showing more detailed interest in the subject, but Tirmidhī's work deserves specific attention here.

Tirmidhī's work clearly demonstrates that a full systematic analysis of sainthood was developing very early in Islamic history. Nearly a century before the first Sufi handbooks appeared, Tirmidhī elaborated a sophisticated, well-integrated theory of the relationships between sainthood and prophethood. Central themes in his work include the nature of God's communication with his Friends, the possibility of intercession, and the various ranks or levels among God's Friends. He begins by exploring the differences in prophets' and Friends' access to divine truth. Prophets receive revelation (*wahy*) in the presence of a spirit (*rūh*) whose task is to signal the terminus of the communication of God's word (*kalām*) and secure the recipient's assent. Saints receive an inspiration (*ilhām*) of supernatural speech (*hadīth*) accompanied by an intense experience of a confirming divine presence (*sakīna*). In addition, a group of lower-ranking saints commune with God intimately but are not privy to the divine speech and the certainty it brings. Their intimate conversation, exalted though it may be, nevertheless leaves them prey to questions about the source of the message. Lacking certainty, these lesser Friends are unable to deliver an authoritative message to their public. People who refuse to accept the Prophetic message are to be considered unbelievers, whereas those who dismiss saintly communications merely miss out on the benefits of the Friend's blessing and spiritual authority. All saints share with prophets the qualities of inspiration, clairvoyance (*firāsa*), and authenticity.

Tirmidhī developed one of the most complete schemes of the cosmic hierarchy of God's 360 Friends, associating varying numbers of them with the "hearts" of major prophets (Adam, Moses, Noah, Abraham) and angels (Gabriel, Michael, Isrāfil). The cosmic hierarchy effectively institutionalizes the notion of intercession, for the Friends are so organized primarily to serve their fellow human beings. Tirmidhī locates at the pinnacle of the hierarchy a figure called the "seal" (*khatm*) of sainthood, clearly establishing an analogy to Muhammad's office as the seal of prophethood. Just as Muhammad brought an end to the line of prophetic messengers, the eschatological seal of sainthood will appear to signal the culmination of human history. The notion that the seal shares most intimately in the prerogatives of prophethood makes Tirmidhī's theory doctrinally problematical, for one might see the need for the seal as an element that dilutes the uniqueness and finality of Prophetic revelation.

Tirmidhī distinguishes other levels among Friends on the basis of their relationships with God. Here he understands the term *Friend* in a very broad sense. The highest of all Friends are intimate with God directly and are utterly steadfast in their spiritual paths. The vast majority relate to God by recognizing what is "due to" God and tend to vacillate in self-discipline and motivation. In this latter category, the lowest are those just beginning the path to Friendship with God as a result of their faith. Above them are those who add good works to faith but whose motives remain largely this-worldly. Some advance beyond delighting in their outward deeds, whereas others manage to transcend most worldly concerns but are nevertheless held back because they are still in love with seeking intimacy with God. In short, only those who are completely free of ego-centered motivation and oriented perfectly to spiritual freedom can attain the higher reaches of Friendship with God.[4]

Ibn ʿArabī's theory of Friendship with God is arguably the most intricate and broadly influential, and perhaps also the most controversial. His systematic treatment turns above all on his interpretation of the complex relationship between prophets and Friends of God. Friends are "heirs of the prophets" in that the two groups share infused knowledge, the ability to bring about change in the physical world through spiritual force alone, and sensory access to the realm of imaginative images. Ibn ʿArabī argues that Friends of God at least equal prophets in number (124,000), though a given prophet might pass along his spiritual patrimony to more than one Friend (thus resulting in a greater number of Friends than prophets). He characterizes some of the major Friends of God as heirs of specific prophets. Ibn ʿArabī regarded himself, for example, as a disciple of Jesus from early on in his own life.

Ibn ʿArabī regarded the cosmic structure of prophethood as the model for that of sainthood. Just as four "pillars" or "pegs" form the hierarchy of Friends of God, four of the prophets function as pillars/pegs (*awtād*): Idrīs, Jesus, Elijah (Ilyās), and Khidr. Paralleling the seven "substitutes" (*abdāl*) among the Friends, Ibn ʿArabī identified Abraham, Moses, Aaron, Idrīs (some figures do double duty in his schema), Joseph, Jesus, and Adam as the prophets who were instrumental in maintaining the seven climes of the cosmos. Ibn ʿArabī expanded on Tirmidhī's view that a seal of sainthood would appear to parallel the seal of prophethood; he identified Jesus as the "seal of universal sainthood" and Muhammad as the "seal of Muhammadan sainthood." He even claimed the title of "seal of God's Friends" for himself.

He then further expanded the notion by introducing the concept of a "seal of children," the last human being to be born.

Ibn ʿArabī argued that prophets enjoy a higher level of communion with God than Friends do and that prophets ascend spiritually as a direct effect of divine light, rather than via a reflection of that light. He suggested that Friends enjoy a "station of proximity" to God that stands just below prophethood but above the station of authenticity (*siddīqīya*).[5]

Finally, Azīz-i Nasafī offers some important insights on the nature and functions of God's Friends and on their relationship to prophets. He says that Friends of God are superior to prophets in their possession of knowledge (though he also acknowledges that prophets are among God's Friends). He suggests a hierarchy in which persons endowed with fundamental knowledge are believers (or philosophers), those gifted with a higher level of knowledge are prophets, and those with the greatest knowledge are Friends of God. Like other theorists, Nasafī takes his cue from traditions that attribute a higher level of knowledge to Khidr than to Moses. Prophets' knowledge equips them to *warn* humankind of impending disaster, whereas Friends are able to *guide* God's people because they comprehend the deeper meanings of all things.

However, Nasafī explains that prophethood is superior to Friendship with God precisely to the degree that prophets share their knowledge of outward realities; Friends, in contrast, keep their inward knowledge to themselves. And because no human being can know everything and thus enjoy perfect Friendship with God, one must acknowledge circumstances in which a Friend of God takes second place to a prophet. Nasafī thus strikes a theoretical balance in a matter of some controversy. Friends need to accept the lead of prophets lest the Revealed Law become subject to dangerous misinterpretation; but prophets need to accept the leadership of Friends in extending the prophetic mission into the postprophetic age. This last point is intimately related to Nasafī's concept of the Perfect Person (*al-insān al-kāmil*), with which he explains the perdurability of paradigmatic intimacy with God after the formal end of divine revelation with Muhammad. Like other theorists before him (especially Rūzbihān Baqlī), Nasafī associates specific groups in the hierarchy of Friends with particular prophets. For example, he links the three hundred *akhyār* with Adam, the forty *abdāl* with Moses, and the seven *abrār* with Jesus.[6]

FRIENDSHIP WITH GOD IN THE SUFI MANUALS

One of the more surprising aspects of the treatment of God's Friends in the great compendia of spirituality is that none of these works discuss in detail

Tirmidhī's seminal concept of the seal of sainthood (*khatm al-walāya*). In fact, though they postdate Tirmidhī's work by well over half a century, the manuals do not mention the notion at all. Even Hujwīrī's discussion of the views of the "Hakīmīya" (by which he means the "followers of Hakīm [at-Tirmidhī])" is silent about the concept. A plausible explanation is that the manual writers were attempting to defend Sufism's teachings from the charge of heresy or innovation. They may have regarded as theologically dangerous Tirmidhī's claim that a "seal" capped the hierarchy of Friends of God just as Muhammad was the seal of prophethood, for it appeared to place sainthood in an adversarial relationship with prophethood. On virtually every other major aspect of the theory of sainthood, however, the handbooks have much to say.

In one of the earliest Sufi handbooks, Kalābādhī notes two varieties of friendship with God. One arises from the absence of enmity with God and is the potential state of all believers. Alternatively, and more rarely, God's direct choice of an individual can safeguard the chosen one from becoming conceited about this preferential treatment. Kalābādhī notes a divergence of opinion about whether Friends of God can be aware of their true spiritual status. Some people argue in the negative, for such knowledge would confer on a human being an undue sense of security, thus undermining his or her status as a servant of God. An authentic godservant must live in the tension between hope and fear. However, one can make a strong argument to the contrary, recognizing that the status of Friendship with God is itself a marvel of grace, so a human being could certainly be gratefully cognizant of this extraordinary blessing. Although Kalābādhī does not attribute the latter position to any particular authorities, he observes that those who hold it are "the greatest and most important," inferring that he himself is so persuaded. Such knowledge, he argues, is the surest defense against personal arrogance.[7]

One of Kalābādhī's contemporaries, Abū Nasr as-Sarrāj, also devoted significant attention to the topic of sainthood, with a chapter on the relationship between Friends and prophets. He refutes the view that sainthood represents a higher level of spiritual development than prophethood, pointing out that the source of such errant speculation is inappropriate exegesis of the Qurʾānic account of the enigmatic relationship between Moses and Khidr (in sura 18). One must take care not to misinterpret the scripture's references to the divine origin of Khidr's knowledge. Though Khidr's knowledge might appear to be superior to that of Moses, one must remember that a saint's prerogatives always reflect the higher status of the principal prophet of the age. Sarrāj identifies Khidr as a Friend of God, rather than as a prophet as some traditions do. He insists that but for the illumination of Moses, Khidr would have had no light to reflect. Friends of God enjoy only ad hoc divine knowledge, whereas prophets continually receive divine inspiration. Though Khidr may appear to be leading Moses in the Qurʾānic story, the two men's essential roles are actually the reverse.[8]

In a chapter on the views of followers of Hakīm at-Tirmidhī, Hujwīrī adds his own interpretation to a summary of Tirmidhī's thought on the subject of sainthood. The author asserts that *walāya* is fundamental to Sufism, though various teachers have advanced diverse theories. He describes the range of meanings of *walāya* (supernatural abilities that belong to God, love or friendship) and *wilāya* (temporal authority) in Qurʾān and hadith. Hujwīrī then discusses the predominant understandings of the term *walī* (Friend) and its plural, *awliyāʾ*. He emphasizes the role of the Friends of God in the divine dispensation, defining Friends as an essential link in the continuity of God's providence. Friends are the heirs of the prophets and God's representatives, and through their spiritual blessing (*baraka*), they are instrumental in ensuring the happiness and success of the faithful. Numbering the Friends at four thousand, Hujwīrī points out that the majority of them are not aware of their status or of that of their fellow Friends, and he says that their identity is unknown to ordinary folk.

Then Hujwīrī breaks down the cosmic "administrative" hierarchy of the Friends into its various already-traditional subcategories: three hundred *akhyār*, forty *abdāl*, seven *abrār*, four *awtād*, three *nuqabāʾ*, and one at the top of the hierarchy known as the *qutb* or *ghawth*. These higher-ranking Friends enjoy privileged awareness of their status and of the identity of the others at the apex of the hierarchical structure. Hujwīrī then discusses the disputed question of whether a *walī* who is aware of saintly status is susceptible to arrogance, and he concludes that the status itself presupposes protection from that pitfall. Thus, he takes exception to the view of the Muʿtazilī systematic theologians that no such distinction can exist among human beings, for all enjoy the same God-given attributes and faculties, and that saintly marvels are not possible for they contravene reason. The Muʿtazilī argument suggests to Hujwīrī that if marvels are indeed inherent in the state of *walāya*, then every believer would be granted them because every believer is a Friend of God by virtue of his or her faith. Hujwīrī rejects any such democratization of the power of marvels.

At this juncture, Hujwīrī addresses the various ways in which several early Sufi shaykhs explain the meanings of *walāya*. His central concerns are the degree of awareness of one's saintly status and the question of whether saints experience fear and hope differently than other human beings.[9] A larger theological question to which Hujwīrī devotes attention is whether

prophets are superior to Friends. On this matter, he insists, spiritual authorities are in general agreement. He points out that all prophets are Friends of
God, but the converse is not the case. Prophethood's spiritual status begins
at the upper limit of saintly spiritual perfection and attainment and moves
upward from there. Whereas prophets remain forever impervious to the
machinations of their ego-souls, saints experience only sporadic protection.

Hujwīrī then dispenses with the errant views of the "anthropomorphists"
on the nature of sainthood. Their opinions are riddled with theologically
unacceptable claims about reincarnation and the superiority of saints over
prophets. Hujwīrī counters that, though contemplative vision (*mushāhada*)
is the ceiling for God's Friends, it is merely the floor for his prophets. Prophets
are prophets throughout their lives, but Friends of God (he implies) must
move toward the culmination of their spiritual state. As a result, when
Bāyazīd presumed to liken his spiritual progress to the prophet Muhammad's
Ascension, he was positing, at best, a rather loose analogy: Muhammad's
experience presupposed a paradoxical coexistence of annihilation and survival, whereas the Friend of God knows the two moments more distinctly.
Whereas prophets' bodies take on a spiritual quality, those of Friends remain
subject to earthly tendencies. Though Prophets come into God's presence in
body and soul, Friends approach in spirit alone.

Finally, Hujwīrī points out that both prophets and Friends are superior to
angels. He refutes the Muʿtazilī view, arguing that grace, not angelic spiritual subtlety and obedience, renders one being superior to another. After all,
Satan possessed angelic properties. Angels can possess knowledge of God on
a par with that of prophets, but this capability does not imply higher rank.
And because human beings who avoid sins must do so only at the price of
overcoming deficits to which angels are not prey, a pure human being must
therefore have attained a spiritual level greater than that of the angels, who
have fewer problems to overcome.[10]

Qushayrī, a contemporary of Hujwīrī, believed that a true Friend of God
is unlikely to regress into a less lofty spiritual estate later in life and that
such a person is shielded from backsliding by the ever-present fear of self-
deception. Friends of God are not protected from sinfulness, however, as
prophets are. According to Qushayrī, essential characteristics of saints in their
ordinary mode of living include sincerity in devotion and religious duties,
affinity to all of creation, patience and acceptance of other people along with
prayer on their behalf, a desire to guide people away from vengefulness, simple respect for others and their belongings, and the grace to hold others in
high regard and speak only good of them.[11]

THEMES IN THEORY: MAJOR THEOLOGICAL ISSUES

Questions about the nature of sainthood and its complex relationships to prophethood constitute only the first and largest category of theoretical issues that Muslim authors have raised. A wide range of questions about the behavior and special qualities of God's Friends, as well as their unique gifts and responsibilities, have drawn the attention of Muslim theorists. Among the most prominent themes are miracles and marvels; clairvoyance, visions, and dreams; intercession, impeccability, and inerrancy; and the visitation of tombs.

Miracles and Marvels

Questions about miracles and marvels are among the more colorful and intriguing topics taken up by Muslim authors. Many of these authors have explored those extraordinary, "custom-shattering" acts commonly called miracles. Writers have nearly always maintained an important distinction between the "evidentiary miracles" bestowed on prophets (see Fig. 28) and the "marvels" or "wonders" granted to Friends of God (see Fig. 29). Saintly marvels have been the subject of considerable discussion and polemic over many centuries.[12] Here I will summarize the views of major early Sufi manual writers who took up the topic, as well as the views of Bāqillānī, an influential Ashʿarite theologian, and early Shīʿī discussions of miracles by imams.

Sarrāj dedicates a whole six-chapter section to the large topic of supernatural phenomena. On the basis of a comment by Sahl at-Tustarī, he divides these occurrences into three types: signs (*āyāt*) that are God's prerogative alone, prophetic or evidentiary miracles (*muʿjizāt*), and saintly marvels (*karāmāt*). Sarrāj's illustrative anecdotes emphasize the necessity of faith in God's power and seem to take for granted that what truthful people claim happened actually "happened." However, he also clearly seeks to underscore the spiritual dimension in both performer and observer. He takes on systematic theologians who object to the concept of saintly marvels on the grounds that such acts imply competition with the prophets. He then details three large differences between prophetic and saintly wonders. First, prophetic miracles aim to persuade the public, whereas saintly marvels ought, ideally, to remain hidden. Second, whereas evidentiary miracles aim to refute the views of nonbelievers, marvels granted to God's Friends seek to help the saints refine their own beliefs. And finally, though the multiplication of supernatural deeds uplifts prophets and advances their causes, it only increases the need for Friends to take care not to be deceived.

FIGURE 29. Muhyī ad-Dīn ibn ʿArabī (d. 638/1240) pours hot coals into a
philosopher's lap to show that God can deprive the coals of their burning
properties. The image offers an example of a Friend's *karāma* (marvel or wonder).
Jāmī, *Nafaḥāt al-uns* (Ottoman, 1003/1595), ©The Trustees of the Chester Beatty
Library, Dublin, T474:306b.

Seeking to ground saintly marvels in ancient sacred tradition, Sarrāj refers (as later manual writers would also do) to marvels bestowed on nonprophets like Mary, the Christian monk Jurayj, and the unnamed people in the Hadith of the Cave (stories told in chapter 4). He regales his reader with illustrations from the lives of important Companions of Muhammad, as well as stories of a dozen early devotees long considered founding figures of Sufism. He argues that every authentic supernatural phenomenon reflects well on Muhammad but acknowledges that the topic is a matter of considerable debate. Sarrāj then lays out a wide spectrum of views on the nature of saintly marvels. Views range from the cautious opinion that the greatest marvel is inner conversion and that outward display is fraught with danger to descriptions that clearly celebrate spectacle and perhaps even shock value. Characters who exemplify the former attitude include Ishāq ibn Ahmad, Abu Hafs, and other Friends who went out of their way not to exercise the powers bestowed on them. Others, like Nūrī and Bāyazīd, had no qualms about pulling out all the stops.

In his last two chapters on the subject, Sarrāj returns to the two issues with which he began his discussion. First, he examines a variety of cases in which Friends speak openly of their marvelous perquisites. Here he includes nearly a dozen accounts of wonders that were observable to those in the Friend's immediate company. He reports that the spiritual states God confers on his Friends are the genuine marvels, even if the general public too seldom recognizes that fact. Sarrāj supports this position with anecdotes that typically feature subtle changes of which few people other than the Friend would be aware.[13]

In another early Sufi manual, Kalābādhī offers important clues to how theories of saintly marvels evolved. Many of his concerns echo those of Sarrāj, but he organizes his material differently. He begins with assorted examples that demonstrate broad agreement about the existence of saintly marvels, as distinct from prophetic miracles. Kalābādhī admits that some people consider talk of such marvels an unseemly, perhaps even heretical, incursion on the prerogatives of prophets. But he insists that such concerns are unfounded, because prophets are distinguished from other persons by qualities far more important than the performance of miracles. Above all, the gift of revelation, whether accompanied by evidentiary miracles or not, is the mark of a prophetic calling. Miracles granted to prophets thus function only to distinguish those whose message is true from charlatans. Kalābādhī distinguishes saints from pretenders to prophethood: Friends of God merely call people to accept the message of true prophets and in no way seek to usurp the prophetic office.

Kalābādhī makes a further distinction between Friends on whom God bestows miraculous powers and enemies of the deity who are allowed to believe that they have extraordinary capabilities. God causes such individuals to be hoist with the petard of their own arrogance and self-delusion, for they imagine that their apparent gift is a result of their own effort and inherent power. Genuine Friends of God, in contrast, respond to manifestations of God's power in them with increased humility, surrender, and self-discipline, qualities that in turn render them still more apt conduits for the display of divine signs. Kalābādhī adds two important distinctions between prophets and Friends. First, saints do not know explicitly the origins of their marvelous deeds, whereas prophets are keenly aware of the divine source of evidentiary miracles. Second, as a result of the first difference, Friends are susceptible to a certain lust for power when they find they can bring about marvels, but God shields prophets from such temptations.

Delving deeper into specific differences between prophetic miracles and saintly marvels, Kalābādhī offers several other important distinctions. Prophetic miracles either bring something out of nothing or alter a thing's inherent nature. Saintly marvels, in contrast, may be a response to the saint's supplication, bring about the perfection of the saint's spiritual state, or result in the exceptional provision of food or other means of survival. When God allows an inauthentic claimant to spiritual authority (such as a prophetic pretender) to manifest a miracle, the action will never be such as would cause religious doubt in those who observe it.[14] Kalābādhī sums up the matter of saintly marvels with a cautionary observation: "The signs of sainthood do not merely consist of external decoration and the manifestation of the extraordinary: its true signs are inwardly, and are the experiences which God puts into the secret heart, experiences which are only known to God and to those who enjoy them."[15]

Several generations after Kalābādhī, Qushayrī likewise dedicated a substantial chapter of his compendium to saintly marvels. He bases his analysis on the principle that, because by definition God controls all of creation, anything God chooses to effect in creation is possible. Furthermore, because saintly marvels betoken authenticity in the individual through whom they are manifest, no such event can occur through a spiritually inauthentic person. Marvels therefore distinguish the genuine from the counterfeit and must constitute some kind of rupture in the natural order to attest to the apparent agent's authenticity. He discusses in some detail the general understanding of differences between prophetic miracles and saintly marvels, and the views he expresses are on the whole consistent with those of Kalābādhī.

Qushayrī, however, marshals more anecdotal evidence and opinions of authorities in support of this view.

Qushayrī emphasizes that the prophets are commissioned precisely to display their miracles, whereas Friends of God are bidden to hide their marvels and to regard them as potential tests and, therefore, nothing to be terribly impressed with. Though Friends often receive marvels in response to a request, the gifts sometimes happen by surprise. Qushayrī believes that a Friend of God might indeed be aware that he or she is a saint. Such knowledge varies from one individual to another, however, and is itself a type of marvel. Every prophet must of necessity manifest miraculous deeds, but a Friend of God need not manifest a marvel to be of saintly rank.

Qushayrī prefaces his lengthy array of anecdotes about saintly marvels with references to a series of hadiths, largely to establish that even Muhammad and his Companions did not hesitate to accept such phenomena. The stories tell variously of a huge boulder miraculously shifting to reveal a means of escape for a group trapped in a cave by a landslide; talking animals and inanimate objects; control over wild beasts; and mysterious modes of communication over impossible distances. Against that legitimating backdrop, Qushayri narrates, in no obviously systematic order, dozens of reports of every conceivable species of marvel. His point, of course, is that saintly marvels are not a newfangled claim but part of a larger dispensation of divine intervention. He ends his collection of anecdotes by observing only that such stories are beyond counting and that he has already recounted more than enough of them.[16]

Hujwīrī offers one of the more theologically sophisticated analyses of marvels and miracles in the Sufi manuals. He prefaces his discussion with the proviso that only individuals whose lives are consonant with Revealed Law are capable of performing "supernatural" acts and that such deeds testify to the individual's authenticity. He notes that Sunnī Muslims generally place greater emphasis on the miracles of prophets than on saintly marvels but argues that the latter differ from the former only in the status of the individual performing them. In this connection, so long as Friends of God do not associate the performance of marvels with pretensions to prophethood, their supernatural deeds raise no difficulties. Hujwīrī makes clear that variation in spiritual status is not inherently linked to the performance of such deeds. Thus, just as one prophet may be superior to another even if both perform evidentiary miracles, so Friends are inferior to prophets even though saints also perform supernatural acts. In both cases, however, supernatural deeds testify to the authenticity of the individual through whom God works.

Moreover, the principal theological function of saintly marvels is to reinforce people's faith in the veracity of their prophet. In other words, because Friends' marvels are meant to underscore God's revelation through Muhammad, they in no way trespass on prophetic turf.

Hujwīrī then turns his attention to specific differences between prophetic miracles and saintly marvels. The former are worked for the benefit of other people, whereas the latter are the Friend's own business. Here Hujwīrī echoes a standard opinion, though he seems to neglect the fairly obvious altruistic element in many saintly marvels. Prophets know that a particular deed is an evidentiary miracle, but Friends can never be sure when a given marvel is in reality a sham meant to deceive or test people's credulousness. Again Hujwīrī emphasizes that the authentic saintly marvel reinforces the prophetic miracle and is never in competition with it. When God allows a saintly marvel to be widely known, this action is a sign of the Friend's particularly lofty status. But if a saint is merely showing off, the apparently marvelous deed is vitiated and is inherently inauthentic.

A miracle or marvel that believers clearly perceive to be genuine undergirds the prophet's (or Friend's) authenticity. Conversely, when believers see through the extraordinary deeds of a charlatan, such as Pharaoh or Nimrod, the counterfeit works only spotlight the impostor's lack of credibility. Hujwīrī explains that believers can tell the difference by discerning contradictions to the creed in the claims of a con artist. Both Pharaoh and Nimrod claimed to be divine, thereby instantly sabotaging any hope of exerting authority among true Muslims. However, Pharaoh and Nimrod both contended with prophets, and distinguishing a fake from a Friend is not easy when both individuals manifest apparently supernatural deeds. Saintly marvels do not inherently provide divine "proofs" as do evidentiary prophetic miracles. Herein lies Hujwīrī's subtlest theological distinction. In this instance, he says, reason, not faith, allows people to distinguish genuine saints from pretenders to sainthood.

Bāyazīd al-Bistāmī, Dhū 'n-Nūn, Ibn Khafīf, Hallāj, and Yahyā ibn Muʿādh ar-Rāzī share Hujwīrī's next concern: a Friend can perform a marvel only while mystically intoxicated, whereas a prophet performs miracles only in a state of spiritual sobriety. Intoxication insures that the Friend is entirely under divine control. Consequently, in some circumstances, a saint may have no option in the manifestation of marvels, and Friends of God may not always be pleased by the way God works through them. In this context, Hujwīrī implicitly links the state in which marvels can occur and the state in which a mystic expresses an ecstatic utterance. He also acknowledges the contrary view of more theologically cautious Sufi authorities (such as Junayd and

Tirmidhī) that marvels can occur only in the state of sobriety, because Friends are sent to help humankind deal with the relatively mundane matters of everyday life.[17]

Before concluding his treatment with a lengthy series of examples, Hujwīrī promises to build a case for the theological soundness of both miracles and marvels on the basis of scripture and tradition (Qurʾān and hadith). He observes that both sources recount numerous stories of miracles and that in more than one instance, miraculous results continued to bless a prophet's people even in the absence of the prophet. He argues that the notion that God's people can enjoy the benefit of saintly marvels long after prophets have come and gone makes perfect sense: distance in time poses no greater difficulty than distance in space, and countless miracles have occurred many miles from the one performing them. Even in the Qurʾān, Hujwīrī notes, one can find evidence of saintly marvels, as when the prophet Solomon's minister Āsaf (himself not a prophet) caused the Queen of Sheba's throne to be transported instantly over a vast distance (27:40). In addition, though Mary the mother of Jesus was not a prophet, the prophet Zakarīya discovered repeatedly that God had wondrously provided her with fruits out of season (3:37). Mary also received the marvel of dates from a barren tree (19:25). Finally, he alludes to the marvel in which a dog spoke to the People of the Cave (known to Christians as the Seven Sleepers of Ephesus), who slept for hundreds of years (18:18).[18]

Systematic theologians have also expressed considerable interest in miracles and marvels. One influential theological treatise on miraculous occurrences is Bāqillānī's *Elucidation of the Difference between Prophetic Miracles and Saintly Marvels, Trickery, Divination, Magic, and Spells*. He first addresses the question of prophetic or "apologetic" miracles (*muʿjizāt*), explaining that such occurrences have to do with things over which human beings have no power. Bāqillānī believes that such evidentiary miracles are necessary proofs of a prophet's claim to have been sent by God. In addition to the fact that only God has power over these actions, miracles must meet three criteria: they must contravene the ordinary or "customary," be effected only by prophets, and involve a challenge to the prophet's adversaries to bring about a similar breach of custom.

Bāqillānī describes saintly marvels or "charisms" (*karāmāt*) as events over which only God has power but which do not serve to establish the veracity of a prophet's claim to divine mandate. They may, however, be similar to prophetic miracles in other respects. Still, not all the amazing feats performed by Friends of God are technically miraculous, because Satan and other enemies of God can perform many attention-getting deeds. Extraordinary and spectacular occurrences can be the result of magic and sorcery, and one must be careful to distinguish the latter from authentic saintly marvels. The author notes that even Muhammad was bewitched on two occasions, but God is the one who allows individuals to fall under such a spell. Skillful tricksters can even appear to give life to the dead, and under some circumstances, God enables a charlatan to appear to have extraordinary powers. God also makes sure that such people cannot work even their usual conjuring or sleight of hand when such tricks would appear to contradict a prophet's claim to divine legitimacy. In such circumstances, God might, for example, cause an impostor to "forget" how to wield his magic or sorcery.

For Bāqillānī, one critical question remains. Apart from the fact that a prophetic miracle is an explicit response to a challenge from unbelievers, what is the effective or discernible difference between an amazing feat performed by a prophet and one performed by a Friend of God? Hagiographic sources rarely make an overt distinction, and even Bāqillānī sees no obvious distinguishing feature. The difference is subtle and depends on what the action suggests about the performer's relationship to the divine source of power. In the prophet's case, the amazing feat is part of a mission from God, whereas in the case of the Friend, it underscores the individual's privileged relationship to God. Saints are incapable of performing marvels merely on a whim; they are instruments of divine choice, with God determining how and when he will make *baraka* available to humankind through them.[19]

Shī'ī thinkers who wrote on the wondrous powers available to the imams offer a final important, but seldom acknowledged, perspective on miracles. As I have suggested throughout this volume, imams have an essential place in the unbroken line of exemplars of devotion. Sources describe unusual powers granted to the imams in direct relationship to their levels of knowledge. They enjoy preferential awareness of both seen and unseen worlds as well as of hidden meanings of divine revelation in all its manifestations. They can communicate with every kind of creature, including inanimate nature. Their miraculous powers include the prophets' ability to wield the ultimate divine name and communicate spiritually with Muhammad. They can restore life to the dead, heal all ailments, and be transported great distances instantly. They can also see and hear the subtlest physical and spiritual signals.

Shī'ī sources generally do not use the term *karāma* to describe the extraordinary deeds of the imams, preferring "amazing things" (*a'ājīb*) and "power" (*qudra*), for example. According to a seminal work by Saffār al-Qummī, *Insight into the Spiritual Ranks*, the imams can pass along certain extraordinary powers to their followers. Such abilities might include healing or clairvoyance. But some signature abilities inherited directly from the prophets are restricted to the imams. These powers generally derive from esoteric knowledge of the ultimate divine name, which consists of seventy-three letters. Various prophets had fragmentary knowledge of the name and thus could perform only certain kinds of miracles. Adam, for example, knew twenty-five of the letters; Noah, fifteen; Abraham, eight; Moses, four; and Jesus, two. Muhammad, however, knew all but the one known only to God. Specific items once owned by prophets also symbolize the special powers of imams in postprophetic times: the cloak of Adam, the cloak of Joseph that had earlier been Abraham's, the staff of Moses along with the Ark of the Covenant and the Tablets of the Law, the seal ring of Solomon, and Muhammad's wondrous sword, Dhū 'l-Faqār. Shī'ī sources, like some Sunnī theological texts, also warn against the potentially serious evil of "natural magic."[20]

Miracles and marvels are perhaps the largest category of extraordinary powers wielded by prophets and Friends of God.[21] But they are by no means the only important type of remarkable gift, as the following sections indicate.

Clairvoyance, Visions, and Dreams

Even the most theologically cautious sources express few reservations about the phenomenon of clairvoyant insight. Anecdotes about Muhammad and his Companions in the hadith celebrate clairvoyance as an important gift. Qushayrī digs deeper and includes a chapter on *firāsa* that begins with a Qur'ānic reference to the ability to "read the signs" in all things, and we may take his views as broadly representative. Clairvoyant insight overtakes the heart unexpectedly with unquestionable authority, illumined by God's light. From the numerous examples that Qushayrī provides, one can conclude that *firāsa* encompasses a range of sixth-sense intimations, from knowing the occupation of a total stranger to discerning people's closely guarded thoughts and becoming aware of events transpiring at a great distance. In a number of stories, it is akin to extrasensory perception. Qushayrī cautions against attempting to develop clairvoyance as a skill; simple openness, allied with sincere faith, is the key.[22] Ghazālī identifies the phenomenon that Qushayrī calls *firāsa* as contemplative vision (*mushāhada*) and associates the power especially with the unique knowledge of Khidr.[23]

Such relative unanimity is not evident in authors' views on matters such as visions and dreams; the concepts of intercession, impeccability, and inerrancy; and the practice of visiting graves. Sarrāj defines "the vision of hearts" as the heart's "gazing upon that which exists in the unseen realm through the lights of certitude in the context of the spiritual realities of the faith." He cites a saying of 'Alī that the heart sees God in the truths of belief.[24] He sets out to correct the mistaken view of some mystics of Syria that their spiritual vision of God in this life is analogous to the ocular vision of God granted to inhabitants of heaven. He tells the story of a group of Iraqi mystics who allowed Satan to dupe them into thinking they were seeing God on the throne, when in reality the figure was only the devil disguised with light. He cautions against too readily believing that God is ever visible to the living, noting that Muhammad's visionary experience (53:11) is a solitary exception.[25]

Kalābādhī also addresses the topic of visionary experience, affirming the standard theological/creedal position that believers will enjoy sight of God in paradise. To demonstrate that such vision is rationally arguable, he glosses a variety of Qurʾānic texts and a hadith on the subject. He explicitly refutes the metaphorical interpretation characteristic of the Muʿtazilī theologians, without identifying them by name. In the present world, however, only the eyes of faith can "see" God. Even the prophet Moses, celebrated as one who spoke with God, was not granted his request to see the Revealer. Apropos of this topic, Kalābādhī briefly takes up the somewhat-disputed question of whether Muhammad saw God during his Ascension. A number of major Sufis, including Junayd, Nūrī, and Kharrāz, take their cue from a saying of the Prophet's wife ʿĀʾisha and deny any such vision. Others, however, allow that Muhammad had the distinction of seeing God in heaven even as Moses's unique grace was to converse with God. A middle position is that the Prophet saw God with the eye of his heart. In the final analysis, Kalābādhī opts for the view that no one sees God in this world and no creature has seen God this side of death.[26]

By the fifth/eleventh century, theologians such as Bāqillānī were incorporating discussions of the "ocular vision of God" in their systematic works. "Standard" creedal statements had long since included references to this celestial experience as an article of faith. Reason, the Ashʿarī thinkers argue, corroborates the revealed truth that believing Muslims will be rewarded with the vision of God after death. According to Bāqillānī, the questions raised by Muhammad's experience of seeing God before his death (during his Ascension) were the triggers for discussion of whether human beings can see God in this life. Some early Muslims, including Muhammad's wife ʿĀʾisha, believed the Prophet saw God "with his heart," but Bāqillānī concurred with the opinion of others that Muhammad saw God with his bodily eyes. Muhammad's experience proves that earthly ocular vision is possible, but Moses's experience proves that the last prophet's privilege was an exception to the rule. Moses asked God pointedly to let him see his Lord (7:143), but God denied his request. The Creator demonstrated his rationale when he reduced a mountain to dust by allowing it to see him. Bāqillānī cites a variety of Qurʾānic texts (10:27, 75:22–23, 83:15) and several hadiths as proof that believers will see God hereafter. He also refutes in considerable detail the arguments of theological adversaries who hold that seeing God with one's bodily eyes reduces God to the level of creatures.[27]

As early as the hadith, Islamic tradition has acknowledged dreams as a mode of access to higher realities, even regarding them as "a share in prophecy."[28] Dreams thus function in the lives of countless ordinary people as a kind of extension of revelation, albeit on a minor scale, beyond the cessation of prophethood. Sufi authors and hagiographers have further developed this fundamental understanding, as evidenced by the ubiquitous use of dream anecdotes.

Qushayrī's *Treatise* devotes a whole chapter to the subject of dreams. He begins by glossing several sayings of Muhammad, the first of which is itself a gloss on a Qurʾānic text (10:64) that refers to "good news in the life of this world and in the next." Muhammad reportedly interpreted the verse as a reference to positive dreams. Another hadith explains that such "positive" experiences are visionary dreams, as opposed to the confusing dreams generated by Satan. In a third tradition, Muhammad assures believers that any dream of him is authentic, for the devil cannot appear in the guise of the Prophet. Qushayrī then describes dreams as either notions that enter the heart or spiritual states that occur to the imagination when one's sleep is not too deep to foreclose such awareness. He further analyzes dream-related experiences, clearly associating dreams with a variety of intrapsychic phenomena. First, he describes several types of sleep, beginning with the least desirable forms (unconscious and habitual, "death's little brother"). Such sleep is inimical to people engaged in the greater *jihād* and is the opposite of knowledge, on the one hand, but paradoxically a bane for Satan, on the other, for it prevents people from going out to sin actively.

Nevertheless, Qushayri notes, the right kind of sleep does have two advantages over the waking state. First, in dreams individuals can encounter Muhammad and his Companions and other deceased ancestors in faith; second, sleep allows access to certain aspects of truth that are unavailable while a person is awake.[29]

Intercession, Impeccability, and Inerrancy

One theologically important question is whether any human has the power to intercede for others in need, either during this life or at judgment after death. The extraordinary pastoral theologian Abū Hāmid al-Ghazālī offers a characteristically insightful perspective on various facets of intercession (*shafāʿa*, advocacy). He cites two sayings of Muhammad that seem to guarantee the Prophet's intercession for everyone who visits his grave in Medina (see the frontispiece). Ghazālī observes further that even individuals who end up in hell as a result of deliberately evil deeds might benefit from the intercession of both prophets and Friends of God. In addition, Ghazālī suggests that even lesser persons might attain sufficient intimacy with God to intercede for their own friends and family members. He explains that individuals might achieve this level of spiritual development by treating all people as God's own, ever aware that even an apparently insignificant individual might in fact be one of God's "hidden" Friends. One can thus rise to the ability to intercede for another merely by extending the smallest acts of kindness to a stranger, thereby meriting God's good pleasure. Uppermost in Ghazālī's mind, however, is the primacy of Muhammad and the prophets as potential intercessors. Prophets enjoy the prerogative of intercession because of their intimate relationship to God as well as their fellowship with the people to whom God sends them. Friends of God, by implication, likewise enjoy intercessory capabilities by reason of an analogous intimacy.[30]

Mainstream systematic theologians, such as Bāqillānī, generally affirm that Muhammad can exercise the prerogative of speaking on behalf of serious sinners before the throne of God. Bāqillānī dispenses with the objections of the Muʿtazilī, who believed that the Prophet might intercede only in the case of nonsinners, people who have sinned in only minor ways, or people who have fully repented. These qualifications are ridiculous and unnecessary, he adds, for they imply that people need to implore God not to act unjustly. Bāqillānī argues, of course, from Qurʾān and hadith, and he dismisses contrary texts as spurious documents or misinterpretations. He even argues that Muhammad's references to interceding for "my community" might include apostates, and he cites a hadith in which Muhammad engages his Companion Abū Dharr. Abū Dharr asks whether a professed Muslim will enter heaven even after fornication and theft. The Prophet responds in the affirmative, adding that even murder and alcoholic intoxication—and Abū Dharr's turning up his nose—will be no barriers.[31]

As we have seen, hagiographic accounts occasionally cast Friends indirectly in the role of intercessors. One obvious example is the work of the beloved legal scholar and Friend Shāfiʿī. Theorists on sainthood are, however, much more reticent to express specific views on the subject than one might expect. Their relative silence on the topic may well arise from an abundance of caution about arguably the most theologically sensitive of all Friend-related questions. Intercession, after all, implies the kind of mediation between God and his creatures that could (critics argue) lead to idolatry. Other "personal" qualities attributed to some Friends (especially to the Shīʿī imams) also pose theological problems, though not necessarily to the same degree that intercession does.

Impeccability and inerrancy, or infallibility (as suggested by the Arabic term ʿisma) are first of all qualities ascribed to prophets, but many authors attribute them to the Shīʿī imams as well. Twelver Shīʿī sources as early as the fourth/tenth century emphasize the need for imams to enjoy the "kindly grace" (luṭf) of divine protection from error, imperfection, and obstinate disobedience to God, because the imam functions as "proof" (ḥujja) of God's presence in human affairs. These elevated qualities are part of God's design to attract people to seek the presence of the imams and those close to them. People are far less inclined to follow a prophet or divine representative who is clearly capable of serious sin or untruthfulness. Shīʿī thought in general takes the notion of prophetic impeccability further than do theologians like Bāqillānī. He and some other Sunnī thinkers held that prophets were capable of even serious sin but were not subject to the sins of unbelief or untruthfulness.[32] The Shīʿī notion of the moral invulnerability and superiority of the imam naturally has had enormous political implications throughout history because it sets the stage for claims of the imam's divine authority, superior to that of a merely human caliph.

Chapter 5 alludes to several aspects of human frailty in the stories of Friends of God. Some theorists, however, extend a modified form of the privileged status of impeccability and infallibility to Friends of God as well as to prophets and imams. Hujwīrī notes that "reform-minded" Sufis (Sahl at-Tustarī, Abū Sulaymān ad-Dārānī and Hamdūn Qassār, for example) believe that a Friend can lose his exalted prerogatives as a result of major sin. But he disagrees, reasoning that because even major sin does not nullify faith, it could hardly nullify a condition that ranks above faith. Hujwīrī points out that though prophets are gifted with sinlessness (maʿsūm), Friends are guarded or kept safe (mahfūz), enjoying a lesser category of divine protection.[33]

Visitation of Tombs

Intimately related to the theme of intercession is the practice of visiting graves, especially those of prophets and Friends. Chapter 7 discusses some of the performative aspects of visitation, and earlier chapters recount scenes of visitation in the tales of individual Friends. Ghazālī offers a more theoretically based recommendation of the visitation of burial places, in his major work of pastoral and mystical theology, *The Revitalization of the Religious Disciplines*. He argues that the practice evokes beneficial reflection on the finitude of human life but can also be a source of spiritual blessing. Indeed, Muhammad's responses to questions about visiting his grave, sometimes delivered in dreams, prompt Ghazālī to recommend the practice. In Ghazālī's many supporting sayings and anecdotes, he emphasizes the reciprocal nature of the visitor's communication with the deceased: when the visitor greets the dead person, his or her greeting is invariably returned. He adds, "The purpose of the visitation of graves is that the visitor should be admonished, and that the one visited should receive benefit from his prayers. The visitor should not neglect to pray for himself and for the one deceased, or to derive a lesson. This latter may only come about through picturing the deceased in one's heart, and the way in which the members have been scattered abroad, and how he shall be raised up from his grave, and that one shall be joining him before long."[34]

Two centuries later, however, Ibn Taymīya took a different tack on the subject. Like Ghazālī, he cites Muhammad's prohibition against burying the dead in houses or holding festivities at his grave, as well as the Prophet's apparent approval of visitation to the graves of ordinary folk (even unbelievers), to make one mindful of death. Creating a festival atmosphere at a grave is excessive and goes far beyond simple, quiet visitation. Embarking on journeys for the express purpose of visitation to either graves or mosques, however, is another matter. Ibn Taymīya cites various opinions against the practice in general, noting that Muhammad allowed exceptions only at his own grave. Ibn Taymīya says that praying at graves can create the erroneous belief that God's power and grace are somehow more accessible there. Offering prayer when passing a grave or wishing peace upon the deceased in passing pose no problem. However, offering supplicatory prayer (*duʿāʾ*) at a grave site in the conviction that such supplications are more likely to be answered there than elsewhere is a serious sin. Ibn Taymīya then dismisses as fabrications stories affirming that even some notable people have made a regular practice of prayer at graves. Responding to other stories in which people claim to have had salutary graveside dreams, he insists that the devil was the one who came to them in their dreams.

In Ibn Taymīya's view, the fundamental problem is that many people believe that prayer at a grave is more beneficial (to themselves as well as the deceased) than prayer elsewhere. They are mistaken. Worse, the practice is not only worthless but causes serious harm. It results in undue attention to maintaining and decorating the burial site, which in turn attracts more people to visit, and so on in an endless cycle of inappropriate practice. A similar problem arises when one memorializes any place the prophet Muhammad or any earlier prophet is believed to have stopped to pray, even momentarily. Identifying such a site as a place for Muslims to congregate for prayer is a fundamental error. He particularly condemns the construction of *mashhads* (martyria, commemorative structures) over graves or *maqāms* (stations, places connected with the presence of a prophet or revered person).[35]

One of the delicious ironies is that today, many people continue to visit Ibn Taymīya's grave in Damascus. Ibn Taymīya was, indeed, a major theological influence on the early modern Wahhābī movement, which has often been inaccurately implicated in twenty-first-century American and European characterizations of Islam as a largely violent tradition. He has thus occasionally been tarred with the same brush as "radical jihadis," and one could argue that Ibn Taymīya has gotten a bad rap for other reasons as well. But he was far too great a contributor to the Islamic tradition to be dismissed through guilt by specious association, and indeed, Muslims have many positive reasons to continue to revere this talented man. Among his dozens of learned and tightly reasoned works is a short volume entitled *The Distinction between Friends of the Merciful and Friends of Satan (Al-Furqān bayna awliyā' ar-rahmān wa awliyā' ash-shaytān)*. As the title suggests, Ibn Taymīya was not opposed in principle to the notion that God singles out certain individuals for distinctive gifts and roles in the divine dispensation, with Muhammad leading the list. Indeed, the Qur'ān mentions *awliyā'* and *wilāya*, describes prophets as the preeminent Friends of God, and names other servants of God who have excelled in piety and nearness to God.

Ibn Taymīya zeroes in on hypocrisy in behavior and in tales of the accomplishments of famous people. Among the most corrosive effects of hypocrisy are the fabrication of traditions in an effort to legitimate excessive claims about ordinary human beings. Such claims, he warns, can only lead to *shirk*, the adoration of beings other than God. Reverent fear of God is the hallmark of Friends of God. They are not set apart from ordinary people by obvious differences, and aggrandizement of Friends of God beyond the status of the prophets is a grave error. Indeed, he suggests, the more an individual goes against the grain, causing a scene with religiously risky behavior, the more obviously such a person is among Satan's friends. Above all, Friends of God model incessant patience, repentance, and the quest for divine forgiveness. Genuine marvels, such as those manifested through the Companions and Followers of Muhammad, are possible only because these extraordinary individuals followed in the footsteps of the last Prophet. Ibn Taymīya makes clear that authentic Friends of God are known by their faith and reverential fear, never by actions arising from a desire for notoriety. One hopes that he can rest peacefully in the knowledge that the fame of his resting place was not his choice.[36]

Notes

ABBREVIATIONS

ASK   Mohamed Kerrou, ed., *L'Autorité des saints: Perspectives Historiques et socio-anthropologiques en Méditerranée occidentale* (Paris: éditions recherches sur les Civilisations, 1998).

CHMI   Françoise Mallison, ed., *Constructions hagiographiques dans le monde indien: entre mythe et histoire* (Paris: Champion, 2001).

CSMM   Henri Chambert-Loir and Cl. Guillot, eds., *Le culte des saints dans le monde musulman* (Paris: Ecôle Française d'Extreme Orient, 1995).

EI2   *Encyclopedia of Islam*, new edition, prepared by a number of leading Orientalists (Leiden: Brill, 1986–c. 2000).

HAI   Abū Nuʿaym al-Isfahānī, *Hilyat al-awliyāʾ wa tabaqāt al-asfiyāʾ*, 10 vols., ed. Saʿīd ibn Saʿd ad-Dīn Khalīl al-Iskandarānī (Beirut: Dār ihyāʾ at-turāth al-ʿArabīya, 2001).

HKN   Hujwīrī, *The Kashf al-Mahjūb*, trans. R. A. Nicholson (London: Luzac, 1976).

HKR   Hujwīrī, *The Kashf al-Mahjūb*, trans. M. W. Rabbani (Kuala Lumpur: A. S. Noordeen, 1997).

HKZ   Hujwīrī, *Kashf al-mahjūb*, ed. V. A. Zhukovskij (Leningrad: Dār al-ʿUlūm, 1999).

HSIJ   Russell Jones, trans., *Hikayat Sultan Ibrahim ibn Adham*, (Berkeley: University of California Press, 1985).

IJMES   *International Journal of Middle East Studies.*

IMH Shaykh al-Mufīd, *Kitāb al-irshād: The Book of Guidance into the Lives of the Twelve Imams*, trans. I. K. A. Howard (Elmhurst, NY: Tahrike Tarsile Qurʾān, Inc, 1981).

KMH ʿAbd ar-Raʾūf al-Munāwī, *Al-kawākib ad-durrīya fī tarājim as-sādat as-sūfīya*, 4 vols. in 2, ed. ʿAbd al-Hamīd Sālih al-Himdān (Cairo: Al-Maktabat al-Azharīya li-Turāth, 1994).

KʿIA Abū Bakr al-Kalābādhī, *The Doctrine of the Sufis*, trans. A. J. Arberry (Cambridge: Cambridge University Press, 1977).

LI Mohammad Ali Amir-Moezzi, ed., *Lieux d'Islam: Cultes et cultures de l'Afrique à Java* (Paris: Autrement, 1996).

LS Abū Nasr as-Sarrāj, *Kitāb al-lumaʿ*, ed. R. A. Nicholson (London: Luzac, 1963).

MAO Shams ad-Dīn Aflākī, *The Feats of the Knowers of God (Manāqib al-ʿārifīn)*, trans. John O'Kane (Leiden: Brill, 2002).

MDI Annemarie Schimmel, *Mystical Dimensions of Islam* (Chapel Hill: University of North Carolina Press, 1975).

MK Denise Aigle, ed., *Miracle et Karāma: Hagiographies médiévales comparées* (Turnhout, Belgium: Brépols, 2000).

MLP Gordon Newby, *The Making of the Last Prophet: A Reconstruction of the Earliest Biography of Muhammad* (Columbia: University of South Carolina Press, 1989).

MSI Grace M. Smith and Carl W. Ernst, eds., *Manifestations of Sainthood in Islam* (Istanbul: Isis, 1993).

MSIT Christian Troll, ed., *Muslim Shrines in India* (Delhi: Oxford University Press, 1989).

MSSA Anna Suvorova, *Muslim Saints of South Asia* (London: RoutledgeCurzon, 2004).

NSJ Douwe A. Rinkes, *Nine Saints of Java*, trans. H. M. Froger, ed. Alijah Gordon (Kuala Lumpur: Malaysian Sociological Research Institute, 1996).

NUJ Jāmī, *Nafahāt al-uns*, ed. Mahdī Tawhīdīpūr (Tehran: Kitābfurūshī-yi Mahmūdī, 1336/1957).

PD Henri Chambert-Loir and Anthony Reid, eds., *The Potent Dead: Ancestors, Saints, and Heroes in Contemporary Indonesia* (Honolulu: University of Hawaii Press, 2002).

QKT Kisāʾī, *The Tales of the Prophets of Kisāʾī [Qisas al-anbiyāʾ]*, trans. Wheeler Thackston (Boston: Twayne, 1978).

QTB	al-Tha'labī, *'Arā'is al-majālis fī qisas al-anbiyā'* or *Lives of the Prophets as Recounted by . . . al-Tha'labī,* trans. William Brinner (Leiden: Brill, 2002).
RQ	Qushayrī, *Risālat al-Qushayrīya,* ed. Khalīl an-Nusūr (Beirut: Dār al-Kutub al-'Ilmī, 1998).
RQG	Qushayrī, *Das Sendschreiben al-Qušayrīs über das Sufitum,* trans. Richard Gramlich (Wiesbaden: Franz Steiner Verlag, 1989).
RQH	Qushayrī, *Risalah: Principles of Sufism,* trans. R. Harris (ABC International Group, 2001).
RS	Vincent Cornell, *The Realm of the Saint* (Austin: University of Texas Press, 1998).
RSG	Safi ad-Dīn, *La Risāla de Safī ad-Dīn ibn Abī 'l-Mansūr ibn Zāfir,* ed. and trans. Denis Gril (Cairo: Institut française d'archéologie orientale, 1986).
RSI	Mahmoud Ayoub, *Redemptive Suffering in Islam* (The Hague: Mouton, 1978).
SAA	Ibn 'Arabī, *Sufis of Andalusia,* trans. R. W. J. Austin (London: Allen and Unwin, 1971).
SC	Allen Roberts, Mary Nooter Roberts, Gassia Armenian, and Ousmane Gueye, *A Saint in the City: Sufi Arts of Urban Senegal* (Los Angeles: University of California, Los Angeles, Fowler Museum, 2003).
SHMC	Catherine Mayeur-Jaouen, ed., *Saints et Heros du Moyên-Orient Contemporain* (Paris: Maisonneuve-LaRose, 2002).
SIG	Ibn Ishāq, *The Life of Muhammad [Sīrat an-nabawīya],* trans. Alfred Guillaume (Oxford: Oxford University Press, 1955).
SM	R. Chih and D. Gril, eds., *Le saint et son milieu* (Cairo: Institut française d'archéologie orientale, 2000).
SML	Carl Ernst and Bruce Lawrence, *Sufi Martyrs of Love* (New York: Palgrave/McMillan, 2001).
SO	Denise Aigle, ed., *Saints Orientaux* (Paris: DeBoccard, 1995).
SSD	Simon Digby, trans., *Sufis and Soldiers in Awrangzeb's Deccan: Malfuzat-i Naqshbandiyya* (Oxford: Oxford University Press, 2001).

SSM   Fritz Meier, "Tāhir al-Sadafī's Forgotten Work on Western Saints of the 6th/12th Century," in *Essays on Islamic Piety and Mysticism* (Leiden: Brill, 1999).

TAA   ʿAttār, *Muslim Saints and Mystics* (excerpts), trans. A. J. Arberry (London: Routledge & Kegan Paul, 1976).

TAE   ʿAttār, *Tadhkirat al-awliyāʾ*, ed. Muhammad Esteʿlāmī (Tehran: Intishārāt-i Zawwār, 2003).

TSV   Shaʿrānī, *Tabaqāt al-kubrā*, trans. Virginia Vacca as *Vite e detti di santi musulmani* (Torino: Unione Tipografico-Editrice Torinese, 1968).

VRT   Christopher S. Taylor, *In the Vicinity of the Righteous: Ziyāra and the Veneration of Muslim Saints in Late Medieval Egypt* (Leiden: Brill, 1999).

WFG   Richard Gramlich, *Die Wunder der Freunde Gottes: Theologien und Erscheinungsformen des islamischen Heiligenwunders* (Wiesbaden: Steiner, 1986).

INTRODUCTION: AN OVERVIEW OF ISLAMIC HAGIOGRAPHY

1. The expression *asātīr al-awwalīn* occurs nine times in the Qurʾān in a variety of contexts (6:25, 8:31, 16:24, 23:83, 25:5, 27:68, 46:17, 68:15, 83:13), typically describing the temporizing of unbelievers. For a useful study of the topic, see Alan Dundes, *Fables of the Ancients? Folklore in the Qurʾān* (Lanham, MD: Rowman and Littlefield, 2003).

2. *Sahīh Muslim.* 5 vols. (Beirut: Dār Ibn Hazm, 1995), 4:1481, tradition 2388. The stories may in fact be intended to function as parables, rather than to suggest that Muhammad actually witnessed the actions.

3. See, for example, James Robson, trans. *Mishkāt al-masābīh* (Lahore: Sh. Muhammad Ashraf, 1975), 2:1271–1382; *Sahīh Muslim*, 4:1423–1566.

4. See *SIG*. Arabic text in Ibn Hishām, *As-Sīrat an-Nabawīya*, 2 vols.(Cairo: Maktabat al-Kulligāt al-Azharīya, n.d.).

5. See, for example, Donald P. Little, "Narrative Themes and Devices in al-Wāqidī's *Kitāb al-maghāzī*," in *Reason and Inspiration in Islam*, ed. Todd Lawson (London: I. B. Tauris, 2005), 34–45.

6. See *QKT* and *QTB* for two excellent translations of tales of the prophets.

7. I am using *TAE* in references to ʿAttār's work. Isfahānī's ten-volume opus (see *HAI*), unlike ʿAttār's much shorter work, gives a great deal of attention to the first several generations of Muslim exemplars. The author dedicates the entire first six volumes to sketches of nearly four hundred Companions, Followers, and Followers of the Followers of the Prophet. On a smaller scale, al-Munāwī's work (see *KMH*) devotes considerable space to the Companions.

8. *SC* 38.

9. *RS* 272–73. Though Cornell explicitly discusses the terms in a Moroccan context, one could argue that his distinction applies to other contexts as well.

10. See Denis Gril, "Saint des villes et saint des champs: étude comparée de deux vies de saints d'époque mamelouke," in *SM,* 61–82.

11. See Jean-Jacques Thibon, "Hiérarchie spirituelle, functions du saint et hagiographie dans l'oeuvre de Sulamī," in *SM,* 13–31.

12. *RS* 274–75. See chapter 11 of this book for further details on relevant cosmological theories.

13. See *RSG* 35–42, for further discussion of this "typology" of holy persons.

CHAPTER 1: BEGINNINGS BOTH HUMBLE
AND SPECTACULAR

1. For extensive lists of a broad range of related "folk" themes, see Hasan M. El-Shamy, *Folk Traditions of the Arab World.* 2 vols. (Bloomington: Indiana University Press, 1995). For example, see "Birth," "Born," "Child," "Children," and so on, listed alphabetically in vol. 2.

2. *TAE* 388.

3. For studies on the general theme in medieval Christian literature, see Michael Goodich, "Childhood and Adolescence among the 13th-Century Saints"; "Una santa bambina, una santa dei bambini: l'infanzia di Elisabetta di Turingia (1207–31)"; and "Il Fanciullo come fulcro di miracoli e potere spirituale (XIII e XIV secolo)," all in *Lives and Miracles of the Saints: Studies in Medieval Latin Hagiography,* ed. Michael E. Goodich (Burlington, VT: Ashgate, 2004).

4. *QKT* 109–110, 163.

5. Ibid., 118–20.

6. Thaʿlabī indicates that his name was Terah originally (Tārīkh in Kisāʾī), but changed to Āzar after he became the custodian of the treasury of Nimrod's pantheon; *QTB* 124.

7. *QKT* 130–38, 160; *QTB* 124–27.

8. *QKT* 214–16; *QTB* 278–80, 282–83.

9. *QKT* 92.

10. *QTB* 441–42.

11. Ibid., 622–25.

12. Ibid., 627–30; *QKT* 326–28.

13. *MLP* 208.

14. *QKT* 329 records that the setting was merely a spring of clear water near a dead tree that became green.

15. *QKT* 330; *QTB* 638–45.

16. *QKT* 289.

17. *SIG* 67–69.

18. Valerie Hoffman, *Sufism, Mystics, and Saints in Modern Egypt* (Columbia: University of South Carolina Press, 1995), 72.

19. *RSI* 70–77.

20. *TAE* 222, 161.

21. Ibid., 73.

22. Ibid., 266.

23. *MAO* 576–81.

24. *MSSA* 114.

25. *SML* 53.

26. *SSD* 182–83.

27. *QKT* 110.

28. Ibid., 290–91.

29. Kisāʾī assigns Abraham this young age. Ibn Ishāq indicates that Abraham was in the cave for no longer than fifteen months when he asked his mother to let him outside to explore, but Ibn Ishāq's account, included in Thaʿlabī, also notes that for the infant Abraham, a day was like a month, and a month equivalent to a year, so he was fifteen years old when he departed the cave. *QTB* 127; *MLP* 68.

30. *QKT* 138–40.

31. *QKT* 216–18; *QTB* 283–87.

32. *MLP* 208.

33. *QKT* 330–32; *QTB* 645–49.

34. *QKT* 321.

35. *SIG* 70–72.

36. *RQ* 383–84; *RQH* 429–30; *RQG* 487–88 See also *HKZ* 291; *HKR* 237; and *HKN*.

37. *TAE* 30–31.

38. Louis Massignon, *The Passion of al-Hallāj*, trans. Herbert Mason, (Princeton, NJ: Princeton University Press, 1982), 1:57.

39. *TAE* 185.

40. John O'Kane, trans., *The Secrets of God's Mystical Oneness* (Costa Mesa, CA: Mazda, 1992), 76–77.

41. Luke 2:25–35.

42. O'Kane, *Secrets of God's Mystical Oneness*, 78–79.

43. *SAA* 109.

44. *MAO* 576–81.

45. Richard McGregor, *Sanctity and Mysticism in Medieval Egypt: The Wafa Sufi Order and the Legacy of Ibn ʿArabī* (Albany, NY: SUNY Press, 2004), 52–53.

46. Denise Aigle, "Un fondateur d'ordre en milieu rural: Le Cheikh Abū Ishāq de Kāzarūn," in *SO*, 186–87.

47. *SML* 53–54.

48. *SSD* 182–83.

49. *SC* 33.

50. *MAO* 581–82.

51. "The Autobiography of al-ʿAydarūs," trans. Michael Cooperson, in *Interpreting the Self: Autobiography in the Arabic Literary Tradition*, ed. Dwight F. Reynolds (Berkeley: University of California Press, 2001), 208–15.

52. See J.-L. Michon, ed. and trans., "L'Autobiographie (*fahrasa*) du soufi marocain Ahmad ibn ʿAjiba (1747–1809)," parts 1–4, *Arabica* 15 (1968): 225–69; 16 (1969): 25–64, 113–54, 225–68. See chapter 2 in part 2, 25, for the account of his earliest infancy.

53. *QKT* 140–41.

54. Ibid., 161–62.

55. Ibid., 167–69.

56. Ibid., 263.

57. Ibid., 321.

58. Ibid., 218–19.

59. Ibid., 291.

60. Ibid., 330–33; *QTB* 649–52; *MLP* 208–9.

61. *SIG* 72–3, 79–81.

62. *IMH* 229–31.

63. Ibid., 279, 297–98, 394–95, 484–90. See *RSI* 78–84 for further details on Hasan's and Husayn's infancies and early youths.

64. *TAE* 223.

65. *RQ* 39–40; *RQH* 31–32; *RQG* 52–53.

66. *TAE* 417–18.

67. Ibid., 497.

68. Ibid., 161; see also *SSM* 423–504, 473, on Shātibī's youthful initiation into asceticism.

69. *SAA* 124.

70. Ibid., 149.

71. *TAE* 476.

72. G. W. J. Drewes, *Directions for Travelers* (The Hague: Martinus Nijhoff, 1977), 10.

73. Devin DeWeese, "Sacred Places and 'Public' Narratives: The Shrine of Ahmad Yasavī in Hagiographical Traditions of the Yasavī Sūfī Order, 16th–17th Centuries," *The Muslim World* 90:3–4 (2000): 359.

74. *MAO* 16; *NUJ* 459–60.

75. *MAO* 17.

76. Ibid., 241.

77. Ibid., 18–19.

78. O'Kane, *Secrets of God's Mystical Oneness*, 97–98.

79. *MAO* 582–85.

80. *TAE* 524–25; *TAA* 244–45.

81. Rūzbihān Baqlī, *The Unveiling of Secrets: Diary of a Sufi Master*, trans. Carl W. Ernst (Chapel Hill, NC: Parvardigar, 1997), 10.

82. Ibid., 10–11.

83. J.-L. Michon, "L'Autobiographie," part 2, 26–27.

84. See also, for example, Istvan P. Bejczy, "The *Sacra Infantia* in Medieval Hagiography," in *The Church and Childhood*, ed. Diana Wood (Oxford: Blackwell, 1994), 143–51.

CHAPTER 2: CONVERSION AND ASCETICISM ON THE
ROAD TO SANCTITY

1. For an interesting quantitative analysis of the relative importance of these aspects of spiritual practice in Moroccan sources, see *RS* 110–13; for discussion of stages of repentance in the Jazūlīya order, see *RS* 181–82.

2. Gerard Manley Hopkins, "The Wreck of the Deutschland," lines 77–78, in *Gerard Manley Hopkins*, ed. Catherine Phillips (Oxford: Oxford University Press, 1995), 100.

3. *TAE* 222.

4. See Richard McCarthy's translation of the *Munqidh* in *Freedom and Fulfillment* (Boston: Twayne, 1980), 61–143.

5. See J.-L. Michon, ed. and trans., "L'Autobiographie *(fahrasa)* du soufi marocain Ahmad ibn ʿAjiba (1747–1809)," *Arabica* 15 (1968): 225–69; and its English version, *The Autobiography (Fahrasa) of a Moroccan Soufi: Ahmad ibn ʿAjiba (1747–1809)*, trans. David Streight (Louisville, KY: Fons Vitae, 1999).

6. Michael Cooperson, trans., "The Autobiography of al-Ḥakīm al-Tirmidhī," in *Interpreting the Self: Autobiography in the Arabic Literary Tradition*, ed. Dwight F. Reynolds (Berkeley: University of California Press, 2001), 119–31.

7. Jamal Elias, trans., "The Autobiography of ʿAlāʾ al-Dawla al-Simnānī (1261–1336)," ibid., 188–93.

8. Another first-person conversion account is that of Muhāsibī (c. 165/781–243/857), in the preface to his *Book of Advice* (*Kitāb an-nasāʾih*); Ahmad az-Zarrūq (846/1442–899/1493), with selections in Ali F. Khushaim, *Zarruq the Sufi* (Tripoli, Libya: General, 1976). A woman named ʿĀʾisha bint Yūsuf al-Bāʿūnīya (d. 922/1516) is also thought to have composed a now-lost autobiographical account. An account by ʿAbd al-Wahhāb ash-Shaʿrānī (897/1492–973/1565), *The Gracious Merits and Virtues Bestowed on Me by God and the Binding Obligation to Recount His Benefits*, has been translated into Italian by Virginia Vacca in *Il Libro dei Doni* (Naples: Istituto Orientale, 1972). See also Dwight Reynolds, "Shaykh ʿAbd al-Wahhāb al-Shaʿrānī's Sixteenth-century Defense of Auto-biography," *Harvard Middle Eastern and Islamic Review* 4:1–2 (1997–98): 122–37. Carl Ernst has translated a thirteenth-century classic by Rūzbihān Baqlī in *The Unveiling of Secrets: Diary of a Sufi Master* (Chapel Hill, NC: Parvardigar, 1997). Fātima al-Yashrūtīya's account of her twentieth-century life appears in Leslie Cadavid, trans. *Two Who Attained* (Louisville: Fons Vitae, 2005).

9. *TAE* 31–32.

10. Ibid., 36.

11. *HKN* 97–98; *TAE* 89.

12. *TAE* 90–91; see also *NUJ* 37–38, and the much fuller account of *HAI* 8:71–119.

13. *TAE* 102–3; *HKN* 103 gives far less detail here. See also *NUJ* 41–43 and the more extensive *HAI* 7:335–55.

14. *TAE* 128–29; however, in *HKN* 105, Bishr had the revelatory dream. See also *NUJ* 48–49 and *HAI* 8:296–316.

15. *TAE* 137–39; *HKN* 100–103 does not include the conversion account; see also *NUJ* 32–37, *HAI* 9:281–330. Yet another type of dramatic conversion to a more fully spiritual life is a kind of ecstatic "ravishing," in which the individual is overtaken by something like a loss of consciousness, or perhaps a "supraconsciousness." Accounts of a number of the great "mystics" feature experiences of this kind. For example, Saʿd ad-Dīn Jibawī (died c. 575/1179), a highway robber in Syria, several times went into a comalike state that lasted as long as a few days. He claims that during these times he encountered Muhammad, who sought to redirect the miscreant; see Éric Geoffroy, "Hagiographie et typologie spirituelle," in *SO*, 91.

16. See also John Renard, "*Al-jihād al-akbar:* A Theme in Islamic Spirituality," *The Muslim World* 77 (1988): 225–42.

17. *TAE* 50; *HKN* 89–90.

18. *HKN* 88; *TAE* 59–60.

19. *TAE* 263; see also *HAI* 7:309–34.

20. *TAE* 324.

21. Ibid., 330–31; *HKN* 110.

22. *HKN* 111–12.

23. *TAE* 465–66.

24. John O'Kane, trans., *Secrets of God's Mystical Oneness* (Costa Mesa, CA: Mazda, 1992), 13–14, 87–90; 133–363.

25. *QKT* 168.

26. Ibid., 254–71. For a fascinating variation on the story of Job, see the very moving Swahili *Utendi wa Ayubu* (*The Epic of Job*), in which Job's wife Rehema plays a much more prominent part than in the biblical account, in J. W. T. Allen, trans., *Tendi* (New York: Africana Publishing, 1971), 370–425.

27. *QKT* 630–34.

28. Ibid., 648.

29. See John Renard, trans., *Ibn ʿAbbūd of Ronda: Letters on the Sūfī Path* (Mahwah, NJ: Paulist, 1986), 101, for the sermon of Hasan; see also Ibn Abū Marwān al-Yahsubī's story about the Prophet and a poor man, *SSM* 449.

30. *SAA* 96.

31. *TAE* 145–46.

32. Ibid., 171.

33. Ibid., 325.

34. Ibid., 378.

35. VRT 92.

36. *RQ* 35, *RQG* 48, *RQH* 28.

37. *TAE* 27.

38. Ibid., 52–53; also *SSM* 443 on Maghribī Friend ʿAbd al-Qādir al-Kindī.

39. *TAE* 76–77.

40. Ibid., 77.

41. Ibid., 113.

42. Ibid., 114; for further stories on Ibrāhīm and food, *TAE* 122–23, 125.

43. Ibid., 143.

44. Ibid., 572.

45. Ibid., 573, and similarly on ʿAbd al-Qādir al-Kindī in *SSM* 445.

46. See *TAE* 38 for a parallel story about Hasan of Basra.

47. Ibid., 572–73.

48. *SML* 156; for more on the shaykh's austerities, see *MSSA* 89–91.

49. *SAA* 102–3.

50. *VRT* 89–90.

51. *TAE* 357–58.

52. Louis Massignon, *The Passion of al-Hallāj*, trans. Herbert Mason (Princeton, NJ: Princeton University Press, 1982), 1:56–7.

53. *TAE* 211–12, which repeats *HKN* 95–96 substantially.

54. *TAE* 390–91; *HKN* 124–25.

55. *TAE* 419.

56. *RQ* 37, *RQG* 51, *RQH* 20.

57. See, for example, *TAE* 168; additional accounts by Tādilī of combat against sexual desire appear in *VRT* 93–95.

58. *TAE* 432.

CHAPTER 3: DREAMS AND VISIONS, VISITORS AND VOICES

1. *TAE* 358.

2. *QKT* 87–88.

3. Ibid., 264.

4. *TAE* 19, 28–29.

5. Ibid., 64.

6. *TSV* 41.

7. *SAA* 124.

8. *QKT* 101, 222, 167.

9. John Renard, *Islam and the Heroic Image: Themes in Literature and the Visual Arts* (Columbia: University of South Carolina Press, 1993), 100–105, 140–45, 205–7, on heirlooms and symbols of prophetic/heroic/saintly lineage; also *IMH* 415–16; and Brannon Wheeler, *Mecca and Eden: Ritual, Relics, and Territory in Islam* (Chicago: University of Chicago Press, 2006), 10–12, 19–46.

10. *QKT* 167–68, 177–78; *QTB* 185–87, 204–9; see also chapter 1 on dreams accompanying the births of prophets and Friends, and Qurʾān 12 for the scriptural account of Joseph.

11. *TAE* 382.

12. *RQ* 414.

13. Richard J. McCarthy, S.J., *The Theology of Al-Ashʿarī* (Beirut: Imprimerie Catholique, 1953), 150–55.

14. Rūzbihān Baqlī, *The Unveiling of Secrets: Diary of a Sufi Master*, trans. Carl W. Ernst (Chapel Hill, NC: Parvardigar, 1997), 19.

15. Safā is one of the two small hills in Mecca between which Hagar ran in

her panic-stricken search for water for her infant Ismāʿīl; pilgrims on hajj imitate Hagar's search by running seven times between the two hills.

16. *KTA* 157–58.

17. Recounted by Munāwī, trans. John Renard, *Windows on the House of Islam* (Berkeley: University of California Press, 1996), 287–90.

18. *TAE* 133.

19. *SSM* 497.

20. *SAA* 84.

21. Ibid., 87–88. Yet another story tells of Ibn ʿArabī's experience in "a kind of sleep," brought on during a session of invocation at which a man was present who was suspected of being a skeptic by others at the session. In the dream, the Prophet appeared to the whole group and affirmed that the stranger was indeed a believer; ibid., 109–110.

22. *TAE* 215–16.

23. Ibid., 216.

24. *NUJ* 81; *TAE* 422, also 425 for another dream about Junayd and Muhammad.

25. Richard McGregor, *Sanctity and Mysticism in Medieval Egypt: The Wafa Sufi Order and the Legacy of Ibn ʿArabī* (Albany, NY: SUNY Press, 2004), 54.

26. *KTA* 158; also in *TAE* 498. See also *SSM* 465–66 on al-Fāʾida's dream in which the Prophet reassures him that his family will be taken care of after he is jailed for speaking out against injustice.

27. *SSM* 454–55.

28. Ibid., 492.

29. *TAE* 574.

30. Kutāmī also recalled that he learned sections of Mālik ibn Anas's collection of hadith, the *Muwattaʾ*, by writing down the lesson in the dream and finding that by morning, he had the passages from memory; *SSM* 456.

31. *MDI* 277, 225. For accounts by Jabartī about Bayyūmī's dream encounters with the Prophet, see William Shepard's translation in Renard, *Windows,* 350–52.

32. *RQ* 417; *RQG* 526; *RQH* 465.

33. *TAE* 140–41.

34. Ibid., 425.

35. Ibid., 169.

36. Ibid., 334.

37. *HKZ* 295; *HKR* 237.

38. *TAE* 214.

39. Ibid., 123.

40. Ibid., 176.

41. *SSM* 464; see also 458 on Gharīb's dream of an angel who slays people who contrive to sell wine.

42. Ibid., 435.

43. *TAE* 389.

44. See McCarthy, *Theology of Al-Ashʿarī*, 170, for an example of how wide-spread this theme is in dream accounts. In this example, a follower of the theologian Abū ʾl-Hasan al-Ashʿarī dreams of a man who had recently died and whom he had given a good burial. When the dreamer asks the dead man how God has dealt with him, the man answers that he has been rejected because of his negative opinion of Ashʿarī. Ashʿarī appears in the dream among his companions and is introduced to the dreamer as one whom God has pardoned.

45. See Leah Kinberg, "The Individual's Experience as It Applies to the Community: An Examination of Six Dream Narrations Dealing with the Islamic Understanding of Death," *Al-Qantara* 21 (2000): 425–44.

46. *TAE* 88, 209, 450–51, 230.

47. Ibid., 136, 209; for dreams about divine mercy and forgiveness, see 329, 389, 221, 230, 451, 594.

48. *RQ* 48; *RQG* 64; *RQH* 39. Similar stories about Sufyān ath-Thawrī (two accounts), Abū Sahl az-Zajjājī, Hasan ibn ʿĀsim ash-Shaybānī, Mālik ibn Anas, Nasrābādhī, Dhū ʾl-Nūn, Shiblī (two accounts), Junayd, an anonymous individual, Abū ʿAlī ad-Daqqāq, Yūsuf ibn al-Husayn, Bishr al-Hāfī (2), and Abū Sulaymān ad-Dārānī appear in *RQ* 413–23; *RQG* 522–35; and *RQH* 465–71. For another sort of pedagogical collection of such accounts, see Abū Hāmid al-Ghazālī, *The Remembrance of Death and the Afterlife*, trans. T. J. Winter (Cambridge: Islamic Texts Society, 1989), 159–68.

49. *TAE* 209–210; *SSM* 485.

50. *SAA* 70. In some accounts of Muhammad's Ascension, the Prophet must choose one of three bowls, variously containing water, milk or yogurt or honey, and wine. He willingly drinks the water and the milk but refuses the wine and is lauded for his sagacity. See, for example, Reuven Firestone's translation of a hadith text on the Ascension, in Renard, *Windows*, 340.

51. *SAA* 101.

52. *SSM* 485. On dreams in other contexts: M. J. Kister, "The Interpretation of Dreams: An Unknown Manuscript of Ibn Qutayba's ʿIbarat al-Ruʾyaʾ," *Israel Oriental Studies* 4 (1974): 67–103; Leah Kinberg, "The Legitimization of *Madhāhib* through Dreams," *Arabica* 32 (1985): 47–79; idem, "The Standardization of Qurʾān Readings: The Testimonial Value of Dreams," *The Arabist: Budapest Studies in Arabic* 3–4 (1991): 223–38; Leah Kinberg, "Literal Dreams and Prophetic *Hadīth* in Classical Islam—A Comparison of Two Ways of Legitimization," *Der Islam* 70:2 (1993): 279–300; Leah Kinberg, "Dreams as a Means to Evaluate *Hadith*," *Jerusalem Studies in Arabic and Islam* 23 (1999): 79–99. Fedwa Malti-Douglas, "Dreams, the Blind, and Semiotics," *Studia Islamica* 51 (1980): 137–61; Sara Sivri, "On Trees, Dreams and Holy Men: Notes on al-Tayyib Sālih's *The Doum Tree of Wad Hamid*," *Edebiyāt* 10:1 (1999): 103–22. On various aspects of visions: Jonathan Katz, "Visionary Experience, Autobiography, and Sainthood in North African Islam, *Princeton Papers in Near Eastern Studies* 1 (1992): 85–118; Marcia Hermansen, "The Study of Visions in Islam," *Religion* 27:1 (1997): 1–5; Marcia Hermansen, "Mystical Visions as 'Good to Think': Examples from Pre-Modern South Asian Sufi Thought," *Religion* 27:1

(1997): 25–43; Bernd Radkte, "Ibrīziana: Themes and Sources of a Seminal Sufi Work," *Sudanic Africa, A Journal of Historical Sources* 7 (1996): 121–27 (on visions of the Prophet).

53. *TAE* 269.

54. Julian Millie, "Creating Islamic Places: Tombs and Sanctity in West Java," *ISIM Review* 17 (Spring 2006): 12–13.

55. *SC* ills. 3.11, 5.5, 5.16. On related bird imagery, see Ignaz Goldziher, "L'oiseau representant l'âme dans les croyances populaires des Musulmans," in *Études Islamologiques d'Ignaz Goldziher*, ed. and trans. G.-H. Bousquet (Leiden: Brill, 1962), 77–80.

56. *KTA* 153–57.

57. Carl Ernst, trans. *Teachings of Sufism* (Boston: Shambhala, 1999), 186–87.

58. The "substitutes" are a category of Friends of God in the cosmological hierarchy whose mission is to mediate divine blessing and marvels and whose identity is known but to a select few. They are called "substitutes," according to some authors, because when one dies another replaces him to maintain a constant number in the category. Authors variously count four, seven, forty, or seventy such beings.

59. Irfan Omar, "Khidr in Islamic Tradition," *The Muslim World* 83:3–4 (1993): 279–94.

60. For exegetical interpretations of Khidr's functions in stories of Moses, see Brannon Wheeler, *Moses in the Qurʾān and Islamic Exegesis* (London: RoutledgeCurzon, 2002): 10–36 and passim.

61. *QTB* 72.

62. *SSM* 470–71.

63. *SAA* 157; on Ibn ʿArabī's other encounters with Khidr, see ibid., 25–29.

64. *SSM* 495.

65. Ibid., 488.

66. *SAA* 151.

67. *Quṭb* is the "pole" or "pivot," the figure at the apex of the cosmological hierarchy, sometimes identified with one or another Friend of God.

68. See, for example, *SAA* 152–53.

69. Al-Ghazālī, *Remembrance of Death*, 99–100.

70. *TAE* 65.

CHAPTER 4: MIRACLES AND MARVELS

1. B. Flusin, "Miracle et hiérarchie," in *Hagiographie, cultures, et sociétés, IVe–XIIe siècles* (Paris: études augustiniennes, 1981), 305.

2. *VRT* 129–67. Richard Gramlich's definitive study of the topic, *WFG* 19–121, discusses the two main categories of the "power" miracle and the "benevolence" miracle.

3. *RS* 115–16; Cornell also reports that though just a bit over half of his sources spoke of paranormal experiences, such events far outnumbered such

criteria for sainthood as moral guidance or charitable giving. WFG 150–92 explores "spiritual" and "physical" powers of Friends, including clairvoyance, knowledge, unique perceptive powers in the first category; and control of breath, need for food, and power over material forces in the second.

4. WFG 193–244 describes, for example, marvels of the Friend's "outward bearing" (including transcending laws of matter, as shown by impassibility, walking on water, casting no shadow). See *RSG* 56–65 for a summary of marvels in Safī ad-Dīn's work. For further studies on marvels of various types and in diverse contexts, see Jane I. Smith, "Concourse between the Living and the Dead in Islamic Eschatological Literature," *History of Religion* 19:3 (1980): 224–36; Leah Kinberg, "Interaction between this World and the Afterworld in Early Islamic Tradition," *Oriens* 29–30 (1986): 285–308; Marcia Hermansen, "Miracles, Language, and Power in a 19th Century Islamic Hagiographic Text," *Arabica* 38 (1991): 326–50. For a North African source dedicated to the marvels of a single Friend of God, see Al-Qushtālī, *Milagros de Abū Marwān al-Yuhānisī (Tuhfat al-mugtarib bi-bilād al-maghrib fī karāmāt al-shaykh Abī Marwān)*, ed. F. de la Granja (Madrid: Al-Maʿhad al-Misrī lil-Dirāsāt al-Islāmīyah, 1974).

5. See, for example, Brandon Wheeler, *Moses in the Qurʾān and Islamic Exegesis* (London: RoutledgeCurzon, 2002), 10–36.

6. *QKT* 94, 97, 146; 97; 99, 103; 121–26; 115–16; *QTB* 104–113, 114–23.

7. *QKT* 145–48, *QTB* 131–35; *QKT* 161 227–30, 233–34 281, 307–8.

8. *QTB* 653–74.

9. On miracles, see John Burton, *Introduction to the Hadith* (Edinburgh: University of Edinburgh Press, 1994), 97–100.

10. *SIG* 178–79.

11. See, e.g., *QKT* 99.

12. *MAO* 40. On miracles of ʿAlī, see *IMH* 229–67.

13. *HKR* 236–37; *RQ* 378; *RQG* 480–81; *RQH* 430–31.

14. *SAA* 90.

15. Ibid., 106–8. Many lesser, though still remarkable, abilities are associated with the devotional activities of some Friends. According to Ibn ʿArabī's account, for example, a woman named Zaynab al-Qalʾīya used to levitate to a great height during her periods of personal prayer; ibid., 155.

16. *TAE* 179–80.

17. Ibid., 180–81.

18. Ibid., 79.

19. *MAO* 405.

20. Ibid., 547.

21. Ibid., 617–18.

22. *SC* 101, figs. 3.17, 3.18.

23. WFG 306–65 analyzes a variety of "miracles involving human beings," including healing, protection, rescue, and provisioning, such as those I discuss in the next several sections.

24. *TAE* 77; for Paul Losensky's translation of this episode in the context of

'Attār's life of Rābi'a, see Michael Sells, ed. *Early Islamic Mysticism* (New York: Paulist, 1996), 151–70; for a translation of Munāwī's version, see John Renard, *Windows on the House of Islam* (Berkeley: University of California Press, 1996), 132–35.

25. *SAA* 83.

26. *TAE* 471.

27. *MSSA* 85.

28. *SSM* 443; *SAA* 67, 148.

29. *TAE* 126; *SSM* 493, 460.

30. *SSM* 493, 496, 442. For more on miracles at sea, see Christophe Picard, "Récits merveilleux et Réalité d'une Navigation en océan Atlantique chez les auteurs musulmans," in *Miracles, prodiges et merveilles au Moyen Age* (Paris: Publications de la Sorbonne, 1995), 75–87.

31. Ibid., 494.

32. Ibid., 442, 474.

33. *SSM* 468–69.

34. *TAE* 179.

35. *SSM* 469.

36. *TAE* 587; variant tales have the companions requesting figs or sweets; *SSM* 497.

37. *SSM* 464–65.

38. Ibid., 484–85.

39. Ibid., 446

40. Ibid., 463; *SAA* 81–82.

41. *SAA* 120–21.

42. *MSSA* 12–14, and Marc Gaborieau, "The Cult of the Saints among Muslims of Nepal and Northern India," in *Saints and their Cults,* ed. S. Wilson (Cambridge: Cambridge University Press, 1983), 303.

43. *TAE* 433–34.

44. *SSM* 486.

45. *NUJ,* 624.

46. *SAA* 150. On certain Friends' specialization in mastery over particular aspects of natural cycles and forces, especially harvests, see, for example, Gaborieau, "Cult of the Saints," 304. *WFG* 366–85 discusses "miracles involving animals."

47. *TAE* 61, 63–64.

48. *SSM* 474–75.

49. *TAE* 126.

50. Ibid., 126–27, 358.

51. Ibid., 127.

52. *QKT* 304–06, 310–11; *QTB* 513–19; *SAA* 144; see also *SAA* 68 for a story about how the Friend Abū Ja'far al-'Uryanī manages to put a pesky jinn in his place.

53. *TAE* 105, 178.

54. *SSM* 485. See, for example, the story about Mālik ibn Dīnār in *TAE* 50. For more on this topic see Catherine Mayeur-Jaouen, "Miracles des saints musulmans et Régne animal," in *MK*, 577–606.

55. *RQG* 507; *RQH* 446; *TAE* 511, 230–31.

56. *TAE* 329; 172; see also 427 on Junayd and the talking dog.

57. Ibid., 392, 74. See also Richard Foltz, *Animals in Islamic Tradition and Muslim Cultures* (Oxford: OneWorld, 2006).

58. John Renard, *Knowledge of God in Classical Sufism* (Mahwah, NJ: Paulist, 2004), 322. Sāriya was a Companion of the Prophet said to be buried in a shrine in the forecourt of the mosque of Hadim Sülayman Pasha (935/1528), located in the citadel of Cairo; Gülru Necipoğlu, *The Age of Sinan: Architectural Culture in the Ottoman Empire* (Princeton, NJ: Princeton University Press, 2005), 97.

59. *VRT* 111–12.

60. *SSM* 481.

61. *TAE* 177.

62. Ibid., 431, 435.

63. *SSM* 462–63.

64. *SAA* 103–4, 142–43.

65. Ibid., 63–64.

66. Ibid., 121.

67. Ibid., 122.

68. Ibid., 153.

69. *MDI* 79; Carl W. Ernst, "Introduction," *MSI*, xxii; *MDI* 211; *TAE* 78.

CHAPTER 5: MERE MORTALS

1. *QKT* 220, 282–83, 317–19.

2. Ibid., 282; *QTB* includes relevant stories about Abraham, Joseph, Job, Moses, Elisha, David, Solomon, Zakarīya, Jesus, and Jirjīs.

3. *QKT* 38–39, 50–51.

4. Ibid., 101; because the donkey was moving slowly with his added burden, Noah had scolded it, saying "Get in, you devil." Iblīs then argued that Noah had unwittingly given him leave to embark! Thaʿlabī (*QTB* 96) explains the situation somewhat differently, reporting that Noah made a "slip of the tongue" by telling the donkey to get in "even if the devil is with you"; *QKT* 195.

5. *QKT* 147; *QTB* 71–73, 160.

6. *MAO* 410–11.

7. Ibn al-Jawzī, *The Book of Professional Storytellers and Raconteurs* [*Kitāb al-qussās wa ' l-mudhakkirīn*], trans. Merlin Swartz, (Beirut: Dar al-Mashreq, 1986).

8. Ibn al-Jawzī, *The Devil's Delusion*, trans. D. S. Margoliouth, serially in *Islamic Culture* 9–12 (1935–38); sections on ascetics, devotees, and Sufis are in 11 (1936): 340–68, 633–47; and 112 (1937): 267–73, 393–403, 529–33; and his sec-

tions on "those who believe in miracles wrought for the glory of the saints" are in 12 (1938): 352–64, 447–57; quoting here 352.

9. *SAA* 97–98.

10. *TAE* 497–98. Hujwīrī includes a shorter version of the account in *HKR* 140.

11. *KTA* 61–66; *TAE* 389, 400, 167–68.

12. *TAE* (2004) 461–62.

13. *LS* 200 (Arabic).

14. *HKN* 360–66; *HKR* 373–77.

15. Jean-Louis Michon, *The Autobiography* (Fahrasa) *of a Moroccan Soufi: Ahmad ibn ʿAjiba*, trans. David Streight (Louisville, KY: Fons Vitae, 1999), 127–40.

16. *TAE* 348–49.

17. Ibid., 378–79.

18. Ibid., 94, 100–101.

19. Ibid., 511.

20. *SSM* 466.

21. *LS* 200.

22. *SSM* 443–44.

23. *TAE* 220.

24. *LS* 199.

25. *TAE* 107–9; *HSIJ* 133–75.

26. *TAE* 574–75.

27. For specific examples in translation, with helpful analysis, see Michael Sells, *Early Islamic Mysticism* (New York: Paulist, 1996), especially 97–150.

28. *SSD* 147–48.

29. *Hamlet*, act 1, scene 2.

30. For more on these themes, see Giovanna Calasso, "Les sourires et les larmes: Observations en marge de quelques textes hagiographiques musulmans," *Al-Qantara* 21:2 (2000): 445–56. Calasso's analysis is based on a hagiographical work by eighth-/fourteenth-century North African Ibn Qunfudh; see also her "La dimension religieuse individuelle dans les texts musulmans mediévaux, entre hagiographie et literature de voyage: les larmes, le émotions, l'expérience," *Studia Islamica* 91 (2000): 39–58; and Halima Ferhat, "Le Saint et son corps: une lutte constante," *Al-Qantara* 21:2 (2000): 457–70.

31. *QKT* 79; *QTB* 83–84, *QKT* 84–91; *QTB* 419–31; *QKT* 267–69, 269, 334–35.

32. *QTB* 164–65.

33. Ibid., 408–10.

34. Abū Hāmid al-Ghazālī, *The Remembrance of Death and the Afterlife*, trans. T. J. Winter (Cambridge: Islamic Texts Society, 1989), 57–74.

35. Ibid., 74–84. Accounts about ʿUthmān and ʿAlī are even simpler and more ordinary.

36. *IMH* 177; see ibid., 10–17 on ʿAlī's murder and grave site.

37. Ibid., 299–378; *RSI* 93–195.

38. Ghazālī, *Remembrance of Death*, 95–96; *RQH* 369 makes a similar observation.

39. Ghazālī, *Remembrance of Death*, 97–106.

40. *RQ* 334–42; *RQG* 418–28, *RQH* 369–77; Sarrāj dedicates a chapter to the "behavior of [God's Friends] at the hour of death," *LS* 209–11; *KTA* 162–64.

41. *TAE* 474.

42. *HKN* 121; also *KTA* 162, briefly, and *LS* 211; *TAE* 360 repeats the story nearly verbatim. For similar brief anecdotes about various figures, see *TAE* 499, 269; *SSM* 437, 438.

43. Th. Emil Homerin, *From Arab Poet to Muslim Saint* (Columbia: University of South Carolina Press, 1994),. 50–52.

44. *MAO* 676–82.

45. *TAE* 591–94.

46. Ibid., 88.

47. Ibid., 99–100.

48. Devin DeWeese, "Sacred Places and 'Public' Narratives: The Shrine of Ahmad Yasavī in Hagiographical Traditions of the Yasavī Sūfī Order, 16th–17th Centuries," *The Muslim World* 90:3–4 (2000): 359–69. The article concludes with another fascinating cycle of marvels in the underground chamber.

49. *TAE* 341, 449–50; see 578 on Ibn Khafīf.

50. Ibid., 135, 220, 127.

51. Ibid., 229–30, 355.

52. *SAA* 158–59; for a similar account on ʿAbd Allāh ar-Rammād, see *SSM* 469–70.

53. *TAE* 158–59.

54. Ibid., 208–9.

55. Th. Emil Homerin, *ʿUmar ibn al-Fārid: Sufi Verse, Saintly Life* (Mahwah, NJ: Paulist, 2001), 307–8.

56. *MAO* 51.

57. Ibid., 543; for stories of lesser-known or anonymous Friends, see *KTA* 162–64.

CHAPTER 6: FRIENDS AND THEIR PEOPLE

1. See *RSG* 69–76 on "shaykhs of the city," discussing relationships between spiritual authority and temporal power; and Catherine Mayeur-Jaouen, "Les Compagnons de la Terrasse, un groupe de soufis ruraux dans l'Égypte mamelouke," in *SO*, 181–209, on the "rural" side of the typology. *MSSA* 59–60 describes two major types: the introverted hermit/scholar/mystic and the more energetic and extroverted intercessor/social worker who is wise to the ways of the world and human passions; *MSSA* 81 contrasts "metropolitan saints," which are a "general type," with Friends, who become more identified with "the colours and forms of the local substratum."

2. André Vauchez, "Saints admirables et saints imitables: les functions de

l'hagiographie ont-elles changé aux derniers siècles du Moyen Âge!" in *Les fonctions des saints dans le monde occidental (IIIe-XIIIe siècle)*, Collection de l'École Française de Rome, vol. 149 (Rome: École Française, 1991), 161–72.

3. See *VRT* 81–108 on such virtues as generosity and availability, and *RSG* 49–52 on fundamental ethical dimensions.

4. *SIG* 86.

5. See Jo-Ann Gross, "Authority and Miraculous Behavior: Reflections on *Karāmāt* Stories of Khwāja ʿUbaydullāh Ahrār," in *The Heritage of Sufism, II: The Legacy of Medieval Persian Sufism (1150–1500)*, 2nd ed., ed. Leonard Lewisohn and David Morgan (Oxford: OneWorld, 1999): 159–71, for more on his ethical legacy.

6. *MSSA* 13; Marc Gaborieau "The Cult of the Saints among Muslims of Nepal and Northern India," in *Saints and their Cults*, ed. S. Wilson (Cambridge: Cambridge University Press, 1983), 302–3.

7. *VRT* 90–91.

8. *TAE* 182, 217.

9. *SSM* 447.

10. Denise Aigle, "Un fondateur d'ordre en milieu rural: Le Cheikh Abū Ishāq de Kāzarūn," in *SO*, 198–201.

11. *MAO* 68–70.

12. For studies of Husayn's martyrdom from various literary and cultural perspectives, see a special issue of *Al-Sirāt* 12 (1986), proceedings of an international conference, especially Syed Mohammad Amir Imam, "The Martyrdom of Husayn b. ʿAlī and the Continuity of Ethical and Moral Concepts," (143–63); and Azim Nanji, "The Imam Husayn: His Role as Paradigm" (164–87).

13. See Allamah Tabatabaʾi, *Shiʿite Islam* (Albany, NY: SUNY Press, 1977), 173–214, for brief accounts of the lives of all twelve imams; William Chittick, *A Shiʿite Anthology* (Albany, NY: SUNY Press, 1981), for prayers attributed to several of the imams; and *RSI* 91–124. For a Shīʿī perspective on the military exploits of ʿAlī, see *IMH* 44–115.

14. *TAE* 28, 435. In another important context, two of the Indonesian Wali Songo—Sunan Gunung Jati and Sunan Kudu—have been especially revered for their roles as warriors in the Islamization of Java. See, for example, Henri Chambert-Loir, "Saints and Ancestors: The Cult of Muslim Saints in Java," in *PD*, 132–40; Henri Chambert-Loir and Cl. Guillot, "Le culte des saints musulmans à Java: Rapport de mission," *La Transmission du savoir dans le monde musulman périphérique* 11 (1991): 9–16; C. Guillot and Henri Chambert-Loir, "Pèlerinage aux Neuf Saints de Java," in *LI*, 203–22; and *NSJ*. For accounts of martyrdom in more recent history, see Sabrina Mervin, "Les yeux de Mūsā Sadr (1928–1978)," in *SHMC*, 285–300; Éric Butel, "Martyre et sainteté dans la littérature du guerre Iran-Irak (1980–1988)," in *SHMC*, 301–18; Pierre Centilivres and Micheline Centilivres-Demont, "Les martyrs afghans par le texte et l'image (1978–1992)," in *SHMC*, 319–34; and Hamit Bozarslan, "La figure du martyr chez les Kurdes," in *SHMC*, 335–47. See also *MSSA* 155–57, 161–62, on Salar Masʿūd Ghāzī (426/1034), also known as Ghāzī Miyān (Master Warrior), and on

interreligious links: Hindus have been among his devotees also, because they identified him with the divine warrior child Krishna, and he was eroticized as a parallel to Rama in relation to Sita. Salar's military banner was the focal point of his cult, along with spears and flags.

15. *SAA* 91–93.

16. *Rasāʾil ilā Imām ash-Shāfiʿī*, 2nd ed. (Cairo: Dār ash-Shayāʾil an-Nashr, 1978). Thanks to Juan Campo for an informal communication on this matter. For advocacy in another cultural setting, see S. L. Pastner, "Feuding with the Spirit among the Zikri Baluch: The Saint as Champion of the Despised," in *Islam in Tribal Societies, from the Atlas to the Indus*, ed. Akbar S. Ahmed and D. M. Hart (London: Routledge & Kegan Paul, 1984), 302–19.

17. See, for example, Devin DeWeese, "Sayyid ʿAlī Hamadānī and Kubrāwī Hagiographical Traditions," in Lewisohn and Morgan, *Heritage of Sufism*, 121–58, especially 153–56.

18. Gross, "Authority and Miraculous Behavior," 164–66.

19. *SAA* 112–14. On this theme in other contexts, see Halima Ferhat, "Sainteté et Pouvoir au Moyen Âge au Maghreb: entre le refus et la tentation," in *ASK*, 239–49; Abdallah Hammoudi, "Sainteté, pouvoir et société: Tamgrout aux XVIIᵉ et XVIIIe siècles," *Annales: ESC* 35 (1980): 615–39; Catherine Mayeur-Jaouen, *Al-Sayyid al-Badawī: un grand saint de l'islam égyptien* (Cairo: Institut française d'archéologie orientale, 1994); Catherine Mayeur, "L'intercession des saints en islam égyptien: autour de Sayyid al-Badawī," *Annales Islamologiques* 25 (1990): 364–88; M. Salim, "The Attitude of Chishti Saints Towards Political Power," *Proceedings of the Pakistan Historical Conference* 2 (1952): 225–29; see *SAA* 147 on a Friend's rejection of a caliph's offer to donate money.

20. Carl Ernst, "Introduction," and Halil Inalcik, "Dervish and Sultan: An Analysis of the Otman Baba Vilayetnamesi," in *MSI*, xxii–xxiv, 209–24. Otmān Bābā was not the only potentially Friend-related disruptive element facing Sultan Mehmet; see A. Yaşar Ocak, "Kalenderi Dervishes and Ottoman Administration from the Fourteenth to the Sixteenth Centuries," ibid., 239–55.

21. See, for example, *SML* 99–101; Simon Digby, "Sufi Shaykh as a Source of Authority in Medieval India," in *Islam et Société en Asie du Sud*, ed. M. Gaborieau (Paris: L'École des Hautes Études, 1986), 57–77, and his "The Sufi Shaykh and the Sultan: A Conflict of Claims to Authority in Medieval India," *Iran* 28 (1990): 71–81; and Richard M. Eaton, "The Court and the Dargah in the Seventeenth Century Deccan," *Indian Economic and Social History Review* 10:1 (1973): 50–63.

22. For treatments of the various groups, see Ahmet Karamustafa, *God's Unruly Friends* (Salt Lake City: University of Utah Press, 1994; reprinted Oxford: Oneworld, 2006); Simon Digby, "Qalandars and Related Groups," *Islam in Asia*, vol. 1, *South Asia* (Jerusalem: Magnes Press, 1984); Katherine Ewing, "A Majzub and his Mother," in *Embodying Charisma: Modernity, Locality and the Performance of Emotion in Sufi Cults*, ed. P. Werbner and H. Basu (London: Routledge, 1998); and Jürgen Frembgen, "From Dervish to Saint: Constructing Charisma in Contemporary Pakistani Sufism," *The Muslim World* 94 (2004): 245–57.

23. On the larger picture of women in Islamic sources, see Gavin R. G. Hambly, "Becoming Visible: Medieval Islamic Women in Historiography and History," in *Women in the Medieval Islamic World: Power, Patronage, and Piety,* ed. G. Hambly (New York: St. Martin's, 1998), 3–28.

24. *TAE* 72.

25. Rkia Cornell, trans., *Early Sufi Women* (Louisville, KY: Fons Vitae, 1999), 46–47.

26. Abū Yaᶜqūb Yūsuf ibn Yahyā at-Tādilī, *At-Tashawwuf ilā rijāl at-tasawwuf,* ed. Ahmad Tawfīq (Ribat: University of Muhammad the Fifth, 1404/1984), 81 (unknown), 193–94 (unknown), 238–39 (Fātima of Andalusia), 277–78 (unknown), 279 (Umm Usfūr).

27. *NUJ* 615–40.

28. For an assessment of various hagiographical treatments of women and a translation of Sulamī's 82 brief lives of holy women, as well as of the 16 of Ibn al-Jawzī's 240 notices on women whose stories Sulamī also recounts, see Cornell, *Early Sufi Women;* for translated accounts from Thaᶜlabī, Munāwī, and Safi ad-Dīn, see Renard, ed., *Windows on the House of Islam* (Berkeley: University of California Press, 1996), 92–95, 130–35, 137–39; and for summaries and translations of accounts from various sources, see Camille Helminski, *Women of Sufism: A Hidden Treasure* (Boston: Shambhala, 2003); Javad Nurbakhsh, *Sufi Women* (London: Khaniqahi Nimatullahi, 2004); Carl Ernst, trans., *Teachings of Sufism* (Boston: Shambhala, 1999), 179–99; ᶜAbd ar-Raᵓūf al-Munāwī, *Les Femmes soufies,* trans. Nelly Amri and Laroussi Amri (St. Jean-de-Bray, France: Éditions Dangles, 1992). For translations of Shaᶜrānī's entries on women, see *TSV* 105; and for the most detailed coverage of this Friend, see Margaret Smith, *Rabiᶜa* (Oxford: Oneworld, 1994).

29. *QTB* 312–16. On a Cairene tomb identified with a certain (apparently another) Āsiya, see *VRT* 84–86.

30. *QTB* 623–27, 638–48; the latter episodes are described in chapter 1 of this book.

31. Two other saintly women from Muhammad's family were Sayyida Nafīsa (see Yousuf Ragib, "Al-Sayyida Nafīsa, sa légende, son culte et son cimetière," *Studia Islamica* 44 (1976): 61–86) and Sayyida Zaynab.

32. For more on Muhammad's wives, see Ghassan Ascha, "The 'Mothers of the Believers': Stereotypes of the Prophet Muhammad's Wives," in *Female Stereotypes in Religions Traditions,* ed. Ria Kloppenborg and Wouter J. Hanegraaff (Leiden: Brill, 1995), 89–107; on various contexts, Helminski, *Women of Sufism,* 5–12; and on the Shīᶜī tradition, see David Pinault, "Zaynab Bint ᶜAli and the Place of the Women of the Households of the First Imams in Shiᶜite Devotional Literature," in Hambly, ed., *Women in the Medieval Islamic World,* 69–98.

33. *HSIJ,* especially 173–75.

34. *MAO* 549–50.

35. *SC* 151–63 and passim.

36. Jean-Louis Michon, *The Autobiography* (Fahrāsa) *of a Moroccan Soufi: Ahmad ibn ᶜAjiba,* trans. David Streight (Louisville, KY: Fons Vitae, 1999), 42–45.

37. *TAE* 136; 333.

38. *SAA* 142, 146–46.

39. *TAE* 140.

40. Nurbakhsh, *Sufi Women*, 131–40, 88–89.

41. *TAE* 84; 86.

42. *MAO* 412.

43. Ibid., 573–74.

44. Ibid., 649–50.

45. Summarized from Katia Boissevain, "Sayyida Manoubiyya de Tunis: sainte musulmane du XIIIe siècle et sainte contemporaine?" in *SHMC*, 247–65. See also Katia Boissevain-Souid, "Saïda Manūbīya: son culte aujourd'hui, quelles specificités?" *Revue de l'Institut des Belles Lettres Arabes (IBLA)* 186:2 (2000): 137–64; and "Pureté rituelle et différenciation sociale dans le culte de Saïda Manoubiya," *Correspondences: Bulletin d'information scientifique de l'IRMC* 69 (2002): 3–10.

46. *SSM* 477. Women often function as tests of a male Friend's virtue. Turkish slave girls play this role in some stories.

47. *MAO* 547. A great deal of recent research on women Friends of God has begun to emerge, especially in the past decade or so. On Female Friends in general, see Michel Chodkiewicz, "Female Sainthood in Islam," *Sufi* 21 (1994): 12–19; and his "La sainteté feminine dans l'hagiographie islamique," in *SO*, 99–115; and D. A. Spellberg, "Writing the Unwritten Life of the Islamic Eve: Menstruation and the Demonization of Motherhood," *IJMES* 28 (1996): 305–24. See the following for a variety of geographical contexts.

In North Africa and Spain: Nelly Amri, "Les Sālihāt du Ve au IXe siècle/XIe–XVe siècle dans la mémoire maghrébine de la sainteté à travers quatre documents hagiographiques," *Al-Qantara* 21:2 (2000): 481–510; M. L. Avila, "Women in Andalusi Biographical Sources," in *Writing the Feminine: Women in Arab Sources*, ed. M. Marin and R. Deguilhem (New York: I. B. Tauris, 2002), and her "Las mujeres 'sabias' en al-Andalus," in *La mujer en al-Andalus: reflejos históricos de su actividad y categorias socials*, ed. M. J. Viguera (Madrid: Ediciones de la Universidad Autónoma de Madrid; Sevilla: Editoriales Andaluzas Unidas, 1989); E. Lapiedra, "Mujeres místicas musulmanas transmisoras de su ciencia en al-Andalus," in *Las sabias mujeres: educación, saber y autoría (siglos III-XVII)*, ed. M. Graña Cid (Madrid: Asociación Cultural Al-Mudayna, 1994); G. Lopez de la Plaza, *Al-Andalus: mujeres, sociedad y religion* (Malaga: Universidad de Málaga, 1992); Manuela Marín, "Retiro y ayuno: algunas practicas religiosas de las mujeres andalusíes," *Al-Qantara* 21 (2000): 471–80; Manuela Marín, *Mujeres en al-Andalus*, (Madrid: Consejo Superior de Investigaciones Científicas, 2000— Estudios Onomástico-Biográficos de al-Andalus, vol. 11); Imed Melliti, "Espace liturgique et formes de l'autorité chez les femmes tījānīya de Tunis," in *ASK*, 133–50; Fenneke Reysoo, "Sainteté vécu et contre-modèle religieux des femmes au Maroc," in *ASK*, 151–62.

In Central Asia: Thierry Zarcone, "La Femme en Asie centrale et les 'regions' du pouvoir (islam et soufisme populaire, culte des saints, chamanisme musulman)," in *Rôle et Statuts des femmes dans les sociétés contemporaines de tradition musulmane* (Paris: Centre des Hautes Études pour l'Asie Moderne, 2000), 157–65.

In South Asia: Netty Bonouvrié, "Female Sufi Saints on the Indian Subcontinent," in Kloppenborg and Hanegraaff, *Female Stereotypes*, 109–22.

CHAPTER 7: FOUNDING FRIENDS

1. Mohammad Kerrou, "Sainteté, savoir, et autorité dans la cité islamique de Kairouan," in *ASK*, 219–38; see also his "Autorité et Sainteté: perspectives historiques et socio-anthropologiques," in *ASK*, 11–38. For various approaches to defending the solid foundations of God's Friends in the traditional religious disciplines, see John Renard, *Knowledge of God in Classical Sufism* (Mahwah, NJ: Paulist, 2004), 65–99, 264–73, 332–74.

2. For the text of one of Ahrār's endowment documents, see Jo-Ann Gross, trans., "A Central Asian *Waqf* of Naqshbandī Master Khwāja Ahrār," in John Renard, ed., *Windows on the House of Islam* (Berkeley: University of California Press, 1996), 231–35. See also David Gilmartin, "Shrines, Succession, and Sources of Moral Authority," in *Moral Conduct and Authority: The Place of Adab in South Asian Islam*, ed. Barbara D. Metcalf (Berkeley: University of California Press, 1984), 221–40.

3. See, for example, Louis Massignon, *The Passion of al-Hallāj*, trans. Herbert Mason (Princeton, NJ: Princeton University Press, 1982); Hamid Dabashi, *Truth and Narrative: The Untimely Thoughts of ʿAyn al-Qudat al-Hamadhani* (Richmond, Surrey: Curzon, 1999); and ʿAyn al-Qudāt al-Hamadhānī, *A Sufi Martyr: The Apologia of ʿAin al-Qudat al-Hamadhani*, trans. A. J. Arberry (London: Allen and Unwin, 1969).

4. S. Soebardi, ed. and trans., *The Book of Cabolek* (The Hague: Martinus Nijhoff, 1975), 35–37; see also 38–45 for three other martyr stories and an analysis of the underlying purpose of the stories; see *NSJ* 15–48 on Siti Jenar, and 123–49 on Pangung.

5. See also the story of Nūrī, *TAE* 468. See Frederick De Jong and Bernd Radtke, eds., *Islamic Mysticism Contested: Thirteen Centuries of Controversies and Polemics* (Leiden: Brill, 1999), on conflict between Friends and authorities presented as representatives of the religious "establishment."

6. Sheila Blair, "Sufi Saints and Shrine Architecture in the Early Fourteenth Century," *Muqarnas* 7 (1990): 35–49; see also Lisa Golombek, "The Cult of Saints and Shrine Architecture in the Fourteenth Century," in *Near Eastern Numismatics, Iconography, Epigraphy, and History*, ed. D. Kouymjian (Beirut: American University of Beirut Press, 1974). For studies of other aspects of the topic, see the following sources.

General: Catherine Mayeur-Jaouen, "Tombeaux, Mosquées et Zāwiya: la polarité des lieux saints musulmans," in *Lieux sacrés, lieux de culte, sanctuaires: approches terminologiques, méthodologiques, historiques et monographiques*, ed. André Vauchez (Rome: Ecole française de Rome, 2000): 133–47; Catherine

Mayeur-Jaouen, "Lieux sacrés, lieux de culte, santuaires en islam: Bibliographie raisonée," ibid., 149–70.

In South Asia: J. M. S. Baljon, "Shah Waliullah and the Dargah," in *MSIT,* 189–97; Mumtaz Currim and George Michell, *Dargahs: Abodes of the Saints,* photos by Karoki Lewis (Mumbai: Marg, 2004); Subhash Parihar, "The Dargāh of Bābā Hājī Ratan at Bhatinda," *Islamic Studies* 40:1 (2001): 105–32; Regula Burckhardt Qureshi, "Samaᶜ in the Royal Court of Saints: The Chishtiya of South Asia," in *MSI,* 111–128; A. R. Saiyed, "Saints and Dargahs in the Indian Subcontinent: A Review," in *MSIT,* 240–56; Iqtidar Husain Siddiqui, "The Early Chishti Dargahs," in *MSIT,* 1–23.

7. For general treatments of communal foundations, see Denis Gril, "Le saint fondateur," in *Les Voies d'Allah: Les ordres mystiques en Islam,* ed. A. Popovic and G. Veinstein (Paris: Fayard, 1996); S. Babs Mala, "The Sufi Convent and Its Social Significance in the Medieval Period of Islam," *Islamic Culture* 51 (1977): 31–52.

In Spain and North Africa : Nelly Amri, "L'occupation par un saint de Tunis (IXe/XVe siècle) de sa future *zāwiya,* d'après les *manāqib* d'Ahmad b. ᶜArūs," in *SM,* 117–36; M. Kisaichi, "Sufi Saints in 12th Century Maghrib Society: Ribat and Rabita," in *Urbanism and Islam,* vol. 4; Proceedings of the International Conference on Urbanism in Islam (Tokyo: The Middle Eastern Culture Center in Japan, 1989).

In Egypt: Doris Behrens-Abouseif, "Change in Function and Form of Mamluk Religious Institutions," *Annales Islamologiques* 21 (1985): 73–93; Leonor Fernandes, "The Zawiya in Cairo," *Annales Islamologiques* 18 (1982): 116–121; Leonor Fernandes, "Some Aspects of the *Zāwiya* in Egypt/Eve of Ottoman Conquest," *Annales Islamologiques* 19 (1983): 9–17; Leonor Fernandes, "The Foundation of Baybars al-Jashankir: Its Waqf, History and Architecture," *Muqarnas* 4 (1987): 21–42; Leonor Fernandes, *The Evolution of a Sufi Institution in Mamluk Egypt: The Khanqah* (Berlin: Klaus Swarz Verlag, 1988); Th. Emil Homerin, "Saving Muslim Souls: The Khanqah and the Sufi Duty in Mamluk Lands," *Mamluk Studies Review* 3 (1999): 59–83; Donald Little, "Nature of Khanqahs, Ribats, Zawiyas under the Mamluks," in *Islamic Studies in Honor of Charles J. Adams,* ed. W. Hallaq and D. Little (Leiden: Brill, 1991).

In Turkey: Doris Behrens-Abouseif and Leonor Fernandes, "Sufi Architecture in the Early Ottoman Period," *Annales Islamologiques* 20 (1984): 103–14; Raymond Lifchez, ed., *The Dervish Lodge: Architecture, Art and Sufism in Ottoman Turkey* (Berkeley: University of California Press, 1992).

In Iran and Central Asia: Anne H. Betteridge, "Muslim Women and Shrines in Shiraz," in *Mormons and Muslims: Spiritual Foundations and Modern Manifestations,* vol. 8, Religious Studies Monograph Series, ed. S. J. Palmer (Provo, UT: Brigham Young University Press, 1983), 127–38; Margaret Malamud, "Sufi Organizations and Structures of Authority in Medieval Nishapur," *IJMES* 26 (1994): 427–42; Javad Nurbakhsh, "The Rules and Manners of the Khanaqah," in his *In the Tavern of Ruin* (New York: Khaniqahi Nimatullahi, 1975).

In South Asia: Fritz Lehmann, "The Sufi Khanqahs in Modern Bihar," in *Islam in South Asia*, vol. 1, *South Asia*, ed. Y. Friedmann (Jerusalem: Magnes/Hebrew University, 1984); Khaliq Ahmad Nizami, "Some Aspects of Khanqah Life in Medieval India," *Studia Islamica* 8 (1957): 51–70; Kerrin Gräffin Schwerin, "Functions and Sources of Income of Muslim Dargahs in India," in *Asie du Sud: tradition et changements. Vth European Conference in Modern South Asian Studies*, ed. M. Gaborieau and A. Thorner (Paris: Centre national de la recherche scientifique, 1979), 279–81.

8. Denise Aigle, "Un fondateur d'ordre en milieu rural: Le Cheikh Abū Ishāq de Kāzarūn," in *SO*, 189–98, 201–05.

9. Jamal Elias, trans., "The Autobiography of ʿAlāʾ al-Dawla al-Simnānī (1261–1336)," in *Interpreting the Self: Autobiography in the Arabic Literary Tradition*, ed. Dwight F. Reynolds (Berkeley: University of California Press, 2001), 191–92. Less interested in the institutional aspects of God's Friends, ʿAttār does not provide much information about the founding habits of the Friends in his anthology, but he does note, for example, that ʿAbd Allāh ibn Mubārak founded two hospices in Merv; *TAE* 212. See the following works on pious foundations and related themes in various contexts.

In South Asia: R. Bilgrami, "The Ajmer Wakf Under the Mughals," *Islamic Culture* 52 (1978): 97–103; Riazul Islam, "Sufism and Economy," *Indian Historical Review* 19 (1992): 31–58; S. Jafri and H. Zaheer, "Landed Properties of a Sufi Establishment," *Proceedings from the Indian History Congress 1986* (Paris: Centre national de la recherche scientifique, 1986); E. A. Mann, "Religion, Money and Status: Competition for Resources at the Shrine of Shah Jamal, Aligarh," in *MSIT*, 145–170; Schwerin, "Functions and Sources of Income," 279–81.

In Iran and Central Asia: Stephen F. Dale and Alam Payind, "The Ahrari Waqf in Kabul in the Year 1546 and the Mughul Naqshbandiyyah," *Journal of the American Oriental Society* 119:2 (1999): 218–32.

In Turkey: Suraiya Faroqhi, "Vakif Administration in Sixteenth Century Konya," *Journal of the Economic and Social History of the Orient* 17 (1979): 145–72; Suraiya Faroqhi, "Seyyed Gazi Revisited: The Foundation as Seen through Sixteenth Century Documents," *Turcica* 13 (1981): 90–122; M. Kiel, "The Türbe of Sari Saltik at Babada-Dobrudja," *Güney Doğu Abrupa Araşlirmalari Dergisi* 6–7 (1977–78): 205–25.

10. *SC* fig. 25, 36.

11. Ibid., fig. 7.2, 166

12. See, for example, texts on religious foundations in Renard, *Windows*, 223–31, 261–66. On traditions that liken the great Ottoman architect Sinan to Sufi Friends of God and even to Khidr (who discovered the water of life), see Gülru Necipoğlu, *The Age of Sinan: Architectural Culture in the Ottoman Empire* (Princeton, NJ: Princeton University Press, 2005), 144–46.

13. Devin DeWeese, "Sayyid ʿAlī Hamadānī and Kubrāwī Hagiographical Traditions," in *The Heritage of Sufism, II: The Legacy of Medieval Persian Sufism*

(1150–1500), 2nd ed., ed. Leonard Lewisohn and David Morgan (Oxford: Oneworld, 1999), 149.

14. *MAO* 41; 29–30 (quote); 37–39; 40.

15. Ibid., 552–53, 645–46, 559. For more accounts of dreams and the founding of institutions, see *VRT* 154–60.

16. *MSSA* 16.

17. Ethel Sara Wolper, *Cities and Saints: Sufism and the Transformation of Urban Space in Medieval Anatolia* (University Park: Pennsylvania State University Press, 2003), 33–35.

18. General treatments on tombs/shrines: Gilmartin, "Shrines, Succession, and Sources"; John A. Subhan, *Sufism: Its Saints and Shrines* (New York: S. Weiser, 1970).

In Spain and North Africa: Maribel Fierro, "El espacio de los muertos: fetuas andalusíes sobre tumbas y cementerios," in *L'urbanisme dans l'Occident musulman au Moyen Âge: aspects juridiques [tables rondes, Madrid, 23 et 24 juin 1997]*, ed. P. Cressier and M. Fierro (Madrid: Casa de Velázquez, 2000).

In Egypt and adjacent regions: Ulrich Braukemper, "Notes on the Islamicization and the Muslim Shrines of the Harar Plateau," in *Proceedings of the Second International Congress of Somali Studies, University of Hamburg, August 1–6, 1983*, vol. 2, *Archaeology and History* (Hamburg: H. Buske, 1984); Th. Emil Homerin, "The Domed Shrine of Ibn al-Farid," *Annales Islamologiques* 25–26 (1989–90): 125–30; Salah el-Tigani el-Humoudi, "The Arab and Islamic Origins of the Tomb and Sacred Enclave in the Sudan," *Sudan Notes and Records* 58 (1977): 107–16; E. Marx, "Tribal Pilgrimages to Saints' Tombs in South Sinai," in *Islamic Dilemmas*, ed Ernest Gellner (Berlin: Mouton, 1985); *VRT*; Caroline Williams, "The Cult of ʿAlid Saints in the Fatimid Monuments of Cairo, Part 1: The Mosque of al-Aqmar," *Muqarnas* 1 (1983): 37–52; Caroline Williams, "The Cult of ʿAlid Saints in the Fatimid Monuments of Cairo, Part 2: The Mausolea," *Muqarnas* 3 (1985): 39–60.

In Turkey: H. T. Norris, *Popular Sufism of Eastern Europe: The Seven Tombs of the Dervish Sari Saltik* (New York: RoutledgeCurzon, 2004).

In South Asia: M. Ali, "Sufi Saints in Pakistan: Main Mausoleums," *Pakistan Studies* 1:1 (1981): 101–10; Syed Hasan Askari, "The Mausoleum of a Saint of the Madari Order of Sufis at Hilsa, Bihar," *Bengal Past and Present* 68 (1949): 40–52; Fredrick W. Bunce, *Islamic Tombs in India: the Iconography and Genesis of Their Design* (New Delhi: D. K. Printworld, 2004); Patricia Jeffrey, "Creating a Scene: The Disruption of Ceremonial in a Sufi Shrine," in *Ritual and Religion among Muslims of the Sufi Sub-continent*, ed. I. Ahmad (Lahore: Vanguard, 1985); R. Kurin, "Structure of Blessedness at Muslim Shrine/Pakistan," *Middle East Studies* 19 (1983): 312–25; P. J. Lewis, "Pirs, Shrines, and Pakistani Islam," *Al-Mushir* 26 (1984): 1–22; J. Lewis, "The Shrine Cult in Historical Perspective," *Al-Mushir* 26 (1984): 54–74; B. Pfleiderer, "Mira Datar Dargah: The Psychiatry of a Muslim Shrine," in *Ritual and Religion Among Muslims in India*, ed. I. Ahmad (Delhi: Manohar, 1981), 193–233; *MSIT*.

In Iran and Central Asia: J. L. Bourgeois, "Afghan Muslim Shrines," *Architectural Review* 168 (1980): 367–69; Masami Hamada, "Islamic Saints and their Mausolea," *Acta Asiatica (Supplement): Bulletin of the Institute of Eastern Culture (Tokyo)* 34 (1978): 79–105; R. D. McChesney, "Architecture and Narrative: The Khwaja Abu Nasr Parsa Shrine—Part 1: Constructing the Complex and Its Meaning, 1469–1696," *Muqarnas* 18 (2001): 94–118; "Architecture and Narrative: The Khwaja Abu Nasr Parsa Shrine—Part 2: Representing the Complex in Word and Image, 1696–1998," *Muqarnas* 19 (2002): 78–107; Maria E. Subtelny, "The Cult of Holy Places: Religious Practices among Soviet Muslims," *Middle East Journal* 43:4 (1989): 593–604; Hongxun Yang, "A Preliminary Discussion on the Building Year of Quanzhou Holy Tomb and the Authenticity of Its Legend," in *The Islamic Historic Relics in Quanzhou*, ed. Committee for Protecting Islamic Historic Relics (Quanzhou: Fujian People's Publishing House, 1985).

In Southeast Asia: John R. Bowen, "Shrines and Power in a Highland Sumatran Society," in *MSI*, 1–14; Denys Lombard, "Autour de la tombe de Kiyayi Telingsing," in *CSMM*, 261–66.

19. Marc Gaborieau, "Cult of the Saints among Muslims of Nepal and Northern India," in *Saints and their Cults*, ed. S. Wilson (Cambridge: Cambridge University Press, 1983), 293–95.

20. Summarized from Desiderio Pinto, "The Mystery of the Nizamuddin Dargah: The Accounts of Pilgrims," in *MSIT*, 112–24.

21. Abū 'l-Hasan al-Harawī (d. 611/1215), *Guide des lieux de Pèlerinage*, ed. Janine Sourdel-Thomine (Damascus: Institut Français, 1953).

22. *VRT* 71–76; see also Josef W. Meri, "The Etiquette of Devotion in the Islamic Cult of Saints," in *The Cult of Saints in Late Antiquity and the Middle Ages*, ed. James Howard-Johnston and Paul A. Hayward (Oxford: Oxford University Press, 1999), 263–85. For other aspects of the cult of Friends, see Marc Gaborieau, "A Nineteenth-Century Indian 'Wahhabi' Tract against the Cult of Muslim Saints," in *MSIT*, 198–239; Marc Gaborieau, "Le culte des saints musulmans en tant que ritual: controverses juridiques," *Archives de sciences sociales des religions* 85 (1994): 85–97.

23. Wolper, *Cities and Saints*, 4 (quote). On related themes in a later Turkish context, see Zeynep Yürekli, "A Building between the Public and Private Realms of the Ottoman Elite: The Sufi Convent of Sokollu Mehmed Pasha in Istanbul," *Muqarnas* 20 (2003): 159–86. The works that follow are additional studies on Friends and the political establishment.

In South Asia: S. F. D. Ansari, *Sufi Saints and State Power* (Cambridge: Cambridge University Press, 1992); Simon Digby, "The Sufi Shaykh and the Sultan: A Conflict of Claims to Authority in Medieval India," *Iran* 28 (1990):71–81; Richard M. Eaton, "Court of Man, Court of God: Local Perceptions of the Shrine of Bābā Farīd, Pakpattan, Punjab," in *Islam in Local Contexts*, ed. Richard Martin (Leiden: Brill, 1982), 44–61; Richard M. Eaton, "The Political and Religious Authority of the Shrine of Bābā Farīd," in Metcalf, *Moral Conduct* and *Authority*, 333–56; Robert Hillenbrand, "Political Symbolism in Early Indo-Muslim Architecture: The Case of Ajmir," *Iran* 26 (1988): 105–17; M. Salim, "The Attitude of Chishti Saints Towards Political Power," *Proceedings of the Pakistan Historical Conference* 2 (1952): 225–29; Alex Weingrod, "Saints and Shrines, Politics and Culture," in *Muslim Travelers*, ed. Dale Eickelman and James Piscatori (Berkeley: University of California Press, 1990).

In Central Asia: Bakhtiyor Babajanov, "Mawlānā Lutfullāh Chūshtī: An Outline of His Hagiography and Political Activity," *Zeitschrift der Deutschen Morgenländischen Gesellschaft* 149 (1999): 245–70; Thierry Zarcone, "Quand le saint légitime le politique: le mausolée d'Afaq Khwâja à Kashgar," *Central Asian Survey* 18 (1999): 225–41.

24. DeWeese argues that a second institutional function of hagiographical accounts is to establish beyond doubt the lineages or spiritual pedigrees of individual Sufis who may have lived great distances in time and space from an order's founder and direct heirs to his authority. See the following studies by DeWeese: "Sacred Places and Public Narratives: The Shrine of Ahmad Yasavī in Hagiographical Traditions of the Yasavī Sūfī Order, 16th–17th Centuries," *The Muslim World* 90:3–4 (2000); "Sayyid ʿAlī Hamadānī and Kubrāwī Hagiographical Traditions"; "The Yasavī Order and Persian Hagiography in Seventeenth-Century Central Asia: ʿĀlim Shaykh of ʿAlīyābād and His *Lamahāt min nafahāt al-quds*," in *The Heritage of Sufism, III: Late Classical Persianate Sufism (1501–1750)*, 2nd ed., ed. Leonard Lewisohn and David Morgan (Oxford: Oneworld, 1999), 389–414; "The *Masha'ikh-i Turk* and the *Khojagan*: Rethinking the Links between the Yasawi and Naqshbandi Sufi Traditions," *Journal of Islamic Studies* 7 (1996): 180–207; and "The Politics of Sacred Lineages in 19th Century Central Asia: Descent Groups Linked to Khwaja Ahmad Yasavī in Shrine Documents and Genealogical Charters," *IJMES* 31:4 (1999): 507–30. For a study of analogous developments in a different context, see Rachida Chih, "Les débuts d'une *tarīqa*. Formation et essor de la Khalwatiyya égyptienne au XVIIIe siècle d'après l'hagiographie de son fondateur, Muhammad ibn Sālim al-Hifnī (m. 1181/1767)," in *SM*, 137–50.

CHAPTER 8: WHERE GOD'S FRIENDS WALKED

1. Abraham Lincoln, "First Inaugural Address," in *The Collected Works of Abraham Lincoln*, ed. Roy P. Basler (New Brunswick, NJ: Rutgers University Press, 1953), 4:271. Lincoln uses the metaphor to connect "every battle-field, and patriot grave, to every living heart and hearthstone," for the chords will be touched again by "the better angels of our nature."

2. The principal differences are that the ʿUmra involves much less time and simpler ritual activities in and around Mecca and can be accomplished at any time of year, whereas the hajj properly occurs only during a specific "season," from the eighth to thirteenth days of the twelfth lunar month.

3. G. E. von Grünebaum, "The Sacred Character of Islamic Cities," in *Mélanges Taha Husain*, ed. A. al-Badawī (Cairo: Dār al-Maʿārif, 1962), 26.

4. Josef W. Meri, *The Cult of Saints Among Muslims and Jews in Medieval Syria* (New York: Oxford University Press, 2002), 142; R. Sellheim on "Fadīla" in *EI2*, 728–29; Amikam Elad, *Medieval Jerusalem and Islamic Worship: Holy Places, Ceremonies, Pilgrimage* (Leiden: Brill, 1995), 6–22 and passim; and Izhak Hasson, "The Muslim View of Jerusalem: The Qurʾān and Hadīth," in *The History of Jerusalem*, ed. J. Prawer and H. Ben-Shammai (New York: New York University Press, 1996), 349–85.

5. *QKT* 61–67; *QTB* 60, 67. Thaʿlabī says that Adam made pilgrimage forty times from India, the land of his origin, and does not link Adam explicitly with the building of the Kaʿba; instead he emphasizes God's direct creation of the House; *QTB* 146–48.

6. *QKT* 99–100, 103; *QTB* 99.

7. *QKT* 151–54; Thaʿlabī includes variant details, such as Gabriel's bringing forth Zamzam by a thrust of his foot and Abraham's retrieval of the Black Stone from Mount Abū Qubays, where God had stored it safely away from the flood; *QTB* 135–54.

8. *QTB* 496–97, 520. Some sources place Iskandar (Alexander the Great), also known as Dhū 'l-Qarnayn (the One with Two Horns) and listed among the prophets, in Mecca as a pilgrim.

9. *SIG* 84–85, 552, 650–52. Thaʿlabī sets much of the story of the prophet Hūd in Mecca and locates his grave there; Kisāʾī focuses less on the Meccan connection and has him buried in Hadramawt, a region spanning the southeast end of the Arabian Peninsula; *QTB* 104–13; *QKT* 113, 116.

10. *TAE* 75–76

11. *MAO* 199–200.

12. *TAE* 105–6. In *HKR* 114, Ibrāhīm took four years to reach Mecca because he encountered the devil disguised as an old man, who tried to discourage him by reminding him he was without food and water. Ibrāhīm resolved to do four hundred ritual prostrations every mile of the way, as a token of his trust in God to provide sustenance.

13. *TAE* 132–33. The story's use in a letter by Ibn ʿAbbād in Morocco, for example, illustrates the widespread popularity of stories of this sort. ʿAttār wrote in Persian two thousand miles to the east a century earlier; Ibn ʿAbbad obtained a somewhat more detailed version from Arabic sources; John Renard, trans., *Ibn ʿAbbād of Ronda: Letters on the Sūfī Path* (Mahwah, NJ: Paulist, 1986), 117.

14. *TAE* 109–10.

15. Ibid., 162–63, 184–85.

16. Ibid., 91–92, 95.

17. Ibid., 123–24.

18. Ibid., 125; *HSIJ* 139–45. *RQH* 440 tells a variation of the pomegranate-tree story, placing it along the road to Jerusalem; in this version, the travelers note that the stunted tree has returned to full health as they pass by on their return journey. The tree became known as the Tree of Worshippers because devout people sheltered beneath it; *RQH* 440. Other stories of Ibrāhīm at Mecca appear in *RQH* 18–19.

19. *TAE* 213–14.

20. *SSM* 486–88.

21. *TAE* 396.

22. *QKT* 304, 321, 330; Elad, *Medieval Jerusalem*, 82–96.

23. Elad, *Medieval Jerusalem*, 111.

24. G. E. von Gruenebaum, *Muhammadan Festivals* (New York: Olive Branch Press,1988), 81–83.

25. See, for example, the story in *MAO* 645, which I cite in chapter 7 in the tale of the visitor to Rūmī's grandson.

26. Elad, *Medieval Jerusalem*, 151–52, 171.

27. Ibid., 145; Rkia Cornell, trans., *Early Sufi Women* (Louisville, KY: Fons Vitae, 1999), 144; *NUJ* 616, 620–21; Javad Nurbakhsh, *Sufi Women* (London: Khaniqahi Nimatullahi, 2004), 57, 66, 88, 109.

28. See, for example, Titus Burckhardt, *Fez, City of Islam* (Cambridge: Islamic Texts Society, 1992); also A. Sebti, "Hagiographie de voyage au Maroc Mèdieval," *Al-Qantara* 13 (1992): 167–79; W. M. J. van Bingsbergen, "The Cult of Saints in North-Western Tunisia; an Analysis of Contemporary Pilgrimage Structures," in *Islamic Dilemmas*, ed. Ernest Gellner (Berlin: Mouton, 1985), 199–239.

29. *SC* 232–33.

30. Ibid., especially 49, 231–43; see figs. 4.19 and 5.30 (121, 143) for visual conflation of the two sacred sites. See also E. Ross, "Touba: A Spiritual Metropolis in the Modern World," *Canadian Journal of African Studies* 29:2 (1995): 222–59.

31. *VRT* 56–57.

32. Ibid., 66. The identities of the inhabitants of these graves vary from one pilgrimage guide to another.

33. Ibid., 20, 27, 34, passim.

34. Ibid., 51.

35. Th. Emil Homerin, *From Arab Poet to Muslim Saint* (Columbia: University of South Carolina Press, 1994), 87–92.

36. Valerie Hoffman, *Sufis, Mystics, and Saints in Modern Egypt* (Columbia: University of South Carolina Press, 1995), 76–77, 86–87, 106–7, 244–45, and passim; R. Strothmann, "Nafīsa," in *EI2*, 7:879. See also Louis Massignon, "La cité des morts au Caire (Qarafa, Darb al-ahmar)," *Bulletin d'Institut Française d'Archaeologie Orientale* 57 (1958): 25–79.

37. Frederick M. Denny, *An Introduction to Islam*, 2nd ed. (New York: Macmillan, 1994), 252.

38. On other sites in the environs of Egypt, see E. Marx, "Tribal Pilgrimages to Saints' Tombs in South Sinai," in Gellner, *Islamic Dilemmas*, 104–31.

39. Meri, *Cult of Saints*, 29–47; Elizabeth Sirriya, "*Ziyārāt* of Syria in a *Rihla* of ʿAbd al-Ghanī al-Nābulusī (1050/1641–1143/1731)," *Journal of the Royal Asiatic Society of Great Britain and Ireland* (1979): 109–13.

40. See Yitzhak Nakkash, *The Shiʿis of Iraq* (Princeton, NJ: Princeton University Press, 1994), especially ch. 6, "Pilgrimage to the Shrine Cities and the Cult of the Saints," 163–83; also Louis Massignon, "Les saints musulmans enterrés à Bagdad," *Revue de l'Histoire des Religions* 58:1 (1908): 329–38.

41. Hoffman, *Sufism, Mystics and Saints*, 73–75.

42. Carl W. Ernst, *Eternal Garden: Mysticism, History, and Politics at a South Asian Sufi Center* (Albany, NY: SUNY Press, 1994). See also Marcia K. Hermansen, "Citing the Sights of the Holy Sites: Visionary Pilgrimage Narratives of Pre-Modern South Asian Sufis," in *The Shaping of an American Islamic Discourse*, ed. E. Waugh and F. Denny (Atlanta: Scholars, 1998), 189–214.

43. *MSSA* 64–70; *SML* 149–50, 152; P. M. Currie, *The Shrine and Cult of Muꜥin ad-Dīn Chishtī of Ajmer* (Delhi: Oxford University Press, 1992): especially 97–140. For more on this topic in South Asia, see: Syed Liyaqat Hussain Moini, "Rituals and Customary Practices at the Dargah of Ajmer," in *MSIT*, 60–75; see also Muhammad Sadiq Dihlawi Kashmiri Hamadani, *The Kalimat as-sadiqin: A Hagiography of Sufis Buried at Delhi until 1614 A.D.*, 2nd ed. (New Delhi: Kitab Bhavan, 1990); Yoginder Sikand, "Ritual and Popular Piety at the ꜥUrs of a Qalandar Dargah in South India," *Journal of the Henry Martyn Institute* 19:1 (2000): 91–103.

44. *Mandala*, originally from the Sanskrit, refers to circles of spiritual power in Hindu and Buddhist traditions. Here the term refers to an area of spiritual potency around a saintly center.

45. Claude Guillot, "The Tembayat Hill: Clergy and Royal power in Central Java from the 15th to the 17th Century," in *PD*, 141–59.

46. For more on the role of Friends in Indonesia, see Henri Chambert-Loir, "Saints and Ancestors: The Cult of Muslim Saints in Java," in *PD*, 132–40; Henri Chambert-Loir and C. Guillot, "Le culte des saints musulmans à Java: Rapport de mission," *La Transmission du savoir dans le monde musulman périphérique* 11 (1991): 9–16; C. Guillot and Henri Chambert-Loir, "Pèlerinage aux Neuf Saints de Java," in *LI*, 203–22. See also H. Chambert-Loir and C. Guillot, "Pèlerinage sur la tombe de Sunan Muria (Colo, Java Central)," *Archipel* 45 (1993): 97–110; James J. Fox, "Ziarah Visits to the Tombs of the Wali, the Founders of Islam on Java," in *Islam in the Indonesian Social Context*, ed. M. C. Ricklefs (Clayton, Australia: Centre of Southeast Asian Studies, Monash University, 1991), 20–38.

47. Summarized from Syed Liyaqat Hussain Moini, "Rituals and Customary Practices at the Dargah of Ajmer," in *MSIT*, 60–75; and Currie, *Shrine and Cult*, 117–63. See also *SML*, especially 85–104, and *MSSA* 70–78 for more on ritual and sacred space at tomb sites.

CHAPTER 9: FRIENDS IN OUR WORLD

1. See, for example, Thierry Zarcone, Ekrem Isin, and Arthur Buehler, eds., *The Qadiriya Order*, vols. 1 and 2 of the annual *Journal of the History of Sufism* (Paris: Maisonneuve, 2000).

2. See, for example, Laurent Metzger, "Le mausolée Habib Noh à Singapour," *Cahiers de Littérature Orale* 49 (2001): 155–65.

3. See *HAI* and *TAE* (2004).

4. See, for example, Syed Hasan Askari, "Contemporary Biography of a Fifteenth-Century Sufi Saint of Bihar," *Indian Historical Records Commission Proceedings* 27:2 (1950): 108–14.

5. I propose the categories here (civic, intellectual, and spiritual) purely for general illustrative purposes, recognizing that considerable overlap exists between them; see Abū 'l-Hasan ʿAlī Nadwī, *Saviours of Islamic Spirit* (Lucknow: Islamic Research and Publications, 1971): citing ix–xiii.

6. See, for example, Michel Chodkiewicz, "La 'Somme des miracles des saints' de Yūsuf Nabhānī," in *MK*, 607–22.

7. See, for example, boxed sets such as *The Life of Muhammad, Mothers of the Believers: Lives of the Wives of Prophet Muhammad*, and *Imām Abū Hanūfa* (Islamic Personalities Series), available online at sites such as www.awakeningusa.com.

8. See *SC*, especially 98–99.

9. Similar observations apply to other two-dimensional images that have historically (though more rarely in recent times) illustrated hagiographical texts or appeared independent of text in albums of miniature paintings and calligraphy. See Cynthia Hahn, "Word and Image: Narrative Problems in Pictorial Hagiography," in her *Portrayed on the Heart: Narrative Effect in Pictorial Lives of Saints from the Tenth through the Thirteenth Century* (Berkeley: University of California Press, 2001), 29–58.

10. See Jürgen Frembgen, "Saints in Modern Devotional Poster-Portraits," *Anthropology and Aesthetics RES* 34 (1988): 184–91.

11. *SC;* and Mohamed Masmoudi, *La peinture sous-verre en Tunisie* (Tunis: Ceres, 1972); see also Zaʾim Khenchelaoui, "Quelques remarques sur la place et l'iconographie de ʿAbd al-Qādir al-Jilānī dans le folklore algérien," *Journal of Historical Studies* 1–2 (2000): 431–41.

12. See Peter Chelkowski, *Taʿziyeh: Ritual and Drama in Iran* (New York: New York University Press, 1979); Samuel Peterson, "The Taʿziyeh and Related Arts," in *Studies in the Art and Literature of the Near East*, ed. Peter Chelkowski (Salt Lake City: University of Utah Press, 1979), 64–87.

13. See Peter Chelkowski and Hamid Dabashi, *Staging a Revolution: The Art of Persuasion in the Islamic Republic of Iran* (New York: New York University Press, 1999), especially 38–65; Shiva Balaghi and Lynn Gumpert, eds., *Picturing Iran: Art, Society and Revolution* (London: I. B. Tauris, 2002); and William Hanaway, "The Symbolism of Persian Revolutionary Posters," in *Iran Since the Revolution*, ed. Barry Rosen (Boulder: Social Science Monographs, 1985), 31–50.

14. *SC*, especially 123–49. Thanks to Allen Roberts for alerting me to a recent development in "lenticular" images of Amadou Bamba and related subjects, producing holographlike 3-D effects when the viewer shifts the image side to side, so that one image seems to morph into another.

15. Thanks to Marcia Hermansen for this information. See also such internet resources as www.sacredsites.com.

16. See *SC* 98–107 for this and similar stories; see also David Robinson, "Beyond Resistance and Collaboration: Amadu Bamba and the Murids of Senegal," *Journal of Religion in Africa* 21 (1991): 149–71.

17. Thierry Zarcone, "The Sufi Networks in Southern Xinjiang during the Republican Regime (1911–1949): An Overview," in *Islam in Politics in Russia and Central Asia (Early 18th — Late 20th Centuries)*, ed. S. A. Dudoignon and H. Komatsu (London: Kegan Paul, 2001), 119–32; and Thierry Zarcone, "Le Culte des Saints au Xinjiang de 1949 à nos jours," *Journal of Historical Studies* 3 (2001): 133–72.

18. In the Buddhist structure stands a *stupa* that purportedly enshrines the ashes of the Buddha, marking the place where he foretold his coming entry into *nirvana*. Vaishali is also the birthplace of the "founder" of Jainism and one of the main "fords" or spiritual crossing-places.

19. See Catherine Servan-Schreiber, "Partage de sites et partage de texts: un modèle d'acculturation de l'islam au Bihar," in *Altérité et identité: Islam et Christianisme en Inde*, ed. J. Assayag and G. Tarabout (Paris: Collection Purusartha [19], 1996), 143–70. Also on the Bihari context, see Catherine Champion, "'Les Meilleurs saints sont musulmans.' La figure de Hātim comme modèle de sainteté dans l'hagiographie islamique indienne: L'exemple du Bihar," in *CHMI*, 385–98. For important research on analogous dynamics in other parts of South Asia, see: Marc Gaborieau, "Cult of the Saints among Muslims of Nepal and Northern India," in *Saints and their Cults*, ed. S. Wilson (Cambridge: Cambridge University Press, 1983), 291–308; Dominique-Sila Khan, "Jāmbhā, fondateur de la sect des Bisnoi au Rajasthan: de l'islam ismaélien à la devotion hindoue," in *CHMI*, 337–64; J. Assayag, "La deésse et le saint: Acculturation et 'communalism' hindou musulman dans un lieu du culte du Sud de l'Inde (Karnataka)," *Annales ESC* 4:5 (1992): 789–813; J. Assayag, "Pouvoir contre 'puissances': Bref essai de démonologie hindoue-musulmane," *L'Homme* 34:131 (1994): 39–55; M. Searle-Chatterjee, "The Muslim Hero as Defender of Hindus: Mythic Reversals and Ethnicity among Banaras Muslims," in "Person, Myth and Society in South Asian Islam," ed. P. Werbner, special issue, *Social Analysis* 28 (1990): 70–79; Stephen F. Dale and Gandadhara Menon, "Nerccas: Saint-Martyr Worship among the Muslims of Kerala," *Bulletin of the Schools of Oriental and African Studies* 41:3 (1978): 523–38.

20. Summarized from Valerie J. Hoffman, "Un cheikh soufi peut-il être un héros moderne? Le cas du cheikh Ahmad Radwān (Egypte)," in *SHMC*, 177–88. For an account of another important, slightly more recent "new Friend of God" (1911–1998), see Rachida Chih and Catherine Mayeur-Jaouen, "Le cheikh Sha῾rāwī et la television: l'homme qui a donné un visage au Coran," in *SHMC*, 189–209.

21. Summarized from Denis Matringe, "La création d'un saint et ses enjeux dans le Panjab pakistanais," in *CHMI*, 399–415. On the story of another contemporary Friend of the Panjab, Muhammad Sadiq (1936–93), see Syed Ishfaq Ali, *The Saints of the Punjab* (Rawalpindi: Pap Board, 1994), 116–26. See also Jürgen Frembgen, "From Dervish to Saint: Constructing Charisma in

Contemporary Pakistan," *The Muslim World* 94 (2004): 245–57, on the rise of various recent local Pakistani figures to the rank of Friend.

22. See, for example, Sossie Andezian, *Expériences du divin dans l'Algérie contemporaine: Adeptes des saints dans la region de Tlemcen* (Paris: CNRS, 2001).

23. In a variation on this first theme, Muslim public figures not clearly associated with traditional institutions can also be elevated through a grassroots movement in which people come to see the individual's spiritual acumen and power—as measured against ostensibly classic norms. One intriguing contemporary religious figure who is currently generating tremendous public interest in Indonesia is ʿAbd Allāh Gymnastiar, better known simply as Aa Gym (b. 1382/1962). Many of his constituents think of him as a *kiai*, a religious scholar with transcendent awareness who can bestow power and blessing on those who seek his tutelage. I thank Anna Gade for this lead.

24. Here I have relied on Henri Chambert-Loir, "Saints and Ancestors: The Cult of Muslim Saints in Java," in *PD*, 132–40; James J. Fox, "Ziarah Visits to the Tombs of the Wali, the Founders of Islam on Java," in *Islam in the Indonesian Social Context*, ed. M. C. Ricklefs (Clayton, Australia: Centre of Southeast Asian Studies, Monash University, 1991), 20–38; and James J. Fox, "Sunan Kalijaga and the Rise of Mataram: A Reading of the *Babad Tanah Jawi* as a Genealogical Narrative," in *Islam: Essays on Scripture, Thought and Society: A Festschrift in Honour of Anthony H. Johns*, ed. P. Riddell and A. Street (Leiden: Brill, 1997), 187–215.

25. Minako Sakai, "Modernising sacred sites in South Sumatra: Islamisation of Gumai Ancestral Places," in *PD*, 103–16.

26. Christian Pelras, "Ancestors' Blood: Genealogical Memory, Genealogical Amnesia and Hierarchy among the Bugis," in *PD*, 117–31. For other aspects of the process of Islamization, see Claude Guillot, "The Tembayat Hill: Clergy and Royal Power in Central Java from the 15th to the 17th Century," in *PD*, 141–59; Michael Feener, "Shaykh Yusuf and the Appreciation of Muslim Saints in Modern Indonesia," *Journal of Islamic Studies* 18–19 (1998–99): 112–31.

27. For more on this perspective on the story of Brawijaya, see James J. Fox, "Interpreting the Historical Significance of Tombs and Chronicles in Contemporary Java," in *PD*, 160–72.

28. Elias Fekih, "Bourguiba, héros national et 'saint laïque' de l'islam contemporain," in *SHMC*, 103–20. Fekih includes a detailed description of Bourguiba's funeral and heroic status post mortem, interpreting the appearance of the naked, almost manic Friend in Bourguiba's dream as a nocturnal continuation of a conflict begun during the waking state, and as a symbol of Bourguiba's inability to deal with his own confusion and ensuing depression. In short, though Bourguiba considered the saint an example of holy folly, at best, the Friend represented Bourguiba's "shadow" and symbol of his irrational side.

29. For studies of contemporary Friends in a variety of other geographic and cultural contexts, see the following works.

In North Africa: Leslie Cadavid, trans., *Two Who Attained* (Louisville: Fons Vitae, 2005); Martin Lings, *A Sufi Saint of the Twentieth Century: Shaykh Ahmad al-ᶜAlawī, His Spiritual Heritage and Legacy* (Berkeley: University of California Press, 1973); M. A. Marcus, " 'The Saint Has Been Stolen': Sanctity and Social Change in a Tribe of Eastern Morocco," *American Ethnologist* 12 (1985): 455–67; Mohamed Brahim Salhi, "Entre subversion et résistance: l'autorité des saints dans l'Algérie du milieu du XXe siècle," in *ASK*, 305–22; D. G. Hatt, "A Tribal Saint of the Twentieth Century," in *An African Commitment: Papers in Honour of Peter Lewis Shinnie*, ed. Judy Sterner and Nicholas David (Calgary: University of Calgary Press, 1992), 3–30.

In the central Middle East: Catherine Mayeur-Jaouen, "Introduction. Grands hommes, héros, saints et martyrs: figures du sacré et du politique dans le Moyen-Orient du XXe siècle," in *SHMC*, 5–34; Étienne Copeaux, "La transcendence d'Atatürk," in *SHMC*, 121–37; Thierry Zarcone, "La fabrication des saints sou la République turque," in *SHMC*, 211–27.

In Central Asia and China: Aširbek K. Mumimov, "Veneration of Holy Sites of the Mid-Sïrdar'ya Valley: Continuity and Transformation," in *Muslim Culture in Russia and Central Asia from the 18th to the Early 20th Centuries*, ed. M. Kemper, A. von Kügelgen, and D. Yermakov (Berlin: K. Schwarz, 1996), 355–67; Ho-Dong Kim, "The Cult of Saints in Eastern Turkestan: The Case of Alp Ata in Turfan," in *Proceedings of the 35th PIAC—1992* (Taipei: n.p., 1993), 199–226.

CHAPTER 10: LITERARY DIMENSIONS

1. See John Renard, *Islam and the Heroic Image: Themes in Literature and the Visual Arts* (Columbia: University of South Carolina Press, 1993), 14–23, on this dual dynamic.

2. See, for example, Brannon Wheeler, *Moses in the Qurᵓān and Islamic Exegesis* (London: RoutledgeCurzon, 2002), 56–64; and Scott B. Noegel and Brannon M. Wheeler, *Historical Dictionary of Prophets in Islam and Judaism* (Lanham, MD: Scarecrow, 2002), 303–5.

3. Qurᵓān 6:25, 8:31, 16:24, 23:83, 25:5, 27:68, 46:17, 68:15, and 83:13. See, for example, Dundes, *Fables of the Ancients?* on oral formula and related theory.

4. See Dwight F. Reynolds, ed., *Interpreting the Self: Autobiography in the Arabic Literary Tradition* (Berkeley: University of California Press, 2001), especially 36–51.

5. On Abū Tālib, see Renard, *Knowledge of God in Classical Sufism* (Mahwah, NJ: Paulist, 2004), 164–90; on Ibn al-Jawzi, see Merlin L. Schwartz, ed. and trans., *Kitāb al-qussās wa'l-mudhakkirīn* (Beirut: Dār el-Machreq, 1986).

6. See *SSD* for full translation.

7. Abū Yaᶜqūb Yūsuf ibn Yahyā at-Tādilī, a.k.a. Ibn az-Zayyāt, *At-Tashawwuf ilā rijāl at-tasawwuf*, ed. Ahmad at-Tawfīq (Rabat: Faculty of Literature and the

Humanities, 1984), 54–81; see also *NUJ* 21–27; and Éric Geoffroy, "Hagiographie et typologie spirituelle,"in *SO*, 89, for more on distinctions of genre.

8. On the relationship of hagiography to the larger category of historiography, see Chase Robinson's tripartite categorization of biography, prosopography, and chronography. Elements of hagiography, as I use the term throughout this volume, occur in all three of Robinson's categories; Chase Robinson, *Islamic Historiography* (New York: Cambridge University Press, 2003), 55–79.

9. These hagiographies include *RSG, SAA, SSM,* and *MAO*.

10. See also Jean-Jacques Thibon, "Hiérarchie spirituelle, functions du saint et hagiographie dans l'oeuvre de Sulamī," in *SM,* 13–32. On a related topic, see Tarif Khalidi, "Islamic Biographical Dictionaries: A Preliminary Assessment," *The Muslim World* 63 (1973): 53–65.

11. For the most detailed English study of the genre, see Jawid Mojaddedi, *The Biographical Tradition in Sufism: The Tabaqat Genre from al-Sulami to Jami* (Surrey, England: Curzon, 2001); see also Ibrahim Hafsi, "Recherches sur le genre '*Tabaqāt*' dans la littérature Arabe," *Arabica* 23:3 (1976): 227–65 and 24:1 (1977): 1–41. In general, one might reasonably conclude that the "generations" genre, with its concern for classification and chronology and its typically restrained approach to elements of the marvelous, is historiography en route to becoming hagiography. Some scholars suggest that whereas many earlier sources gather material about Friends from across Islamdom, latter works often limit their coverage geographically or institutionally, focusing on Friends from a particular town or region or on those who belonged to specific legal schools or Sufi orders.

12. On the *tadhkira* genre, see Marcia Hermansen, "Religious Literature and the Inscription of Identity: The Sufi Tazkira Tradition in Muslim South Asia," *The Muslim World* 87:3–4 (1997): 315–29; Marcia Hermansen and Bruce Lawrence, "Indo-Persian Tazkiras as Memorative Communications," in *Beyond Turk and Hindu: Rethinking Religious Identities in Islamicate South Asia,* ed. David Gilmartin and Bruce B. Lawrence (Gainesville: University of Florida Press, 2000), 149–75. Related works meant for a narrower public include the Persian *Assemblies of the Lovers (Majālis al-ʿUshshāq)* and Hilālī's *Qualities of the Lovers (Sifāt al-ʿāshiqīn),* and Fuzūlī's Turkish *Garden of the Felicitous (Hadīqat as-Suʿadāʾ).*

13. *SAA* and *SSM*.

14. See RSG passim.

15. For more on the beginnings and evolution of hagiographical literature, especially the full-biographical type, see Denise Aigle, "Sainteté et miracles en islam médiévale: l'exemple de deux saints fondateurs iraniens," in *Miracles, prodiges et merveilles au Moyen Âge* (Paris: Sorbonne, 1995), 47–73; and Thierry Zarcone, "L'hagiographie dans le monde turc," in *SO,* 55–67. See also Michel Chodkiewicz, "Le sainteté feminine dans l'hagiographie islamique" (99–115); and D. Gril, "Le miracle en islam, critère de la sainteté?" (77–80), both in *SO,* to compare the two lives of Shādhilī.

16. Bruce Lawrence, *Notes from a Distant Flute* (Tehran: Imperial Iranian Academy of Philosophy, 1978), 27–28.

17. For more on the *malfūzāt* form in India, see Syed Hasan Askari, "Tazkira-i Murshīdī, a rare Malfuz of the Fifteenth Century Sufi Saint of Gulbarga," *Indian Historical Congress Proceedings* 15 (1952): 179–89; Khaliq Ahmad Nizami, "Historical Significance of Malfuz Literature of Medieval India," in his *On History and Historians of Medieval India* (Delhi: Munshiram Manoharlal, 1983). See also Bruce B. Lawrence, "Biography in the 17th century Qādirīya of North India," in *Islam and Indian Regions,* vol. 1, ed. A. L. Dallapiccola and S. Zingel-Ave Lallamant (Stuttgart: Franz Steiner, 1993), 399–415. For a similar work on Sharaf ad-Dīn Maneri, see Paul Jackson, trans., *Khwān-i pur niʿmat: A Table Laden with Good Things* (Delhi: Idarah-i Adabiyat-i Delli, 1986).

18. See, for example, *Signs of the Unseen: The Discourses of Jalaluddin Rumi,* intro. and trans. W. M. Thackston, Jr. (Putney, VT: Threshold, 1994).

19. Tirmidhī, *The Concept of Sainthood in Early Islamic Mysticism: Two Works by al-Hakīm al-Tirmidhī,* trans. Bernd Radtke and John O'Kane (London: Curzon, 1996).

20. See further, Cemal Kafadar, "Self and Others: The Diary of a Dervish in Seventeenth Century Istanbul and First-Person Narratives in Ottoman Literature," *Studia Islamica* 69 (1989): 121–50; and Louis Pouzet, "Remarques sur l'autobiographie dans le monde arabo-musulman au Moyen-Âge," in *Philosophy and the Arts in the Islamic World,* ed. U. Vermeulen and D. de Smet (Leuven: Peeters, 1998), 91–107.

21. Jean-Louis Michon, *The Autobiography (Fahrasa) of a Moroccan Sufi: Ahmad ibn ʿAjiba,* trans. David Streight (Louisville, KY: Fons Vitae, 1999).

22. For analysis of six examples of the type, see Jonathan Katz, "Visionary Experience, Autobiography, and Sainthood in North African Islam, *Princeton Papers in Near Eastern Studies* 1 (1992): 85–118.

23. Leili Anvar-Chenderoff, "La genre hagiographique à travers la *tadhkirat al-awliyāʾ* de Farīd al-dīn ʿAttār," in *SO,* 39–53; my translation from 39.

24. See ibid., 41–48, on didactic and poetic functions and the relationships between miracle and metaphor.

25. Heshmat Moayyad and Franklin Lewis, trans., *The Colossal Elephant and His Spiritual Feats: Shaykh Ahmad-e Jam: The Life and Legend of a Popular Sufi Saint of 12th Century Iran* (Costa Mesa, CA: Mazda, 2004), citing 69–70.

26. Ibid., 68–409, quoting from 68–73.

27. Ibid., 71.

28. S. Soebardi, ed. and trans., *The Book of Cabolek* (The Hague: Martinus Nijhoff, 1975), 73.

29. Franz Rosenthal, *A History of Muslim Historiography* (Leiden: Brill, 1952), 216.

30. Thaʿlabī's comments bring to mind the observation of the biblical Book of Wisdom that "passing into holy souls from age to age, she [Wisdom] produces friends of God and prophets," Wisdom 7:27.

31. *QTB* 3–5.

32. Zeren Tanindi, *Siyer-i Nebi* (Istanbul: Hurriyet Foundation, 1974), 10.

33. Abū 'l-Hasan ad-Daylamī, *Sīrat-i Abū ʿAbdallāh ibn Khafīf ash-Shīrāzī*, ed. Annemarie Schimmel (Ankara: Turk Tarih Kurumu Basimevi, 1955), 36; and A. Schimmel, "Ibn Khafīf: An Early Representative of Sufism," *Journal of the Pakistan Historical Society* 6 (1958): 147–73; A. Schimmel, "Zur Biographie des Abu ʿAbdallah ibn Chafif ash-Shirazi," *Welt des Orients* 2:1 (1955): 193–99.

34. Mahmūd ibn ʿUthmān, *Firdaws al-murshīdīya fī asrār as-samadīya*, ed. Fritz Meier (Leipzig: F. A. Brockhaus, 1948); Fritz Meier, *Die Vita des Abu Ishaq al-Kazaruni* (Leipzig: F. A. Brockhaus, 1948); A. J. Arberry, "The Biography of Shaikh Abu Ishaq al-Kazaruni," *Oriens* 3 (1950): 163–72.

35. Muhammad ibn-i Munawwar, *Asrār at-tawhīd*, trans. John O'Kane (Costa Mesa, CA: Mazda, 1992), 63.

36. *MAO* 679–80; see also 681–82.

37. *TAE* 5–10. See also A. G. Ravan Farhadi, *Abdullah Ansari of Herat: An Early Sufi Master* (Surrey, England: Curzon, 1996), 45–47, on the benefits of stories of Friends for beginners in the spiritual life.

38. *RS* 276–85, quoting 276.

39. Frederick M. Denny, "'God's Friends': The Sanctity of Persons in Islam," in *Sainthood: Its Manifestations in World Religions*, ed. Richard Kieckhefer and George D. Bond (Berkeley: University of California Press, 1988), 69–95.

40. Éric Geoffroy, "Hagiographie et typologie spirituelle," in *SO*, 89; André Vauchez, "Saints admirables et saints imitables," in *SO*, 161–72. Shaʿrānī structures his biographical sketches in nine chapters, treating the Companions of the Prophet; ascetics of the second and third generations (during the Umayyad and early ʿAbbāsid caliphates); the founders of the four Sunnī law schools; holy women of the second and third Islamic centuries; mystics of the third, fourth, and fifth centuries; founders and heads of Sufi orders in Syria, Iraq, Egypt and North Africa in the sixth and seventh Islamic centuries; Sufi leaders during the Mamlūk dynasty in North Africa and Egypt, featuring the early Shādhilīya; teachers and friends of Shaʿrānī himself; and an appendix that arranges sayings of great saints thematically; *TSV* passim; see also M. Winter, *Society and Religion in Early Ottoman Egypt: Studies in the Writings of ʿAbd al-Wahhāb al-Shaʿrānī* (New Brunswick, NJ: Transaction Books, 1982); J. C. Garcin, "Index des Tabaqāt de Shaʿrānī," *Annales Islamologiques* 6 (1966): 31–94.

41. *TAE* 49.

42. Ibid., 139; for more on Dhū ʿn-Nūn, see *KMH* 1:400–15; *HAI* 9:281–330.

43. *HKZ* 109, *HKR* 102, *HKN* 89; more extensive accounts of Mālik appear in *KMH* 1:277–82; *HAI* 2:320–45.

44. For one approach to the study of anecdotes, see Riazul Islam, "Towards a Methodology of Sufic Studies: Case Study of Anecdotes," in his *Sufism in South Asia* (Delhi: Oxford University Press, 2002), 1–67.

45. Thanks to Catherine Scine of Saint Louis University for suggesting the comparative table of stories. For similar parallel uses of anecdotes in Hujwīrī and ʿAttār, see stories about the following characters: Habīb al-ʿAjamī's call (*TAE* 62–63, *TAA* 37–38, *HKZ* 107, *HKR* 101, *HKN* 88–89); Fudayl ibn ʿIyād's con-

version (*TAE* 89, *TAA* 53–55, *HKZ* 119, *HKR* 108–09, *HKN* 97); Bishr's conversion (*TAE* 128–29, *TAA* 81, *HKZ* 130, *HKR* 115, *HKN* 105); Sarī's conversion (*TAE* 331, *TAA* 167, *HKZ* 137, *HKR* 121, *HKN* 110); Ahmad Khidrūya's visit to Bāyazīd (*TAE* 349, *TAA* 174, *HKZ* 150, *HKR* 129, *HKN* 118); Abū Hafs and Jewish sorcerer (*TAE* 391, *TAA* 192–93, *HKZ* 105, *HKR* 132, *HKN* 124); Junayd and the devil (*TAE* 426, *TAA* 205, *HKZ* 142, *HKR* 136, *HKN* 129–30); Samnūn and wealthy woman (*TAE* 512, *TAA* 241, *HKZ* 173, *HKR* 142, *HKN* 137); Khayr an-Nassāj's death (*TAE* 547, *TAA* 252, *HKZ* 183, *HKR* 149, *HKN* 145). Many of these stories also appear in slight variants in *NUJ*. For parallel stories of Muʿādha al-ʿAdawīya in Sulamī and Ibn al-Jawzī, see Rkia Cornell, trans., *Early Sufi Women* (Louisville, KY: Fons Vitae, 1999) 88, 264.

46. See, for example, Donald Little, "Narrative Themes and Devices in al-Wāqidī's *Kitāb al-maghāzī*," in *Reason and Inspiration in Islam*, ed. Todd Lawson (London: I. B. Tauris, 2005), 34–45, for further study of similar issues.

47. One could also argue, as I suggest in chapter 7, that the establishment of lineage as a method for legitimating the authority of individual Friends and related institutions is an important function. See, for example, Devin DeWeese, "The Politics of Sacred Lineages in 19th Century Central Asia: Descent Groups linked to Khwaja Ahmad Yasavī in Shrine Documents and Genealogical Charters," *IJMES* 31:4 (1999): 507–30; Bradford G. Martin, "Shaykh Uways bin Muhammad al-Barawi: A Traditional Somali Sufi," in *MSI*, 225–38; Julia A. Clancy-Smith, "The Man with Two Tombs: Muhammad ibn ʿAbd al-Rahman: Founder of the Algerian Rahmaniyya, ca. 1715–1798," in *MSI*, 147–70; David B. Edwards, "The Political Lives of Afghan Saints: The Case of the Kabul Hazrats," in *MSI*, 171–92.

48. Jürgen Paul, "Au début du genre hagiographique dans le Khorassan," in *SO*, 15–38, citing 21; and also his "Hagiographische Texte als historische Quelle," *Saeculum* 41 (1990): 17–43.

49. Geoffroy, "Hagiographie et typologie spirituelle," especially 84–86.

50. DeWeese, "Sayyid ʿAlī Hamadānī and Kubrāwī Hagiographical Traditions," in *The Heritage of Sufism, II: The Legacy of Medieval Persian Sufism (1150–1500)*, 2nd ed., ed. Leonard Lewisohn and David Morgan (Oxford: Oneworld, 1999), especially 149–53, quote from 149–50. See also Jamal Elias, "A Second ʿAlī: The Making of Sayyid ʿAlī Hamadānī in the Popular Imagination," *The Muslim World* 90:3–4 (2000): 395–420. Conversion of nonbelieving beings, whether spirit, animal, or human, is a significant motif in hundreds of stories. Demons and those curious characters called jinn often function as (pardon the expression) devil's advocates against Friends of God. But even these staunchest advocates of evil—or in the case of the loose-canon jinn, with their more generic type of potential mischief—are no match for the presence of the Friend; see DeWeese, "Sayyid ʿAlī Hamadānī," 150.

51. Billy Collins, *Sailing Alone around the Room: New and Selected Poems* (New York: Random House, 2002), 16.

52. Nimrod Hurvitz, "Biographies and Mild Asceticism: A Study of the Islamic Moral Imagination," *Studia Islamica* 85:1 (1997): 41–65.

CHAPTER 11: THEOLOGICAL DIMENSIONS

1. For an example of saintly typologies in traditional hagiographical texts, see Eric Geoffroy, "Hagiographie et typologie spirituelle," in *SO*, 90–98.

2. For brief general treatments of the topic, see *VRT* 80–89, *TSV* 8–10, and Hermann Landolt, "Walāyah," *Encyclopedia of Religion* (New York: Macmillan, 1987), 15:316–19.

3. *NUJ* 121.

4. Summarized from Tirmidhī, *The Concept of Sainthood in Early Islamic Mysticism: Two Works by al-Hakīm al-Tirmidhī*, trans. Bernd Radtke and John O'Kane (London: Curzon, 1996); and Richard McGregor, *Sanctity and Mysticism in Medieval Egypt: The Wafa Sufi Order and the Legacy of Ibn ʿArabī* (Albany, NY: SUNY Press, 2004). As McGregor points out (16, 20–26), Ibn ʿArabī's elaboration of the theory of the seal posits the need for multiple seals of sainthood to go along with the various types of sainthood and clarifies the superiority of the prophet by indicating that prophets possess all the attributes of the highest saints in addition to their uniquely prophetic prerogatives. Another of the early contributions to the developing concept of the role of the *walī* is that of Junayd; see, for example, Ahmet Karamustafa, "Walāyah according to al-Junayd (d. 910)" in *Reason and Inspiration in Islam*, ed. Todd Lawson (London: I. B. Tauris, 2005), 64–70.

5. Summarized from Michel Chodkiewicz, *Seal of the Saints: Prophethood and Sainthood in the Doctrine of Ibn ʿArabī*, trans. Liadain Sherrard (Cambridge: Islamic Texts Society, 1993); see *RSG* 65–67 on saintly hierarchies. See also Stephen Hirtenstein, "Universal and Divine Sainthood: The Meanings and Completion of God's Friendship," *Journal of the Muhyiddin Ibn Arabi Society* 4 (1985): 7–23. For the theoretical contributions of Rūzbihān Baqlī, see Carl Ernst, *Ruzbihan Baqli: Mystical Experience and the Rhetoric of Sainthood in Persian Sufism* (Surrey: Curzon, 1996).

6. Summarized from Lloyd Ridgeon, *ʿAzīz Nasafī* (Surrey, England: Curzon, 1998), 178–99. For another theoretical perspective that sees a parallel between the two types of divine emissaries (prophets/*anbiyāʾ* and messengers/*rusul*) and two types of Friends (righteous ones/*sālihūn* and authentic ones/*siddīqūn*), see Richard J. A. McGregor, "The Concept of Sainthood According to Ibn Bākhilā, a Shādhilī Shaykh of the 8th/14th Century," in *SM*, 33–50; see also McGregor's "A Medieval Saint on Sainthood," *Studia Islamica* 95 (2002): 95–108.

7. *KTA* 57–62.

8. *LS* 422–24.

9. *HKZ* 265–72; *HKR* 220–27.

10. *HKZ* 303–6; *HKR* 241–45.

11. *RQ* 381–82; *RQH* 427–29.

12. See, for example, Maribel Fierro, "The Polemic about the *karamat al-awliyaʾ* and the Development of Sufism in al-Andalus (4th–10th/5th–11th

Centuries)," *Bulletin of the Schools of Oriental and African Studies* 55 (1992): 236–49.

13. *LS* 315–33.

14. *KTA* 57–61.

15. Ibid., 66; see 153–61 for further examples.

16. *RQ* 378–412; *RQH* 423–59.

17. See also Bernd Radtke, "Al-Hakim al-Tirmidhi on miracles," in *MK,* 287–99.

18. *HKZ* 272–81; *HKR* 227–41; *HKN* 218–35.

19. Summarized from Abū Bakr al-Bāqillānī, *Kitāb al-bayān ʿan al-farq bayn al-muʿjizāt wa'l-karāmāt wa'l-hīl wa'l-kahāna wa's-sihr wa'n-nāzijāt,* ed. Richard McCarthy, S. J. (Beirut: Librairie Orientale, 1958), passim. On the prophetic side of the question, see Peter Antes, *Prophetenwunder in der Ashʿarīya bis al-Ghazālī (Algazel)* (Freiburg: Klaus Schwarz, 1970). See also Denise Aigle's general overview in "Sainteté et miracles en islam médiévale: l'exemple de deux saints fondateurs iraniens," in *Miracles, prodiges et merveilles au Moyen Âge* (Paris: Sorbonne, 1995), 47–73.

20. Mohammed Ali Amir-Moezzi, *The Divine Guide in Early Shiʿism: The Sources of Esotericism in Islam* (Albany, NY: SUNY Press, 1994), 16–17, 91–97.

21. See also *WFG* 13–138 on "Theological Aspects of Miracles" and 386–450 on other theoretical dimensions, including means of effecting miracles, purposes and results, techniques for dealing with unintentional or unwanted marvels, and various attitudes toward miracles.

22. *RQ* 266–74; *RQH* 281–91; *KTA* 57.

23. See, for example, Renard, *Knowledge of God in Classical Sufism* (Mahwah, NJ: Paulist, 2004), 322–26.

24. *LS* 350.

25. *LS* 428–29.

26. *KTA* 24–27.

27. Summarized from Bāqillānī, *Kitāb at-tamhīd,* ed. Richard J. McCarthy, S.J. (Beirut: Librairie Orientale, 1957), 266–79 (chapter "Ocular Vision of God"); and Richard J. McCarthy, S.J., "Al-Bāqillānī: Muslim Polemist and Theologian" (PhD dissertation, Oxford University, 1951), vol. 1, 155–64. See also McCarthy, *The Theology of Al-Ashʿari* (Beirut: Imprimerie Catholique, 1953), 45–52. For a Shīʿī perspective, see G. Vajda, "La Problème de la vision de dieu (ruʾya) d'après quelques auteurs šīʿites duodécimains," in *Le Shīʿisme imâmite* (Colloque de Strasbourg, 6–9 May 1968; Paris: n.p., 1970), 31–54.

28. McGregor, *Sanctity and Mysticism,* 18.

29. *RQ* 413–23; *RQH* 461–72.

30. Abū Hāmid al-Ghazālī, *The Remembrance of Death and the Afterlife.,* trans. T. J. Winter (Cambridge: Islamic Texts Society, 1989), 113, 210–16.

31. Summarized from Bāqillānī, *Kitāb at-tamhīd,* 365–77 (chapter on intercession); and McCarthy, "Al-Bāqillānī: Muslim Polemist and Theologian," vol. 1, 150–55. See also a dream narrative in which the theologian Abū 'l-Hasan al-

Ash'arī appears and is introduced to the dreamer as one whom God has pardoned. The dreamer says, "And I *think* that they said 'And God has constituted him intercessor for his companions'" (my italics); in McCarthy, *The Theology of Al-Ash'ari*, 170. See also Catherine Mayeur, "L'intercession des saints en islam égyptien: autour de Saÿyid al-Badawī," *Annales Islamologiques* 25 (1990),364–88.

32. Abdulaziz Sachedina, *Islamic Messianism: The Idea of the Mahdi in Twelver Shi'ism* (Albany, NY: SUNY Press, 1981), 106, 135–38; Wilferd Madelung, "'Isma," in *EI2*, 4:182–84, sums up a wide spectrum of views on the degree of protection and on whether the conferral of divine protection occurred before or only after prophetic mission.

33. *HKZ* 283, 307; *HKR* 232, 245.

34. See Ghazālī, *Remembrance of Death*, 111–20, quoting 118.

35. Summarized from M. Memon, *Ibn Taymiyya's Struggle against Popular Religion* (Paris: Mouton, 1976), especially 259–307; and Niels Henrik Olesen, *Culte des saints et pélerinages chez Ibn Taymiyya, 661/1263–728/1328* (Paris: P. Geuthner, 1991).

36. Ibn Taymīya, *Al-Furqān bayna awliyā' ar-rahmān wa awliyā' ash-shaytān*, ed. Ahmad Hamdī (Jidda: Dār al-Madanī, 1372/1952).

Index

Entries include death, or fl., dates of major figures, where available, and brief English equivalents of technical terms. Names of Arabic and Persian origin, as well as non-English technical terms, are given with full transliteration, including sub-linear dots not used in the text.

Text: 10/13 Aldus
Compositor: BookComp, Inc.
Printer and binder: Thomson-Shore, Inc.